SCOTLAND'S FIRST OIL BOOM

32

SCOTLAND'S FIRST OIL BOOM

The Scottish Shale Oil Industry, 1851 to 1914

John H. McKay

JOHN DONALD

First published in Great Britain in 2012 by
John Donald, an imprint of Birlinn Ltd

West Newington House
10 Newington Road
Edinburgh
EH9 1QS

www.birlinn.co.uk

ISBN: 978 1 906566 50 0

The publishers gratefully acknowledge the support of
BP plc towards the publication of this book

British Library Cataloguing-in-Publication Data
A catalogue record for this book is available on request from the British Library

Typeset by IDSUK (DataConnection) Ltd.
Printed and bound in Britain by Bell & Bain Ltd, Glasgow

Contents

List of tables

Appendix 1

Appendix 2

Introduction

At its peak in the years before the Great War, the Scottish shale oil industry gave employment to some 10,000 people and was a major factor in the economy of the Almond Valley. In relation to the 1888 Glasgow Exhibition, 'The late Dr James "Paraffin" Young was claimed with pride by Glasgow as the father of an important industry'.[1] However, it was never comparable in size with the engineering, coal, iron and steel industries in that period. Indeed, in considering its growth up to 1866, a historian of the industry's early years has described it as 'little more than a valuable case study for the industrial archaeologist'.[2] However, a detailed study of the industry can be justified on a number of grounds.

In discussion of the difficulties faced by Scottish industry in the period before the Great War, shale oil has been cited as an example of the successful identification of opportunity and the application of new techniques to the problems of modern industry.[3] It is also the case that the industry survived, often with considerable success, from the 1850s to 1919, in competition with natural petroleum, first from the United States and latterly from Russia and the Far East. Competition from the United States was particularly intense. The relative success of the shale industry in meeting this challenge in the late 1860s is acknowledged by historians of the American oil industry: 'To some extent the relative decline of the British imports of refined was conditioned by competition from the domestic shale oil industry'.[4] It is intended here to examine the factors which enabled the Scottish industry to maintain this competition until the Great War.

It is also true that the shale industry made a significant contribution, in the period up to the Great War, to Scottish demands for illuminating oil and to those of the United Kingdom for wax candles. The industry was also important in time of war, particularly during the Great War. At the end of this conflict the surviving companies were persuaded to combine forces and become a subsidiary of the Anglo-Persian Oil Company, of which the British government was the majority shareholder at the time. Until the middle of the twentieth century, the mines and works contributed largely to meeting Scotland's requirements for oil products.

The industry was also important enough to merit the reporting of its directors' reports and annual meetings in the major Scottish newspapers of the time, especially the *Scotsman* and *Glasgow Herald*. It was one of the industries featured in the *Scotsman* with an annual report on its achievements and prospects. In some of these it was described as an important Scottish industry.[5]

One last, and possibly most important, reason for a study of the development of the industry is that it provided a valuable recruiting ground for expertise in oil for the Anglo-Persian Oil Company (later successively known as the Anglo-Iranian Oil Company, the British Petroleum Company, and today as BP plc). As the shale industry declined, many of its workers were recruited for the Grangemouth petrochemical works, and for the refineries at Llandarcy in Wales and Abadan in Iran. This trend is perhaps best illustrated by the career of William Fraser. His father, also William Fraser, was the founder and for many years managing director of the Pumpherston Oil Company. Fraser junior followed his father into the company, becoming joint managing director at the age of 28 when his father died in 1916. With the amalgamation of the shale companies in 1919, Fraser became managing director of Scottish Oils Limited, and in 1923 a director of the parent company, Anglo-Persian Oil Company Limited. A.D. Chandler, in *Scale and Scope*, takes British Petroleum as an example of a successful British company and identifies its chairman, Professor (later Lord) Cadman, as the person responsible for this success.[6] Cadman acknowledged freely a debt owed to Fraser who was his deputy for 13 years and who succeeded him as chairman in 1941. Fraser presided over the company during the troubles with Iran in the early 1950s and has been credited with the relatively favourable outcome for the company's interests.[7] The industry that produced such a man is obviously worthy of extended study.

Part 1 The development of the industry

1862–1877

The Scottish shale oil industry developed to its fullest extent in the valley of the River Almond which, for much of its length, formed the boundary between what were then the counties of Midlothian and West Lothian. Here were found extensive beds of carboniferous limestone or oil shale. There was, in the earlier stages of the industry's life, some exploitation of shales associated with coal seams in Lanarkshire, Ayrshire and, more extensively, in Renfrewshire. The main emphasis was in the Lothians, particularly in the Almond valley, where works and mines were developed from Tarbrax, just over the county boundary in Lanarkshire to Dalmeny on the shore of the Firth of Forth. The Lothian shale beds extended under the Forth into Fife and there was, until the early 1890s, some relatively successful exploitation, particularly at Burntisland. The seams also appeared around Loanhead to the south-east of Edinburgh and were the basis of a successful operation until this was curtailed by serious water problems.

The industry developed from the work of James Young, a Scottish chemist working in Manchester. From 1847 he refined lubricants for the cotton industry from a seepage of crude oil in a Derbyshire coal mine. When this source of raw material failed, he turned his attention to the dry distillation of coal, finding a suitable raw material in the cannel coal seam at Boghead near Bathgate in West Lothian.

By 1851, Young, in partnership with fellow chemist Edward Meldrum and Manchester lawyer Edward W. Binney, had established works near Bathgate which retorted cannel coal and refined the resulting crude oil. The firm, E.W. Binney & Company, monopolised the United Kingdom oil trade for some years because of the rigorous enforcement of Young's carefully drawn patent. In the years up to the expiry of the patent in 1864, the company's works were reorganised and expanded several times.

The industry and its methods

The initial raw material, cannel coal or shale, first had to be mined. The cannel coal at Bathgate was exploited by James Russell & Son using the normal methods of the time. When the industry began to use shale in the first half of the 1860s, the geology of the area became important. The shale seams have four major and many minor faults, along with much folding of the strata.[1] This had both favourable and unfavourable consequences. In the early years of the industry, it was possible for small operators to obtain supplies from the many outcrops by open cast working, or by shallow drift mines or adits.[2] As the industry developed, shale was mined from deeper seams in much the same way as coal and other minerals.

Shale is a carboniferous limestone rock which does not contain oil as such. It contains carbon, hydrogen, nitrogen and sulphur. By a process of destructive distillation, the various elements are made to produce crude oil, ammonia and crude naphtha.[3] The cannel coal or shale required to be heated to what Young described as a 'low red heat'.[4] Steuart later gave a more precise definition of this as being between 630 and 730 degrees Fahrenheit.[5] In the Bathgate works of E.W. Binney & Company, the apparatus first used was a modified horizontal coal gas retort. These were set in coal-fired ovens. The volatile products were driven off and condensed in 16 to 24 hours.[6] The throughput was 6 or 7 hundredweights per 24 hours per retort.[7] The Bathgate works initially had six benches each of five retorts.[8]

The first advance in technology occurred after about two years, when vertical retorts were introduced. H.R.J. Conacher describes the retorts constructed at Addiewell in 1866 as having a throughput of 25 to 30 hundredweights of shale per day,[9] a substantial improvement on the earlier horizontal version. The vapours from the retorts passed through atmospheric condensers and produced crude oil, ammonia and crude naphtha. There was also a substantial quantity of permanent gas. In the early stages this was allowed to escape to the atmosphere, but it was later used as a fuel in various operations, including the heating of the retorts themselves.[10]

The crude naphtha was refined into solvents for the paint and other industries. The ammonia liquor initially disposed of as a waste product was a considerable problem in the local water courses. In the mid-1860s it was found to be a useful fertiliser, and some works began to treat the ammonia liquor to produce sulphate of ammonia in crystalline form.[11]

The crude oil was refined by distillation followed by treatment with sulphuric or hydrochloric acid to remove impurities in the form of tar. In some works this was disposed of as waste, again to the detriment of local streams and rivers. In some, the acid tar was used in the conversion of the ammonia liquor to sulphate of ammonia. After treatment with the acid, an alkali, normally caustic soda, neutralised any residual acid in the crude oil. The various fractions forming the saleable products were then obtained by further distillations and chemical treatment.

At first, the main product was lubricants for the textile industry. A secondary product was naphtha, used in the paint and rubber industries. The lighter fractions were originally a handicap, because the saleable products could not be produced in isolation. However, there was some scope for their use as burning oil, and the invention in the mid-1850s of suitable, cheap lamps made burning oil into the most important product of the early industry.[12] A third product began to assume some importance. Solid paraffin had until the mid-1850s been little more than another waste product, but the introduction of a candle-making machine provided an outlet for paraffin wax. By 1864, at the Bathgate works, the products derived from 1 ton of Boghead cannel coal were 80 gallons of burning oil worth £10; 10 gallons of lubricating oil worth £2.50; and 20 pounds of paraffin wax worth £1.[13] In 1864 the products of cannel coal yielded a gross profit of nearly £12.[14] Burning oil made up nearly three quarters of the value of the products. For the three years up to 1864, the profit from the Bathgate enterprise averaged £57,000.[15]

The Scottish oil mania

Competition inspired by such profit margins was inhibited to some extent by Young's patent. This did not cover the distillation of oil shale, as distinct from cannel coal, but it did relate to the refining of crude oil and restricted the development of the shale industry until its expiry in 1864. Despite this, from 1860 to 1863, 23 concerns were established to exploit the oil shales, and from 1864 there occurred what has been described as a 'Scottish oil mania'.[16] It has been stated that by 1865–6 there were probably 120 firms of varying size in operation in Scotland.[17] Conacher notes that this figure is frequently quoted for 1865, but that it should be taken as referring to the whole period – he considered that there was a maximum of 50 firms at any one time.[18]

In the valuation rolls for the counties of Midlothian, West Lothian and Lanarkshire for the period from 1861–2 to 1875–6, 43 works, operated at various times by 51 different concerns or individuals, can be identified (Tables 1.1(a) and 1.1(b)).

Ten of these were limited companies, eight of which were formed to take over pre-existing concerns. Only two were established to initiate new enterprises: in 1861–2, the only works was that of E.W. Binney & Company at Bathgate, while in 1862–3 Robert Bell commenced a small operation at Stewartfield near Broxburn in the eastern part of Uphall parish. In 1863–4 there was the first manifestation of the 'Scottish oil mania'. Six new works were established: three in or around Broxburn, two in or near West Calder, and one near Mid Calder. By 1866–7 the number of works in operation had risen to 26, reaching its highest total of 27 in the following year. There was a sharp decrease to 21 in 1868–9, suggesting that the 'oil mania' had possibly lost momentum. However, there were again 27 works in operation in 1869–70. In 1870–1, seven works stopped production, but there were five new operations, leaving 25 active works. Thereafter there was a steady decline

Table 1.1(a) **Works in operation in the Almond Valley, 1861–1876**

Year	Existing	New	Stopped	Restarts	Total
1861–2	1				1
1862–3	1	1			2
1863–4	2	6			8
1864–5	8	3			11
1865–6	11	7			18
1866–7	18	10	2		26
1867–8	26	5	4		27
1868–9	27	3	10	1	21
1869–70	21	1	1	6	27
1870–1	27	5	7		25
1871–2	25		2	2	25
1872–3	25		2		23
1873–4	23	2	5	1	21
1874–5	21		5		16
1875–6	16		6		10
	252	43	44	10	261

to ten works in operation in 1875–6. In this period, only two new works were established and three restarted, in contrast to 20 stoppages.

Up to 1864–5, ten new works were established, all with annual values of £200 or less. This group comprised 18 out of 27 works in 1867–8; 11 out of 21 in 1868–9; and 16 out of 27 in 1869–70. Thereafter numbers declined, until in 1875–6 only one remained. Even in the year 1867–8, when they numbered 18 of the 27 works in operation, their aggregate annual value was only 20 per cent of the total. More substantial concerns, with annual values between £201 and £1,000, first appeared in 1865–6, when three were counted. Numbers rose to 11 in 1872–3 and 1873–4, but declined to four in 1875–6. In 1866–7, their annual value was 57 per cent of the total, indicating a substantial contribution to the industry's production. This remained relatively true until 1874–5, when it fell to less than 20 per cent. The first works with an annual value of more than £1,000 was the Bathgate works of E.W. Binney & Company, which reached £1,020 in 1863–4. This works was valued at £2,012 in 1864–5 and £2,143 in 1866–7, when it belonged to Young's Paraffin Light & Mineral Oil Company Limited. Works with annual values greater than £1,000 made up 26 per cent of the total annual value in 1866–7 and 40 per cent in 1867–8. Thereafter, they never constituted less than 50 per cent. In 1874–5, this had risen to 76 per cent; and in 1875–6, to 85 per cent.

Table 1.1(b) Annual values of works in the Almond Valley, 1861–1876

Year	Annual value (£)									
	1–200		201–1000		1001–2000		2001–3000		Over 3000	Total
	No.	AV	No.	AV	No.	AV	No.	AV	No.	AV	
1861–2		1	891								891
1862–3	1	50	1	905							955
1863–4	7	503			1	1020					1523
1864–5	10	641					1	2012			2653
1865–6	14	858	3	1024			1	2012			3894
1866–7	15	1308	10	4629			1	2143			8080
1867–8	18	1801	7	3576	1	1409	1	2143			8929
1868–9	11	994	7	2831	2	2453	1	2143			8421
1869–70	16	1922	8	3414	2	3095	1	2143			10574
1870–1	12	1171	10	4707	1	1456	2	4543			11877
1871–2	13	1684	9	4397	1	1491	1	2143	1	3130	12845
1872–3	9	918	11	5435	1	1829	1	2143	1	3205	13530
1873–4	6	655	11	4990	2	3112	1	2143	1	3205	14105
1874–5	5	590	6	2645	3	4063	1	2143	1	4116	13557
1875–6	1	30	4	1651	4	5615			1	3600	10896

Butt identifies 1866–7 as the end of the 'Scottish oil mania'.[19] This examination of the Almond Valley valuation rolls lends some support to this, as the 44 stoppages all occur in that or in subsequent years. However, over the same years 16 new works appeared, and ten of those that had stopped were restarted. The demise of the 'mania' in the Almond Valley appears to have been protracted. The valuation rolls also confirm the process of concentration in larger units identified by Steuart.[20] Of the ten surviving works, two – at Bathgate and Addiewell – were the property of Young's company, while four – Uphall, Hopetoun, Starlaw and Benhar – belonged to the Uphall company. The Oakbank, Dalmeny and West Calder companies owned one each. James Liddell & Co. owned a small works at Hall Farm near Broxburn.

It is clear, therefore, that by 1876 the shale oil industry in the Almond valley provided a less than favourable environment for smaller concerns. In 1876, the number of works in operation in the Almond valley had fallen to ten from a peak of 27 in 1867–8 and 1869–70. Liddell's small works at Broxburn stopped in the next year, and the more substantial enterprise of the West Calder Oil Company Limited stopped in 1878. The reasons for the decline were complex, and included increased

levels of imports from the United States, domestic overproduction and, more prob-
lematically, a general decline in the United Kingdom economy following the end of
the Great Victorian Boom.[21] One of the features of this 'Great Depression' was a
general fall in prices from 1873 to 1895. Saul points out that the prices of sugar and
petroleum fell most heavily – in the case of petroleum, because of the opening of
new wells.[22] It seems clear, therefore, that a major adverse influence on the Scottish
industry was the growth in American oil production.

American Oil: British and European markets

Contemporary opinion was that imports of American oil seriously affected the
Scottish oil industry. At the first annual general meeting of Young's Paraffin Light
& Mineral Oil Company Limited, the directors' report referred to an extreme
depression in the price of oil caused principally by large importations from
America, and by failures in the home industry which had released large quantities
of oil for forced sale.[23]

A brief outline of the American industry would be helpful here. The first oil well
was struck by Edwin L. Drake on 28 August 1859. There was a rush of prospectors
to the area, but it was not until 1861 that it became clear that supplies of crude oil
were sufficient to support an expanding refining industry. In 1862, production was
3 million barrels; in 1870 5 million; and in 1873 nearly 10 million barrels. However,
the new industry faced considerable difficulties. Important among these was transport to refineries and markets. The first strike was in a remote area of northwestern Pennsylvania, which was poorly served by rail and other transport links.
In the early stages, crude oil was transported in barrels, and handling and freight
charges were high: in 1860, they could run to as much as $11 per barrel; another
estimate, in 1862, was $8 per barrel. However, by 1866, crude oil was being
delivered to railway depots by 'gathering' pipelines, and in some instances transported by rail tank cars, which reduced handling and freight charges by 5 cents per
gallon.[24]

In 1864–5, refinery capacity in the United States was 11,680 barrels (400,000
gallons) per day. By 1872–3 it had risen to 47,600 barrels (1,666,000 gallons) per
day.[25] Steuart gives a figure of 25 million gallons as the annual production of shale
crude oil in Scotland in 1871, equivalent to 15 days' throughput of the American
industry.[26] Scottish shale oil had a formidable adversary.

The American oil industry was in a peculiar position relative to other American
industries. Almost from the start it depended heavily on exports. In 1862, 95,000
barrels – or 28 per cent of the refined product – was exported; in 1866 this rose to
1,416,000 barrels (69 per cent). Of the exported illuminating oil, 80–85 per cent
went to Europe.[27] The reason for this emphasis on exports is clear: the domestic

market was simply not large enough. The population of the United States in 1860 was 31 million, rising to 38 million in 1870; 50 million in 1880; and 63 million in 1890.[28] Neighbouring countries were also relatively small potential markets: in 1870, for example, Canada's population was only 3.736 million.[29] The production of illuminating oil in the United States from 1873 to 1875 averaged 6,529,500 barrels per annum, or about 274 million American gallons.[30] This equates to just over 7 gallons per head of the population per annum. In the period 1883–5, production rose to 15,171,400 barrels, or 637,198,800 American gallons – slightly over 10 gallons per head of population. Over the decade from 1874 to 1884, per capita consumption of illuminating oil in the United States rose from about 1.5 gallons to 3.6 gallons.[31]

It is clear that there was, in terms of the United States domestic market, a substantial over-production which, however, found a ready outlet in Europe. The population of Europe in 1850 was 266 million, and in 1900 it was 401 million.[32] The United Kingdom population stood at 29 million in 1861; 31 million in 1871; 35 million in 1881; 37 million in 1891; and 41 million in 1901.[33] Europe, therefore, had a population six or seven times larger than the United States. Its population was not the only factor that made it an attractive market, though. In 1860, north-west Europe had 11.1 per cent of the world's population but 29.3 per cent of its income; North America, in contrast, had only 3.1 per cent of population and 14.8 per cent of income.[34]

In the third quarter of the nineteenth century, the economies of western European countries had reached an advanced stage. There was, consequently, a growth in numbers of the various groups required to administer the bodies associated with these new economies. The professional middle class in the United Kingdom expanded from the 272,000 enumerated in the 1851 census to 684,000 in 1871.[35] The lower middle classes grew at the same time, with the number of clerks rising from 92,000 in 1861 to 370,000 men and 19,000 women in 1891.[36] Over the same period, the Net National Income per head of population rose from £18.3 in 1855 to £37.8 in 1890.[37] It has been estimated that the number of income tax payers – i.e., those in receipt of an income of over £160 per annum – in 1860 was 280,000. In 1880 the number rose to 620,000, and in 1913 to 1,190,000.[38] In 1880 this group was made up of professionals such as doctors and solicitors, and of wealthier individuals. By the end of the nineteenth century it included skilled mechanics, bank and county council clerks, teachers, police inspectors and commercial travellers, among others.[39]

Despite the level of poverty revealed by Booth's study of London and Rowntree's of York, it is clear also that the last quarter of the nineteenth century was a period of relative prosperity for those belonging to the working class who were lucky enough to be in employment. Peter Mathias suggests that money wages almost doubled between 1850 and 1910, while prices, particularly food prices, fell in the period from 1874 to 1900.[40] This improvement was not experienced by all of the working classes: Fraser argues that real wages did not uniformly improve over the period.[41] There were substantial variations between skilled, semi-skilled and unskilled workers, although it is true that substantial numbers of workers were able to progress from low paid to better rewarded jobs because of the growth in opportunities in service industries and in local and national government. He also points out that there were regional variations, and that the available general indexes take no account of short time and irregular working which was a feature of some industries. However, he concludes that: 'The general picture, none the less, is of a substantially improved standard of living for the mass of the population in the 1870s, 1880s and 1890s.'[42] Wilson and Thomson conclude that the period 1870–1914 saw a 50 per cent increase in the purchasing power of the urban worker.[43]

It is evident, therefore that there existed in Europe, and in particular the United Kingdom, a market for some of the luxuries of life. One of these was artificial light. Up to the eighteenth century, tallow, animal, vegetable and fish oils were the only sources of such light. In the early part of the century, sperm oil, which burned well in lamps, was introduced. It was later found to contain a material for candles which became and remained the standard by which all candles were judged. However, sperm oil and candles were expensive and remained available only to the wealthier sections of society.[44] The labouring classes in Britain depended on rush lights and candles, and economies had to be made in these by going to bed as soon as darkness fell.[45]

The discovery of petroleum and the development of the shale oil industry, there-fore, took place at a time of considerable change in British and European society. The second half of the nineteenth century was a period of rising, or at least stable, money wages for those in employment. At the same time prices were falling. Hours of work were controlled in many industries, allowing more time for leisure activi-ties such as reading, which was increasingly provided for by the more frequent publication of newspapers and new publications, often specifically directed at working people.[46]

Reading, especially in the winter months, required adequate, inexpensive artifi-cial light, and the mineral oil industries were able to supply this, although the effect on this market of introducing mineral burning oils was not immediate. Williamson and Daum refer to Young's 'premium prices'[47] and it is true that, until he sold his interests to the limited company in 1866, Young was able to charge between 2 shillings and 6 pence (£0.125) and 3 shillings and 6 pence (£0.175) per gallon for burning oil.[48] In the first year of the limited company (1866), the average price dropped to 23.21 pence (£0.096).[49]

One suggestion for strong European demand is that:

> European experience with artificial illuminants began a half-century or more before the birth of the modern petroleum industry. High costs of illuminating materials had limited lamplight to the homes of the wealthier classes, but as American-made kerosene became available at relatively low prices, lamplight began to spread gradually among the middle and lower income groups in the society.[50]

An 1892 description of a village shop provides evidence of this spread: 'The newsvendor is generally the "merchant" of the place. His dingy shop has on one side chunks of cheese and tubs of butter side by side with paraffin oil and coils of brown twist'.[51]

Gas provided the main competition for oil lamps and candles until relatively late in the nineteenth century, when electricity was introduced. By the end of the nineteenth century there were nearly 1,000 gas works in Britain.[52] In 1881 there were one and a half million gas consumers out of a total of six million houses in Britain.[53] However, this left four and a half million households without gas. In London the number of gas consumers rose from 293,029 in 1887 to 1,283,278 in 1914. This increase was partly caused by a fall in prices, which made gas possible for working-class households, but also by the introduction of the incandescent mantle.[54] The increase in working-class consumers was assisted by the introduction of pre-payment meters.[55] Even in London, however, oil remained a source of light in some working-class homes in the years before the Great War. In 39 budgets collated by Maud Pember Reeves from 1909 to 1913, 26 included expenditure on gas and ten on oil. Two budgets had spending on gas and oil, and one spent on gas and candles.[56]

Oil lamps also offered the advantage that no permanent installation was required. They were thus preferred by many middle-class households because they provided better illumination than gas for detailed work such as reading or sewing. There was also a considerable price advantage.[57] A contemporary tribute is worth quoting in full:

> It is a striking testimony to the value of the paraffin lamp that it has not only been adopted in the country in place of all others, but that it has superseded the use of gas even where that illuminator is available. If this is due in part to fashion, it is also due to the greater pliancy with which the lamp lends itself to decorative effect. In this way Young's invention has shared in and helped to promote the improvement in taste which has been so marked during the last twenty years.[58]

The available company records show that the Scottish companies were concerned about American competition. In 1871, the directors of the Oakbank Company reported that reduced prices were due to heavy continental stocks of American oil. This also supports the view that the Scottish companies were interested in European sales as well as in the home market.[59] In 1874 it was stated that: 'The future of the oil trade is controlled by the American supplies of petroleum.'[60] In 1875, the directors of Young's company opined that prices were entirely controlled by American oil.[61]

The severity of this pressure on the Scottish industry is amply demonstrated by the growth in imports of petroleum from 361,746 gallons in 1861 to 5,584,208 gallons in 1862. Imports of refined petroleum more than doubled from 2,929,687 gallons in 1864 to 6,352,109 gallons in 1870.[62] Imports increased to 29,460,718 gallons of refined petroleum in 1878.[63]

American competition was not limited to quantity. Reporting to the AGM on 18 June 1872, the Young's directors set out clearly the advantages enjoyed by American petroleum over the shale product:

> Such Oil as was made at Bathgate when the Business was taken over from Mr Young, and even that was made during the first two or three years of the Company's existence, could not now be sold in quantity and to advantage in Foreign markets. Petroleum can be easily refined so as to be nearly colourless and inodourous, whereas Shale Oil can only be brought to this condition with much difficulty and expense; and though mere colour is no test of the value of these Oils as an Illuminant still Petroleum is sold in quantities so much larger than Shale Oil, that its want of colour has come to be looked on as an evidence of purity, and no Burning Oil is saleable at a full price unless it is nearly white.

Alterations had been made in the Bathgate works to enable the company to produce burning oil of the required colour. Although this 'new' oil sold at a higher price, the cost of production was greater.[64]

Another aspect of the American competition was the relative importance of crude oil and refined burning oil. American statistics show that in 1864, exports of American oil to England consisted of 109,598 barrels of crude oil and 88,167 of illuminating oil. By 1866, the amount of crude oil had risen to 128,364 barrels, but illuminating oil had reached a total of 230,853 barrels. In 1867, exports of crude oil to England fell to 35,142 barrels, while those of illuminating oil rose to 428,917 barrels. Despite an increase to 60,529 barrels in 1868, exports of crude to England fell sharply to 9,550 barrels in 1869; 4,714 barrels in 1870; 28,197 in 1871; 5,435 in 1872; and 16,168 in 1873.[65]

The reasons for this sharp decrease are twofold. The abandonment of the gold standard by the United States during the Civil War meant that export transactions were made on very favourable exchange rates. The advantages were greater on the more valuable refined product than on the crude oil.[66] Crude was also much more difficult to ship in barrels. It generally contained salt water and other elements that tended to dissolve the sealants used in lining barrels, resulting in considerable leakage. In the early 1860s, estimates of such losses ranged from one tenth to one third of shipments. Crude oil also had a lower initial boiling point than refined oils, and oil from flowing wells contained some gas. These factors led to pressure building up in barrels, resulting in explosions and fires. Crude oil was much less safe during transportation.[67]

The sharp decrease in imports of American crude oil after 1866 meant that refineries using imported crude oil were deprived of their main source of raw material, and this led to the demise of the British refining industry.[68] These refineries had been an important outlet for the numerous small shale crude oil concerns in Scotland. A contemporary estimate was that crude oil produced at 38 Scottish works was refined in Scotland, in Wales and on the continent.[69] For example, the Forth Bank works at Stirling, built in 1864 by George Shand & Company, had in 1866 a throughput of some 40,000 gallons per week of American crude and Scottish shale oil.[70] It ceased trading in 1871.[71] The collapse of these refining concerns reduced the market for shale crude oil to the few refining companies within the shale industry itself. This must have been a factor in the process of concentration in the industry identified by Steuart as commencing in the early 1870s.[72]

It is difficult to arrive at an accurate figure for the production of the early Lothians shale companies. Steuart states that in 1871, 51 works in Scotland produced 25,000,000 gallons of crude oil per year.[73] At this stage, shale crude oil lost almost 40 per cent in refining.[74] This indicates a production about 16 million gallons of finished products per year. Another contemporary estimate is 21,800,000 gallons of crude oil.[75] In 1872, the directors of Young's company reported to shareholders that American exports of petroleum exceeded 150 million gallons per year, while the 'Shale Burning Oil made in Great Britain was only about 8,000,000 Gallons, or slightly over Five per cent of the exports of Petroleum from America'.[76] In 1871, America exported to England 378,617 barrels (12,494,000 gallons) of illuminating oil, about 50 per cent more than the British shale production. Over 96 million gallons were sent to Europe.[77] The British shale producers had interests in the continental market as well as in the United Kingdom. Ledger No. 2 of Young's company covered a period from 1869 to 1872 and contains accounts headed 'Paris Sales', 'Foreign Sales', 'Paris Import Duty' and 'Foreign Sales Charges'. Ledger No. 1 of the Oakbank company has a large number of accounts for addresses in Italy, Austria, Germany, Holland

and Scandinavia. These interests were obviously affected by the large American imports.

American competition also influenced product prices. At the expiry of Young's patent in 1864, the price of the industry's main product, burning oil, was between 2 shillings and 6 pence (£0.125) and 3 shillings and 6 pence (£0.175) per gallon. By 1866 it had fallen to 1 shilling and 8 pence (£0.083).[78] The average price achieved by Young's company for burning oil fell from 23.21d. (£0.097) per gallon in 1866 to 15.61d. (£0.065) by 1872–3.[79] In 1875, the Oakbank company directors reported to shareholders that prices realised for burning oil had been, in 1870, 14.15d. (£0.059) per gallon net in tanks; in 1875, the price had fallen to 8.02d. (£0.033). In 1876, the price fell further to 7.12d. (£0.030).[80]

Such low prices might well have been reflected in the profits of the companies. The dividends of four of the limited companies are given in Table 1.2.

Young's company paid dividends every year after its formation until 1876, except in 1868 when a loss of £13,026 on the year's working was attributed to the great depression in the trade. The best performances were in 1870 and 1872, when 10 per cent was paid. Over the same period the Oakbank company paid a dividend in each year after its formation in 1869, except for 1875. This loss was attributed to low

Table 1.2 Dividends of shale oil limited companies, 1867–1876

Year	Company							
	YP		OOC		UMOC		DOC	
	%	£	%	£	%	£	%	£
1865	5	7265						
1868	nil	nil						
1869	5	24671						
1870	10	37134	5	875				
1871	7.5	33497	10	3527				
1872	10	47851	15	6000	10		12.5	1131
1873	6.5	31235	15	6000			nil	nil
1874	7.5	36496	10	4000				
1875	5	24331	nil	nil			5	945
1876	9	43796	7.5	3189	2.5	2750	6	1134

YP: Young's Paraffin Light & Mineral Oil Company Limited, founded in 1866
OOC: Oakbank Oil Company Limited, founded in 1869
UMOC: Uphall Mineral Oil Company Limited, founded in 1871
DOC: Dalmeny Oil Company Limited, founded in 1871
Sources: Uphall and Dalmeny companies, company reports in the *Scotsman*; Young's company, Shareholders' Minute Book No. 1 (SHMB 1); Oakbank company, General Minute Book (GMB).

prices, but it was reported that a profit made on manufacturing operations had been overturned by a loss on commercial transactions, including purchases of petroleum for resale.[81] The Dalmeny company passed its dividend in 1873 largely because the benefits of improved prices had not materialised, owing to prices dictated by contracts entered into in the summer of 1872.[82]

It seems clear, therefore that three companies were able to maintain a reasonable level of profitability despite the American competition and other problems. Their performance in the years after 1872 may well have been influenced by declining domestic competition. The number of works in operation in the Almond Valley fell from 23 in 1870–1 to ten in 1875–6. The fourth concern, the Uphall Mineral Oil Company, paid only two dividends in the period.

Even at their highest level, the smaller concerns made up only a minor part of the industry in the Lothians. In 1862, when shale was first exploited, the dominant firm was that of E.W. Binney & Company, and this continued to be the case after it became Young's Paraffin Light & Mineral Oil Company Limited in 1866. The break-up of the partnership which led to the formation of this company also served to bring into being another major concern. Young's partner, Edward Meldrum, along with a local coal master, George Simpson, formerly a partner in the Caledonian Oil Company at Fauldhouse, set up works at Starlaw, near Bathgate. Later, this enterprise was merged with a plant at Uphall Station, owned by Peter McLagen, a local landowner. The combined concern was incorporated in 1871 as the Uphall Mineral Oil Company Limited.

At Oakbank, near Mid Calder, the local landowner, S.B. Hare, together with Sir James Simpson, the discoverer of the anaesthetic properties of chloroform, and William McKinlay, formerly manager of Russell's cannel coal mine at Boghead, set up a small works which was, in 1864, incorporated as the Mid Calder Oil Company Limited. It was later taken over and expanded by the Oakbank Oil Company Limited.

In 1871, these three firms were mentioned in the Fourth Report of the Rivers Pollution Commissioners as using a total of 453,500 tons of shale per annum.[83] This is 56.7 per cent of Steuart's figure of 800,000 tons used in the UK in 1871. Steuart also refers to the impossibility of obtaining full and reliable data on the production of the industry, and states that he provides approximate estimates only.[84] The figures given in the Rivers Pollution Report must also be treated with caution. The report states that in 1871 Young's company produced 3,785,000 gallons of burning oil. The company's own figure for the year ending 30 April 1871 was 2,657,659, and for 1872 it was 3,209,908.[85]

It is clear that in 1876 these three firms occupied a dominant position in the Lothians industry. Of the ten works in operation in 1875–6, two were owned by Young's company; four by the Uphall company, one each by the Oakbank,

Dalmeny and West Calder companies, and one by James Liddell & Company. Young's works had annual values totalling £5,486; those of the Uphall company £2,523; the Oakbank company £1,200; the West Calder company £1,200; the Dalmeny company £457; and James Liddell & Company £30. The smallest operation, the Liddell works at Hall farm, Broxburn, was associated with a larger enterprise in the west of Scotland, and in any case ceased operations in the following year. The remaining companies were relatively large, and the smallest of these, the Dalmeny Company, had an annual value of £457. However, size was no guarantee of survival. The West Calder Company failed in 1878. The companies that survived into the next phase of the industry's development were Young's, Oakbank, Uphall and Dalmeny. Three of these were completely vertically integrated. They mined shale, retorted it and refined the crude oil. It is possible that the growth of these firms was a factor in the demise of the smaller enterprises.

Although oil production in the Broxburn area had virtually ceased by 1876, Robert Bell continued to mine shale there for sale to the other companies.[86] Shale production in the east of Scotland area in 1876 was 454,892 tons.[87] Production and distillation of shale continued in other areas of Scotland. The reports of the Inspectors of Mines list shale mines in Lanarkshire (1); Ayrshire (2) and Renfrewshire (8), producing 86,381 tons of shale. Of this, 76,943 tons was mined in Renfrewshire.[88] The Clippens Oil Company at Linwood, James Liddell & Company at East Fulton, and the Abercorn Oil Company at Inkerman can be identified as oil producers in that area.[89] The relatively small operations at Tarbrax in Lanarkshire, Capeldrae in Fife and Straiton in Midlothian appear to have been suspended at this time.[90]

1877–1887

Trading conditions improved in 1876 and 1877. The value of the products of a ton of shale at Oakbank works rose by 21 per cent from 229.465 pence (£0.95) in 1876 to 278.009 pence (£1.15) in 1877. Production increased. At 581,351 tons, shale output in the East of Scotland District was 27 per cent greater than in 1876. Young's company's production of finished oils, etc, increased by 31 per cent from 4,493,362 gallons in 1876 to 5,886,436 gallons in 1877. The number of miners employed by the five surviving concerns rose from 644 in 1876 to 751 in 1877. Profits and dividends recovered. In 1876, Young's company paid 9 per cent, and in 1877 17.5 per cent. The Dalmeny Company paid 6 per cent and 15 per cent, while the Oakbank Company paid 7.5 and 25 per cent. The Uphall company paid 7.5 per cent, an increase from 2.5.[1]

The shale oil industry seemed about to enjoy some prosperity during a period of decline in the British economy. The years immediately after 1873 marked the end of what has been described as the Great Victorian Boom[2] and the start of what has become known as the Great Depression. However, the Great Depression has been described as a 'myth'. Saul suggests that, from 1865 to 1875, real wages rose by 33 per cent and remained relatively stable until 1888.[3] Bowley calculated that over the period there was a rise of 1.11 per cent per annum, while Feinstein calculates that the rise was 1.24 per cent.[4] This enabled working people to enjoy a more varied diet.[5] It is also possible that this improvement in living standards was reflected in the demand for illumination, in this case burning oil. At any rate, the average per capita consumption of kerosene in Europe rose from approximately two thirds of a gallon to nine tenths of a gallon between 1874 and 1884. In the United Kingdom, consumption in 1874 was 640 imperial gallons per 1,000 of population; in 1884 it had risen to 1,084 imperial gallons, a considerably greater increase.[6] This was no doubt a factor in the increased prosperity of the Scottish industry. In 1884, the local newspaper was able to state that the Scottish industry was making substantial gains in the English, Irish and Antwerp markets, and also in Norway and Sweden.[7] In 1888 it was stated that

> The increase of the consumption of oil for illuminating purposes, which is greatly in excess of the increase in population, is a feature of importance to those engaged in the trade as it will probably require the combined power of

America and Russia for many years to come to meet the demand for what is now a necessary requirement of civilised life.[8]

This increase in consumption occurred in a period of considerable price reduction. The wholesale price of American oil in London per gallon rose from about 17 cents in 1875 to just over 24 cents in 1876, but fell back again almost as quickly to just over 12 cents in 1879, and was as low as 11 cents in 1883 and 1884.[9] At Oakbank works, this was reflected in the price of burning oil: in August 1876, it averaged 7.919 pence per gallon; in January 1877, 11.893 pence; and in October 1877, 8.104 pence. The average for November 1877 to April 1878 was 7.93 pence. Over the next six months to October 1878, it fell to 5.919 pence and the price hovered around the 4–5 pence mark until 1884, falling below 4 pence during 1883 and reaching a low point of 3.047 pence in May of that year.[10]

It is interesting to note the Young's chairman's statement that over the year to 30 April 1876, the 'profits from burning oil were, owing to the excessive competition of petroleum, only one sixth of what they had formerly been'.[11] Even at the low prices current during that year, some profit, however small, had been earned on burning oil.

It is against this pattern of falling prices for burning oil, hitherto its main product, that the shale industry's performance over the next decade must be examined. At Oakbank, the value of the products of a ton of shale fell from the peak of 278.009 pence in 1877, to 175.664 pence in 1885, having reached a low of 172.032 pence in 1882.[12] Over this period the companies paid dividends as shown in Table 2.1.

Diversification

The maintenance of such levels of profitability against the background of low prices for burning oil is explained by several factors. In 1864, at the expiry of Young's patent, burning oil was very much the most important element in the Scottish industry's

Table 2.1 Dividends, 1877–1884: companies active before 1877

Company	Year							
	1877	1878	1879	1880	1881	1882	1883	1884
Young's	17.5	17.5	12.5	8	5	6	4	6
Oakbank	25	15	20	20	7.5	1.125s.*	2.25s.*	7.5
Uphall	7.5	2	4	6	3.5	4	3.5	
Dalmeny	15	15	15	15	15	25	30	20

* Shillings per share.
Source: Newspaper reports of company affairs; BP Archive, YP, SHMB 1, y.e. 30 April 1883.

production, making up nearly three quarters of the value of its products. In the year ending 30 April 1868, burning oil made up 50.94 per cent of Young's company's sales, and 51.33 per cent in 1869. In the year ending 30 April 1872, Young's sales of products amounted to £399,205. Of this total, burning oil made up 52 per cent, paraffin wax 16.04 per cent, candles 15.79 per cent, lubricating oil 10.71 per cent, sulphate of ammonia 3.15 per cent, and naphtha 2.30 per cent. In 1875, the value of the Oakbank company's products was made up of 43.19 per cent of burning oil, 20.58 per cent of lubricating oil, 29.06 per cent of paraffin scale and 7.16 per cent of sulphate of ammonia.[13] It is clear that, by the mid-1870s, although burning oil remained the major factor in the industry's sales, solid paraffin and candles had become important.

Up to 1877, there was relatively little competition from America in lubricating oils and paraffin, but from then onwards imports of these commodities began to increase.[14] In 1874 American exports of lubricating oil to Europe totalled 27,800 barrels (973,000 gallons), in 1879, 55,200 (1,932,000 gallons) and in 1884 the figure was 238,400 barrels (8,344,000 gallons). In 1874, the United Kingdom took 83 per cent of these imports; by 1884 its share had fallen to 51 per cent.[15] It is worth noting that in 1872 American exports of burning oil were nearly twenty times as large as the total British shale production. It is of also interest that the proportion of American burning oil exported averaged 75.1 per cent of production in 1873–5, 70.4 per cent in 1878–80 and 69.0 per cent in 1883–5. In the same periods the proportion of lubricating oils exported was 12 per cent in 1873–5, 23.8 per cent in 1878–80 and 31.5 per cent in 1883–5.[16] Even at this last date, there seems to have been less pressure on the British industry from American lubricating oil than burning oil.

Figures for lubricating oil show that the Oakbank company produced 200,000 gallons in 1875, while Young's company in 1872 produced 418,764 gallons.[17] These outputs combined make a total of over 600,000 gallons, or roughly two thirds of American exports to Europe in 1874.[18] It is also the case that in 1872 American exports of burning oil were nearly twenty times as large as the total British shale production. There can be little doubt that the shale companies' production of lubricating oil increased over the next decade, although probably not to the same extent as American exports. In the year ending April 1879, Young's company produced nearly 1.25 million gallons of finished liquor – the raw material for lubricating oil; in the same year, the Oakbank company produced 268,000 gallons of lubricating oil.[19] At about 1.5 million gallons, the total is not far short of the American exports to Europe in 1879. By 1884 American exports to Europe had increased fourfold to over 8 million gallons, of which over 4 million gallons were imported into the United Kingdom. Between 1879 and 1884, shale production in Scotland had doubled,[20] and with it, no doubt, the shale companies' production of lubricating oil, not quite keeping up with imports.

There is some evidence that the Scottish shale companies were concerned with promoting sales of lubricating oil at this period. The Oakbank directors in 1876 placed the production of lubricating oil in the hands of their chemist with the promise of a bonus of £50 on the attainment of certain standards.[21] At any rate, the fall in price of lubricating oil over the period of eight years after 1876 was not quite as steep as that in burning oil. In 1869 the price averaged 1 shilling per gallon; in 1882 it was 7.5 pence, 62.5 per cent of the 1869 figure. Over the same period, burning oil fell from 15 pence per gallon to 4.3 pence, 28.66 per cent of the former price.[22]

A similar pattern prevailed with the other major product, paraffin scale, from which was produced wax for candle-making and other uses. In 1869, scale was priced at 30 pence per gallon; in 1875 at Oakbank the price was 30.5 pence, and in 1882 it had fallen to 19.2 pence.[23] The fall in this case was 36 per cent, comparable with that in lubricating oil and considerably less than in burning oil.

It is clear that the shale companies were aware of this factor. In 1874, Young's directors reported that sales of burning oil had fallen off because of 'unprecedentedly large importations of Petroleum into the home and continental markets, and to the unusually low prices at which it was disposed of'. At the same time, they stated that it was intended to increase the sales of lamps, candles and lubricating oils, the disposal of which was not 'controlled to the same extent as the Burning Oil by American supplies'. It was hoped that a steady profitable trade could be developed.[24] The chairman of the company was able to report in 1876 that

> the business was on a broader and less fluctuating basis, because new outlets had been discovered for those products which were not entirely controlled by American importations and because products which were formerly residual and useless had recently been utilised and made marketable.[25]

In 1877, the directors reported that two ether freezing machines had been installed. These would make it unnecessary to store untreated oils in hot weather, and would also 'enable a larger percentage of solid Paraffin to be obtained, and, while increasing the specific gravity of the lubricating oils, will prevent them freezing in the winter', This was successful, and in the following year it was decided to convert two existing air freezing machines to ether machines.[26] In 1879, the chairman of the company, in proposing a dividend of 12.5 per cent, commented on the continuing severe pressure on the price of burning oil and said that he thought it 'fortunate that the company were so much less dependent on the prices of burning oil than they were at one time'.[27]

The Oakbank company also diversified. In 1877, the AGM was informed of the installation of a freezing machine, and in 1880 it was reported that the company now had plant for refining paraffin scale into wax.[28] It is possible, however, that the Oakbank company was not under the same pressure from its shareholders as Young's company. The paid-up capital of Young's in 1878 was £486,625, while that of the Oakbank company was £45,000. The 17.5 per cent dividend paid by Young's represented £0.3655 per ton of shale used. In the year ending 8 May 1878, the Oakbank company paid royalties on 51,453 tons of shale, and paid a dividend of 15 per cent, amounting to £6,750, or £0.1312 per ton of shale. In 1878 the value of the products of a ton of shale at Oakbank was £0.954. In Young's company, the equivalent figure was £2.023.[29] Young's usage of shale was rather more than four times greater than that of the Oakbank company, and some economies of scale might be expected. However, it remains clear that the larger company had to be significantly more efficient in its operations to enable the payment of dividends approximating, in percentage terms, that of the smaller concern.

By 1879, two of the surviving refining companies had been successful in modifying their product base to withstand American competition in burning oil. Young's sales in the year ending 30 April 1879 were made up of 27.67 per cent of burning oil and 43.73 per cent of wax and candles; in the same year, the Oakbank company's sales comprised 28.65 per cent of burning oil, 25.06 per cent of wax and scale, and 15.05 per cent of lubricating oil.[30] The Oakbank company at this time refined a considerable quantity of American residuum – crude oil from which the lighter fractions had been distilled. The products from this contributed 11.13 per cent of the total sales.[31]

Over the period 1872–9, Young's production of burning oil had remained very much the same, but the company had achieved substantial increases in products not yet subject to the fierce American competition suffered by burning oil. Finished liquor production was almost three times the 1872 figure, naphtha two and a half times, crude paraffin four times, while refined paraffin was nearly 30 per cent up and sulphate of ammonia had increased by just over half.[32]

A comparison of Young's profit and loss accounts for 1872 and 1879 reveals that the amount of profit earned by burning oil was £49,534 in 1872, but that in 1879 there was a loss of £4,308. In the case of paraffin, there was a profit in 1872 of £30,471, and in 1879 it was £83,083.[33] It is clear that, by 1879, the profitability of the company depended on solid paraffin rather than burning oil.

Costs of production

In 1874, the Young's directors reported higher costs because of increased wages and prices of materials, but that this had recently been reversed. They referred to a reduction of waste in refining and other improvements at the works which would reduce costs.[34] Similar statements were made each year between 1875 and 1879. In

1881, the chairman of the company was able to claim that, because of the reduction in prices, the company's receipts for the year set against the prices of 1873 were less by £246,687. Deducting the dividend of £31,235 paid in 1873, he was able to say that £215,452 was a 'result and a measure of the improvements, consisting of reduced costs and increased output, which have been carried out since that time, without any addition to the capital account'.[35]

In the year ending 30 April 1872, the production costs of burning oil at Young's Bathgate works amounted to 11.548 pence per gallon; in 1879 this had been reduced to 6.432 pence. At the more modern Addiewell works, the costs were 9.097 pence in 1872 and, in 1879, 6.073 pence per gallon. There were similar reductions in the costs of other products at both plants.[36]

The costs of production fell into three parts. The crude oil was refined in much the same way as natural petroleum, although the process of destructive distillation of the shale produced tars and other impurities that required a treatment that was not necessary in refining natural petroleum. Conacher states that a good grade of petroleum could be refined with a loss of 5 per cent on the crude oil used. For shale crude oil in the early 1870s, the average yield of finished products was about 61 per cent.[37] D.R. Steuart, the chief chemist of the Broxburn company, states that the loss in refining in 1885 was 30 per cent, but that it had been reduced to about 26 per cent in 1889.[38] G.T. Beilby, the chief chemist and later manager at the Oakbank oil works, has estimated that in 1869 refining costs represented about 5 shillings and 6 pence per ton of a shale yielding 30 gallons per ton, or about 2.2 pence per gallon of crude oil. He also estimated that this had fallen to 3 shillings and 6 pence per ton or 1.4 pence per gallon of crude oil by 1882. These figures are not radically different from those of the American refiners in the 1870s and early 1880s.[39] The major difference in costs between the shale producers and the American refiners lay in the mining and retorting of the shale. The shale industry made strenuous efforts to minimise these.

In 1873 the 524,095 tons of shale produced in the United Kingdom were valued at £262,047, or 10 shillings per ton (£0.50). In 1882 it was reported that, in Scotland, 994,487 tons were produced, valued at £298,346 or 6 shillings per ton. By 1894 the cost of Scottish shale had fallen to 5 shillings per ton. There were minor fluctuations thereafter, but the cost was 5 shillings and 6 pence per ton in 1910.[40]

Over the period, this was a considerable saving to the oil companies and no doubt assisted the revival of those companies that survived after the mid-1870s. Within this general decline, there were considerable short-term fluctuations both over time and between companies. In 1875 the directors of the Oakbank company reported that in the year ending March 1874, shale had cost 6 shillings and 3 pence (£0.3125) per ton; in 1875, 7 shillings and 8 pence (£0.3833); and it was expected to cost no more than 5 shillings and 6 pence (£0.275) in the current year.[41] In the year ending 30 April 1872, Young's used 149,273 tons of 'good shale' at 8 shillings and 6 pence (£0.425) per ton; and 4,486 tons of 'inferior shale' at 4 shillings and 11.03 pence (£0.245) and 10,761 tons at 3 shillings and 7.11 pence (£0.18).[42] In May 1883, the Addiewell retorts were supplied with thick shale at 6 shillings and 3.7 pence per ton, and 'lower' shale at 5 shillings and 9.4 pence per ton.[43]

How had this decline in a major cost factor come about? A major element in the cost of shale was miners' wages, which were paid at piece rates. In 1877 the Broxburn miners were paid 1 shilling and 4 pence (£0.066) per ton; in 1887 the rate had risen to 2 shillings (£0.10).[44] The tonnage rate fluctuated around that level until the Great War. It appears that wages cannot have contributed to any great extent to the sharp fall in shale costs outlined above.

Royalties were payable to the owners of mineral rights in the land from which the shale was extracted. In 1870 the Oakbank company paid a lordship of 1 shilling per ton to S.B. Hare of Calderhall.[45] Young's company owned the mineral rights to some lands. Those at Polbeth had been granted to the company by James Young at the time of its formation; others, at Muirhall and Breichmill, were purchased in 1870.[46] The lordships of these were credited to the company's mineral fields and property accounts. Much of the company's shale was, however, derived from the property of local landowners. In 1872 the company paid one landlord 10 pence per ton of 22.5 hundredweights, to another 9 pence, and, to their largest source, 1 shilling and 3 pence per ton of 20 hundredweights.[47] The rates of lordship tended to fall as time went on. Sometimes this was the result of a landlord sympathetic to a company's difficulties. In 1875, the Oakbank rate was reduced to 9 pence per ton so long as burning oil remained below 11 pence per gallon.[48] The Pumpherston company leased a shale field at 8 pence per ton in 1884.[49]

It is not possible to quantify the cost of carrying the shale from the mines to the retorts, except, to some extent, comparatively. In the early stages of the industry, shale would sometimes be carried to retorts over long distances, sometimes miles.[50] As the industry developed, retorts and mines were placed in closer proximity to reduce costs, although the older companies continued to have some problems in this respect. Young's works at Addiewell, and particularly at Bathgate, were situated at some distance from the company's main sources of shale at Polbeth and Westwood. This difficulty was, to a certain extent, overcome when the company constructed a railway connecting Polbeth and Westwood to Addiewell and to a link with the Morningside and Coltness branch of the North British Railway.[51] The retorts were then supplied with shale conveyed in wagons drawn by the company's own locomotives. Similarly, the Oakbank company's mine was about a mile from the oil works. A complete connection by railway between the mine and works was not possible until 1886, when the mineral landlord withdrew his objections to the railway passing through his grounds.[52]

Variations in wage rates and royalties were responsible only for relatively minor year-to-year changes in the cost of shale. The main cause of the reduction from around 10 shillings per ton to 6 shillings per ton was the adoption of more efficient mining methods. Up to the mid-1870s, the Dalmeny, Uphall, Oakbank and Young's companies mined their shale by means of 'long wall faces'. This involved working the full breadth of a seam. Access roads some 7 feet wide were driven to reach the seam at intervals of about 12 or 13 yards. The shale was brought down by blasting and removed to the roadheads to be filled into hutches for transport to the surface. As the face advanced, the access roads were extended by a system of wooden pillars filled with waste material from the shale. The space between the pillars was also used to accommodate waste material. Any excess of waste was disposed of in the space left after the removal of the shale. In working a seam of any size, the system involved a number of 'brushers' or 'roadsmen' whose function was to deal with the extension of the access roads and to ensure that the waste was properly disposed of. These were 'oncost' men, a charge on the companies, with their wages paid at a daily rate.

By the mid-1870s, the seams in the Broxburn area were found to be suitable for working by the 'stoop and room' method. The mines at West Calder and Oakbank continued to be worked by the 'long wall face' because they were mostly not more than 3 feet in thickness. The 'stoop and room' method involved driving a 'main dook' or 'drift' into the seam until it reached its boundary. At intervals along this 'dook', 'levels' were driven out, again to the edge of the seam. From these, 'upsets' were driven at intervals to connect each 'level' with the next. In this way, a system of connecting tunnels was constructed throughout the whole of the accessible seam. The tunnels were the 'rooms' and the pillars left between them were the 'stoops'. This was known as the first working and, when it was complete, the stoops were removed, generally starting with those at the furthest part of the seam and working back to the dook head. At both stages, the whole depth of the seam was taken out.[53]

In 1886 in the county of Linlithgow, 1,601 underground workers produced 901,776 tons of shale, while in the county of Midlothian 1,530 miners produced 570,523 tons. In Linlithgow, all except 43 miners were employed in stoop and room workings, while, in Midlothian, 596 men worked long wall faces. In Linlithgow the average per man was 563 tons and in Midlothian, 372 tons, a clear indication that the stoop and room method was the more productive.[54]

Until 1875, all the shale mines in operation were worked by long wall faces. In 1876, Robert Bell at Broxburn had three mines worked by the stoop and room method. In 1877, his successor, the Broxburn Oil Company Limited had five mines all working 6-foot seams by the stoop and room method. In the same year, the Uphall company converted its four mines to the new system, and in 1878 the Dalmeny company was also working by stoop and room. Only the West Calder company, Young's and Oakbank remained on the long wall system.[55] Two of the surviving companies and a major new concern had adopted the stoop and room system, and this undoubtedly made a contribution to cost reductions in those companies. The Oakbank and Young's companies, however, were, by reason of the thinner seams available to them, compelled to adhere to the less productive long wall system. It is possible – indeed probable – that Bell's conversion to the stoop and room system enabled him to carry on mining shale for sale to the refining companies at competitive prices.

The next step in shale oil production was the retorting or distillation of the shale to produce crude oil. According to Conacher, 'the search for technical improvement is probably exhibited most strikingly by the development of the retort'.[56] By 1889, Redwood's list of patents for apparatus used in the industry numbered 112 – 63 of which related to retorts.[57] As stated earlier, the first advance in technology was the adoption of the vertical retort, shortly after the firm of E.W. Binney & Co. was founded. This, however, was not the end of the matter. Beilby describes vividly the manner in which the vertical retorts were worked when he arrived at Oakbank works in 1869:

> The proper principles for setting and firing retorts had not yet been arrived at, and the waste of coals and of retorts was prodigious. The furnaces were relatively enormous, while the ovens in which the retorts stood were narrow and confined. The flame and hot gases from these powerful furnaces were led directly round the lower parts of the retorts, but to protect them from the keen action of the flame these parts were surrounded with fireclay covers moulded to the shape of the retorts. Coals were shovelled into the fires often at the rate of 6 cwts. for every ton of shale distilled, the combustion requiring a powerful chimney draught, which dragged large quantities of the powdery ash of the coal into the narrow channels surrounding the retorts, rapidly closing them as well as adhering to the hot surface of the retorts forming a non-conducting layer to overcome, which involved more and more vigorous firing. Naturally the life of the retorts themselves was short, they generally bulged a little below the centre, and became hopelessly burned and cracked, sometimes even in 6, 9, or 12 months, especially if, at any time, the firemen had the run of a better class of coal than they had been accustomed to.
>
> The crude oil, costing 4d. or more per gallon, suffered a loss of 40 per cent, on refining, and only contained about 7 per cent of paraffin scale; an oil which today would be considered by any refiner too dear at 1d. per gallon.[58]

From 1868 onwards, experiments were made to improve the vertical retort in attempts to reduce costs, improve the quality of the crude oil and assist the industry's response to American competition.[59] The most important of these were carried out by William Young (not related to James Young), manager of the Clippens works at Paisley, and Norman Henderson, manager of the Oakbank works. Each produced a retort that made use of the residual carbon in the shale as fuel, thus reducing the cost of heating the retorts. In addition, they returned to James Young's original concept of distillation at a 'low red heat',[60] which produced a more easily refined crude oil. There was an extended and often acrimonious disagreement between Young and Henderson as to the original conception of the design. The dispute was taken to the courts, and eventually settled in Henderson's favour by the court of session.[61]

A major difference in the two retorts was that Young's required skilled supervision to achieve its full potential, while Henderson's did not make 'too many demands on the skill and attention of the labourer'.[62] George Beilby also later stated that:

> Hitherto, retorts had been a perpetual source of weakness, and in the older works a large staff of bricklayers and fitters were continually at work repairing and renewing the retort benches, pulling down the worn out and rebuilding the new. Now, at last, it was felt that a kind of finality had been reached, and that the fortunate manager who possessed these retorts would be able to leave them in charge of his subordinates, and devote his skill and energy to perfecting the other apparatus of the oil work.[63]

The new retort was charged directly from hutches bringing the shale to the retorts. Previously shale had been dumped on a platform, from which it had to be shovelled into the retorts. Spent shale was discharged directly into hutches for transport to the spent shale bing. There were significant savings in labour costs. The use as fuel of permanent gas produced by the retort cut the amount of coal used by about half.[64] Henderson estimated that crude oil from his retort cost 2.31 pence (£0.00962) per gallon compared with 3.27 pence (£0.0136) from the best available vertical retorts, a reduction of nearly 30 per cent.[65]

Henderson's new retort was patented in 1873, and a trial bench of 28 was erected at Oakbank works in 1874.[66] In 1875 it was reported to the shareholders that the Henderson retort produced crude oil at a cost one halfpenny less than the old vertical retorts. It was proposed to convert to the new retort as soon as possible.[67] However, this decision was never implemented: in 1878, the shareholders were informed that it was not intended to add to the retort conversion, as the present works could cope with all that was required.[68] The directors' report also recommended a dividend of 15 per cent, following one of 25 per cent in the previous year. With that kind of performance, the directors were no doubt able to justify their decision. The Oakbank company confined itself to relatively successful efforts to improve the performance of the old vertical retorts.[69]

The other surviving companies also persevered with older equipment, and for some years this was successful, with good dividends paid. However, as conditions changed these companies found it necessary to adopt the new retort to cope with American competition. The Uphall Company erected 96 at its Uphall works in 1880, while Young's company had installed 576 by 1883.[70]

The companies were also careful to reuse material from obsolete plant. The Uphall company in 1877 enlarged its refinery by removing plant from Benhar which had not been in operation for some years.[71] The Oakbank company in 1886 dismantled a bench of old retorts and reused the bricks in the construction of new railway between the pit and the works.[72]

Expansion of the Scottish industry

The better trading conditions after 1877 inspired competition from within Scotland. This took two forms. In 1878, Thomas and James Thornton, who had ceased working at Breich and Leavenseat near West Calder, resumed operations and by 1879 they were employing 23 men above ground and 143 underground.[73] There were also a number of new concerns, including some that were taking over works and mines closed in the period up to 1876. The first and most important, the Broxburn Oil Company Limited, was registered in November 1877 to take over the shale lease from Robert Bell, as well as the numerous small works in and around Broxburn that had all fallen into his hands.[74] These had a motley collection of horizontal and old vertical retorts, which were used for some months. Even in the relatively favourable trading conditions of 1877–8, though, they could not be made profitable:

> After mature consideration of different descriptions of retorts, and comparing the results of a most exhaustive series of experiments, obtained from various sources, the Directors decided to erect 200 Henderson's Patent Retorts, which, in their opinion, form the most desirable, having regard more especially to saving of fuel and labour, cheapness of maintenance, & superior quality of the oil produced, giving, as it will, a high yield of lubricating oil & solid paraffin which are the most remunerative products – the efficiency of Retorts in these respects your Directors regarded as a matter of the utmost importance to the success of the Company.[75]

At the same time, a little over £30,000 was spent on the refinery, which was to be capable of dealing with 4 million gallons of crude oil per year.[76]

Henderson estimated that crude oil from his retort cost almost 30 per cent less than that from the older vertical retorts. It can also be shown that this crude oil suffered a smaller loss in refining. In the first full year of operation, ending on 31

March 1880, the company refined 3,938,077 gallons of crude oil to produce 2,554,836 gallons of refined products, a loss of 35.12 per cent. Crude oil from earlier retorts produced only 61 per cent of refined products. In later years, this improvement was maintained and increased. In the year ending 2 April 1884, 7,796,663 gallons of crude oil produced 5,442,205 gallons of finished products, a loss in refining of 30.2 per cent. In 1887, the chairman of the Clippens company claimed that at the company's Straiton works the yield of finished products was 73 per cent, while at its Renfrewshire works the yield was 69.20 per cent.[77]

Contemporary critics cited the proportion of solid paraffin extracted from the crude oil as another measure of a company's efficiency. This had become an increasingly valuable product. In the year ending 30 April 1878, Young's company processed 9,680,000 gallons of crude oil to produce 729,425 gallons of paraffin scale, 7.54 per cent of the crude oil used.[78] The earliest production figures for the Broxburn company are for the year ending 30 March 1881. In that year, 4,670,950 gallons of crude oil were used to give 470,224 gallons of paraffin scale,[79] 10.07 per cent of the crude oil used – a significant improvement on the earlier figures for Young's.

Unfortunately, it is not possible to estimate this superior production of paraffin scale in money terms. The Broxburn company in the year in question sold its paraffin as crude, unrefined scale, while Young's sold most of its production as refined wax and candles. However, it is possible to compare the performance of the two companies in more general terms. The directors' reports to the shareholders of both companies contain, for the years up to 1883, details of the value of products sold. This, when associated with the dividends paid, will allow a comparison of the respective performances.

It cannot be positively asserted that the improved performance was entirely due to the new retorts. The Broxburn company was also equipped with a new refinery costing upwards of £30,000. The company also appears to have obtained its shale more cheaply. In the year ending 30 March 1879, 134,879 tons of shale were used at

Table 2.2 Comparative performance of Broxburn and Young's companies

Year	Broxburn			Young's		
	Sales £	Dividend £	Dividend/Sales %	Sales £	Dividend £	Dividend/Sales %
1880	155388	37500	24.13	409821	38930	9.50
1881	201705	37500	18.59	421898	29197	6.92
1882	236668	44937	18.99	430657	29197	6.78
1883	298491	44937	15.05	420593	19465	4.63

Source: BP Archive, YPLMO, SHMB, passim; BOC, GMB 1, directors' reports dated 10 May 1881 and 9 May 1887.

Broxburn at a cost of 4 shillings and 6 pence per ton (£0.225).[80] In the year ending 30 April 1879, Young's Addiewell works used 166,749 tons at a cost of £51,680 6s. 2.38d. (£0.309) per ton.[81] What is clear, however, is that the new company was an immediate and phenomenal success. In the year 1879–80, its first full year of operation, 3,982,489 gallons of crude oil were manufactured, £155,388 of products were sold, and at year end (31 March 1880), the company paid a dividend of £37,500, 25 per cent of the paid-up capital. This level of dividend was repeated each year until 1886, and the company's operations were expanded up to 1885: in 1884–5, 8,459,000 gallons of crude oil produced sales of £309,776.[82] The older companies now had significant competition from within the Lothians shale field.

From 1877 onwards a number of other new concerns were established, and some defunct works were restarted, sometimes under different ownership. The net result of this was that, in 1882 in the Eastern District of Scotland, ten concerns employed 1,876 underground workers. In 1876, seven companies, of which two had given up by 1882, employed 957 men underground.[83] Activity in the industry had almost doubled over the period.

In 1882 there were two relatively large companies. Young's company had 617 underground miners, 32.89 per cent of the total, while the Broxburn company had 460, 24.52 per cent. These two concerns made up more than half the industry. The remainder consisted of one very small concern, the British Oil and Candle Company Limited, which had assumed control of the refinery at Lanark and the crude works at Tarbrax. This ceased trading in 1883.[84] The seven remaining companies were somewhat larger, employing between 68 and 168 underground workers. The largest was the Uphall company, but it was closely followed by the Thornton Brothers at Hermand, the Oakbank and Dalmeny companies, and the Clippens works at Straiton.[85]

There was also some continuing activity in Renfrewshire and Ayrshire. The Clippens Oil Company, with works and mines near Paisley, had been incorporated in 1878, and the Walkinshaw Oil Company Limited[86] was formed in 1880 to take over the works and mines in Renfrewshire of the Abercorn Oil Company and of James Liddell and Company. The Clippens works in 1877–8 had an annual value of £1,800; in 1883–4 this rose to £4,000.[87] A significant expansion of the industry in that area is indicated.

As indicated above, the Broxburn company paid dividends of 25 per cent for some years. The Burntisland company was from the start equipped with the Henderson retort, and it was similarly successful for the first years of its existence. Dividends of 20 per cent in 1883, 1884, 1885 and 1886 were paid.[88]

Young's company had erected 576 Henderson retorts by 1883, and the Uphall company built 96 in 1880, but these two companies and the Dalmeny and Oakbank companies continued to rely to some extent on 'more or less improved vertical retorts'.[89] Young's company in fact retained 324 vertical retorts, 'which will one day have to be superseded'.[90] In 1884, the Linlithgow Oil Company Limited set up works and mines, equipped with Henderson retorts, said to be capable of distilling upwards of 400 tons of shale daily.[91] In 1885, an unincorporated partnership, James Ross & Company, started work at Philpstoun, also near Linlithgow, and was from the first equipped with Henderson retorts.[92]

Early in 1883 an annual production of 37 million gallons of crude oil was claimed. Ten years before, 22 million gallons were produced by about twice the number of works.[93] This expansion took place in a climate of continuing competition from American imports. In the 1860s and 1870s, this had had severe effects on the prices of burning oil, and this continued to an even greater extent in the 1880s. In 1882 the directors of the Broxburn company reported that prices were the lowest ever known in the trade; the following year the Oakbank shareholders were told that the prices of refined oils had reached the lowest point in the history of the trade; and in 1885 the directors' of Young's company reported that the average prices of shale products were lower than in any previous year.[94] What was of some concern was that paraffin scale was now affected. The Young's directors, in their report to the 1881 general meeting, explained a reduced dividend by saying that 'America has been sending to this country a quantity of scale, which not only seriously affected the Company's prices for the year, but rendered it necessary, as a matter of prudence, greatly to reduce the valuation of the stock therof on hand'.[95]

There is some evidence that the Scottish companies were not overly concerned about American competition. Early in 1883, in a report on the 'Scotch Mineral Oil Trade' in the local newspaper, it was claimed that even if American crude oil were supplied free, and if no profit was made in refining, the costs of barrels, transport etc. would amount to 4 pence per gallon for burning oil, and that Scottish companies would be able to compete at that level. It was also said that the price of paraffin scale had risen from 3 pence to 4½ pence per pound and this, together with sulphate of ammonia at £20 per ton, would compensate for any deficiency in burning oil.[96] In fact, Table 2.3 shows that the shale companies managed to pay dividends during this period, although those of some of the older concerns were reduced.

At the same time it was stated that American oil had deteriorated in quality, while Scottish oil had improved and 'is now in some cases actually superior to the best brands of petroleum, both as regards burning qualities and high flash point – the latter being the test of safety.' It was also claimed that very little American oil was used in Scotland, and that efforts were being made to increase sales of Scottish oil in other parts of the United Kingdom. The superiority of the Scottish product does not appear to have been universally acknowledged. A stockbroker's report on the industry's performance in 1884 claimed that the board of the Midlothian

Table 2.3 Dividends, 1877–1884: all companies

Company	Year							
	1877	1878	1879	1880	1881	1882	1883	1884
	%	%	%	%	%	%	%	%
Young's	17.5	17.5	12.5	8	5	6	4	6
Oakbank	25	15	20	20	7.5	1.125s.*	2.25s.*	7.5
Uphall	7.5	2	4	6	3.5	4	3.5	
Broxburn			9	25	25	25	25	25
Burntisland							20	20
Dalmeny	15	15	15	15	15	25	30	20
Clippens							5	10

* Shillings per share
Source: Newspaper reports of company affairs; BP Archive, YP, SHMB 1, y.e. 30 April 1883.

company had 'admitted the inferiority of some of the products sent out, but threw the blame on the workmen.'[97]

Further development of retorts

The industry continued to grow in the period up to 1889. Shale production increased from 1,130,729 tons in 1883 to 1,986,990 tons in 1889.[98] Experiment with the retorting process had continued, despite the almost universal adoption of the Henderson version. The Oakbank company did not add to its small bench of Henderson retorts but altered the older vertical retorts to produce the same 'low red heat' and to improve the quality of the crude oil. This was successful to the extent that the resulting crude oil contained 10 or 11 per cent of paraffin scale, an improvement of 2 per cent. Coal consumption and the cost of repairs were reduced.[99] However, the yield of sulphate of ammonia fell from 15 pounds to 12 pounds per ton. Steuart considered that the Broxburn shale contained nitrogen equivalent to 70–90 pounds of sulphate of ammonia per ton, but acknowledged that the Henderson retorts at Broxburn could extract no more than one fourth of this.[100]

By the late 1870s, sulphate of ammonia had become important as a product not subject to foreign competition. It was thought that American and Russian petroleum had been produced by the action of heat on organic deposits, and that any nitrogen had been lost. In the oil-shale deposits these organic remains had not been subjected to this action, and the nitrogen was made available by the retorting process.[101]

In 1881 George Beilby, the manager of the Oakbank works, and William Young, manager at Clippens, jointly patented a new type of retort designed to increase the output of ammonia while retaining a good yield of crude oil. This consisted of a cast-iron portion 12 feet long, in which the shale was heated to a temperature suitable for oil recovery. The shale then passed into the lower part of the retort, which was constructed of firebrick to resist the much higher temperature required for the optimum production of ammonia. The Young & Beilby retorts were heated by their own permanent gas supplemented by coal gas retorts set in the benches. The heating of the retort entirely by gas was necessary to maintain closely the different temperatures.[102]

This Young & Beilby retort, together with the healthy dividends paid by the Broxburn company in particular, inspired the formation of a number of new concerns. In 1883, five companies were established. The Westfield Oil Company in Fife had only a short existence, being one of the concerns promoted by the ubiquitous George Simpson. The Bathgate Oil Company had a similar short life. The Pumpherston Oil Company, the West Lothian Oil Company and the Lanark Oil Company were founded as serious contenders in the use of the new retort, although the latter two were handicapped by the involvement of George Simpson. In 1884, the Holmes company and the Linlithgow company were formed, followed the following year by the incorporation of Thornton's West Calder enterprise as the Hermand Oil Company Limited.[103] All of these concerns opted to use various versions of the new retort, except Linlithgow, which settled on the Henderson retort as having been responsible for the success of the Broxburn company. A private partnership, James Ross & Company, set up crude oil works at Philpstoun, near Linlithgow, also using the Henderson retort.

The net result was that, in 1886, the Inspector of Mines for the Eastern District of Scotland listed 12 concerns actively engaged in working shale. They employed 3,401 underground workers, nearly double the number employed by the industry in 1882.[104] In addition it is known that Walkinshaw mined shale in Renfrewshire, and the Annick Lodge Company in Ayrshire.[105] There was a similar increase in the amount of shale mined in Scotland, up from 994,487 tons in 1882 to 1,699,144 in 1886.[106] Of the individual companie,s it should be noted that British Oil & Candle had ceased trading, Midlothian Oil had been taken over by Clippens, and the Uphall company had been absorbed by Young's. Young's remained the largest concern, but Broxburn's position as second in the industry was challenged by Clippens . These three companies employed more than half the underground workforce, but the remaining nine concerns were relatively substantial, the smallest employing 100 men underground. Three – Burntisland, Linlithgow and Pumpherston – each employed 200–300. The industry had continued its consolidation into larger units.

From 1883 to 1885 eight new limited companies and a private partnership were formed. The Bathgate and Westfield companies had only very short lives, and the Lanark only lasted two years, but Pumpherston eventually became the industry leader. The Holmes, Linlithgow and Hermand companies survived into the twentieth century, but the West Lothian was wound up in 1892. At the same time some existing concerns took steps to counter the fall in product prices by expansion. In 1884, Young's absorbed the Uphall Oil Company Limited and commenced a programme of reorganisation and expansion based on Uphall works and shale fields in West Lothian.[107] In 1886, the shareholders were told that 'developments and expansions of the last three years at Newliston, Uphall and Hopetoun have cost the aggregate sum of £134,559'.[108] In 1884 the Oakbank shareholders were told by the directors that, although the capacity of the works had been increased from 1¼ million gallons of crude oil per year at the formation of the company to 2 million gallons, it was necessary to increase it further by one half to enable the company to compete with its larger neighbours.[109] In 1885, it was agreed that, to provide for the necessary expansion, the company should be wound up and reorganised. As a result, the directors were able to report in 1887 that the new company now had works with a capacity of 4 million gallons of crude oil per year.[110] In 1887, 232 underground miners were employed, an increase from 119 in 1886.[111] In 1885 the Clippens Company took over the Midlothian Oil Company Limited and continued its transfer of mining and retorting operations from Renfrew to Loanhead. The chairman of the company stated that, in the year ending 31 March 1886, sales of the company's products had realised 15 per cent less than in the previous year, but that a better result was hoped for because production had been increased by one third.[112] The Broxburn company increased its throughput of crude oil from 3,938,077 gallons in 1879–80 to 9,231,500 in 1886–7.[113]

In 1886, the directors of the West Lothian company explained a debit balance by stating that, with the exceptionally low prices of products, only companies that could economise by manufacturing in quantity could hope to make a reasonable profit.[114] However, one of the newer companies did set out to emulate the older concerns in economies of scale. In 1886, William Fraser, the managing director of the Pumpherston company, in explaining the need for a further issue of shares, was reported as saying that

> their reasons for thus issuing the new shares were that the subscribed capital was £76,500, while the expenditure to 30th April, 1886 was £118,000, . . . which . . . was nearly double what they had contemplated at the formation of the company, and the works were something like two and a half times the extent of what had been intended when the company was formed. The reason why they had gone into this materially increased expenditure had been to meet the continued reduction in prices. He had had the curiosity to turn up the prices at about the time when this company was formed, and he found the difference in money value of their products was no less than the astonishing

sum of £40,000. It would at once be observed that something had to be done in order to meet that heavy and continual drop in the price, and their directors wisely, as he believed, thought that the proper way was to extend the works, both in order to reduce the cost of production and to increase the business. He had no doubt that the action of the directors in this matter would meet with the approval of the shareholders. It was the course that every company in the oil trade had adopted that had been successful.[115]

The entry of new companies alongside the expansion of existing concerns greatly increased competition within the industry at a time of growing threat from imports. In 1886, the Young's directors reported that 'within the last three years paraffin scale has fallen £12, sulphate of ammonia £6 and lubricating oil £3 per ton respectively. These items represent a difference of £120,000 per annum to this company'. They went on to add that this was caused by 'over production from new oil companies and by inexperienced and necessitous sellers.'[116] There were references to keen competition in the reports of the directors of the Broxburn and Oakbank companies.[117]

The newer companies also experienced problems. In 1887, the Linlithgow chairman complained that 'other companies had made contracts for scale at higher prices than were obtainable when the Linlithgow Oil Company came into the market, and to this exclusively the directors attributed the differences revealed by the published balance sheets'.[118] In 1889, the directors complained of the difficulty of breaking into the market for candles; the Candlemakers' Association made no concessions to facilitate introduction to the market.[119]

New companies, overproduction and lower prices

Every company was adversely affected by the problems of the second half of the 1880s. This is reflected in the dividends paid.

The best illustration of the pressure on prices is perhaps the performance of the Broxburn company. For the year 1881–2, a dividend of 25 per cent was paid: £44,937, or 18.99 per cent of total sales of £236,668. For 1885–6, the dividend was again 25 per cent and £44,937, but only 14.27 per cent of sales of £315,865. Over the same period the amount of crude oil produced rose from 7,236,682 gallons to 9,231,500, an increase of 27.56 per cent. In the following year the dividend was reduced to 15 per cent – £29,962 – only 11 per cent of sales of £271,235. In the year ending 2 April 1884, the company's London Candle account shows sales of 159,556 dozen pounds for £42,335: 63.68 pence per dozen pounds. London wax sales totalled 341,509 pounds and £4,999: 3.51 pence per pound. In the year ending 28 March 1888, the corresponding figures were 267,571 dozen pounds and £48,973: 43.93 pence per dozen

Table 2.4 Dividends, 1885–1887

Company	1885	1886	1887
Young's	8	8	nil
Oakbank	nil	nil	nil
Broxburn	25	25	15
Burntisland	20	20	7
Dalmeny	25	25	20
Clippens	12	7.5	nil
Holmes	10	8	5
Hermand	nil	86/7	nil
Linlithgow		10	nil
Pumpherston	10	10	nil
West Lothian	15	nil	nil
Walkinshaw	nil	nil	nil

Source: Newspaper reports of company affairs.

pounds, a fall of 31 per cent; 929,081 pounds of wax were sold for £5,820: 1.50 pence per pound, 43 per cent of the 1884 price. Over the same period, the price realised for burning oil in London remained virtually steady: 6.09 pence per gallon in 1884; 6 pence in 1888.[120] Burning oil seems to have reached and maintained a low level over the period, but there was a definite pressure on the prices of candles and wax, although the figures indicate a considerable increase in the quantities sold.

By 1887, all of the companies were facing difficulties. Only the Broxburn, Burntisland, Dalmeny and Holmes companies had anything to divide in 1887, and their dividends were reduced from previous years. Newspaper reports of annual meetings all mention problems. The Clippens chairman referred to the past year as a time 'when prices of products had reached the lowest level known in the Scottish oil industry'. In particular he stated that the price of wax, 'their most valuable product, had fallen to a much lower point than had ever been known in the history of the trade', attributing this to 'the sudden increase of production which took place two or three years ago'.[121]

There is, however, some evidence that savings had been made in an effort to cope with the lower prices. It was reported in January 1886 that such 'savings in working expenses have quite counterbalanced them (the low prices), and placed, it is said, such concerns as Broxburn, Burntisland, Clippens and Young's above all anxiety'. The report went on to state that the proportion of paraffin scale derived from the crude oil was at its highest level ever, and that the yield of sulphate of ammonia was also higher. An improvement described as the 'simultaneous process of distillation' had been patented by Norman Henderson of the Broxburn Company. It was claimed that this had reduced the cost of refining by a halfpenny per gallon, worth over £17,000 to the company on a throughput of 8,459,000 gallons of crude oil.[122]

There were some gloomy forecasts from commentators outside the trade. In a circular to investors, an Edinburgh firm of stockbrokers, in discussing the market for oil shares stated that: 'Parties connected with the various companies profess to minimise the effect of the coming crisis in the Oil Trade, but that it will be severe is beyond question, and that it is not remote is evident from the refusal of prices to move up with others.'[123] In a comment on what was said to be 'not the first time in its history that the Scotch Oil Trade has passed through a crisis', it was noted that, ten years earlier, there had been 50 concerns producing burning oil in Scotland. The price of this had been as much as 3s. 6½d. per gallon in December 1865, and as late as January 1873 it was selling at 1s. 9¼d. per gallon. It was now available at 5½d. per gallon; less for some qualities. It closed by stating that the Scottish oil companies had sold oil at a loss, which was made up by the prices obtained for the other products.[124]

There were some casualties. In December 1884 the Lanark directors' report showed a loss of nearly £6,000; a liquidator was appointed on 2 December 1886.[125] The Walkinshaw directors complained that, unless the balance of an issue of preference shares was taken up, the uncalled capital of £1 10s. per share would require to be called up.[126] The company meanwhile had to contend with an indifferent shale field and difficulties with its leases. It ceased mining and retorting in 1886 but continued to refine purchased crude oil, although there were difficulties in obtaining supplies at suitable prices. In 1887 the shareholders were informed that the works were at a complete standstill.[127]

Apart from reducing dividends, the reaction of some refining companies was to look favourably on suggestions of co-operative action to maintain prices at profitable levels. The newer concerns certainly took this view – the Pumpherston and Burntisland directors supporting it strongly – and there was also some adverse comment on the attitude of the older concerns. William Fraser, managing director of Pumpherston, said that: 'The want of an arrangement had been caused by the old companies refusing to hold out the hand of friendship to the young companies.'[128] The West Lothian directors made a statement about

the efforts recently put forth by them, in concert with most of the others in the trade, to arrive at a mutual understanding or combination amongst the Scottish companies, in view of the present extremely depressed state of the industry, in order to the prevention of undue competition in price between these companies themselves – an effort in the first instance confined to paraffin scale, but conceived on a basis broad enough to have afterwards included the other products. This effort was defeated by the representatives of one of the companies, after long and earnest negotiations and representations made by the others, refusing to join in the proposed combination, mainly on the ground that they hoped to attain their ends by the collapse of some of the other companies, and in a similar manner, an effort subsequently made to effect an arrangement with the American producers was thwarted.[129]

It is not clear which company was the target of this accusation. At the Broxburn company's annual general meeting, a shareholder complained of the continual reduction in the value of sales and suggested that 'this company and one or two of the big companies had some idea of extinguishing the small companies'. At the same AGM it was reported that Mr Kennedy had attended a candlemakers' meeting at which an agreement had been made, only for it to break down within a week. He stated that, with over 60 candlemakers in the country, it was not possible to regulate prices. He had also attempted to secure agreement among the eight producers of paraffin scale, but this too had fallen through, because of a lack of unanimity. Since then he had been in correspondence with the Standard Oil Company to look for an agreement between that concern and the companies in Scotland; they had replied favourably, but considered that the time was not right.[130]

It is clear, however, that the largest company, Young's, was against the proposal. In June 1887, the chairman's statement to shareholders referred to the

refusal of the directors to join in a scale syndicate last November. There were two schemes submitted. One would have seriously injured the company's large and long standing connection by preventing direct negotiation with customers for solid paraffin; and while the other admitted of this, it contained clauses which the board believed would be inimical to the interests of the company. By a draft article it was proposed to establish an association to consist of one member from the board of each company – the board to determine at what prices paraffin scale should be sold; and it was further proposed that in a place selected and set apart within the premises of the several companies, or in a separate store, as the joint committee might determine, all surplus scales should be stored – the parties storing being entitled to a cash advance of three fourths of the nominal value until sold and accounted for. With regard to the necessary funds for carrying out the proposal of the committee representing the various companies were to raise money for which they were to become jointly and severally liable.

The directors were advised that this scheme was wholly *ultra vires* of the directors, and so declined to enter into it. The shareholders were told, however, that another scheme was under consideration, to which the board had assented in principle.[131]

Despite this apparent discord, a Scottish Mineral Oil Association had been in existence since 1883. This had aims similar to those of associations among Clydeside employers at this period: i.e., agreement on prices and wages.[132] On 29 June 1887, it held a meeting, but without representatives from the Broxburn, Clippens and Oakbank companies, a letter from the Broxburn company explaining that it would take no part in the scheme of amalgamation. Two schemes were considered by the meeting and remitted to a committee for consideration and report. One of the them, submitted by the secretary of the West Lothian company, Mr Hoey, gave a committee of company representatives the power to fix product prices, quality and output, with provision for penalties for non-compliance. It is hardly surprising that two of the largest companies had reservations about this.[133]

Comment in the press concentrated on what had been achieved. Walker & Watson, in their July circular, referred to an agreement to set the price of burning oil at 5–5½ pence per gallon and expressed the hope that similar arrangements for other products would follow. The circular went on to state that: 'A proposal to effect a general amalgamation, the benefits of which to the trade at large would be very material, has fallen through owing to the disinclination of the sounder companies to ally themselves with those that are in difficulties.'[134]

The most important outcome of the meeting was confirmation of an earlier decision to reduce wages at the mines and works, due to take effect the following Thursday. This was implemented throughout the industry except by the Holmes, Clippens and Oakbank companies. Holmes was under contract to supply crude oil to the Pumpherston company; the Oakbank concern had recently been comprehensively reorganised and was unable to make a stand, while Clippens claimed that an equivalent reduction had been made indirectly.[135] Apart from these concerns, the result was a general strike by the miners and oil workers.

Initially the employers stood united, but this began to break down early in August. The Dalmeny and Pumpherston companies conceded half the reduction, and their men returned to work; Pumpherston incurred the Mineral Oil Association's displeasure. By mid-September, the Linlithgow company was able to resume.[136] The *West Lothian Courier* (*WLC*) of 24 September 1887 reported an end to the strike at Philpstoun and Burntisland. On 28 September, a meeting of the Scottish Mineral Oil Association was informed that the shale miners had agreed to resume work at the full reduction, with the exception of those employed by the Broxburn company. In effect, the miners had decided to deal with Broxburn first, taking on the others later. The association members agreed to support the Broxburn company with supplies of shale or crude oil; at the same time, the striking Broxburn miners received monetary support from those working at other mines. The Broxburn strike continued for some weeks, finally ending in December when the company undertook to reduce the cut in wages by a half by 1 January 1888.[137]

As the strike moved to a close, commentators became concerned with the effects of influences inside and outside the industry. The strike started at a time of year when activity in the market for oil products was at its lowest, and there is an illuminating comment in the 'Commercial and Monetary' column of the local newspaper:

> Most of the oil works in Scotland are still practically closed, neither directors nor workmen showing much desire to bring about a termination of the dispute, save on their own terms. It is an open secret that the position of many of the companies, and the heavy stocks of finished products held by them, for which a profitable price could not be obtained, made a cessation of work a desirable thing. The result has been to clear out these stocks and to increase the value of some, at least, of the articles produced. It cannot be said, however, that the demand is excessive, or that buyers are yet prepared to pay such prices as would put the trade on a firm basis. There is little doubt that a few weeks more of the present restriction will materially alter the position of affairs. Mineral oils and wax are essential features of modern life, and would not be dispensed with by any class of society, even if they cost double what they do at present.[138]

In September the local newspaper printed an article from the *Scottish Leader* in which the columnist forecast that Russian oil would be a feature of the United Kingdom market in the coming winter. The restriction of production in Scotland caused by the strike would render supplies sufficient only to meet the demand in Scotland, leaving little for Ireland and the north of England. It was further claimed that candlemakers were beginning to realise that American imports were insufficient for their needs.[139]

At this time, the Russian industry had secured a substantial foothold in the European market. Its share of European imports of illuminating oil rose from 2.8 per cent in 1884 to 19.3 per cent in 1889. Imports of oil from Russia to the United Kingdom rose from 2.7 million gallons in 1886 to 8.3 million gallons in 1887 and 20.8 million gallons in 1888. It was reported that an advertisement had appeared in the *Glasgow Herald* indicating that Nobel Brothers had appointed an agent in Glasgow for Russian burning.[140]

On 27 August 1887, the *West Lothian Courier* reported that, in America, the July prices were lower than at any time since 1882, although there seemed to have been a falling off of crude oil production. In an earlier edition, the newspaper mentioned that:

> Rather unpleasant advices for the Scotch Oil Trade are said to have been received from the United States. As is known, efforts for a time have been

pushed towards securing the co-operation of the Standard Oil Company in raising the price of paraffin scale, the decline in the value of which has contributed chiefly to the present depressed state of our national industry. It is said that the Standard Company has informed its correspondents here that it cannot enter into any agreement of the kind indicated. It prefers to retain freedom of action, and that has lately been exemplified by an offer of scale on the London market at 1½d the pound – the lowest price ever quoted.[141]

However, in October, Mr Kennedy, managing director of the Broxburn company, held out hope that the Standard Oil Company would come to some arrangement.[142] In December the *Courier* reported that, contrary to expectations of some in the United Kingdom, the restriction scheme (see below) in America appeared to be working, and that prices in New York were higher. It was also claimed that America had no scale to offer, and that this would have a beneficial effect on prospects for the Scottish companies.[143]

Towards the end of the year, after the strike ended, press comment became more optimistic. Prices were higher than they had been for more than a year, and it was said that stocks were low, particularly of lubricating and burning oil. This was said to be due largely to the effects of the strike, but it was noted that the restrictions agreed in America in November were beginning to have a beneficial effect. It is of interest that sulphate of ammonia was 'hardening' because of the improved position of the sugar trade; it is also worthy of note that the Dalmeny company declared a dividend of 20 per cent for the year ending 9 November 1887.[144] This company produced only crude oil and sulphate of ammonia, and it is tempting to suppose that the profit earned was at the expense of companies such as Broxburn, whose mines and retorts were at a standstill because of the strike. This is supported by results for the year ending in March/April 1888. Of the refining companies, only Pumpherston, Oakbank and Broxburn paid anything (3, 6 and 5 per cent respectively).

At the end of 1887 the future of the industry was uncertain, although there were signs of some improvement in prices. It remained, however, very much at the mercy of American petroleum and its dominant position in United Kingdom and European markets.

3

Paraffin wax and Standard Oil, 1888–1899

How did such a small industry, split into a dozen competing concerns, survive against competition from the American giants and growing imports from Russia? Why, also, was Standard Oil concerned about competition from this minnow? In considering the events of the next few years, it must be borne in mind that the shale industry's profitability was now firmly linked to the price of paraffin scale and wax. In 1864, 74 per cent of E.W. Binney & Co.'s sales had been derived from burning oil, and only 7.4 per cent from solid paraffin. In 1872, burning oil provided 52 per cent of Young's sales revenue, while sales of candles and wax amounted to 31.83 per cent. By 1879, burning oil, although it remained a substantial element, contributed only 27.67 per cent of the sales revenue; candles and wax were by now the largest part of sales at 43.73 per cent. There was a slight adjustment of the balance by 1889, but wax and candles remained the largest element in sales revenue at 36.28 per cent against burning oil at 33.82 per cent.[1] Developments in the American refining industry are also important.

Changes in American refineries

Until the late 1870s, apart from a few concerns converted from the coal oil industry, American refiners had mainly concentrated on producing illuminating oil. The heavier fractions left after its extraction, known as 'residuum', were sold to specialist refiners producing lubricating oils and wax principally for the American home market. The wax was used in candle-making and match manufacture, as sealants for the preservation of foodstuffs, and in chewing gum.[2] Some of this 'residuum' was exported, and some used by British refiners. The Dee Oil Company of Saltney in Cheshire used £50,000 worth annually to produce candles, other paraffin wax products and lubricating oils worth £150,000.[3] Residuum also figures in the shale oil industry: in the twelve years up to 1884 many shiploads were processed at Oakbank.[4] In the year ending 26 March 1879, 12,001 barrels of residuum, costing £8,029, were used to produce 1,775 hundredweights of scale, 8,691 hundredweights of various oils and 77 tons of coke, yielding a profit of £3,267.[5]

The major influence on the development of the American oil industry was that of John D Rockefeller and Standard Oil. In 1873, Standard Oil controlled about 10 per cent of American refining capacity; by 1878, it was over 90 per cent. This virtual monopoly was not completely maintained, but in 1884 some 77 per cent of refining capacity remained under Standard's control. The many and varied plants acquired during this push for dominance required considerable reorganisation, and this occupied Rockefeller and his associates until the formation of the Standard Oil Trust in 1882.[6] Part of this reorganisation was the large-scale manufacture of lubricants and other by- products, although the main product remained illuminating oil. By 1881, according to Nevins, the Cleveland works consisted of six units that manufactured kerosene and naphtha; oils, greases and paints; and wax and candles. Nevins also states that for some years Standard found it difficult to sell its huge stocks of paraffin, but also cites the *Oil Paint and Drug Reporter* of 3 August 1881 as stating that Standard's paraffin and wax were so good that British candle-makers were largely dependent on them.[7] Rockefeller had recruited a German chemist, Herman Frasch, who in the mid-1870s produced 'a new wax for British candle-makers'.[8]

While the Scottish industry was feeling the effects of internal competition, culminating in the strike of 1887, the American oil industry also had problems. Despite a decline in production in 1884, stocks of crude oil remained high and remained so until early in 1887. The price of crude oil fell from an average of 84 cents per barrel in 1884 to about 62 cents per barrel in mid-1887. This was despite concerns about the ability of the Appalachian fields to maintain production sufficient to meet the needs of refiners. In 1884, Standard refineries had a capacity of 96,000 barrels per day of crude oil out of a total US capacity of 124,000 barrels. As the major refiner, Standard was obviously concerned about the long-term future of its raw material. Standard and the crude oil producers agreed to limit output for a period of 12 months from 1 November 1887. The purpose was to raise the price of crude to profitable levels, but it also had the effect, after the agreement ended in November 1888, of encouraging new drilling and exploration, which secured the long term future of crude oil supplies.[9]

This limitation of output coincided with the ending of the strike in the Scottish industry, and the consequent reduction of American supplies together with the shortage of home-produced products led to some improvement in prices at the end of 1887. By the end of the year it was said that production was unequal to the demand. The town of Grantown-on-Spey was said to be virtually in darkness because of the lack of oil. In America production of crude oil had fallen to levels not seen for ten years. Stocks of American oil in European ports had fallen by over 100,000 barrels, and in London stocks had fallen from 91,000 barrels to 72,000. In mid-January, prices were said to have improved since the previous January by 1½d. per gallon for burning oil, by £1 10s. per ton for lubricating oil, by ⅜d. per lb for scale, and by £2 10s. per ton for ammonia.[10]

Solid paraffin and candles: American and Scottish producers

In the United Kingdom, solid paraffin was used principally for the manufacture of candles and nightlights. Young's company installed candle-making machinery in 1866.[11] At first only the best qualities were made, 'but though these were at once introduced into use at the Royal Palaces and among Purchasers of the Highest Rank, the demand was so limited that there was no room for a large production. Second Class qualities at a lower prices to meet the ordinary and more extensive demand were accordingly introduced.'[12] The material used became known as 'semi-refined' paraffin, and in a report on exhibits at the 1887 Jubilee Exhibition at Manchester, its recent introduction was said to have almost annihilated the composite and tallow candle branch of the industry.[13]

Initially the advent of burning oil as an illuminant had a slightly adverse effect on the candlemakers. The sales of Price's Patent Candle Company from 1857 to 1861 had been 46,905 tons. In the years 1862–6, 43,609 tons were disposed of, a fall of 7 per cent. However, the company soon recovered and in the 1882–6 period, 80,205 tons were sold. In the mid-1880s Price's was said to be the largest refiner of paraffin in the world, using 19,000 tons of raw materials to produce annually some 18,000 tons of candles and other wax products, with a value of £700,000. The total production of candles in the United Kingdom was given as 27,000 tons of paraffin candles, 7,500 tons of which was made from stearin. Price's raw materials were stated to be scale from Scotland and America. In 1880, 5,051,800 pounds of candles were exported from the United Kingdom; in 1888, this had doubled to 10,830,900 pounds, and in 1894 exports almost doubled again to 19,250,900 pounds. In 1907, 100,425,00 pounds of candles were produced in the United Kingdom, of which 31,788,700 pounds were exported.[14] The home and export markets were obviously maintained in the first decade of the new century.

This had obvious attractions for both the Scottish shale companies and the American producers. Young's company, the largest in the Scottish industry, in the year ending 30 April 1884, sold candles worth £180,925. The Broxburn company, in the year ending 2 April 1884, disposed of candles with a value of £116,629. The total sales of candles of almost £300,000 made the Scottish industry a significant force in the candle industry. Young's exhibit at the International Inventors' Exhibition in London in 1885 claimed an annual production of 6,000 tons of solid paraffin, 4,000 tons of this being sold as candles.[15] The 2,000 tons sold as wax no doubt made a significant contribution to the raw materials used by independent candle manufacturers.

In 1883, the Scottish shale production amounted to 1,130,729 tons, and by 1888 this had risen to 2,052,202 tons.[16] Scottish production of solid paraffin must have risen accordingly: in fact, it was in excess of 24,000 tons.[17] Over the period, imports of paraffin from America also increased: in 1877, they amounted to 10,413 hundred-weights (520 tons), valued at £22,006, or £2 11s. per hundredweight; in 1888 the total was 340,441 hundredweights (17,022 tons), valued at £437,228, or £1.28 per hundred-weight.[18] There were also smaller importations of paraffin from Germany and other countries, and from 1885 from Burma and other British dominions, but up to the end of the century this import market was dominated by American producers.[19]

Agreements with Standard Oil

At the end of 1887, the Scottish industry had just emerged from the damaging strike. Although product prices had improved, the companies remained concerned about prospects and were obviously nervous of the increased American competition. At the same time, the American producers wanted to exploit their export markets to the full. However, in the case of solid paraffin, as opposed to burning oil, the advantage did not lie entirely with the Americans. Russian petroleum yielded no solid paraffin, and American never more than 1 or 2 per cent, while Scottish shale crude oil produced about 12 per cent.[20] However, paraffin imports were, in the late 1880s, sufficiently large to cause concern among the shale oil companies. They therefore welcomed a visit to Scotland by Edward T. Bedford, described in a newspaper report as 'one of the partners of the Standard Oil Company' and 'the authorised delegate to this country of the great oil raisers in the United States'. In fact, Edward T. Bedford was the 'Bedford' of Thompson & Bedford, a subsidiary company of Standard Oil which was responsible for the distribution of lubricants throughout the United States and Europe. In 1892 he was described as its president, and although not a partner in Standard Oil he was very senior within the organisation, becoming a director in 1903.[21] His presence in Scotland in 1888 indicates that Standard Oil had begun to regard the Scottish shale companies as serious competitors in the market for paraffin scale and wax. The result of Bedford's meetings with the companies was an agreement on minimum prices of hard scale and semi-refined wax with power, if required, to reduce production in Scotland and exports from America. A further agreement was made between the Scottish refining companies for minimum prices for burning oil. A third arrangement among candlemakers fixed minimum prices, discounts and other matters.[22]

These agreements were not achieved without difficulty. The Oakbank company had doubts, one of its main concerns being to secure its supplies of American residuum from which it manufactured specialist cylinder oils for marine engines.[23] The strength of feeling among the other concerns is indicated by a condition in the agreement that candlemakers would not purchase wax from the Oakbank company if it refused to join. The company eventually agreed. The chairman of the Linlithgow company, in describing this agreement to shareholders, referred to the Standard Oil Company as 'the largest sellers of scale in the world. The bulk of the wax candles made in London and throughout England are made from this scale, and Mr Bedford was therefore able to use his great influence on behalf of the Scotch proposal, that the candlemakers should co-operate with them in their efforts to reorganise the trade.'[24]

In January 1889, after some initial opposition from Oakbank, it was agreed to continue the agreement for another year. In 1890, the Scottish companies' proposal for an increase in minimum prices was said to have been answered by Standard urging that prices be kept at a moderate level to stimulate consumption. At the same time, it was reported that Standard intended to send to Great Britain 4,000 tons more wax than in the previous year. However, there was an extension for a further year with an increase of a halfpenny per pound in the minimum prices for all kinds of solid paraffin. It was also claimed that, although imports from America had not decreased, demand in the United Kingdom had greatly increased. The agreements were renewed in 1891 for a further year, with a similar increase in minimum prices.[25]

A report on the Scottish Mineral Oil Companies for 1889 has a number of points of interest. It states that burning oil was the companies' chief source of profit and that the restriction and price-fixing arrangements by the Scottish Mineral Oil Association had increased prices by up to 1¾d. per gallon. It described the association as, at first, a rather dubious experiment, going on to note: 'But the alliance proved unexpectedly robust; and it not only endures still, but is extending its powers and functions, as if determined to become a settled and lasting institution.' It had in fact decreed another increase in the price of burning oil of ½d. or ¾d. per gallon. The report also pointed out that the consumption of Scottish burning oil was confined mostly to Scotland, but that producers were at liberty to sell elsewhere at whatever price was obtainable, and stated that: 'The outside market to Scottish producers is, however, of little importance comparatively, being for the most part in the possession of American petroleum, which seldom gets scarce enough or rises high enough in price to offer the Scottish product a chance, although occasionally it does.' It discussed the threat of a 25 per cent increase in imports of American scale, but stated that this danger was thought to be over and that a delegate from America was imminently expected to arrange an extension of the agreement. A small increase in price was expected, as was increased competition from two new ventures in the home industry. A new company – presumably the Caledonian Oil Company Limited – had been formed to work an old Lanarkshire shale field, and the Hermand company, hitherto producing crude oil only, proposed to enter the refining side of the industry.[26] This did not come to pass, but the company agreed to amalgamate with the Walkinshaw company, which had in 1886 been compelled to cease production because of problems with its shale field, although its refinery was still in working order.[27]

It is of interest that, in 1888, 340,441 hundredweights (17,022 tons) of American paraffin were imported into the United Kingdom, while the figures for 1889, 1890 and 1891 were 306,338 hundredweights (15,316 tons), 489,149 hundredweights (24,457 tons), and 543,110 hundredweights (27,155 tons) respectively.[28] It seems clear that in the first year of the agreement American shipments were reduced, but thereafter they increased sharply, reaching in 1891 almost 60 per cent above the 1888 level. Scottish shale production fell from 2,052,202 tons in 1888 to 1,986,990 tons in 1889; in 1890 it increased to 2,180,483 tons; and in 1891 to 2,337,932 tons, a 14 per cent increase from 1888.[29] It seems that, after the first year, there was no need to restrict production or importation.

There is some evidence to support the statement that demand in the United Kingdom increased. Candle exports increased from 10,830,900 pounds valued at 52.68 pence per dozen pounds in 1888, to 13,556,800 pounds with a value of 55.56 pence per dozen pounds in 1890.[30] The Scottish companies' need for the arrangements with the Americans and the candlemakers is amply demonstrated by the results declared in the early part of 1888, shown in Table 3.1.

Only the Oakbank, Broxburn, Dalmeny, Hermand and Pumpherston companies paid dividends in 1888, the financial year covering the period of the strike. Oakbank was emerging from a period of serious reconstruction, and any dividend was a hopeful sign. Broxburn had borne the brunt of the miners' strike, which ended in November 1887, and its directors felt it necessary to make provision for

Table 3.1 Dividends, 1888–1891

Company	1888	1889	1890	1891
Young's	nil	7	7.5	9
Oakbank	6	8	5	5
Broxburn	5	15	15	15
Burntisland	nil	nil	nil	
Dalmeny	20	20	20	nil
Clippens	*	5	nil	nil
Holmes	nil	4	5	*
Hermand	7.5	17.5	*	*
Linlithgow	nil	nil	nil	nil
Pumpherston	3	10	10	10
West Lothian	nil	nil	nil	nil
Caledonian				5

* No information available.
Source: Newspaper reports of company affairs.

depreciation from the company's substantial reserve fund, making it possible to pay a dividend of 5 per cent. This unusual piece of finance attracted some adverse comment. The Dalmeny company had another successful year ending in November 1887: the directors were able, after crediting a new works account with £1,500 from revenue, to devote £3,780 to paying a dividend of 20 per cent. Hermand was in the process of reorganising the works taken over from Mr Thornton, and the dividend of 7½ per cent was regarded as satisfactory. The Pumpherston company, after making full provision for depreciation, a deficit from the previous year and interest charges, paid 3 per cent – a respectable performance in view of the state of trade. It was also stated also that a bench of 80 Young & Beilby retorts had been erected to replace the crude oil hitherto purchased from the Holmes company. A further bench of retorts was needed to replace this completely, but it had been decided not to proceed because of the agreements, which might entail production restrictions.[31]

Profitability improved in the financial year ending in March/April 1889. Three more companies managed to pay dividends: Young's (7½ per cent); Holmes (4 per cent); and Clippens (5 per cent). The shareholders of the Burntisland, West Lothian and Linlithgow companies received nothing. Of the rest, Dalmeny again paid 20 per cent; Broxburn managed 15, up from 5; Oakbank 8, up from 6; Hermand 17½, up from 7½; and Pumpherston 10, up from 3.

The performance even among companies not paying dividends improved during the year. The directors of most concerns expressed in their reports appreciation of the agreements made between the Scottish companies, with the American producers, and between the candlemakers. These agreements exercised a beneficial influence on the trade, and were renewed for another year. The extent of the benefit can be gauged from the statement by the managing director of the Broxburn company that 'in comparing the prices realised with those of the previous year, there was an increase in values amounting to £30,182.10.5'.[32] The Oakbank company is mentioned as a reluctant participant because, it was said, of 'continued friction between the companies on the restriction of output question'.[33] The Linlithgow company chairman commented to shareholders that 'the formation of a candle makers' association had not proved an unmixed good to the Company', while the Burntisland company had also found it difficult to break into the market for candles, but was hopeful of prospects for the coming year.[34]

Among the successful concerns, Young's was emerging from a drastic reorganisation of its capital. It was also completing the absorption of the Uphall company that had commenced in 1884, and the replacement of its Henderson retorts with the Pentland version. A dividend of 7½ per cent was a reasonable result. In their report, the directors complained that the Scottish Mineral Oil Association's restriction policy had operated unfairly on Young's. The restriction had been based on a period when their works' reorganisation had temporarily reduced production, and an unsuccessful appeal had been made to the association. The Clippens company paid 5 per cent, despite continuing difficulties with water in the pits. All of the successful companies, with the exception of Oakbank, referred to the various agreements between the Scottish companies, Standard Oil and the candlemakers, but possibly the most interesting point was made in the Broxburn and Pumpherston directors' reports. Both referred to the economies effected by adopting the continuous distillation process patented by Norman Henderson, the Broxburn manager. D.R. Steuart, the Broxburn company's chief chemist, stated that the cost of refining when the company began in 1879 was 1.38d. per gallon of crude oil; in 1889, it had fallen to 0.77d.[35]

The renewal of the agreements in 1889, 1890 and 1891 meant that the Scottish industry survived, and to some extent prospered, in these years. Table 3.1 shows that Broxburn, Pumpherston, Oakbank, Dalmeny and Young's paid relatively good dividends in these years. The other companies simply survived.

Breakdown of the agreement and renewal of unregulated competition

This was the position in Scotland at the beginning of 1892, when renewal of the agreements was discussed. The American producers' circumstances had, however, changed. The 'Great Shut-Down', which had restricted crude oil output in America, ended on 1 November 1888, and there was a considerable increase in production in 1889 and subsequent years. Also, Standard Oil had developed the Frasch process for refining the sulphur-contaminated crude from the Lima field in Ohio, and this made available large quantities of crude oil hitherto only suitable for fuel oil.[36] By September 1890, a new refinery, which became one of the largest in the world, was in operation at Whiting, Indiana. Initially concentrating on kerosene, gasoline and naphtha, the plant had, by 1893, begun manufacturing paraffin and candles in quantity.[37]

The sheer scale of oil production in America became in the 1880s a significant threat to the shale concerns. The amount of crude oil processed in American refineries rose from an average of 7.65 million barrels in 1873–5 to 27.6 million barrels in 1889. The Lima field development offered the prospect of further increase. In fact, 44.3 million barrels were refined in 1894 and 49.7 in 1899.[38] Even allowing for the smaller proportion of scale in American crude, the massive increase in the quantity processed meant an equally large increase in the amount of solid paraffin produced. In addition, the Pennsylvania crude gave only 1 per cent of scale, but the Lima crude oil produced 1.75 per cent, a significant increase.[39]

It has been estimated that in 1888 American production of paraffin wax was 53 million pounds, or 23,660 tons. Of this 36,006,000 lbs, or 16,074 tons, was exported, indicating that, in the case of this product, the American industry was as dependent on exports as it was with regard to illuminating oil and other liquid products. In

1889, the value of the industry's products had reached $85 million. In 1889, 15,101 tons of paraffin was exported from the USA, valued at $2.03 million.[40] At 2.39 per cent of the total value of products, this is a not insignificant contribution from what was essentially a by-product.

The arrangements with the Americans meant that the Scottish companies had to accept the reductions in production which had seriously affected some of their concerns. In the year ending 30 April 1889, the Young's directors complained that they had experienced a reduction of 1 million gallons, while the Burntisland directors complained that the 'restriction of production of crude oil and scale, ordered by the Oil Association in terms of the agreement with the American scale producers, has caused a considerable diminution in the amount of the sales of the company's products during the year.'[41] This year was one in which there was a reduction in American scale and wax imports. A comparison with Scottish production of the previous year, ending March/April 1888, is not informative because of the effects of the miners' strike in 1887. However, shale production in Scotland in 1886 was 1,699,144 tons; and in 1888 this rose to 2,052,202 tons,[42] not indicating a general compliance with the association's request. The Broxburn company, in fact, in the year ending 30 March 1887, processed 9,186,874 gallons of crude oil; in the year ending 3 April 1889, 10,453,153 gallons were refined.[43]

In 1889 shale production was 1,986,990 tons, a fall of about 3 per cent. In 1890 it rose again to 2,180,483 tons, and in 1891 to 2,337,932 tons.[44] Oakbank, Broxburn, Pumpherston and Young's, in the financial year ending in spring 1889, had total sales of scale, wax and candles of £310,066. In the year ending in spring 1892, the total was £449,247, an increase of 45 per cent.[45] In 1888, 17,022 tons of American paraffin valued at £437,228 were imported, and in 1891 it was 27,155 tons valued at £777,572 – a 60 per cent increase in quantity and 77 per cent in value.[46] It is clear that the Scottish companies had benefited from the agreement, but the American industry even more so.

At the beginning of 1892, further negotiations secured the extension of the agreement between Standard Oil and the Scottish companies until 31 March 1893. The memorandum of agreement states that Scottish production for the previous year had been 24,900 tons, and American imports 24,320 tons. It was agreed that for the ensuing year, Scottish production should be limited by 10 per cent to 22,400 tons, and that the reduction be added to the American wax imports to make a total of 26,800.[47] In the parliamentary Annual Statement of Trade of the United Kingdom with Foreign Countries and British Possessions for the Year 1891, imports from America amounted to 27,115 tons.[48] The difference may be accounted for by the fact that the agreement was between the Scottish producers and American interests represented by Standard Oil along with the Tidewater Oil Company: there may well have been exports by American producers outside this group.

Difficulties arose almost immediately. At a meeting of the Scottish Mineral Oil Association on 2 March 1892, the Pumpherston and Stanrigg companies drew attention to 'the necessity for providing for the altered conditions arising out of the largely increased American production.'[49] Mr A. Fraser, secretary and general manager of the Pumpherston company, stated that Mr Bedford's original proposal had involved creating new markets in other countries for the surplus of American wax. It was now clear, he claimed, that a large part of that surplus was to be absorbed by displacement of Scottish scale from markets hitherto held by the Scottish companies. A further difficulty arose from the high quality of semi-refined wax offered by American producers. During the summer of 1892, discussions took place among the Scottish companies, but this did not result in a course of action acceptable to all parties. The main stumbling block was the different interests of companies that had candleworks and those limited to selling their product as scale or wax.

In the year ending 30 April 1892, Young's derived 55.8 per cent of its wax-related revenue from candles, 28.6 per cent from wax and 15.6 per cent from scale. In the same year, Broxburn had 70 per cent of this revenue from candles and 30 per cent from wax. Oakbank's sales were all of refined wax. Pumpherston sold 52.8 per cent as scale and 47.2 per cent as refined wax, realising 2.87d. and 3.52d. per pound respectively. Oakbank had an average of 3.49d. per pound for its sales of refined wax, while Broxburn achieved an average of 4.16d. per pound for candles sold by its London branch.[50] There was a significant bias in favour of the more vertically integrated concerns.

I.T. Redwood, in his 1897 book on the shale industry, ascribed the industry's difficulties to a lack of investment in new refining methods that would facilitate competition with 'go-ahead foreign manufacturers', as well as over-competition among the companies. He also claimed that 'the industry would have, by this time, been practically a thing of the past had not the Standard Oil Company of America tried to act as a mediator between the several companies, and got them to combine and work amicably together, with a view to maintaining such prices as would enable them to pay the dividends due to their trusting (but often sadly disappointed) shareholders'. Without a combination of companies and changes in management, he suggested that, 'we would be left to mourn the loss of one of Scotland's most important industries.'[51]

This assessment of Standard's role must be viewed with caution. Faced with the greatly increased production of scale and wax from the new Whiting refinery, there can be little doubt that Standard wished to control the European market in wax, as it already did in burning oil. On 7 February 1893, John Fyfe, managing director of Young's company, and William Kennedy of the Broxburn company travelled to London, to meet Mr Bedford and Mr Usmar of Standard Oil. Fyfe reported: 'We sat until midnight discussing all matters connected with the present position and future prospects of the Mineral Oil Trade in America and Scotland.' Bedford explained that it was now Standard's policy to maintain existing low prices for scale, and that he expected American exports to Europe in the coming year to be about 35,000 tons, and 'if the market should be able to absorb a greater quantity the Standard Oil Trust will have no difficulty in supplying it'. The possibility was discussed of the Standard Oil Trust taking an interest in the two Scottish companies by investing in preference shares and debenture stocks. Bedford indicated his cautious approval, but thought it would depend on Scottish production of solid paraffin being reduced from 24,000 tons to 14,000 tons. Mention was also made of the possibility of the purchase of a works 'with a view to breaking up so as to terminate its career finally'. Bedford also 'both frankly and feelingly admitted that it was his disagreeable message of thirteen months ago which had worked such havoc even amongst the few good companies in Scotland'. He went on to say that he had nothing but friendly feelings towards them, and that if the scheme proposed were found to be of mutual advantage he would very pleased 'to be in alliance with Mr Kennedy and myself'.[52]

That Standard Oil regarded the Scottish producers as significant competition was made clear in 1897 when an emissary approached Kirkman Finlay of the Burmah company with a proposal for a joint price war 'to knock the Scotch [shale oil] trade on the head'. This was rejected.[53]

The deciding event was the decision made on 8 September 1892 to wind up the Burntisland company. Over 600 tons of the company's hard scale was held as security for cash advances. The Mineral Oil Association was asked to purchase this to avoid the adverse effect on the market of its uncontrolled disposal. The association was unable to agree on a solution for this and the problem of large stocks of scale and wax, which were said to be, at 31 August 1892, 4,000 tons more than at the same time in 1891.[54] In their annual report, the directors of the Linlithgow company complained that their working capital was insufficient, 'mainly owing to the large stocks of scale and wax, for which a free outlet cannot in the meantime be obtained'.[55] The Pumpherston company's stock of scale rose from £2,343 in the year ending 30 April 1891 to £15,927 in 1892.[56]

Pumpherston left the association and immediately started to sell scale and wax at lower than the agreed prices; the company's general meetings of 1893 were told of reductions in product values. The Broxburn managing director spoke of a fall of around one third.[57] This was a very serious matter for the Scottish industry. For some years, scale, wax and candles had been one of the most important sources of revenue. From 1892 up to the end of the century, apart from 1895 when a shortlived attempt was made to revive the agreement with the Americans, the Scottish shale companies existed in a completely free market, with competition from the American producers and with new sources of liquid and solid products in the Far

East. Imports of American paraffin rose to 37,205 tons in 1893, and the price fell from £1.43 per hundredweight in 1891 to £1.05. By 1898 imports had reached 45,379 tons and the price had fallen to £0.85.[58]

The West Lothian company ceased trading early in 1892 and was subsequently wound up. The Burntisland company went into voluntary liquidation in September 1892 and was the immediate cause of the breakdown of the agreements; an unsuccessful attempt was made to reorganise it as a new company. Clippens also went into voluntary liquidation in December 1892, but a new company was incorporated in June 1893, which carried on operations until 1897 when a serious dispute with the Edinburgh Water Trust caused the stoppage of the company's works and mines. The directors of the Hermand company, in 1893, reacted to the difficulties facing the trade by closing their works and mines to wait for better times. The company was reconstructed and the works reopened in 1899.[59] The rest of the industry survived, although for some concerns it was for a limited time only.

It is clear from Table 3.2 that the Scottish industry experienced great difficulty after the failure of the agreements. Seven refining companies entered the contest, but the Clippens concern was, in 1897, compelled to close for reasons unconnected with the oil trade. This left six refining companies and three making crude oil only. In addition, the private partnership James Ross & Co. continued to mine shale and produce crude oil at Philpstoun, near Linlithgow.

The two largest refining concerns in 1890 were Young's and Broxburn, which employed 734 and 698 underground workmen respectively. Pumpherston had 336, Oakbank 290, Linlithgow 273 and Caledonian 164. In 1896 Young's underground workforce grew to 847, Broxburn fell slightly to 660, and there were increases at Pumpherston to 582, Oakbank to 302, Linlithgow to 300, and Caledonian to 250.

Table 3.2 Dividends, 1892–1900

Company	1892	1893	1894	1895	1896	1897	1898	1899	1900
Young's	5	nil	nil	nil	nil	nil	nil	nil	nil
Broxburn	10	nil	nil	5	7.5	7.5	7.5	8.5	15
Pumpherston	10	nil	nil	5	5	nil	nil	nil	20
Oakbank	nil	nil	nil	nil	5	nil	nil	5	7.5
Linlithgow	nil	nil	nil	nil	nil	nil	nil	nil	nil
Caledonian	*	*	*	*	*	nil	*	nil	*
Clippens	nil	nil	nil	nil	*	nil			
Holmes	nil	nil	nil	nil	nil	nil	nil	nil	
Dalmeny	nil	10	*	*	*	7.5	5	nil	nil

* Information not available.
Sources: Company reports in *Scotsman*, *Glasgow Herald* and *West Lothian Courier*.

The crude oil producers had also increased in size: Dalmeny from 130 men to 164, Holmes from 109 to 126, and Ross from 53 to 164, indicating that some of the refining concerns were increasing purchases of crude oil.[60] In 1896, the Linlithgow company agreed to purchase for five years the output of the Holmes company.[61] In the same year, the Oakbank company contracted for some years to buy the whole crude oil output of the Dalmeny company[62]

The importance of sulphate of ammonia in the industry's survival

At this period, sulphate of ammonia became an increasingly important element in sales. It also figured largely in the by-product profile of the iron and steel industry.[63] It had become an important source of nitrogen in agriculture, although initially very little was used by British farmers and much of the production of shale works, gas works, and so on was exported to Germany, where it was used in a heavily subsidised sugar beet culture.[64] Sulphate of ammonia was also considered to be the best artificial fertiliser for sugar cane – although the relatively poor condition of that industry in the West Indies inhibited its use to some extent.[65] A vigorous publicity campaign in the early twentieth century helped to persuade British agriculture to use sulphate of ammonia to provide half of its needs for nitrogen.[66]

In 1879, sulphate of ammonia made up 5.71 per cent of the Oakbank sales; by 1891 this had risen to 11.2 per cent. At Young's in 1879, sulphate of ammonia contributed 4.87 per cent of sales; in 1891, it was 11.47 per cent. In 1891 sulphate of ammonia made up 31.91 per cent of Pumpherston's sales, making it the most important part of the company's revenue.[67]

Production increased in the mid-1880s with the introduction of the Young & Beilby retort. Pumpherston was equipped with this from the start, and Oakbank had been one of the first to convert. Young's installed 1,024 Pentland retorts – a version of the Young & Beilby – by 1892. The Broxburn company in 1891 decided to open mines at Drumshoreland, south of Broxburn, and to erect a crude oil works equipped with a new retort designed by the works manager, Norman Henderson.[68] The Pumpherston directors announced the intention to acquire the works and shale fields at Seafield near Bathgate, formerly the property of the Bathgate Oil Company, 'which are to provide the crude oil supplies hitherto purchased from outside sources'. This would ensure 'ample supplies of crude oil at a very favourable cost'.[69] The work was completed in 1892.[70] The Oakbank company had earlier built a new bench of retorts, prompting the chairman to comment that the installation was made 'not so much with the view of increasing production – though also with that view – as that they might keep up full production in the event of any of the retorts getting out of repair'.[71] This may well have been a contributory factor in the disagreement with the other members of the association.

All four of these companies were confident enough of the future in the early 1890s to engage in expansion. This continued even after the breakdown of the agreements and the severe fall in the price of scale and wax. The Broxburn company pressed on with the building of the new crude oil works at Roman Camp, which came into full production in the middle of 1893. All of the old retorts at Broxburn had been replaced by December 1894. Oakbank in 1893 increased production by about one third by the purchase of crude oil.[72] Young's, the largest of the refining concerns, simply maintained or only marginally improved its production.

The Linlithgow company had a rather less happy experience over these years. It had been established to use the original Henderson retort, but this was found unsatisfactory in its sulphate of ammonia yield. One bench of retorts was altered in the year ending April 1889, and the erection of Young & Beilby retorts was recommended by an extraordinary general meeting in April 1890. However, over the next few years, the company had difficulty in financing the necessary developments. An issue of preference shares was only partly subscribed.[73]

1900–1914: New retorts and expansion

The four major refining companies managed to survive the troubles of the 1890s, although only the Broxburn company consistently paid dividends. The turning point in the fortunes of the industry again involved a further development of the retort. In 1896, a bench of a new retort was erected at the Seafield works, and after a few months results were such that the Pumpherston company decided to replace all the existing retorts and to acquire the Deans works and mines formerly worked by the West Lothian company. Two benches of the new retorts were to be erected at the Deans works.[1]

Hitherto, it had been the received opinion that retorts had to be relatively small in circumference to allow the heat to reach all of the shale. In 1894 and 1895 James Bryson, the Pumpherston works manager, patented a retort that had a diameter of 3 feet at its largest section.[2] The spent shale was removed at regular intervals from the bottom of the retort, ensuring a slow and even progress through the retort. This, combined with enlargement of the diameter towards the bottom, caused a lateral movement in the shale, ensuring that the whole content of the retort was exposed to heat. The capacity was 5 tons per day, or about three times that of previous plant. It was heated, after initial firing, entirely by the permanent gases produced from the shale. Bryson claimed that the cost of retorting a ton of shale had been reduced from the 22 pence per ton of the Young & Beilby retort to 12 pence per ton. In the year ending 31 March 1899, Oakbank processed 106,671 tons of shale in Young & Beilby retorts at a cost of £10,743, or 24.17 pence per ton. In the same year, 73,974 tons were dealt with in the new Bryson retorts at a cost of £4,341, 14.08 pence per ton, not radically different from Bryson's claim.[3]

The new retort was immediately adopted. Pumpherston had 208 in use by December 1897, two benches at Seafield and two at Deans. A further two benches were installed at Pumpherston in August 1898. Oakbank erected a bench in January 1898 and completed a second, the renewal of its entire retorting plant, by 1900. Young's had replaced all of its Pentland retorts by 1901. The Broxburn company was somewhat slower to adapt. The general meeting in May 1902 was informed that the work to replace the retorts had begun two months previously; the retort renewal at Broxburn was reported in May 1905, and at Roman Camp in May 1906. In 1907 it was reported that another bench of retorts was under construction at Broxburn to keep the mines fully employed. A further bench was completed in 1911.[4] There seems to have been a steady increase in the company's production in the period up to the Great War.

Young's did not initially increase its plant. In 1904 the shareholders were told that it was not the board's policy to increase production beyond the standard set at the amalgamation with the Uphall company in 1883. Increased production might be difficult to dispose of in a bad year. Nevertheless, it was also reported in 1904 that an additional bench of retorts was being built at Uphall to maintain production when retorts were being cleaned or repaired.[5] In 1907 a new bench was built to compensate for shales producing smaller yields of liquid products.[6]

From 1899 to 1913, Young's underground mining workforce rose from 812 to 930, a 14 per cent increase. Over the same period, Broxburn increased its workforce from 703 to 919, a 31 per cent increase. In the year ending 29 March 1899, the company used 478,472 tons of shale; in 1913 it was 646,441 tons, an increase of 35 per cent. However, crude oil production increased by only 13 per cent from 12,226,025 gallons to 13,806,562 gallons. Purchases of crude oil increased from 1,261,054 gallons in 1899 to 4,432,827 gallons. Total throughput of crude oil increased by 35 per cent. It is clear that shales less productive of crude oil were in use at the later period, but this was compensated for by an increase of purchased crude oil. There was also a considerable increase in productivity in the mines. In 1899 in the East Scotland District, 3,374 underground miners produced 2,206,408 tons of shale – 654 tons per man; in 1913, 4,384 men produced 3,279,903 tons – an average of 748, and an increase of 14.37 per cent.[7]

The really striking increases in production occurred at Oakbank and Pumpherston. Oakbank had completely replaced its Young & Beilby retorts with the new Bryson version by 1900, and in 1902 the company began constructing mines and a crude oil works near Winchburgh in West Lothian. At the same time, extensions were made to the Oakbank refinery. Although the company remained the smallest of the four refining concerns, this expansion meant an increase in shale processed from 180,645 tons in 1899 to 428,031 tons in 1913. Over the same period, crude oil purchased increased from 2,595,090 gallons from the Dalmeny company to 4,474,890 gallons from Dalmeny and James Ross & Co., making a total throughput of 13,599,699 gallons, more than double the quantity refined in 1899.[8]

The Pumpherston company had completed two benches of the new retorts at each of its three works by 1898. In 1902 a third bench was installed, making seven in all. In 1908, the shareholders learned that the Deans works were undergoing large extensions.[9]

In 1904 the Tarbrax Oil Company Limited was formed to take over the works and mines at Tarbrax formerly worked by the Caledonian Oil Company, which had gone into liquidation in February 1903. This company, although a separate entity, had the same directors as the Pumpherston company. The shares were offered to

Pumpherston shareholders, and were taken up by them, except for a very small number of preference shares. The whole output of crude oil was to be refined at Pumpherston. Initially there were two benches of the Bryson retorts, but in 1906 a third was added and in 1909 a fourth. In 1912 it was decided that the two companies should formally merge. Pumpherston had become the largest company in the industry. In 1899, 554 men were employed underground; in 1913 there were 1,279 underground miners, well over double the previous number.[10]

There were, however, some casualties. The Hermand works had been closed for some years because of the condition of the trade. The company was reconstructed in March 1899 and the works restarted, but results were unsatisfactory because of the worn-out plant;[11] £25,000 of 7 per cent preference shares were offered to the public to finance the building of new retorts, but only £18,154 was subscribed and it was not possible to build a full bench. Despite efforts towards further reconstruction to secure fresh capital, the company went into voluntary liquidation in June 1902. The company's works were bought by Pumpherston company in 1903, and in 1904 it was reported that the retort plant had been removed to the Seafield works.[12]

The Linlithgow company struggled through the last decade of the nineteenth century. In 1900 the chairman reported to the annual meeting that more modern retorts were needed, but that it was not possible to ask the shareholders for the required funds while the future of the industry remained doubtful. It was decided to wind up the company in February 1902. This was associated with the demise of the Holmes company, which was placed in liquidation in 1900.[13]

The reasons given for some companies' lack of success illustrate some of the problems faced by the industry, besides that of foreign competition. The Dalmeny company, which had regularly paid dividends of 20 per cent and more, on one occasion disappointed its shareholders. In December 1890 the directors reported that a fire had broken out in a shale seam in October, and it had been necessary to close part of the mine. In December 1891 it was reported that the problem required the workings to be flooded: this had resulted in a loss for the year of £1,902.[14]

In addressing the annual general meeting in May 1891, the Clippens chairman explained the company's poor results for the previous few years. The Pentland Main seam of shale, although rich in products, had peculiarities in its roof and pavement which required great care in working. The seam was exploited successfully from 1882 to 1886, when a 'crush' took place.[15] Although this was overcome, there was a sudden inrush of water and the workings were flooded to a depth of 250 feet. This was not cleared until that financial year. The extra cost of mining shale from the old crushed working was about £30,000 and contributed largely to the poor performance.[16]

The net result of all the changes within the industry and within the various companies was that, as the country approached the Great War, the Scottish shale

Table 4.1 Dividends, 1900–1914

	Company				
	Young's	Oakbank	Broxburn	Pumpherston	Tarbrax
Ordinary	267,152	239,401	379,521	592,553	33,585
Preference		32,241	90,000	96,000	19,444
Debenture Bonds	250,980				
Contingent Dividends	70,500				
Totals	588,632	271,642	469,521	688,553	53,029

oil industry – or, at least, its strongest concerns – had survived and prospered. Shale production had increased by almost 50 per cent from 2,206,408 tons in 1899 to 3,279,903 tons in 1913. A grand total of £2,071,377 in profit was distributed by the industry in the period 1900–14.

The industry owed its survival to a number of factors, some of which will be explored in more detail in later chapters. There was an element of good fortune in that it enjoyed certain advantages over foreign competitors: the relative richness of the crude oil as a source of paraffin scale, and the presence in the shale of large quantities of nitrogen. These advantages were exploited to the full by the efforts of management figures such as William Young, Norman Henderson, George Beilby, James Bryson and others. The overall management of the successful concerns by men like William and Archibald Fraser, William Kennedy, John Fyfe and John Wishart was also important. This aspect of the industry's success will be discussed in chapters 13 and 14.

At this point it is sufficient to assess how the industry adapted to changing markets over the years from its foundation in 1851. Burning oil was the most important product until the 1870s, when it was overtaken by scale, wax and candles. In the decade before the Great War, sulphate of ammonia became the largest seller. This indicates an ability to adapt to trading conditions. It is also true that in 1864 the products of one ton of cannel coal fetched a total of £13 10s. (£13.50);[17] in 1869 one ton of shale gave products valued at £1 4s. 11d. (£1.25), and in 1897, 10s. 11d. (£0.55).[18] By 1911, the Oakbank directors reported that the products of a ton of shale fetched only 9s. 10¾d. (£0.49). The company was, however, able to provide a dividend of 5 per cent; in the same year, Pumpherston paid 30 per cent on its ordinary shares.[19] The shale companies had obviously made significant improvements in efficiency.

The value of Young's products at various periods is given in Table 4.2.

It has been claimed that by the late 1870s American kerosene dominated the British market, until the importation of Russian oil threatened this 'comfortable

Table 4.2 Young's: relative value of different products in selected years

	Burning oil %	Lub. oil %	Wax etc %	Candles %	Naphtha %	Sulphate of ammonia %	Lamps %
1864	74	19	7				
1872	52	11	16	16	2	3	
1889	34	13	6	25	4	7	5
1901	23	14	13	20	7	18	5
1913	20	13	14	11	6	32	4

Source: BP Archive, YP Ledgers and Journals.

American monopoly'.[20] It has also been asserted that the Anglo-American Oil Company, set up by Standard Oil in 1888, 'monopolized the British oil trade'.[21] The Americans may in fact have enjoyed a major share of the British market, but it was not by any means a monopoly. In 1891, 130,615,360 gallons of petroleum oils were imported into the United Kingdom. Of these 82,035,621 gallons (62.8 per cent) were from the United States; 46,835,116 (35.86 per cent) from Russia; and 1,744,623 (1.34 per cent) from other countries.[22] Information given in the *Journal of the Society of Chemical Industry* provides a basis for calculation of the Scottish industry's production of oils in 1891:[23] 2,337,932 tons of shale yielded 25.09 gallons of crude oil and 1.73 gallons of naphtha per ton, a total of 62,703,336 gallons, which gave 34,624,782 gallons of various refined liquid oils – 26.50 per cent of the volume of oils imported, or 20.95 per cent of the total volume of oils used in the United Kingdom in 1891 and 42.20 per cent of imports from the United States. In 1913 imports of oils amounted to 488,106,963 gallons.[24] In the same year the Scottish industry produced 45,168,875 gallons, or 9.25 per cent of the volume imported.[25] Even in 1913 the Scottish industry made a significant contribution to the British oil trade. In 1890, it was stated that the bulk of the shale industry's production of burning oil was sold in Scotland.[26] In 1913, 18,069,681 gallons were delivered by the four Scottish concerns, 12,072,930 to Scotland (66.81 per cent). The remainder was delivered almost equally to England and Ireland (17.44 per cent) and foreign destinations (15.75 per cent).[27] It seems that the companies had, in fact, retained their local market.

In the build-up of armaments in the early years of the twentieth century, the Admiralty was interested in using fuel oil in place of coal. By 1905, the Royal Navy had become the 'leader in the field of burning oil among the navies of the world'. The Admiralty in 1910 purchased 20,000 tons of Scottish shale fuel oil to encourage 'a domestic source of supply'. In 1919 the Anglo-Persian Oil Company, in which the government was a majority shareholder, was persuaded, for similar reasons, to acquire the Scottish shale oil companies.[28]

The shale industry, by the start of the Great War, had survived a number of serious crises largely by concentrating on a small number of relatively large concerns. This involved creating a large number of limited companies, and dissolving most of them. These companies, and their capital, shareholders and management, will be discussed in later chapters.

Part 2 Capital employed

Introduction

In industry, successful enterprises are able to combine technical innovation, labour and capital to make the most of opportunity. Opportunity, labour and technical innovation in the shale industry are dealt with elsewhere. This section will consider the amount and sources of capital involved in the new industry.

It has been said that:

> Manufacturing enterprises, until the end of the nineteenth century, very rarely raised money on the London or provincial stock exchanges. This was partly because much manufacturing could begin in a small way. Where large amounts of capital were needed at the outset to sink the mine, dig the canal, lay the railway, capital was raised at first through partnerships, but then through companies publicly quoted on the stock exchange.[1]

The shale oil industry was established and developed to its greatest extent before the Great War, and seems to have followed the pattern outlined by Ackrill. In 1914 the industry consisted of Young's Paraffin Light & Mineral Oil Company Limited, the Oakbank Oil Company Limited, the Dalmeny Oil Company Limited, the Broxburn Oil Company Limited, the Pumpherston Oil Company Limited, and the private partnership of James Ross & Company. These were the six survivors of 63 concerns initiated in the Almond Valley since 1851, of which 21 had been limited companies and 42 individual entrepreneurs or private partnerships.[2] Ten of the limited companies and 41 of the private concerns were formed in the period up to 1877, and from then until 1904, eleven limited companies and one private firm came into existence.[3] In terms of numbers, the industry was, in its early stages, predominantly one of private concerns. After 1877 it consisted almost entirely of limited companies. Of the 41 private concerns set up before 1877, only three survived after that date, and two were converted to limited companies.[4]

1851–1877

Individual entrepreneurs and partnerships, 1851–1877

Even in its early years, the industry required considerable capital investment. Because of the absence of records, an exact figure cannot be placed on the amount of such investment by individuals and partnerships, but a newspaper of the time estimated that £150,000 had been spent on the various works around Broxburn by 1865.[1] It is also known that the eight partners in the Caledonian Oil Company at Benhar, near Whitburn, invested a capital of £30,000.[2]

The earliest and largest of the concerns was E.W. Binney & Company at Bathgate. Its cost in 1851 was possibly about £3,000: this included six benches, each of five horizontal retorts, at £60 per bench, together with the associated condensing and refining plant, and it probably produced about 200,000 gallons of oil per year. By 1864, when the partnership of E.W. Binney & Company was dissolved, production had increased to about 2 million gallons, substantial expansion having occurred in 1859 and 1860. On the dissolution of the partnership, it was agreed that Young should pay £32,000 for the works.[3]

In 1871 the works at Dalmeny was valued at £3,591. This included 24 vertical retorts and ancillary equipment valued at £2,204, 21 horizontal retorts at £352, and the mine at £950.[4] In 1871, the rateable value of this works was £164. If, as seems reasonable, a relationship is assumed between the rateable value and the capital investment involved, it might be deduced that the capital involved in the various concerns in the Almond Valley not operated by limited companies was of the order of £100,000.[5] This, however, is based on the valuation of an existing works which had, very probably, suffered some depreciation. The value placed on the vertical retorts was, in fact, less than two thirds of the new price ruling in 1871.[6] Capital investment in private concerns in the Almond Valley may therefore have been considerably higher than £100,000, and may well have been as much as twice that amount.

Who provided this finance? In the case of the first major firm, E.W. Binney, the three partners were James Young, Edward Meldrum and Edward William Binney, who was a Manchester lawyer with an interest in geology. He provided, directly or through his professional contacts, the bulk of the capital for the Bathgate works.[7] For the remaining concerns, the major source of information is again the Valuation Rolls, which provide the names of all property owners, tenants and occupiers in the area. These have yielded the names of 51 men who had been individual operators or members of partnerships. For 39 of them, a previous or concurrent occupation or designation was given; they are grouped according to occupation or designation in Table 5.1.

Allocation to the different groups was relatively simple, although some cases presented a little difficulty. The resolution of these difficulties sometimes produced additional information about the individual concerned. For example, Ebenezer Fernie was eventually designated as a business man, but it became clear that he had, prior to his involvement in the Scottish industry, been very much concerned in oil manufacture in England and Wales. He had also accumulated a considerable fortune by speculation in mineral leases.[8] Robert Calderwood, the occupier of an oil works at Drumcross, near Bathgate, was described in the Memorandum of Association of the Oakbank Oil Company as an oil manufacturer.[9] Before his entry into the oil industry he had been a colliery manager, a colliery engine keeper and a coal miner.[10]

There were ten merchants. Nine of them were members of partnerships and one, Robert Fraser, was the lessee of an oil works at Drumcross, near Bathgate, where he sublet the working to Robert Calderwood. None of the merchants had any obvious local connection. Three were located in Edinburgh, six in Glasgow and the west of Scotland, and for one no address was given in the Valuation Roll. Eight were described simply as merchants, one as an oil merchant and one as a coal merchant.

Of the eight coal, iron and lime masters, five had local connections. George Gray was the lessee of the lime works at Leavenseat near West Calder, in association with which he mined and retorted the local shale. He was also involved in coal mining

Table 5.1 Individual entrepreneurs and members of partnerships

Designation	Number
Merchant	10
Coal, iron and lime masters	8
Landowners	4
Members of professions	4
Manufacturers	4
Chemists	2
Clerks	2
Business man	1
Colliery manager	1
Mineral borer	1
	39

in the adjacent parish of Carnwath in Lanarkshire. George Simpson was a coal master at Benhar, near Whitburn in West Lothian, where he was a partner in the Caledonian Oil Company. In partnership with Edward Meldrum, he established the Boghall works near Bathgate and was later a partner in the Uphall Mineral Oil Company. The Watson Brothers of Armadale and the Grangepans firm of John Nimmo & Sons were both coal masters on a considerable scale, and engaged in oil manufacture as a secondary activity. The Thornton family of Crofthead, near Fauldhouse, West Lothian were farmers, coal masters and lime masters.

The landowners were all local men. Andrew Walker exploited the shales on his estate of Hartwood, near West Calder from 1869 to 1873. Robert Stewart worked the shales on his land as a member of a partnership. John P. Raeburn of Charlesfield, near Mid Calder, and Peter McLagen of Pumpherston were also substantial land-owners. The professional men included a Wishaw general practitioner, two bankers – one of whom was also a property factor – and a lecturer in geology. Among the manufacturers were, from Glasgow, an iron tube manufacturer and one man simply described as 'manufacturer'. A family of iron founders from Bathgate and a Broxburn bone meal-maker completed the list from industry. The two chemists listed in Table 5.1 were James Young and his partner Edward Meldrum, and the two clerks were the sons of the Earl of Rosebery's factor, himself a substantial figure in local agriculture. These two young men, therefore, could be said to be closely associated with the landowning and agricultural section of society. The business man was E.W. Fernie, while the craftsmen were a carver and gilder and a retired coach builder, both from Edinburgh.

The relatively small amounts of capital involved in the small concerns during the early stages of the industry would have been well within the resources of such individuals. It is, because of the lack of records, not possible to state categorically whether these men did or did not borrow the necessary finance. However, it is clear that the initial capital investment made by individuals and members of partnerships came from already established elements of society.

Limited liability

The considerable success enjoyed by surviving concerns in the first decade of the twentieth century, and the record of failure in other companies, suggest that the industry might be a suitable case study on the performance of British industry since the middle of the nineteenth century.[11] The predominance of limited liability places such a study firmly in the context of the limited company. The shale oil industry developed at a time of major change in the capital structure of the United Kingdom. The Companies Acts of 1856 and 1862 made generally available the benefits of incorporation and the limited liability of individual shareholders.

From 1862 to 1875, ten limited companies were set up in the Almond Valley, and seven elsewhere in Scotland. Investment in limited companies is, at first sight, much easier to quantify than that in private concerns. Details of paid-up capital are given in the company files and have been extracted to form Table A in Appendix 1.[12] This, among other things, gives for each year from 1863 to 1913 the cumulative total of investment in the limited companies. In this case the discussion is not confined to the Almond Valley, but includes all limited companies traced in the Scottish oil industry. The companies were found by a search of the BT2 repertory of dissolved companies in the National Archives of Scotland. To these were added the names of the three companies which have not yet been dissolved, and the Pumpherston company, which remained in existence until the late 1990s. Forty-three limited companies were found to have been registered in the period up to 1914.

Any discussion of limited liability in Scotland in the nineteenth century must be set in the context of Professor Payne's analysis of the 2,625 companies formed in Scotland between 1856 and mid-1895 and dissolved by 1970.[13] This analysis, in the form of a table, shows that 38 companies were classified in category 326, the shale oil industry, while my analysis produces a figure of 40 limited companies in the industry over the same period. The difference may be accounted for by the fact that one oil company was initially registered in 1876 as the Straiton Estate Company Limited; Professor Payne's table has, in all probability, included this under a different classification. His table also lists no registrations of shale oil companies in 1869, while this present work shows that the Oakbank company was registered in that year. It is also the case that of the three companies registered in 1893 one, the Oil Gas Enrichment Company, was not related to the shale industry. We are left, therefore, with 39 companies registered in the shale industry up to 1895.

Professor Payne's analysis ends in mid-1895, and his table, as discussed above, includes all companies registered between 1856 and mid-1895, not solely those dissolved by 1970. It therefore includes the four shale companies, which survived as subsidiaries of Scottish Oils Limited. Between 1895 and 1919 four more shale oil companies were formed, and were also dissolved by 1970. The present analysis is therefore initially concerned with 43 limited companies formed in the shale industry between 1856 and 1919. James Ross & Company Limited, registered in 1919, was the incorporation of the partnership James Ross & Company, which was carried out simply to facilitate the formation of Scottish Oils Limited.

Professor Payne set out to show the number of companies formed in each year, their objectives, how long they lasted, why they ceased to exist, how much capital was involved, and what relationship, if any, there was between the size, length of life and growth of companies.[14] It is my intention to examine the companies in the shale industry in that context, using the same sources, the files of the dissolved companies and any available additional sources, such as newspaper reports and any company records that have survived.

Starting with the length of life of the companies, it is necessary to establish the dates of commencement and cessation. Payne suggests the date of incorporation as an obvious starting point for all companies; the date of cessation requires more consideration. In some cases, a resolution to wind up the company voluntarily was made in general meeting; in others, a court order was obtained for a compulsory winding up. These may clearly be accepted as the date of cessation of business. Some companies were taken over or absorbed as going concerns by other companies, and the date of takeover may be accepted. Some companies, as Payne suggests, simply withered away, to be dissolved under the provisions of Clause 7 (4) of the Companies Act, 1880 by an announcement in the *Edinburgh Gazette*. In such cases, Payne suggests that the date of cessation be assumed as 12 months after the submission of the last annual return of capital and shares; these submissions would have been expected to continue if the company had remained in operation. A last category was abortive concerns. Payne provides four definitions of 'abortive', only two of which concern us here: a company whose capital was not subscribed for, or which made no returns to the registrar after the issue of the certificate of incorporation.[15]

These rules were followed with respect to the shale concerns, with the exception of the four companies not dissolved before 1970. Young's Paraffin Light & Mineral Oil Company, the Oakbank Oil Company (1886), and the Broxburn Oil Company remain in existence today, and the Pumpherston Company lasted until the late 1990s. However, virtually all of the ordinary shares of the companies were acquired in 1919 by Scottish Oils Limited, a subsidiary company of the Anglo-Persian Oil Company, and the companies from then on were controlled by Scottish Oils, and ultimately by Anglo-Persian (later Anglo-Iranian and, latterly, British Petroleum). The date of termination in these cases is taken as 1919.[16]

Payne provides an analysis of the average length of life of dissolved Scottish companies by year of incorporation.[17] It is useful to set the shale companies against this. Only 34 of the 40 shale oil companies are shown in Table 5.2, and only those years in which a shale company was formed are included. The Glentore Oil Company (1866) submitted no documents to the registrar after the initial registration, and was regarded as having ceased to exist 12 months later. The Oil Gas Enrichment Company (1893) was regarded as not relevant to the shale industry. The Scottish Mineral Oil and Coal Company Limited issued no shares and was treated as abortive.[18] The four companies not officially dissolved before 1970 were also excluded, as Payne's analysis includes only dissolved concerns.

Payne states that only 7 per cent of Scottish companies formed up to 1895 were 'abortive', and in the case of the shale industry, only one of the 40 companies was deemed as such. In England, by contrast, in the first twenty-five years of limited liability, about one third of companies were unable to find shareholders. Payne suggests that the Scottish investor was cannier than the English,[19] an assertion that will be discussed later, with particular reference to the career of George Simpson.

Table 5.2 sets the shale companies against the Scottish companies as a whole in terms of longevity. The relatively small number of shale companies in any given year makes it difficult to make valid comparisons with the overall Scottish picture. In only two years were more than two shale companies registered: in 1866, eight were registered and enjoyed an average length of life of 6.5 years, while Scottish companies overall amounted to 36 with an average life of 18.8 years; and in 1883, four shale companies were registered and enjoyed an average existence of 4.1 years, while 105 Scottish companies averaged 13.3 years.

Payne shows that that the average life of Scottish companies incorporated in any year up to 1895 was never less than 11.3 years. In 35 of these 40 years, the average was 13–22 years. For the 34 shale companies, it was 7.7 years. The four companies not dissolved until after 1970 were given a notional date of cessation as 1919, and when

Table 5.2 Longevity of Scottish limited companies and shale oil companies

Year	Payne (all Scottish companies)			Shale companies		
	Number of companies	Average length of life		Number of companies	Average length of life	
		Months	Years		Months	Years
1862	33	226.7	18.9	1	18.9	1.6
1864	27	157.7	13.1	1	42.0	3.5
1866	36	225.7	18.8	8	78.2	6.5
1869	17	330.4	27.5	1	203.6	17.0
1871	43	253.1	21.1	3	137.0	11.4
1872	78	171.4	14.3	1	71.0	5.9
1876	60	190.0	15.8	2	79.6	6.6
1878	56	160.6	13.4	2	108.7	9.1
1880	66	245.4	20.5	2	75.8	6.3
1881	71	224.7	18.7	1	132.1	11.0
1882	104	185.0	15.4	1	38.8	3.2
1883	105	159.6	13.3	4	48.8	4.1
1884	101	212.8	17.7	2	205.8	17.2
1885	72	175.2	14.6	2	54.9	4.6
1890	124	194.9	16.3	1	119.6	10.0
1893	169	186.5	15.5	2	120.6	10.1

these companies are included, the average length of life of the shale companies is increased to 11.6 years, still substantially less than the Scottish average. Payne shows that, at the end of 1895, 1,755 of the 2,936 (59.77 per cent) companies registered in Scotland up to that point remained in existence.[20] Ten out of 40 shale companies survived: i.e., only 25 per cent. Further examination of the performance of the shale industry in this respect will be carried out in consideration of its management.

Payne also concludes that the size of a limited company had a 'negligible influence on its expectation of life in its original form'.[21] Of the 17 companies formed in the shale industry from 1862 to 1875, one was abortive. Of the remaining 16, only six survived beyond 1877, when the industry began to emerge from a period of difficulty. Of these, two were wound up in 1878 and one in 1881, leaving only three survivors.[22] Of the 13 'failures', five had a paid-up capital of £5,000 or less; two between £5,001 and £10,000; three between £10,001 and £25,000; one £26,890; one £138,540; and one £199,850. The 'failures' were spread fairly evenly through the size range. However, it must be noted that all six companies with a capital of £10,000 or less were wound up; so, too, were three out of four that had a capital of between £10,001 and £25,000, one out of two with a capital of between £25,001 and £50,000, and two out of three with a capital of over £50,000. The last two had paid-up capital of £138,540 and £199,850 respectively. The last company was the Uphall Mineral Oil Company, which was wound up to allow a reduction of capital to £170,000. The new company, the Uphall Oil Company, was identical to the old in all respects, except for the cancellation of £30,000 of the shares originally issued to the vendors. It continued to operate the same works and mines, and it seems appropriate for it to be considered a 'survivor' rather than a 'failure'. The four companies that survived into the next phase were Dalmeny, with a capital of £18,900, Oakbank with £45,000, Uphall with £170,000, and Young's with £486,625. Two of these were relatively small, one large and one very large. One was below the average for Scottish companies – £33,500 – one not far above, but one five times the average, and one fourteen times the average.[23] It seems, therefore, that, for the early shale companies, size may well have been a factor in survival.

Payne discusses the effect of large proportions of uncalled capital on the stability of limited companies, citing a suggestion that this was in fact a negation of the principle of limited liability.[24] He is concerned here with the relationship between called-up capital and nominal capital. His analysis suggests that, in the years between 1862 and 1875, the ratio was never more than 50 per cent, and in 1866 it was as low as 31.5 per cent.[25] In the early shale companies, registered between these dates, the position was as shown in Table 5.3.

Over the period 1862–75, the proportion of called-up to nominal capital in the shale industry at 69.4 per cent was substantially greater than that for Scottish industry as a whole. This ranged from 31.5 per cent in 1866 to 50 per cent in 1862.

Table 5.3 Nominal, issued and called-up capital: shale companies formed between 1862 and 1875

	Nominal £	Capital issued £	Called-up £	Called-up to Nominal %	Called-up to Issued %
Broxburn Shale	20000	16000	10000	50	62.5
Mid Calder (a)	10000	8500	8500	85	100
Young's (b)	600000	572500	486625	81.1	83.5
Capeldrae (c)	1400	1400	1400	100	100
Scottish	20000	7000	2800	14.0	40.0
Glasgow	25000	25000	23750	95.0	95.0
Dalserf	50000	25100	24125	48.25	96.1
Monklands Oil Refining	10000	8000	2400	24.0	30.0
Monklands Oil & Coal	50000	5000	5000	10.0	100.0
Glentore (d)	1400	1400	1400	100.0	100.0
Airdrie (e)	10000	7500	3750	37.5	50.0
Oakbank (f)	20000	20000	20000	100.0	100.0
Uphall (g)	250000	200000	181742	72.7	90.9
Dalmeny	27000	27000	18900	70.0	70.0
Midlothian Mineral	75000	26890	26890	35.9	100.0
West Calder (h)	160000	138100	105670	66.0	76.5
	1329800	1089390	922952	69.4	84.7

Notes

(a) Before its demise in 1869, the capital was twice increased until in 1866 it stood at: Nominal, £25,000; Issued, £25,000; Called-up, £22,129.

(b) At its formation in 1866, Young's issued 5,825 £100 shares, a total of £582,500. Between then and 1870, 100 shares were declared forfeit, and in the balance sheet for the year ending 30 April 1870, the issued capital was shown as £572,500. The company called up its capital at intervals over the period 1866–71, using temporary loans from banks to pay Young's price for the assets. By 1871, £85 per share was paid-up, a total of £486,625, and this remained the position until the amalgamation with the Uphall company in 1884 (source: BP Archive, YP, SHMB 1, Fos 111, 123, report after Fo. 189). Throughout this part, Young's issued capital is taken as £572,500.

(c) In 1876, called-up capital was £5,000. Resolution to increase nominal capital to £40,000 was never acted upon.

(d) Called-up capital assumed to be the same as issued.

(e) In 1869, a further call increased called-up capital to £7,500.

(f) By 1876 capital had been increased to £60,000 nominal and issued, with £40,000 in fully paid shares and 20,000 £1 shares, with 5 shillings called-up, a total of £45,000 in called-up capital.

(g) By 1876, when the company was reorganised, the remaining unpaid capital had been called up, making the called-up capital £199,850; £150 was 'unpaid'.

(h) By 1875, the remaining uncalled capital had been called up, making the called-up capital £138,540; £60 was 'unpaid'.

The proportion of called-up to *issued* capital in the case of the shale industry is 84.7 per cent. Payne describes the difference between these two proportions as a 'technical difference';[26] it may well, however, be a little more important. The uncalled portion of *issued* capital was freely available to the directors of a company. Any shareholder unable or unwilling to pay calls found his shares liable to forfeiture. The availability of the *unissued* shares as a source of funds was limited to their appeal to investors.

The usefulness of uncalled capital is illustrated by the Uphall company, which experienced difficulties leading to a reorganisation in 1876. In the period immediately before this the uncalled capital of £2 per share on the 9,129 shares not issued as fully paid up was called up. Similarly, in the case of the West Calder company, wound up in 1878, the £3 per share on 10,860 shares not issued as paid up was called up in 1874 and 1875.[27] These two companies also illustrate the practice of vendors being allocated fully paid-up shares with no uncalled liability. In the case of the Uphall company, 10,871 shares of £10 each were issued on this basis to the three vendors. The West Calder company's vendor received 3,000 fully paid £10 shares. This raises the point that it may be more appropriate to consider the ratio of *uncalled* capital to nominal and issued capital rather than that of called-up capital. In the case of the Uphall company, initial uncalled capital of £18,258 was the responsibility of 143 holders of 9,129 shares. The three vendors held 10,871 shares with no uncalled liability. For the West Calder company, 138 holders of 10,860 shares had an uncalled liability of £3 per share or £32,580, while the vendor held 3,000 fully paid £10 shares. The agent for the vendor in the case of the West Calder company was one of the original directors; the three vendors of the Uphall company were all members of the board.

Uncalled capital was also useful to the directors as security for loans. In 1886, the Oakbank company was granted a loan of £15,000 by the Clydesdale Bank on the security of the uncalled element of its new shares.[28]

Capital investment in limited companies

Table A (see Appendix 1) shows, for any given year, the amount of 'paid-up' capital invested in the individual companies: the total for each year and a cumulative total. Also shown is the amount of capital lost by dissolution or by reductions of capital. This again gives the amounts for individual companies: the total for each year and a cumulative total. Finally, for each year there is a figure for the 'net active capital', the difference between the cumulative totals of invested and lost capital.

Information about capital is found in the files of the Registrar of Companies.[29] The files consist of the documents required by law to be lodged at various stages in a company's existence. They include the Memorandum of Association (a statement of the aims of the company); the Articles of Association (the rules governing the conduct of its business); Notice of Situation of the Registered Office; copies of resolutions regarding changes in capital or Articles of Association; and, most importantly for the present purpose, the annual returns of capital and shareholders, known as the Summary of Capital and Shares (SCS). This document provides information on the nominal, issued and paid-up capital. These were not necessarily identical. A company might be incorporated with a given level of capital expressed as a number of shares each of a specified denomination. For one reason or another, not all of the shares might be issued, or not all of the value of the issued shares might be called up. For instance, the Lanark Oil Company was set up in 1883 with a nominal capital of £130,000 in £10 units. Only 10,000 shares were issued, and only £9 was called on each. The company's issued capital was therefore £100,000 and its paid-up capital £90,000.[30]

At the end of 1876, a total paid-up capital of £1,020,509 (initial investment plus new shares and fresh calls) had been invested in the limited companies in the oil industry (see Appendix 1, Table A). Taken together with investment by individuals and partnerships, the overall total of investment at this stage may have been as high as £1.2 million. This is not the whole story. A number of the limited companies were formed to take over the works and activities of already established concerns. In the case of the 17 companies registered between 1862 and 1876, shares with a paid-up value of £162,720 were issued in payment or part-payment for assets trans-ferred to the companies. In addition, cash payments amounting to £460,490 were made (see Appendix 1, Table B). This indicates that, of the £1,020,509 invested in limited companies up to 1876, £623,210 (61.07 per cent) was in respect of already existing works, plant, etc. This may well be an underestimate. The Summary of Capital and Shares was not required to show the issue of shares not paid for in cash until 1885.[31]

It cannot be argued that these payments were an insuperable burden. Two of the companies involved, Young's and the Dalmeny, survived until the 1919 amalgama-tion, although in the case of Young's, the £400,000 paid for the works was frequently cited as a major cause of the concern's later difficulties. The Uphall Mineral Oil Company also survived to be reconstructed in 1876, with a reduction of capital of £30,000 of the vendors' shares. However, three concerns – the Dalserf Coal Coke & Oil Company, the Midlothian Mineral Oil Company and the West Calder Oil Company – were wound up.

Looking at the industry in more general terms, Table B (Appendix 1) gives, for three periods – 1862–70; 1871–76; 1877–1914 – the total amounts of capital involved at the initial formation of the various shale companies. The nominal capital is stated in the Memorandum of Association. The amount of issued capital at initial formation has been derived from the first SCS submitted after incorporation. In the case of 11 of the 13 companies formed between 1862 and 1869, this document was submitted within 12 months after incorporation, and the amount of issued capital stated has been accepted as the initial issued capital of the companies. One company did not submit an SCS, and its issued capital is taken as the amount of the shares taken up by the subscribers. One company was abortive. In the absence of prospectuses for most of the companies, it is not possible to ascertain how much of the initial nominal capital was intended to be issued. Three of the companies issued all of the nominal capital. In one, 80 shares out of 100 were issued, but the remaining 20 were reserved for the mineral landlord.[32] In three of the companies, the initial issued capital was in the form of shares held solely by the subscribers, and this did not change over the life of the companies. In three concerns, most of the issued shares were held by the subscribers, and a small number only were issued to other parties. The proportion of nominal capital issued by these six companies ranged from 10 per cent to 85 per cent, and only £37,400 of £110,000 nominal capital (34 per cent) was issued. The shares of ten companies were held by small numbers of holders: the largest was 15, and in some cases only the subscribers were involved. Two companies had larger numbers of shareholders (see Table 8.1 (b)).

The Dalserf Company was formed on 19 September 1866 with a nominal capital of £50,000. The first SCS, dated 10 July 1867, shows that only £25,100 of this had been issued. It is possible to conjecture that the whole nominal capital had been offered, but that it had not been taken up, although 32 individuals were listed as shareholders. Young's company is the only one of the 13 for which a prospectus has been found.[33] This indicates that the whole nominal capital of £600,000 was to be issued and had in fact been taken up without being offered to the public. The first SCS submitted some seven months after incorporation shows issued capital of £582,500.

For the five companies incorporated between 1871 and 1876 the first SCS was accepted as the source for the initial issued capital in only two cases. The first SCS of the Uphall company was submitted on 8 June 1871, less than six months after incorporation. Only 4,545 of the 9,129 available shares had been taken up. All of these had been issued when the second SCS was submitted on 4 June 1872. The Midlothian Oil Mineral Company had some difficulty with forfeited shares in its first year, and again the second SCS was used. Four thousand shares in the Straiton company shown as issued were at first held by a director on behalf of the company; this was corrected in the second SCS, when 800 were shown as issued and 3,200 remained unissued.[34]

For the companies formed after 1876 the first SCS was taken as the source for the issued capital, except in the following cases. The Broxburn company's file was not readily available and the issue of shares to shareholders was derived from the directors' minute book, which shows that all 16,500 shares had been taken up by 24 July

1878, some nine months after incorporation.[35] The Binnend company originally had shares of £10 nominal value. Before the submission of the second SCS, the nominal value of the shares was reduced to £3. The second SCS is regarded as the more appropriate source. In two other cases – the Midlothian and Holmes companies – the second SCS is adopted. The first SCS in both cases was submitted within a few months of incorporation, and the whole of the shares offered had not been taken up.

Some prospectuses were found that show the number of shares offered. In a few cases it is possible to see that, despite the favourable climate, some companies had difficulty in placing all the offered shares. The Walkinshaw company, incorporated on 14 October 1880, offered 12,000 shares, of which 1,764 had been issued to the vendors. When the first SCS was submitted, only 11,062 shares had been taken up. The full 12,000 were not subscribed for until 1884. The Bathgate company invited subscriptions for 3,500 £10 shares, of which only 2,260 were taken up. The company failed shortly after flotation. The Holmes company offered 6,750 £10 shares, of which only 5,625 were taken up. The prospectus indicated that the company was to engage in refining, and the shortfall in take-up of the shares may well have been one reason for the company remaining a crude oil producer. The Linlithgow company was offered as 17,300 £10 shares, with a further 2,700 reserved for the vendors. Only 12,600 shares were taken up, and the vendors accepted a reduction to 1,400 shares. The directors considered that, although this did not come up to their expectations, the capital subscribed would be enough for the requirements of the company. The remaining shares were successfully issued two years later.[36]

From 1862 to 1870, 12 companies had at their formation a total nominal capital of £826,400, issued capital of £697,400, and paid-up capital of £589,750: 71.36 per cent of nominal and 84.56 per cent of issued capital. From 1871 to 1876, five companies had a nominal capital of £612,000, issued capital of £448,790, and paid-up capital of £367,502: 60.05 per cent of nominal and 81.89 per cent of issued capital. From 1877 to 1914, 20 companies had nominal capital of £2,266,000, issued capital of £1,747,100, and paid-up capital of £1,494,977: 65.97 per cent of nominal and 85.57 per cent of issued capital. Over the period as a whole from 1862 to 1914, 37 companies were formed with nominal capital of £3,704,400, issued capital of £2,893,290, and paid-up capital of £2,452,229: 66.20 per cent of nominal and 84.76 per cent of issued capital (see Appendix 1, Table B).[37]

In the earliest period, from 1862 to 1870, shares issued for considerations other than cash amounted to only £12,500, or 2.12 per cent of the total paid-up capital. However, the data for this period are somewhat distorted by Young's paid-up capital of £486,625, or 82.51 per cent of the total for the 12 companies. The only cash payment of £400,000, equal to 67.82 per cent of paid-up capital, was the payment to James Young. It represented 82.19 per cent of the paid-up capital of Young's company.

For much of the life of the company, this payment was a substantial burden, leading to considerable difficulty for the directors and shareholders. The valuation, with hindsight, was obviously optimistic, but what can be known of the transaction illustrates to some extent the frame of mind of investors in the industry in the early years of limited liability. In 1868 the shareholders were told that: 'Owing to the great depression of the trade almost from the date of formation of the company it has become evident that to meet the engagement of paying off Mr Young's claims, more of the capital must be called up: the prospect of settling them out of the profits to any extent having for the present at least failed to be realised.'[38] It seems that the company purchased the assets hoping to be able to defray at least part of the cost out of profits. In view of the profits earned by Young and his partners in the early 1860s, this may not have seemed unreasonable to potential investors.

In the period 1871–6, cash payments to vendors represented 27.84 per cent of paid-up capital, while shares not paid for in cash amounted to 40.88 per cent. This period also saw a change in the shareholding structure. In the earlier period, the number of shareholders was generally small, sometimes limited to the subscribers to the Memorandum of Association. The largest number was the 74 shareholders of Young's. The Dalserf Coal Coke & Oil Company had 35, and this concern is the first to differentiate between types of shares: 500 B deferred shares were issued to the three vendors as part-payment for the transferred assets. These were not to receive a dividend until the A shareholders had received a dividend of 20 per cent.[39]

During 1871–6, the companies were larger, five having a total nominal capital of £612,000, of which £448,790 was issued and £367,502 was paid up: an average of £122,400 nominal, £89,758 issued, and £73,500 paid up (see Appendix 1, Table B). There were 461 shareholders, excluding vendors: an average of 92, with a minimum of 61 and a maximum of 138. Unfortunately, no details are available for the transfer of the assets in the case of the Straiton Estate Company. The shares issued as part-payment for the assets of the Midlothian and Dalmeny companies were not distinguished from the other shares of the companies. The Uphall Company acquired the assets from three vendors for a total of £90,000 in B and C shares with dividends postponed to the A shares. Five hundred and fifty A shares were allocated with respect to interest on the purchase price, and a further 1,500 A shares were issued as fully paid with respect to the purchase of the Northern and Caledonian Oil Works at Fauldhouse.[40] This also indicates that the promoters, at any rate, had considerable optimism about the prospects of the industry in 1871. Their mood was probably shared by the investing public. Fifty shareholders had subscribed for 4,545 A shares by June 1871, and by June 1872, 99 held 9,129 (the total available for issue) with £8 called on each.[41]

The West Calder company paid £80,000 for the assets acquired, of which £50,000 was to be paid in cash and £30,000 in B shares postponed to the A shares.

B shares were not to be sold until five years after the formation of the company. It is clear, therefore, that by this time investors required some guarantee as to the bona fides of company promoters.

In the last period, from 1877 to 1914, 20 companies were incorporated with nominal capital of £2,266,000, issued capital of £1,747,100, and paid-up capital of £1,494,977. The average was £113,300 nominal, £87,355 issued, and £74,748 paid-up, in each case not radically different from the average of the five companies incorporated in the previous period (see Appendix 1, Table B). The largest number of shareholders was the 328 of the Linlithgow company; the smallest Clippens' seven and the British Oil & Candle's eight. These were essentially conversions from private partnerships to give the partners the benefit of limited liability. British Oil & Candle ceased to exist and was replaced by the Lanark, a public company. In 1882, Clippens financed expansion by an increase in capital and had 141 shareholders.[42] All of the concerns operating in the industry after 1877 were public limited companies, except James Ross & Company, which remained an unincorporated partnership.

In the last period, shares worth £597,889, 39.99 per cent of the total paid-up capital were issued free to vendors (see Appendix 1, Table B). It must be noted here that the Hermand company, incorporated in 1890 to take over the old Hermand and Walkinshaw companies, had a nominal capital of £350,000, of which £315,000 was issued to the shareholders of the two companies as payment for the assets taken over.[43] The New Hermand Company, formed in 1899 to reorganise the failing Hermand company, had a nominal capital of £70,000, of which £51,355 was issued free of charge to the shareholders and creditors of the old company with respect to their interest in the mines, works, etc; £366,355 of the £597,889 of shares not paid for in cash was in respect of these transactions.[44]

At the same time, cash payments to vendors of £262,066 made up 17.53 per cent of the paid-up capital, a substantial reduction on both of the previous periods.

Finance for expansion

Those industrial and commercial joint-stock companies that were established in the late nineteenth and early twentieth centuries, and which did obtain a stock exchange quotation, were almost entirely the conversion of established businesses, already provided with their capital rather than new concerns seeking to raise finance. In fact their appearance seems to owe at least as much to demands from the public for suitable investments as to the desire of the captains of industry to release ownership and control to a publicly quoted joint-stock company.[1]

As R.C. Michie points out, many of the shale companies were, of course, conversions, but most required, in addition to the capital already represented by works, etc, fresh capital to fund consolidation and expansion. Over the period 1862–1914, the initial paid-up capital of the industry amounted to £2,452,229. Of this, £760,609 was in shares issued free to vendors in part-payment for assets transferred. The sum of £722,556 was paid in cash to these same vendors, making a total payment for assets of £1,483,165: 60.48 per cent of the initial paid-up capital. The remainder, £969,064 or 39.52 per cent of the paid-up capital, was available for any expansion or working capital (see Appendix 1, Table B). These concerns therefore seem to fall a little short of Michie's analysis. A large proportion of the initial paid-up capital was spent on already existing plant, etc, but nearly half of this was found from capital subscribed by new shareholders. There was also something left over to fund new capital projects.

The industry did expand, particularly from 1877 to 1913, when shale production rose from 684,118 tons to over 3 million tons, a more than fourfold increase.[2] This was partly due to the formation of new companies such as Pumpherston, Holmes and Linlithgow, set up to develop 'green field' sites which had not hitherto been exploited to any significant extent. However, there was considerable expansion of existing concerns after conversion to limited company status and substantial capital was involved. Expansion was, in fact, cited in some cases as a reason for conversion.

New ordinary shares in established companies

The company files for lapsed companies, shareholders' minute books for three of the four 'live' companies and newspaper reports of meetings show that, from 1862 to 1914, ordinary shares with a paid-up value of £954,290, additional to companies' initial capital, were issued. Calls on the unpaid element of shares totalled £482,962; and preference shares with a paid-up value of £452,256 were issued. In all, a total of £1,889,508 of additional capital was raised (see Appendix 1, Table C). The preferred method, judged solely by the relative amounts, was clearly the issue of new ordinary shares. The Broxburn company (formed 1879) paid dividends of 25 per cent in each year from 1880 to 1886. In 1879–80 it produced and refined 3,982,489 gallons of crude oil; by 1884–5 this had more than doubled to 8,459,000. The finance for this was secured by the issue of new ordinary shares in 1880 and 1884.[3] In September 1880, 3,500 £10 shares were issued to pay for new machinery, and also for the acquisition of the Benhar works at Fauldhouse. These were issued at a price of £15, for which the buyer received a £10 share with £8.50 paid up, a premium of £6.50 per share. These shares were all taken up before the issue of the next Summary of Capital and Shares on 1 June 1881.[4] In May 1884, 2,350 new £10 ordinary shares were issued at a price of £22 per share with £8.50 paid up, a premium of £13.50 per share. These were all taken up before the date of the next SCS, 3 June 1885.[5] These new issues demonstrate that the investing public had considerable confidence in the Broxburn company.

Some other concerns had similar, if less spectacular, experiences with new issues. The Burntisland company paid dividends of 20 per cent from 1883 to 1886. In May 1884 capital was increased by 2,000 £10 shares, which were issued at £14 for each share with £8.50 paid up, a premium of £5.50. This was to pay for additional retorts. In May 1886, a further issue of 3,000 £10 shares was made at a price of £12 for each share with £8.50 paid up, a premium of £3.50. In 1885, the directors of the West Lothian company were able to issue 2,500 shares at a premium of £1 per share. In June 1883 the Midlothian company was able to secure a premium of £1 on the issue of 3,000 shares.[6] The take-up of these issues lends support to the idea that 'not only was capital available in abundance for any feasible investment, but that investors were actively seeking any suitable outlet for the funds they had at their disposal.'[7]

Other companies issued new shares at par. Sometimes it is not possible to be completely sure that the capital raised was spent on expansion, although in most cases the raising of new capital occurred at the same time as such development. Over the period from February 1882 to May 1884 the Clippens company increased its paid-up capital from £135,000 to £198,750. At the same time the company expanded its operations into the east of Scotland with the construction of mines and crude oil works at Pentland in Midlothian.[8] The Oakbank company increased its paid-up capital between 1869 and 1882 by £48,000, and over the same period the works' capacity increased from 1.25 million gallons of crude oil to 2 million gallons, and a paraffin refinery was added. The same company in 1901 issued new paid-up shares to the value of £85,000 to fund the development of shale fields at Duddingston, and a new crude oil works near Winchburgh.[9] It is not possible, because of the lack of many companies' records, to make a precise assessment of the amount of new capital raised for such purposes, but it may well have been in excess of £500,000.

We can be more certain of the amounts of new capital raised for other purposes. Young's company in 1884 issued new shares to the value of £119,000 to take over the Uphall Oil Company Limited. Between 1888 and 1892, Young's issued new shares to the value of £125,856 in redeeming the Convertible Debenture Stock created in the crisis that affected the company in 1887. In 1885, Clippens took over the works and mines of the Midlothian company for a consideration, which included £33,850 in fully paid-up Clippens shares. The Pumpherston company absorbed Tarbrax in 1912, issuing shares with a paid-up value of £25,500.[10] A total of £178,350 of new capital was expended in this way.

At the same time as taking over the Tarbrax company, Pumpherston modified its capital structure. At the 1912 general meeting, the directors were asked to consider dividing the shares because of their high stock exchange value. At the same time, a shareholder stated that he disliked holding shares with an element of uncalled capital.[11] The result of these representations was a proposal to pay from reserves and from profits a bonus of £1 3s. (£1.15) per ordinary share. The uncalled element of the ordinary shares was called up, and shareholders were offered one fully paid share at par for each ordinary share held. The effect of this was to increase the ordinary capital of the company by £130,000 plus the call of £19,500 on the existing ordinary shares.

Overall, therefore, whereas £958,067 of the new shares issued by the oil companies was invested in works expansion or the development of activities, £434,206 of the new shares can be identified as having been used for other purposes.

Uncalled capital

£482,962 was raised by calls on the uncalled element of shares. In its reorganisation of 1887, Young's called up 10s. (50 pence) of the £1 10s. (£1.50) uncalled on each share, a total of £35,625. This was to assist in the reduction of the shares from £10 to £4 with £3 called.[12] In 1892 the directors were authorised to issue a new debenture stock to replace one falling due on 31 July 1892.[13] In 1893 it was reported that, owing to the depression in the trade, this issue had been unsuccessful and that in consequence it had been found necessary to make a final call of £1 per ordinary share, a sum of £113,202. The calls made by Young's company were therefore all related to restructuring of capital.

Uncalled capital was the most certain source of finance for the directors. Shareholders were committed to pay up to the full nominal value of their holding. Failure to pay led to forfeiture of the shares, and companies in trouble were able to use this as a last resort. In fact, in the shale industry, apart from the £19,500 called up by the Pumpherston company in 1912 at the request of its shareholders, all of the calls on shares, subsequent to those made at the setting up of companies, were made by directors of concerns in difficulties of one kind or another. In all cases, except that of Young's described above, the companies concerned were subsequently wound up. Only two, the Oakbank and Uphall companies, were successfully reconstructed.

Preference shares

Preference shares were fixed-interest shares carrying a preference, often cumulative, over ordinary shares in terms of dividend. Where the original owners of a concern sought the protection of limited liability while at the same time retaining control, the ordinary shares were issued to the vendors and any additional capital was raised by the issue of non-voting preference shares.[14] In the shale industry only one concern, the Tarbrax company, issued preference shares at the time of incorporation. This concern was set up by the Pumpherston directors, and the share capital, ordinary and preference, was sought from the Pumpherston shareholders.

The Pumpherston company itself issued £91,690 of preference shares in 1890 to finance expansion, including the development of mines and works at Seafield. The total issue was £100,000, but £8,310 was issued to William Fraser as the seller of the works, etc. In 1908 the Oakbank company issued £100,000 of preference shares to finance new mines and additions to the works, as well as to capitalise a floating loan of £28,472. This last was also the predominant factor in the Broxburn company's decision in 1887 to issue £100,000 of preference shares to pay off £ 85,106 of short-term debt. In 1912, Pumpherston issued £50,000 of preference shares to replace the same amount of Tarbrax shares, and in 1896 the Dalmeny company issued £18,900 of preference shares as part of a reorganisation of capital. The remainder of the £452,256 of preference shares issued by the industry was spent in efforts to secure the survival of companies in difficulty. In 1883, Walkinshaw experienced difficulty with its shale fields and offered £60,000 of 6 per cent preference shares to finance necessary development. Only £28,000 was taken up, and in 1885 the directors decided to call up the remaining ordinary capital. In the early 1890s, the Linlithgow company experienced problems with retorts not suitable for its shale; £50,000 of 7 per cent preference shares were offered, but only £27,206 was taken up. An offer of £30,000, of which only £18,150 was taken up, was made in an abortive attempt to revive the New Hermand Oil Company in 1900.[15]

Borrowing, bank loans and debentures

The shale companies also raised money for capital projects by other means. The published accounts of many of the concerns contain items described as 'interest on debentures and loans'.[16] The short-lived West Lothian company reported payments of interest on debentures and loans of £655 in 1888, rising to £1,135 in 1889 and remaining over £1,000 until 1891. Interest rates at the time were not unduly high. The Broxburn company had substantial borrowings at 3.5 and 4 per cent, which had been replaced by 6 per cent preference shares. The West Lothian company's liability may have been anything from £15,000 to £25,000, depending on the rate of interest, equivalent to from one fifth to one third of the company's paid-up capital. The Burntisland company paid interest of £1,828 in 1884, rising to £4,238 in 1888, £6,606 in 1889 and £6,648 in 1890. Much of this was in respect of £100,000 of 6 per cent debenture bonds issued in 1887–9 to consolidate loans of £56,200 and to provide working capital. This was equal to 58.8 per cent of the company's share capital. In 1884, Clippens paid £2,000 as interest on £40,000 of debenture bonds, a rate of 5 per cent. In 1886, interest of £3,912 was paid on £90,075 of heritable and debenture bonds, an average of 4.34 per cent. In 1890 this rose to £5,492, and in 1891 to £6,795. When the company was liquidated and reconstructed in 1892–3, it was stated that there was £135,200 of debenture stock and £53,602 of convertible debentures: a total of £188,802, equal to 73.44 per cent of the share capital. After the reduction of capital authorised in 1892, the debenture stock represented 243 per cent of the share capital of £77,670. The Linlithgow company paid £1,470 interest on debentures and bank overdraft in 1887; this rose to £5,004 as interest on debentures, temporary loans and debenture stock, and by 1901, when the company was in its last throes, it had fallen to £2,636.[17]

Among the more successful companies, the Broxburn company's General Minute Books provide details of borrowings, and it is possible to relate this to developments in the company. In 1879 borrowings amounted to £4,272, rising rapidly over the next few years to £85,106 in 1887, when £100,000 of preference shares was issued to consolidate this debt. In 1891 it was decided to construct mines and a crude oil works at Roman Camp, south of Broxburn, to exploit the Drumshoreland shales with a new retort designed by Norman Henderson, the works manager. It was proposed to pay for this by using the company's reserve fund of £27,000 and by temporary loans to be repaid from year to year, with equivalent sums being written off as depreciation from the capital account.[18] The necessary borrowing reached £64,557, its highest level, in 1895. From 1893–5 the company, in addition to completing the new crude works at Roman Camp, had replaced the older model Henderson retorts at the Broxburn works. The borrowing needed for this was paid off by 1900. A similar sequence of events took place in the first decades of the twentieth century. In 1909 the shareholders were informed that the directors were 'spending a very large amount on the works' to put the company on a par with one paying a dividend of 50 per cent.[19] In 1910 the directors referred to a new bench of retorts and the installation of electrical power; in 1911 there is mention of new retorts and new mines in the Dunnet seam.[20]

Similar relationships between borrowing and capital expenditure can be found in the other leading companies. In 1885, the Pumpherston company paid £361 in interest on loans; in 1886 the sum was £2,012, and in 1887 it rose to £3,741. The original cost of the company's works was £72,000, but the expansion necessary to meet competition had increased this to £130,000 by 1887. The difference was eventually partly made up by the issue of new ordinary shares to the value of £34,000. However, in the interim, arrangements were made for an overdraft of £8,000 with the Union Bank of Scotland, Glasgow. This was raised to £16,000 in November 1884. In 1885 an overdraft of £26,000 was negotiated with the British Linen Company, which was to take over the Union Bank overdraft of £16,000. At the same time it was reported that loans had been made by William Fraser, managing director, of £1,500; James Wood, chairman, £1,000; and Robert B. Tennent, director, £500. In June 1885, it was agreed to issue £30,000 of debentures at 5 per cent. These were not well received, and in December 1885 the secretary commented on the difficulty of raising money by debentures. It was agreed that the directors would give their names as additional security for borrowings. Overdrafts of £26,000 with the British Linen Company and £13,000 with the Union Bank were extended to the end of 1886. In March 1886, a loan of £5,000 was arranged with the London & Yorkshire Bank. In July 1886, an overdraft repayment was requested by the British Linen Company, and a loan of £7,200 was arranged with the National Bank. At the same time the board was informed that a loan of £4,000 by Messrs W. & A. Fraser, due on 6 August, had been extended for a further three months. In December 1886, an £8,000 debenture bond was agreed with the British Linen Company. Overdrafts of £15,037 with the Union Bank and £30,960 with the British Linen Company were reported on 1 February 1887.[21] At the same meeting, the capital account of the company was set out as:

Capital required at present	£180,000
Amount possessed	£173,260 made up of
Shares	£107,220
Debentures	£17,040
Loans	£31,000
Bills	£18,000

Some of this debt had been paid off by 1892, when only £1,756 was paid in interest charges. However, from 1893 onwards such charges increased, standing at over £4,000 from 1896 to 1903.[22] During this period, the company more than doubled its crude oil capacity by the construction of virtually new works at Seafield and Deans, and by the modernisation of the retorts at its Pumpherston works. Depending on the interest rate, such payments indicate borrowings of anything from £65,000 to £100,000: 30.9 per cent to 47.5 per cent of the company's share capital. Indeed, it represented from 58.8 to 90.5 per cent of the ordinary share capital. However, by 1907 the whole of this debt had been paid off.[23]

The Oakbank company, the smallest of the four surviving concerns, consistently borrowed sums which in 1889 amounted to £9,169 and in 1900 reached £25,144, or 37.25 per cent of the paid-up capital.[24] During the 1890s, the company expanded its activities and this no doubt influenced the amount of borrowings. Major extensions were carried out in the first decade of the twentieth century, financed mainly by the successful issue of ordinary and preference shares. However, borrowing rose steeply from £25,465 in 1901 to £59,333 in 1911, remaining at over £40,000 until the start of the Great War.[25]

Young's company, the oldest concern and for much of the industry's history its largest, commenced business in 1866, having agreed to pay James Young £400,000 for the Bathgate works and a partially built new works at Addiewell, near West Calder. As indicated earlier, the directors of the new limited company expected to be able to pay much of this over a period of years out of profits. This proved to be impossible, and two loans of £80,000 each were arranged with the Union Bank and the Clydesdale Bank, to be repaid in instalments by 1 March 1871. This required calls on the uncalled element of the company's ordinary shares. The called-up capital was £231,550 in 1868 and rose to £486,625 in 1871. Although these loans were paid off, the company continued to rely on borrowed money to a considerable extent. In 1872, creditors included £50,000 of debentures and cash loans of £42,602. In 1880, debentures of £50,000 remained outstanding and loans had risen to £66,649. In 1881, as a consequence of erecting 288 Henderson retorts, cash loans had risen to £152,295, while debentures remained at £50,000. The chairman told the shareholders that the company expected the excess of depreciation over capital outlay to allow for the repayment of these amounts over a few years.[26]

The takeover of the Uphall company in 1884 involved considerable reorganisation and extension of the company's Uphall and Hopetoun works. By 1887 the company's debt had risen to £262,300 of debentures and £263,962 of cash on deposit: a total of £526,262, a sum almost as great as the paid-up capital of £605,625. The company was reorganised in 1887, with a severe reduction in capital to £285,000. A debenture stock convertible into ordinary shares was created, which existed until 1892 alongside mortgage debenture bonds in excess of £200,000. When the convertible debenture stock became due for repayment in 1892, a similar bond was offered as a replacement but it was not popular, with only £62,473 being taken up. The directors were compelled to call up the remaining £113,202 outstanding on the ordinary share capital.[27] The debenture stock was reorganised in 1896–7, and thereafter consisted of £150,000 of 5 and 6 per cent mortgage debenture bonds, and £150,000 6 per cent mortgage debenture bonds with contingent dividend rights.[28] This total of £300,000 was 66 per cent of the company's paid-up capital.

In the shale industry, it appears that most companies had recourse to debentures and other borrowings when in need of money for capital projects. Only in the case of Young's did this become a permanent part of capital structure, where it equalled 66 per cent of paid-up capital, considerably in excess of the 40.58 per cent of the share capital of companies listed in *Burdett's Official Stock Exchange Intelligence*.[29]

The relationship between equity capital and fixed interest stock is summed up in Table 6.1.

As the table indicates, in the period 1862–70, all of the capital was in the form of ordinary shares. In the second period (1871–6), £25,000 of debentures were issued by the West Calder company. The last period, from 1877 to 1914, was one of significant expansion. Out of a total paid-up share capital of £2,802,595, £433,356 was in preference shares: 15.46 per cent of the total. Debentures of £755,220 equalled 26.95 per cent of the total paid-up share capital. In 1895, preference shares constituted 22.46 per cent of the aggregate paid-up share value of all companies listed in *Burdett's Official Stock Exchange Intelligence*, and the value of debentures equalled 40.58 per cent.[30] The position of the shale industry in this respect was not radically different from that of commerce generally. Table 6.1 also shows that the industry fits closely with Cottrell's conclusion that over the 30 years before the Great War, companies began to issue preference shares and debentures as well as ordinary shares.[31] In 1913, preference shares made up 30 per cent of the issued capital of London quoted companies, with debentures and loan stocks constituting another 22.4 per cent.[32]

It has not proved possible to find equivalent data for Scottish industry as a whole but, over the period 1884–1905, 35 Scottish brewing companies issued £3,109,000 in ordinary shares, £2,381,000 in preference shares and £431,000 in debentures.[33] Preference shares made up 43.37 per cent of the share capital, and debentures equalled 7.85 per cent. The proportion of preference shares is considerably greater than in the shale industry, and that of debentures much less. However, it seems that

Table 6.1 Paid-up equity capital, preference shares and debentures

Period	Paid-up ordinary shares £	Paid-up preference shares £	Total paid-up share capital £	Debentures £
1862–70	1060212			1060212
1871–6	460030	18900	478930	25000
1877–1914	2369239	433356	2802595	755220
1862–1914	3889481	452256	4341737	780220

Table 6.2 Capital of the four surviving refining companies in 1919

Company	Ordinary shares £	Preference shares £	Total paid-up share capital £	Debentures £
Young's	452808		452808	300000
Broxburn	199750	100000	299750	
Oakbank	176750	100000	276750	100000
Pumpherston	285500	150000	435500	50000
	1114808	350000	1464808	450000

the total proportion of fixed interest stocks is much the same. The paid-up ordinary shares of the Steel Company of Scotland from 1888 to 1895 amounted to £446,040 and debentures to £250,000, equal to 56.05 per cent of the paid-up capital: again, not radically different from the shale and brewing industries.[34]

The final capital of the four refining companies which survived up to the amalgamation in 1919 is considered in Table 6.2.

Preference shares constituted 23.89 per cent of the total paid-up share capital; debentures, 30.72 per cent. There was considerable variation between the companies: 33.36 per cent of the Broxburn company's share capital was in fixed-interest preference shares; 34.44 per cent of the Pumpherston company's was in preference shares, and debentures equalled 11.48 per cent of paid-up share capital; Young's company had debentures equal to 66.25 per cent of paid-up share capital; and 36.13 per cent of Oakbank's paid-up capital was in preference shares, while its debentures equalled 36.13 per cent. The high proportion of fixed-interest securities in the last two companies might explain lower dividends on ordinary shares.

Working capital

Thus far only fixed capital, or the finance necessary to provide the mines, works, etc, has been considered. Like any other industry, the shale companies also required a sufficient working capital. The special conditions applying to the shale companies are perhaps best described in the words of the Oakbank directors at an extraordinary general meeting in 1874, when it was stated that the capital of the company was represented as follows:

Sunk in plant	£34,000
Stock of shale, oil in process	£15,000
Barrels	£3,000
Stores	£1,000

This totals £53,000. The paid-up capital was only £40,000, and it was stated that there was no working capital left, and that there never had been. By working capital, as distinguished from the sunk capital, was meant

> the necessary sum to pay cash for coals, plant, wages etc. so as to wait for the returns for the products manufactured by the company. The shareholders must know that from the month of February till September almost no burning oil is consumed. The whole produce therefore of burning oil for eight months is sold and delivered in four months, and, as it is generally sold on a credit of two months, the actual returns for the manufactured oil, are only in hand for the previous year in January, February and March of the succeeding year. In an ordinary year the value of this stock of oil at September would be £10,000 to £12,000 above what the stock would be in March following.[35]

The necessary finance had until that point been provided by the directors: in 1871, it was £11,200; in 1872, £7,200; and in 1873 £7,929. It was resolved that a credit to a maximum of £10,000 was to be arranged with the Clydesdale Banking Company to replace this obligation to the directors.

There was indeed a marked preponderance of deliveries in the winter months, and this continued to be the case. In the 12 months ending in March 1897, the Oakbank company's sales from April to August 1896 made up 25.87 per cent of the total for the year. The remaining seven months accounted for 74.13 per cent, and 35.92 per cent was delivered in the three months from November to January.[36] Young's sales followed a less marked pattern. In the 12 months ending in April 1895, 25.2 per cent of sales took place in the four months from May to August; 74.8 per cent occurred in the remaining eight months, with 28.49 per cent pertaining to the three months from November to January.[37] The imbalance here is less pronounced than in the case of Oakbank, and the difference may have been the result of different sales organisations. Young's had a number of branches throughout the United Kingdom, while Oakbank relied more on agents. This will be considered more fully in a later chapter.

Relationship with the banks

It is clear that at different times borrowed money played a significant part in financing development and the introduction of new technology to the shale industry, as well as in the provision of working capital. A press comment in 1887 claimed: 'There is not a Scotch oil company, possibly with the exception of Young's Paraffin, which is not in need of money, either for working capital expenses, or to take the place of borrowed cash calls falling due.'[38] The sources of these borrowings can be somewhat obscure. It is true that in its early years Young's was able to rely on the Union and Clydesdale banks for substantial temporary loans to tide the company over until calls on shares became available to extinguish the debt to James Young. The experience of the Young's and Pumpherston companies indicates that debenture bonds were a source of finance for capital projects. It is also clear that these two companies were able to call on three of the Scottish banks for support in their formative years. Young's is known to have borrowed £46,250 from the Clydesdale Bank in 1868, and in the same year the bank also provided credits for the Mid Calder Mineral Oil Company.[39] The Clydesdale's relationship with the industry continued until at least 1897. Credits were provided for the Stanrigg and Oakbank companies, and the bank took up £20,000 of Young's company's debentures.[40] Unfortunately, only the earliest directors' minute books for each of the four surviving companies have survived, and only occasional references to bank loans are made in the published reports. The Linlithgow company included an overdraft with the Union Bank in its statement of interest paid in 1899; Oakbank noted a bank overdraft of £7,743 in its published accounts in 1887.[41] It remains clear, however, that the Scottish banks were not unwilling to offer assistance to the shale companies.

The policies of English banks in the late nineteenth and early twentieth centuries have been criticised for not meeting the financial requirements of manufacturers. In particular, they were alleged to have been reluctant to provide firms with more than working capital.[42] Mathias has stated that, in Britain, 'the city to a large extent had its back turned to industry'.[43] This view has recently been re-examined, and it has been shown that there were significant similarities between English and continental, especially German, banking practices with regard to industry, particularly with respect to overdrafts or the 'rolling over' of short-term loans.[44]

The development of the stock exchanges in London and provincial cities in the 1840s provided a new source of long-term capital, leaving the banks a position as short-term lenders. However, the Scottish banks continued to be involved in medium- and longer-term advances to industry, secured on land owned by business proprietors or on business premises.[45] This continued into the period after the introduction of general limited liability. The Bank of Scotland in 1879 had loans to 38 business totalling £2,730,000. It advanced a total of £6,572,598 to merchants and manufacturers in 1879, and £5,271,565 the following year.[46] It seems, therefore, that Scottish banks were prepared to assist commerce and manufacture, and the belief that 'no borrower with adequate prospects and security was ever turned away' is founded in fact.[47] Indeed, it was considered by some in the banking sector that 'all the banking disasters in Scotland can clearly be traced to too intimate a connection between the management of the banks and the mercantile section of the community'.[48]

British banks have also been criticised for not taking an active interest in the conduct of their industrial customers' business.[49] The only evidence of such involvement in the shale industry again centres on the Clydesdale Bank. Sir James King was chairman of the Clydesdale at intervals from 1874 until 1911. He was also a director of Young's from its formation until his death in 1911, and chairman from 1900 to 1907.[50] George Readman, manager of the bank 1852–80 and managing director 1886–7, was briefly auditor of Young's company, with a seat on the board. He was later the first chairman of the reorganised Oakbank company, resigning because of his management commitments at the bank but re-elected to the Oakbank board in 1888.[51]

The shale industry – at least its more prosperous concerns – certainly seems to have been able to rely on support from the Scottish banks.

Investment financed from within firms: depreciation, maintenance and repair

The importance of finance from the banks may also have been exaggerated. Cottrell discusses the place of retained profit in financing expansion; Collins, in introducing his consideration of banks and industrial finance, contends that industry was largely financed from within itself.[52] In the case of the shale industry, the limited companies, in the main, derived their initial capital from appeals to the investing public. However, a rather different story emerges in consideration of the investment needed to ensure the continued success of the various firms. As described above, some of this was secured, mainly on a temporary basis, from banks, as well as from loans by private individuals. However, companies legislation made it possible for directors to make provision out of profits for depreciation and other contingencies before declaring a dividend. In the late nineteenth century, the charging of depreciation was the subject of debate among accountants and others, and most British companies were not required to depreciate their assets.[53] Indeed railway companies have been cited as frequently forgetting about depreciation 'when the maintenance of the dividend required such a sacrifice.'[54] Systematic depreciation of machinery was rare in the worsted industry.[55] In Scottish industry, Beardmore, one of the largest engineering concerns, made only 'nominal allowance for depreciation' up to 1909.[56] In 1900, a Glasgow chartered accountant remarked: 'It is not unusual to find the balance sheet of a limited company docquetted as correct "subject to provision for depreciation" when the auditor does not consider sufficient allowance has been made for fixed capital exhausted during the year.'[57]

The model Articles of Association in the First Schedule of the 1862 Act, Table A, simply stated (Article 74):

The Directors may, before recommending any dividend, set aside out of the Profits of the Company such Sum as they think proper as a reserved fund to

meet Contingencies, or for equalizing Dividends, or for repairing or maintaining the Works connected with the Business of the Company, or any part
thereof; and the Directors may invest the Sum so set apart as a reserved Fund
upon such Securities as they may select.

Among the shale companies, nine adopted the article set out in Table A; seven
adopted an article similar in effect to that quoted above; nine provided for a reserve
fund that could be used in the business of the company; and three set up a reserve
fund that specifically mentioned depreciation. Four companies imposed on the
directors a requirement to set aside out of profits for depreciation a specific sum
based on the capital account.

Before looking in detail at the shale companies' performance in relation to
depreciation, it should be noted that most published company accounts included a
statement that 'maintenance and repair' had been taken into account before the
balance had been struck. In some cases, the amount spent was also given. In the
nine years from 1886 to 1894, Pumpherston's expenditure on maintenance and
repair rose from £4,941 to £13,574, reflecting the increase in capacity.[58] After 1894
no cash figures are given. Even the poorest performing companies made this provision. In the course of its short life, the West Lothian Oil Company set aside, out of
revenue £25,573, an average of £3,653.[59]

The most complete information is that for Young's . In the 18 years from its foundation in 1866 to the amalgamation with Uphall in 1884, the company spent, out of
revenue, £287,883 on the maintenance and repair of its works and mines: an average
of £15,993 per annum. From 1885 to 1887, £53,494 was spent, an average of £17,831;
from 1889 to 1900, £248,192, an average of £20,682 per annum; from 1901 to 1904,
£118,933, an average of £29,733 per annum.[60] After 1904 no cash figures are provided.
Also after 1900, this expenditure is described as 'maintenance and renewal'. This,
together with the marked increase over the previous years, suggests that some of
the expenditure was devoted to replacing plant, something that might well have
been debited to capital account. In 1903 this account amounted to £28,588, of which
£4,432 was in respect of new boilers and other plant renewals. Additional refrigerating and sweating plant costing £10,477 was erected during the year and debited to
revenue over three years.[61]

Renewal and replacement of plant was provided for by setting aside from
revenue, before declaring a dividend, a sum described as depreciation. This was
sometimes prescribed in the Articles of Association as a percentage of the firm's
capital. The Broxburn company's Article 78 required that depreciation of 5 per cent
be charged to the revenue account before any dividend was declared.[62] At the same
time, it was open to companies to charge to their capital accounts expenditure on
new or additional plant. Over the years from 1879 to 1903, it can be shown that the

Broxburn company charged to its capital account a total of £625,195, including the original costs of the works. Over the same period, the revenue account was debited with depreciation to the amount of £396,750.[63] The net depreciated cost of the works was therefore £228,445. The paid-up capital in 1903 was £299,750. This was unchanged from 1888, when £100,000 of preference shares was issued.[64] It is clear that this concern was able to finance its capital expenditure from its own resources.

The published accounts of the other surviving refining concerns also show that depreciation was charged against revenue (see Table 6.3).

The position of the less successful concerns was obviously very different, since they had all failed by the early years of the twentieth century. However, when the state of their income and expenditure accounts allowed, some minor provision for depreciation and retort renewal was made. The Linlithgow company, from 1886 to 1901 set aside a total of £15,540 for depreciation, and in 1895 wrote off from revenue £1,675 of capital expenditure. From 1885 to 1897 the Holmes company wrote off £8,967 for depreciation and £4,779 for renewal of retorts. The West Lothian company from 1886 to 1891 set aside £8,921 for depreciation.[65]

The uses to which the depreciation account could be put are not entirely clear. It has been suggested that if depreciation were treated as a reserve derived from profits, it could in later years be used as such in case of need.[66] Two of the four companies discussed here, in fact, at various times, accumulated reserve funds distinct from depreciation accounts. That of the Broxburn company, amounting to £27,467, was put towards the financing of the Roman Camp crude oil works in 1891. In 1912, Pumpherston had a reserve fund of £110,000, which was used to fund the restructuring of the company's capital and the absorption of the Tarbrax company.[67] It seems clear, therefore, that the successful companies in the shale industry had no need to make use of their depreciation accounts in bad years. In fact, depreciation was provided for by all four companies in all but a few years in the period 1866–1914.

All four companies in their published reports indicated each year that provision from revenue had been made for works and plant maintenance and repair. The depreciation account was therefore available for expenditure to keep plant up to date. That it was also used to finance development and expansion of the four companies' activities is clear from the published reports. In addition to showing the amount set aside for depreciation, these reports discussed, often in some detail, capital expenditure incurred during the year. In 1879, the Broxburn company disclosed capital expenditure of £22,550, which included 88 Henderson retorts, a significant extension to the works. This was greater than the unexpended portion of the original capital, and the excess was to be met out of depreciation.[68] In 1891 the directors proposed that the expenditure on the new crude oil works at Roman Camp be met partly from the reserve fund and partly by temporary loans which would be repaid from 'year to year, and a sum equal to the amount repaid will yearly be written off for depreciation on capital expenditure. In this way the whole cost of the work will be met without any addition ... to the capital of the company.'[69]

Broxburn was fortunate in that, in 1881, it was able to issue 3,500 new £10 ordinary shares with £8 10s. paid at a price of £15 each, a premium of £6 10s. per share, a total of £22,750. This sum was added to the usual depreciation and written off the company's capital account. A similar transaction in 1885 yielded £31,725, which was again written off as depreciation. This was a very prudent treatment of share premiums which, until 1948, could be used for a variety of purposes, including the payment of dividends. Robert Bell surrendered 750 fully paid shares in the company in renegotiating the terms of his sale of the assets. With a nominal value of £7,500, these were sold by the directors in 1882 for £18,000. This was again written off as depreciation.[70]

In 1889, Pumpherston reported capital expenditure of £3,348 on 48 workmen's houses, £1,553 on the sinking of a new mine, and £2,886 on plant connected with Henderson's patent continuous distillation process. In 1900 the directors reported that £13,978 of capital expenditure had been incurred in mining development, additional workmen's houses at Deans works, and in extending the refinery at Pumpherston, all indicating some expansion of the company's activities. The shale companies therefore clearly enjoyed periods of prosperity that enabled them to expand their activities from within their own resources. The effects of this use of depreciation are clearly set out in the chairman's address to the Broxburn shareholders in 1891. He pointed out that capital expenditure for the year was £17,819, while depreciation of £17,051 had been written off. The effect was that the net balance of capital expenditure remained virtually the same as in the previous year, but the works 'have been improved and extended; a new mine has been opened up; a bench of new retorts has been erected; additional mineral wagons have been purchased; and a number of foremen's cottages have been built'.[71]

Retort renewal and plant improvement

At the same meeting, in seconding the adoption of the report, treasurer Richmond of Glasgow expressed concern that the need for such levels of depreciation was greater in the shale industry than in other trades because of the rapid change and obsolescence in some of the machinery involved.[72] This was particularly true of the retorts. Over the period 1851–1914, the retorts used had changed from horizontal to vertical, to Henderson and similar types, to the Young & Beilby and its variants, and, finally, to the different developments of the Bryson or Pumpherston retort: five different versions of the plant used in one of the most important stages of production. In their operation, retorts were subject to extremes of temperatures and dealt with large quantities of the basic raw material, leading to considerable wear and tear. The Oakbank chairman, in proposing to set aside sums each year for retort renewal, said that experience showed that retorts 'needed renewing, or at least thorough overhauling, once at least every seven or ten years.'[73] In 1896, the Broxburn chairman expressed the view that the average life of retorts was ten years.[74]

One result was that the companies started to set aside out of revenue what became known as 'retort renewal accounts'. These appeared as early as 1884 in the Young's accounts.[75] By the 1890s, expenditure on retorts was often debited to revenue by means of such accounts or by other devices. Between 1890 and 1896, Young's spent £95,520 in changing its whole retort plant. The chairman commented that the company had created three new crude oil works out of revenue.[76] Subsequently, in the years 1900–9 and 1913–14, £178,685 was set aside from revenue in a retort renewal fund.[77] From 1896 to 1914, Oakbank set aside a total of £95,799 for retort renewal.[78] In 1899 the directors stated that it was thought prudent to pay for the new retorts out of revenue: they would improve the efficiency but not the capacity of the works, and therefore the 'cost cannot equitably be charged to capital'.[79] Broxburn, from 1894 to 1914, set aside £201,416 from revenue for retort renewal; while Pumpherston, in the five years up to 1904, spent £64,922 on retort replacement.[80] Subsequently, payment for new retorts was included in sums written off to an 'Improved Plant Account', which included such items as the installation of electric power at the Pumpherston works and an extension to the refinery. In 1908, it was reported that £149,109 had thus far been expended out of revenue for retort replacement and improved plant, which is 'strictly speaking, capital expenditure'.[81]

Young's, from 1908 onwards, also deducted from the revenue account sums for 'exceptional outlay at works'. In 1908, this comprised mechanical stokers, fuel economisers, multitubular heaters and continuous distillation plant all intended to improve fuel economy.[82] From 1908 to 1914, such expenditure totalled £57,839.[83]

It is clear that the successful concerns in the shale industry were able to maintain and expand their activities in the period up to 1914. In the 1880s, the Broxburn, Burntisland, Midlothian, West Lothian and Pumpherston companies were able to finance such development by the issue of additional ordinary shares. In the 1890s, the only addition to share capital was Pumpherston's issue of preference shares. The companies that expanded operations at this time relied on borrowing and money derived from profits. This situation continued in the first decades of the twentieth century. Expansion financed by the issue of ordinary and preference shares was confined to the Oakbank company's venture at Niddry Castle and Duddingston. Also, the promotion of the Tarbrax company was a thinly veiled expansion of Pumpherston's activities.

However, in this period much of the expansion was financed from the profits of the companies themselves. It is instructive to examine the published accounts for the companies in one year during this period. Pumpherston in 1909 reported a balance at the credit of its profit and loss account of £131,089. From this was deducted £10,000 for depreciation and £41,758 for expenditure on improved plant, a preference dividend of £6,000 and an ordinary dividend of 50 per cent – £55,250 – leaving a balance of £18,084 to be carried forward.[84] The Broxburn company, out of a balance of £88,880, set aside for depreciation £13,801; a preference dividend of £6,000; a 17.5 per cent ordinary dividend of £34,966; income tax of £1,747; £12,000 to retort account; £10,000 to reserve (making this account £70,430); and writing down consols to 84 per cent, £2,120, leaving a balance of £8,255 to be carried forward.[85] Young's, out of a credit balance of £120,500, set aside for depreciation £20,000; retort reserve fund, £10,000; for exceptional outlay at works, £15,434; interest on debenture bonds, £16,732; 7 per cent dividend on ordinary shares, £31,696; contingent dividend of 8 per cent on B debenture bonds, £12,000, leaving £14,637 to be carried forward.[86] Oakbank, from a credit balance of £53,885, devoted £1,658 to interest on loans; £2,241 to a preference dividend; £25,500 to a 15 per cent ordinary dividend; £14,000 to depreciation; and £5,000 to retort renewal, leaving £5,486 to be carried forward.[87]

Of particular interest here is the fact that Young's balance of £120,500 was very little short of the £131,098 belonging to the industry leader, Pumpherston, which was able to pay a dividend of 50 per cent on its ordinary shares with £55,250. Young's managed only 7 per cent with £31,696. It had an ordinary share capital of £452,808 compared with Pumpherston's £110,500, and it also had to pay interest of £16,732 on its debenture bonds, along with a contingent liability of £12,000 on half of these. These figures illustrate the difficulties faced by Young's because of the price paid for the assets in 1866 and the expedients adopted to cope with the problems of 1887.

The shale industry was able in its profitable years to devote considerable sums to development. The setting aside of profits for depreciation and other capital projects can be shown to have provided finance from within the companies, as shown in Table 6.3.

This gives a grand total of £2,591,575, considerably greater than the funds derived from increase in capital.

There was in British industry generally a fall in profit levels in the period from 1870 to 1909, and it is possible that this led to a shortage of internal and external funds for investment.[88] The position in the shale industry is not clear-cut. On the one hand there were a number of failures at various times. Those at the end of the nineteenth century were obviously influenced by a shortage of capital for investment in new technology – the dramatically improved retorts. On the other hand,

Table 6.3 Capital expenditure financed from internal sources, 1866–1914

Company	Depreciation	Retort renewal/plant improvement	Capital projects written off from revenue
	£	£	£
Young's	704927	271204	47647
Broxburn	549954	200416	
Pumpherston	245280	280881	
Oakbank	168252	97020	26174
	1668413	849521	73641

the four companies that survived to 1919 were able to finance these improvements – in part, at least – from profits.

The Broxburn company in 1893 had paid-up capital of £299,750 and a throughput of 10,964,274 gallons of crude oil. In 1913 capital remained the same but throughput had risen to 17,239,389 gallons, an increase of 57.23 per cent.[89] In 1893, Pumpherston's paid-up capital was £180,860, and it refined 5,883,632 gallons of crude oil. In 1913, the capital was £435,500: £149,500 of this resulted from a bonus to shareholders in the reorganisation of 1912–13. The capital, compared to 1893 was, therefore, £286,000, an increase of 58.13 per cent. The company's throughput in 1913 was 22,682,843 gallons, an increase of 285.52 per cent.[90] In 1893, Oakbank's paid-up capital was £67,500, and the company dealt with 4,147,366 gallons of crude oil. In 1913 the relevant figures were £270,000 and 13,599,689 gallons: an increase of 300 per cent in capital and 227.91 per cent in throughput.[91] Unfortunately, similar data are not available for Young's.

These figures indicate that, over the period, the Broxburn company achieved a significant increase in production financed entirely from its own internal resources. At the same time, Pumpherston had an almost fourfold increase in through put, funded by a mixture of external and internal finance. The increase in capital was partly due to the completion of the issue of preference shares in 1896,[92] and partly to taking over the Tarbrax company in 1913. These two companies show that, in the shale industry, there was no shortage of finance derived from profits. The experience of the Oakbank company indicates that it was possible to secure external funding by the issue of fresh shares: there was some confidence in the industry on the part of the investing public. However, it cannot be said that this was an industry-wide experience. These three companies were survivors of an industry in which the great majority of concerns had failed. Some of the reasons for this failure will be explored in a later chapter dealing with the management of the industry.

Four refining companies and two concerns producing crude oil only lasted up to the amalgamation in 1919. They were the survivors of 43 limited companies established in the industry between 1862 and 1904. Before leaving our consideration of the capital employed, it is necessary to look at how much of that capital was lost.

Capital Lost

The writing down of capital: reconstructions

Payne suggests that, up to 1895, £3.2 million of the Scottish companies' capital was lost by writing down. He further suggests that this was largely confined to overseas ventures and shipping companies.[1] The amount lost in this way by the shale industry was as follows:

Lanark	1885	£40,000
West Lothian	1886	£25,000
Clippens	1892	£180,480
Total		£245,480[2]

This represents 7.67 per cent of the total for all Scottish companies dissolved before 1895, and is a not insignificant proportion of this total figure. Large sums were also written down by two companies which were not dissolved until after 1895. In 1887, Young's reduced its capital by £427,500, and in 1894 the Linlithgow company wrote its capital down by £100,000.[3] In all, £772,980 of capital was lost in this way in the shale industry. In all cases except that of Young's, writing down capital was a prelude to dissolution.

We pass on to a consideration of losses incurred in reconstruction, by winding up and restarting as a new company. The first of these was the winding up in 1876 of the Uphall Mineral Oil Company with a paid-up capital of £200,000, and its rebirth as the Uphall Oil Company with a capital of £170,000. The £30,000 represented the C shares of the company. Along with £60,000 of B shares, this made up the price paid for the assets taken over from the vendors in 1871. The B and C shares were postponed to the A shares, which had been paid for in cash. In terms of dividends, none had ever been paid on the B and C shares.[4]

When dissolved in 1885, the Oakbank Oil Company had a paid-up capital of £90,000.[5] The new company had a nominal capital of £90,000. The shareholders of the old company agreed to accept £45,000 for their shares; the old company therefore lost £45,000 of its capital in the reconstruction.[6]

Takeovers and amalgamations

Five companies were sold or amalgamated. The takeover of the Straiton Oil Company by the Midlothian company valued the concern at £66,000, of which £28,000 was held to be satisfied by Midlothian's assumption of a bond secured over the estate. The remaining £38,000 was to be paid out of the capital of the new company.[7] It is possible therefore that the Straiton shareholders did not lose the entire value of their holdings. A little more information is available for the subsequent acquisition of these works by the Clippens Oil Company. The price paid to Midlothian was £80,000, plus £7,082 for the stock in trade. This was settled by the bond of £28,000 secured on the property that Clippens was assuming, the transfer to the Midlothian of 3,385 fully paid shares in Clippens at the price of £14 10s. (£14.50) per share (i.e. £49,082), and £10,000 in cash: a total of £87,082.[8] A press comment stated that the Midlothian directors, after paying the company's debts, would have some £27,000 to divide among the shareholders, 54 shillings (£2.70) per £10 share (£8 paid). Midlothian shares stood at 40 shillings (£2) on the Glasgow stock exchange.[9] The shareholders appear to have suffered a loss of £53,000.

In 1884, the Uphall Oil Company was taken over by Young's, which took over debts amounting to £18,822 and assumed liability for debentures of £45,000. Uphall's paid-up capital was £170,000. The shareholders were given £10 shares (£8 10s. paid) in Young's for each Uphall A share and each Uphall B share of £10 (fully paid).[10] The total value of these shares was £119,000, and so it can be seen that the Uphall shareholders lost £51,000 on the paid-up value of their shares. However, the B shares were originally issued to the vendors of the company as fully paid. They had never received a dividend and it may be said, therefore, that the Uphall vendors at last received £25,500 for the works transferred in 1871.

The Hermand and Walkinshaw oil companies agreed to amalgamate in 1890. The Hermand capital consisted of 3,000 £10 shares with £8 10s. paid up, and 9,000 £10 shares with £1 paid up: a total of £34,500. Walkinshaw's capital was made up of 12,000 ordinary shares of £10, all paid up, and 2,800 preference shares of £10 each, all paid up except for an unpaid call of £150: a total of £147,850. The new company, the Hermand Oil Company, had a nominal capital of £350,000 in £1 shares. The holders of the £8 10s paid shares in the old Hermand company received 25.08 fully paid £1 shares in the new company for each share; those holding £1 paid shares received 22.4 £1 shares, with 15 shillings paid up for each share. The holders of Walkinshaw's £10 ordinary received one fully paid £1 share in the new company. Holders of preference shares received ten £1 fully paid shares. The Hermand company was therefore valued at £226,440, and the Walkinshaw at £40,000: a total of £266,440. The Walkinshaw shareholders lost £107,850, while those of the Hermand saw their shares revalued to £226,440 from £34,500.[11]

This transaction is, in the absence of any further information, not easily understood. The seemingly unbalanced treatment of the old Hermand £8 10s. paid and £1 paid shares may have been related to the latter's liability for a call of 5 shillings on each new share. This was in fact called up in 1892. more than one fifth, of these shares – 42,279 – were forfeited because of non-payment.[12] The works and mines were closed down to wait for better conditions shortly thereafter, and in 1899 the company was reconstructed as the New Hermand Oil Company Limited, with a nominal capital of £70,000. The old company had 272,721 £1 shares all fully paid up. These were to be exchanged for shares in the New Hermand at the rate of one £1 share (16s. 8d. paid up) for five shares in the old company; 51,355 shares were taken up, indicating that some shareholders had no wish to accept a call liability. The company did not prosper, and in 1905 the liquidator reported that, after realising the whole assets of the company, £519 was available for a first and final dividend to the ordinary creditors.[13] It seems clear, therefore, that investors in the original Hermand and Walkinshaw companies lost their entire investment.

The Pumpherston company formally absorbed Tarbrax with effect from 30 April 1912. The £50,000 of Tarbrax preference shares were exchanged for similar Pumpherston shares, with the option of payment in cash. The £85,000 of ordinary shares were exchanged at the rate of three Pumpherston ordinary shares of £1 (fully paid) for ten £1 (fully paid) Tarbrax shares.[14] Pumpherston shares stood at £11 0s ¾d and Tarbrax at 35s 6d, a very good result for the Tarbrax shareholders.[15]

Liquidations, windings up and dissolutions

Peter Payne suggests that dissolved companies fell into five groups:

1. Abortive
2. Sold, amalgamated or reconstructed
3. Wound up compulsorily, or under supervision, or by reason of liabilities – in short, insolvent
4. Wound up voluntarily, without any reason being given, usually because the company's prospects were unfavourable or, more rarely, because the company had fulfilled the purpose for which it was started
5. Dissolved in disregard of legal forms, or unknown, and struck off the Register under the provisions of Section 7 of the Companies Act of 1880 or the similar clauses of subsequent Acts.

He also considers that an estimate of capital lost to shareholders might be made by using the following assumptions, arrived at 'using empirical (if spotty) evidence'.[16] Of the sum raised by abortives, 50 per cent was completely lost to the shareholders.

Companies sold, amalgamated or reconstructed lost 20 per cent of their share capital, while those wound up compulsorily lost 90 per cent and firms wound up voluntarily lost 50 per cent. Firms dissolved in disregard of legal forms under clause 7 (4) of the Companies Act 1889 – i.e., those that simply withered away – lost 100 per cent of their share capital.

For the shale industry, evidence is a little more plentiful, although it also remains 'spotty'. In the period from 1863 to 1881, 13 of the companies formed before 1877 were dissolved. One of these was considered abortive, having never issued shares beyond those taken by the subscribers. Three were dissolved under clause 7 (4) of the Companies Act 1880 – in Payne's terms, they 'simply withered away'. Their total capital was £31,029, and the assumption is that all of this may be regarded as lost. However, in the case of the Mid Calder Mineral Oil Company Limited, it is known that their Oakbank works and mines were purchased by the Oakbank company in 1869 for £5,600 plus £1,300 for stocks of oil and shale, a total of £6,900.[17] It is not stated whether the purchase was made directly from the Mid Calder company; it was certainly not bought as a going concern, the works being one of those that stopped production in 1867–8. However, it is at least possible that the money received for the works was not all absorbed in paying creditors, and that something might have been left for the shareholders.

Nine of the concerns are considered to have been wound up voluntarily. The Capeldrae Oil & Coal Company Limited, although a resolution for voluntary winding up was passed on 9 December 1878, was eventually dissolved under Clause 7 (4) of the Companies Act, 1880. Similarly, on 24 December 1869 the shareholders of the Monklands Oil Refining Company passed a resolution to wind up voluntarily, but the company was subsequently dissolved under Clause 7 (4) of the Act. Apart from the decision to wind up the company, it was also resolved that the directors should sell the 'whole works, plant and other property belonging to the company' to James Struthers & Company of Rochsoles Colliery, Stand, near Airdrie. James Struthers held 100 shares in the company and was one of the three directors.[18]

The remaining seven concerns were all wound up in accordance with the legislation. The Broxburn Shale Oil Company's shareholders simply put forward 'as a Special Resolution, within the meaning of the 51st clause of the Companies Act, 1862, that this company be forthwith wound up', and this was followed by a final meeting on 13 February 1866. A similar resolution was adopted in 1868 by the Scottish Oil Company's shareholders, with the addition of a clause appointing a liquidator. The Glasgow Oil Company resolved in 1873 that 'this company be wound up, and wound up voluntarily'. In 1881, the Monklands Oil & Coal shareholders resolved that 'it has been shown to the satisfaction of this meeting that the Monklands Oil & Coal Company Limited cannot by reason of its liabilities, continue its business, and that it is advisable to wind up the same'. Similar decisions were taken in respect of the Midlothian Mineral Oil Company.[19]

The Dalserf Coal Coke & Oil Company is of particular interest. Article 97 of the Articles of Association prescribed that: 'In the event of losses being sustained to an extent exceeding one third of the Capital, as instructed by any Balance, or successive balances, then, and in that case, the Company may be dissolved and its affairs wound up, upon a written requisition to that effect, made and subscribed by Shareholders to the extent of one half of the Capital.'[20] In 1868, it was resolved

> That in respect of the circumstances referred to in the minute of the last meeting which had just been read, and more especially of the loss sustained to an extent beyond one half of the capital of the Company and of the Requisition for a Voluntary Winding which had been subscribed to the extent of one half of the said capital, it be as it is hereby resolved that the affairs of the company be wound up voluntarily in terms of the provisions contained in the Companies Act, 1862.

Two liquidators were appointed, and they reported to a general meeting on 19 July 1869 that a surplus of £1,505 remained to be divided among the shareholders.

The case of the West Calder Oil Company is also of interest because it passed a special resolution to enter into voluntary liquidation on 22 March 1878. This was overtaken by an order for voluntary winding up under the supervision of the court. In 1888, the liquidator reported that dividends on claims to the amount of £16,956 had been paid.

The cases of these two concerns suggest that it might be over-generous to assume the loss of only half of the capital of companies voluntarily wound up.

Of the companies dissolved after 1881, six were wound up voluntarily. The Annick Lodge company resolved on 4 November 1889 to wind up because, by reason of its liabilities, it could not continue in business. The British Oil & Candle Company resolved on 4 August 1883 to confirm the sale of the company's property as effected by the directors, and subsequently, on 9 May 1885, a final meeting was held to wind up the company.[21]

The remaining four companies present a little more difficulty. The Bathgate company's dissolution involved a petition to the court as well as a decision to seek a voluntary liquidation.[22] The Binnend company was one of George Simpson's enterprises: incorporated with a nominal capital of £130,000 in 1878, all of the shares were issued with £3 called on each, but unpaid calls totalled £3,480. In 1880 the shares were reduced to £3 each, fully paid. On 17 October 1881, a special resolution to wind up was adopted, and the winding up was completed on 1 June 1882. In 1881 the works and associated lands were sold to John Waddell for £60,000:

£20,000 for the lands and £40,000 for the works.[23] It seems possible that money was available to enable the shareholders to recover their investment.

The Clippens company had, early in 1892, reduced its capital from £258,150 to £77,670: 25,890 shares of £3 each, fully paid. On 29 December 1892 an extraordinary resolution to wind up was adopted.[24] This resulted in the formation of a new company, also called the Clippens Oil Company Limited, incorporated on 23 June 1893 to take over the old company. The new company took over the debentures issued by the old, but with an interest rate reduced from 5 to 3 per cent. The debenture trustees were given 500 £1 A shares in the new company. Ordinary creditors, including holders of £2 convertible debentures, received £1 fully paid ordinary shares in the new company. Shareholders in the old company received one deferred paid-up share of 1 shilling for each share held. The new company had a paid-up capital of £91,959, consisting of £500 in A shares, £90,165 in ordinary shares issued to creditors, and £1,294 in deferred ordinary shares issued to the ordinary shareholders of the old company. The ordinary share capital of £258,150 in 1891 had been reduced to £1,294. The company worked on for some years, until it was closed down because of water problems in the mines and a dispute with the Edinburgh Water Company. The company was eventually wound up in 1911, with the debenture holders not being paid in full.[25]

The Burntisland Oil Company resolved on 8 September 1892 that the company be wound up voluntarily. On 26 September, the court directed that the voluntary winding up should continue under its supervision. It was subsequently proposed that a new company be formed to take over the assets. This was registered on 25 March 1893, and had a nominal capital of £155,000 consisting of 120,000 £1 preference shares and 35,000 £1 ordinary shares. The debenture holders of the old company received fully paid preference shares in the new company to the full value of debentures held. The unsecured creditors received fully paid preference shares in the new company equal to one half of the sums due to them. The ordinary shareholders received two fully paid ordinary shares in the new company for each £10 share in the old company.[26] These Ordinary shareholders therefore saw their investment reduced by 80 per cent.

In the event, there is no evidence that the new company ever worked the mines and works, and it was wound up voluntarily by a resolution adopted in 1896. The stock of products was held as security for advances amounting to just under £18,000.[27] The only assets in the liquidation would therefore be the works and mines. The mines were seriously affected by a 'crush' in 1891, and it is clear from other liquidations that oil works realised little more than break-up value in such circumstances. In 1881, in the course of the liquidation of the West Calder Oil Company, its works, pits and mineral leases, which were said to have cost upwards of £100,000, were acquired by Young's for £17,752.[28] In 1901, the New Hermand company issued £18,154 of preference shares to finance a bench of the modern retorts then coming into use. When the company was liquidated in 1905, the entire assets of the company realised £8,727.[29]

The Linlithgow company entered into voluntary liquidation by a resolution passed on 13 February 1902. This was subsequently, as in the case of the West Calder company, overtaken by a petition for supervision. The net result was that, on 16 November 1904, the liquidator reported that £15,969 was available for division among ordinary creditors at the rate of 4s. 7⅝d. in the pound on a rankable debt of £68,901. Again, there was nothing left for the shareholders.[30]

The experience of these six concerns, especially Clippens and Linlithgow, casts some doubt on the assumption that only half of a company's capital was lost in the case of voluntary dissolution.

Four of the companies were wound up compulsorily, and these provide a little more information concerning their demise. The Westfield company was one of George Simpson's promotions, and a petition to wind up was lodged on behalf of a creditor on 27 January 1886. The resulting liquidation produced funds of £1,072 against preferential debts of £730 and ordinary debts of £6,016. The liquidator's report specifically stated that there was no surplus falling to the shareholders.[31] The West Lothian company was wound up on a petition of creditors dated 20 November 1891. In 1894 it was reported to the court that the works and mineral leases had been sold at a price insufficient to cover the debentures; after paying £291 of preferred claims, there remained only £446 for the ordinary creditors, whose claims amounted to £45,842.[32] The Holmes company was wound up by order of the court on 27 October 1900 in response to a petition by the mineral landlord. On 16 November 1903, the liquidator reported that he had realised the whole assets of the company, amounting to £1,200. There was obviously nothing left for the shareholders.[33]

The Lanark company was wound up in consequence of a petition by the Commercial Bank of Scotland. The liquidator's report states that the company's assets amounted to £84,172, which included £83,648 for the works and mines. This was the book value after depreciation of £21,109. Total liabilities were £36,221. The end result fully illustrates the difficulties faced by companies in this industry in such circumstances. The liquidator attempted to sell the works, etc to pay off the secured debts and leave something for the unsecured creditors. No offer was received. The Lanark works was held as security for a bond of £10,646 by the Commercial Bank, and was put up for sale by 'public roup' four times at the upset price of £15,000, before being sold on 18 July 1888 for £4,000. There were debentures of £13,980, secured over the works at Tarbrax and Lanark but postponed to the debt to the bank. The Tarbrax works were sold to the mineral landlord for £3,000, who accepted £1,500 in settlement of claims amounting to £6,000. The net result was that the Commercial Bank lost about £6,000 of its loan to the company;

the debenture holders received £580, leaving them some £13,500 out of pocket. There was nothing left for the unsecured creditors and, obviously, nothing for the shareholders, some of whom were also debenture holders.[34]

It is clear, therefore, that with regard to compulsory dissolutions, and to those carried out under supervision, the experience of the shale company shareholder was that nothing could be expected out of a company's failure.

Dividends as compensation for lost capital

Payne suggests that the losses borne by shareholders in dissolved concerns might have been compensated for by dividends received – not simply from the dissolved companies, but from shares held in a 'diversified portfolio'.[35] In the case of the shale industry, it is clear that dividends were paid to shareholders of some companies. In the case of the majority of those formed before 1870, no information is available: company records have not survived, and most companies had very small numbers of shareholders. They were essentially what became known as private companies, and their reports and meetings were not covered in the press. For the later companies, we must rely, in the main, on reports of their activities in the financial columns of the *Scotsman*, the *Glasgow Herald* and the *West Lothian Courier*. However, for Young's, Broxburn and Oakbank, we are fortunate to have access to minute books of the shareholders' annual general meetings.

The available data show that, from 1867 – the first year in which Young's company declared a dividend – to 1919, when the four surviving limited companies were absorbed into Scottish Oil Limited, a total of £4,013,234 was paid in dividends on ordinary shares of the various companies. Of this, £1,143,797 came from Young's; £448,734 from Oakbank; £1,025,845 from Broxburn; and £1,103,290 from Pumpherston: i.e., £3,721,666, or 92.7 per cent, was derived from the four concerns that survived into the amalgamation. Over the same period, £457,614 was paid in dividends on preference shares. Again, the bulk of this, £433,131, was paid by the four survivors.

Table A (Appendix 1) shows that, by 1913, £4,341,737 had been invested in limited companies in the shale oil industry. The five limited companies still surviving in 1914 had between them a paid-up capital of £1,514,758. Failures and reductions of capital among the survivors accounted for a loss of £2,826,979 of investment.[36] Some of this may have been recovered by shareholders at liquidation, but the above analysis of individual concerns indicates that this would have been a small amount at best. However, it is clear that the dividends paid exceeded to a considerable extent the amount of lost capital. The value of the shares in the surviving concerns must also be taken into account. In 1919, when they were acquired by Scottish Oils, the ordinary shares of the companies were valued as follows:

Pumpherston	285,500 shares @ £5	£1,427,500
Broxburn	235,000 shares @ £2	£470,000
Oakbank	200,000 shares @ 37s. 6d.	£375,000
Young's	113,202 shares @ 63s.	£356,586

This gives a total of £2,629,086.[37]

The preference shares were left in the hands of the shareholders and amounted to a further £350,000. In addition, Young's had £300,000 worth of 99-year debenture bonds, which were left in the hands of the holders; £150,000 of these had a contingent dividend entitlement. To secure the abandonment of this liability, the Anglo-Persian Company offered the holders 20 7 per cent shares in Scottish Oils for the abandonment of the right in each £100.[38] These debentures therefore had an additional value of £30,000. The four companies had a total value of £3,309,086.

Overall, it is clear that, by 1919, the industry as a whole had profited to some extent. Ordinary dividends of £4,013,234, and preference dividends of £457,614 added to the value of the surviving concerns – £3,309,086 – is a total of £7,779,934: 78.5 per cent more than the £4,341,737 invested in the industry. Almost the whole of this had been accrued by the four surviving companies and would, of course, have been of little consolation to shareholders in the failed concerns.

Speculation

The identity of shareholders will be explored in a later chapter, but it is appropriate here to consider whether all of the original shareholders actually lost anything in the companies' failures. It has been estimated that in 1856, one third of transactions on the Glasgow stock exchange were speculative, and that by 1914 this had risen to about three quarters of transactions. There was considerable activity in shale oil shares in the 1880s on the Glasgow and Edinburgh exchanges.[39] The case of the Burntisland company is of particular interest. The company was incorporated on 5 September 1881 and submitted its first Summary of Capital and Shares on 28 December 1881. This listed 195 shareholders of 12,000 shares. Eighteen shareholders transferred their complete holdings, amounting to 675 shares, in the period up to 28 December 1881. Another 11 shareholders transferred a part of their holdings, amounting to 342 shares. In all, 1,017 shares were transferred. On 2 January 1883 the second SCS was submitted, showing that 4,647 of the shares held at 28 December 1881 had been transferred by 94 shareholders. The third SCS dated 4 June 1883 shows that a further 1,691 of these shares had been transferred by 38 holders. By 9 June 1884, 1,805 more had been disposed of by 28 holders, and by 14 June 1886 a further 825 shares had been transferred by 17 shareholders. In all,

8,968 of the shares held on 28 December 1881 had been transferred by 177 of the then shareholders.[40]

It is possible, by using the daily lists of share prices in the newspapers, to form an estimate of the value of these shares at the time of transfer. In the nineteenth century, share transactions on the stock exchange were not completed until the end of the 'account' in which they were made. There were two 'accounts': in the middle and at the end of each month. A transaction in shares was normally completed and the transfer registered with the company involved within three or four days of the end of the 'account'.[41] It seems, therefore, that a transfer recorded on a particular date in the SCS would refer to a transaction that had taken place some days, and possibly more than two weeks, previously. This presents some difficulty in assessing possible payments for transferred shares. However, movements in the Burntisland share price over the period occurred over relatively long periods. For example, between 28 December 1882 and 26 February 1883, the price rose from £15 1s. 2d. to £16 1s. 4d., rising further to £21 7s. 8d. by 25 April 1883. It remained at around that figure until the end of 1883, with a short-lived peak of £25 1s. 4d. in September. After 26 January 1884, there was a gradual decline to £15 1s. 2d. on 24 December 1884, and thereafter a small recovery to between £16 1s. 2d. and £18 3s. 8d. between February and June 1885. It seems, therefore, appropriate to value transferred shares by the price quoted at the end of the 'account' before the date of transfer: it seems likely that this will provide a reasonable approximation of the sums involved.

The transfers listed in the Summaries dated 28 December 1881 and 2 January 1883 have not been taken into account here. It is not until the one dated 4 June 1883 that it becomes clear that the shares were paid up to the extent of £8.50 for the whole period covered by the SCS. It has been estimated, as described above, that shares listed as transferred on that SCS had a stock exchange value of £13,494 in excess of the £8.50 paid-up on each share; those listed on the SCS dated 9 June 1884 standing at £21,734; and the SCS of 8 June 1885, £3,469.[42] In a period of less than four years from the formation of the company, a total profit of £38,000 could have been made by share dealings. It must also be assumed that the 4,647 shares listed as transferred in the SCS dated 2 January 1883 were not disposed of at a loss, and that a possibly substantial profit was generated here also.

The £38,000 was shared by 83 shareholders, but there were some very substantial individual transactions. James Steel, a Broxburn company director, transferred 370 shares on 4 May 1883; 170 on 27 June and 2 July 1883; and 80 on 10 June and 1 September 1884. He made a putative profit of £7,677. John Waddell transferred 550 shares on 22 February 1884, with a gain of £7,150.

The SCS dated 4 June 1883 also shows that, over the period from 2 January to 4 June 1883, 29 holdings comprising 904 shares were transferred by people who had not held shares on 28 December 1881: these shares had therefore been acquired and disposed of in the period between the two dates. A further 215 shares had been transferred by people who had not held shares on 2 January 1883: again, these were acquired and disposed of during the period covered by the SCS.

It is clear, therefore, that shares in this company were the subject of considerable speculation. Some significant amounts were involved, but there were some small 'investors'. Of the shares shown in the SCS of 4 June 1883 as transferred by holders on 28 December 1881, one person disposed of 370 out of a holding of 620; one disposed of 200; and two disposed of 100, both complete holdings. At the other end of the scale, three holders disposed of complete holdings of 5 shares; one of 5 shares out of 10; and six of complete holdings of 10 shares.

This pattern of speculation in the shares of new companies appears in other companies. The Midlothian company was incorporated on 22 March 1882. The first SCS, dated 17 July 1882, shows no transfers, but the second, dated 10 July 1883, shows that there were 85 transfers, totalling 4,272 of the original shares.[43] After the shares became paid up to the extent of £8 on 16 August 1882, the price rose to £10 on 23 December 1882 and reached a high of £11 7s. 8d. on 9 January 1883. It fell to lows of £9 13s. 16d. and £9 15s. 16d. on 27 March and 8 May 1883.[44] At these prices, the share disposal would not have attracted as great a profit as those of the Burntisland company; nevertheless, a gain of £2–£3 over a short period on an investment of £8 was substantial. In addition, there were 59 transfers of 3,055 shares by people who had not held shares on 17 July 1882. These shares were acquired and disposed of during the period covered by the SCS.

The West Lothian company was incorporated on 5 October 1883. The first SCS dated 15 February 1884 shows that 50 shareholders had transferred 1,135 shares up to that time.[45] The next SCS, dated 20 February 1885, shows that a further 207 holders of the original shares had transferred 5,010 shares in the period from 16 February 1884 to 20 February 1885. In addition, 39 people had acquired and disposed of 1,370 shares over the same period. This company was not the subject of such profitable speculation as the two discussed above. However, the £7 paid shares did trade at above that price from October 1884 to November 1885, reaching a high of £10 and maintaining £8 or £9 for periods of some weeks during this time.

The shale companies in the hierarchy of Scottish limited companies

Before leaving consideration of the industry's capital, it is appropriate to consider the position of the surviving shale oil companies within the hierarchy of limited companies in Scotland. Scott and Hughes list Scotland's 64 largest non-financial companies in 1904–5. The cut-off point is an issued capital of £300,000. Young's company and the Broxburn company were placed at nos 53 and 64 respectively.[46] The Pumpherston company, with an issued capital of £230,000, and the Oakbank with £200,000, would not have been far behind. Pumpherston and Oakbank expanded significantly in the next few years, and by 1913 had issued capital of £435,500 and £300,000 respectively.[47]

The nominal value of issued capital is not an exact measure of a company's actual worth. In 1919, the four surviving refining companies, along with James Ross & Company, were amalgamated to form a new company, Scottish Oils Limited. The ordinary shares of the four refining companies were valued at £2,629,086, of which £1,427,500 was to be paid for those of the Pumpherston company. A company that had been ranked behind Broxburn and Young's in 1904–5 was now valued at more than the combined worth of the other three companies. Scottish Oils Limited in 1920–1 was ranked ninth of 72 non-financial companies in Scotland.[48] The shale industry, although not approaching in size any of the major heavy industries, must be considered a significant element in the Scottish economy.

Part 3 Shares and shareholders

8

Size of shareholdings

It has been shown that the paid-up capital of the limited companies comprised £3,889,481 in ordinary shares, £452,256 in preference shares and £780,220 in debenture bonds (see Chapter 6, Table 6.1). Ordinary shares made up 89.58 per cent of the total, and it is appropriate to consider the size of shareholdings and what can be established about their ownership. Tables 8.1(a)–(d), 8.2(a)–(d) and 8.3(a)–(d) provide data regarding various aspects of the shareholdings at the time the companies were incorporated.

The nominal value of 198 shareholdings of net issued capital totalled £694,900, an average of £3,510. The nominal value of issued shares for Young's is given here as £582,500. This is based on the first Summary of Capital and Shares. In consideration of the industry's capital in Part 2. the issued capital is taken as

Table 8.1(a) Limited companies: nominal and issued capital, denomination of shares, 1862–1869

Year	Company	Capital				
		Nominal £	Issued cash £	Not paid in £	Net issued £	Denomination of shares £
1862	Broxburn Shale	20000	16000		16000	200
1864	Mid Calder Mineral	10000	8500		8500	100
1866	Young's PL & M	600000	582500		582500	100
1866	Capeldrae Oil & Coal	1400	1400		1400	10
1866	Scottish	20000	7000		7000	10
1866	Glasgow	25000	25000		25000	50
1866	Dalserf Coal, Coke & Oil	50000	25100	12500	12600	10
1866	Monklands Oil Refining	10000	8000		8000	10
1866	Monklands Oil & Coal	50000	5000		5000	10
1866	Glentore Mineral	10000	1400		1400	100
1866	Airdrie Mineral	10000	7500		7500	500
1869	Oakbank	20000	20000		20000	50
		826400	707400	12500	694900	

Table 8.1(b) Limited companies: number of shareholders, average holding, largest holding and proportion of net issued capital, 1862–1869

Year	Company	Shareholdings			
		Number	Average holding £	Largest net issued £	Percentage of capital
1862	Broxburn Shale	15	1067	6400	40.00
1864	Mid Calder Mineral	7	1214	3100	36.47
1866	Young's PL & M	74	7871	100000	17.17
1866	Capeldrae Oil & Coal	7	200	200	14.29
1866	Scottish	7	1000	1000	14.29
1866	Glasgow	9	2778	6250	25.00
1866	Dalserf Coal, Coke & Oil	32	393	1000	7.94
1866	Monklands Oil Refining	12	667	2000	25.00
1866	Monklands Oil & Coal	9	556	2250	45.00
1866	Glentore Mineral	7	200	200	14.29
1866	Airdrie Mineral	9	833	1500	20.00
1869	Oakbank	10	2000	5000	25.00
		198		128900	18.55

Table 8.1(c) Limited companies: shareholdings with a nominal value of £1,000 or more, proportion of net issued capital, 1862–1869

Year	Company	Shareholdings		
		No. £1000 or more	Nominal value £	Percentage of net issued capital
1862	Broxburn Shale	4	12400	77.50
1864	Mid Calder Mineral	4	7400	87.06
1866	Young's PL & M	74	582500	100.00
1866	Capeldrae	–	–	–
1866	Scottish	7	7000	100.00
1866	Glasgow	8	24500	98.00
1866	Dalserf Coal, Coke & Oil	6	6000	47.62
1866	Monklands Oil Refining	3	4000	50.00
1866	Monklands Oil & Coal	2	3350	67.00
1866	Glentore Mineral	–	–	–
1866	Airdrie Mineral	5	5500	73.33
1869	Oakbank	4	17000	85.00
		117	669650	96.36

Table 8.1(d) Limited companies: smallest shareholding, number of holdings with a nominal value of £100 or less, total nominal value and proportion of net issued capital, 1862–1869

Year	Company	Shareholdings			
		Smallest £	No. £100 or less	Nominal value £	Percentage of net issued capital
1862	Broxburn Shale	200	–	–	–
1864	Mid Calder Mineral	100	1	100	1.18
1866	Young's PL & M	1000	–	–	–
1866	Capeldrae	200	–	–	–
1866	Scottish	1000	–	–	–
1866	Glasgow	1250	–	–	–
1866	Dalserf Coal, Coke & Oil	50	7	600	4.76
1866	Monklands Oil Refining	50	1	50	0.63
1866	Monklands Oil & Coal	100	4	400	8.00
1866	Glentore Mineral	200	–	–	–
1866	Airdrie Mineral	500	–	–	–
1869	Oakbank	500	–	–	–
			13	1150	0.17

Table 8.2(a) Limited companies: nominal and issued capital, denomination of shares, 1871–1876

Year	Company	Capital				Denomination of shares £
		Nominal £	Issued cash £	Not paid in £	Net issued £	
1871	Uphall Mineral	250000	200000	108710	91290	10
1871	Dalmeny	27000	27000	4510	22490	10
1871	Midlothian Mineral	75000	26890	7000	19890	5
1872	West Calder	160000	138100	30000	108100	10
1876	Straiton Estate	100000	56800		56800	1
		612000	448790	150220	298570	

Part 3 Shares and shareholders

Table 8.2(b) Limited companies: number of shareholders, average holding, largest holding and proportion of net issued capital, 1871–1876

Year	Company	Shareholdings			
		Number	Average holding £	Largest £	Percentage of net issued capital
1871	Uphall Mineral	99	922	10000	10.96
1871	Dalmeny	64	351	2000	8.89
1871	Midlothian Mineral	99	231	3500	14.56
1872	West Calder	138	783	5000	4.63
1876	Straiton	61	1016	11100	18.50
		461		31600	10.58

Table 8.2(c) Limited companies: number of shareholdings with nominal value greater than £1,000, nominal value and proportion of net issued capital, 1871–1876

Year	Company	Shareholdings		
		No. £1000 or more	Nominal value £	Percentage of net issued capital
1871	Uphall Mineral	28	81440	89.21
1871	Dalmeny	7	8000	35.57
1871	Midlothian Mineral	5	9000	37.43
1872	West Calder	54	87700	81.13
1876	Straiton	22	50450	84.08
		116	236590	79.24

Table 8.2(d) Limited companies: smallest shareholding, number of holdings with a nominal value of £100 or less, total nominal value and proportion of net issued capital, 1871–1876

Year	Company	Shareholdings			
		Smallest £	No. £100 or less	Nominal value £	Percentage of net issued capital
1871	Uphall Mineral	50	14	1350	1.48
1871	Dalmeny	30	14	940	4.18
1871	Midlothian Mineral	5	56	3475	17.47
1872	West Calder	50	22	2250	2.07
1876	Straiton	100	14	1400	2.33
			120	9415	3.15

£572,500. In 1870, the balance sheet shows that 100 shares with a nominal value of £10,000 had been forfeit.[1]

Four hundred and sixty-one holdings of net issued capital amounted to a total of £298,570 – an average of £648.

There are problems with the Uphall data. Although the company was incorporated on 26 January 1871, the agreement with the vendors was not concluded until 19 May. The first SCS was submitted on 8 June 1871, and only 4,545 of the 11,000 A shares were taken up. It was thought necessary to base the analysis of this company on the second SCS, dated 4 June 1872.[2] The company was formed to take over from a partnership of Edward Meldrum, Peter McLagen and George Simpson. Payment was in the form of 9,000 B and C shares deferred to the 11,000 A shares. However, 550 fully paid A shares were issued to the partners in respect of interest; 1,500 fully paid A shares were also issued to Simpson in part-payment for works at Benhar and Fauldhouse, acquired by the company in a separate transaction. A total of 2,050 fully paid A shares were issued. On 5 August 1871 the three vendors transferred 179 A shares to the company, presumably in adjustment of the interest due to them.[3] This left 1,871 fully paid A shares in the hands of the vendors. The SCS dated 4 June 1872 shows that 11,000 A shares had been issued: 1,871 with £10 paid and 9,129 with £8 paid. This figure, 9,129 remains constant in succeeding returns and has been accepted as the basis for the nominal value of net issued capital, £91,290, given in Table 8.2(a). Simpson transferred 791 of the fully paid shares allocated to him.[4] It is not possible to trace these to their new holders, and the analysis of shareholders is based on an assumption that the 1,871 fully paid shares remained in the hands of the vendors.

The net issued capital in most cases is taken as the nominal value of the issued capital less the value of shares not paid for in cash. However, in the case of the Lanark company the only available SCS is dated 6 January 1886, more than two years after incorporation.[5] It is not possible to identify the shares issued to Simpson as part of the price paid for the assets. The SCS does indicate that Simpson owned shares at some point, and it has been assumed that he did in fact receive these shares. Otherwise, the shareholder profile discussed later has been constructed on the basis of holdings at 6 January 1886. The situation is further obscured by the fact that 16,047 shares were recorded as transferred in the year up to that date.

In the case of the West Lothian company, Simpson was allotted 1,500 shares as part of the purchase price. However, because of the high level of applications he agreed to give up these shares for issue to applicants.[6] With regard to the Holmes Company, the vendor sold a portion of the paid-up shares, and these cannot be traced;[7] again the profile has been based on the complete shareholdings of the company.

Table 8.3(a) Limited companies: nominal and issued capital, denomination of shares, 1877–1885

Year	Company	Capital				Denomination of shares
		Nominal £	Issued cash £	Not paid in £	Net issued £	£
1877	Broxburn	165000	165000	65000	100000	10
1878	Clippens	150000	120000	100000	20000	100
1878	Binnend	39000	39000	2900	26100	3
1880	British Oil & Candle	15000	12000		12000	10
1880	Walkinshaw	120000	110620	17640	92980	10
1881	Burntisland	120000	120000	3000	117000	10
1882	Midlothian	100000	70000		70000	10
1883	Westfield	25000	25000	6000	19000	10
1883	West Lothian	100000	75000		75000	10
1883	Bathgate	50000	22600	10000	12600	10
1883	Pumpherston	130000	90000	20000	70000	10
1883	Lanark	130000	100000	30000	70000	10
1884	Holmes	100000	56250	6250	50000	10
1884	Linlithgow	200000	140000	14000	126000	10
1885	Annick Lodge	12000	11775	5500	6275	5
1885	Hermand	140000	28500	9000	19500	10
		1596000	1185745	299290	886455	

Note: In the case of the British Oil & Candle Company, the vendor, Peter Dow, held 200 shares, but it is not clear whether these were vendors' shares. The Midlothian company was formed to take over the assets of the Straiton company, and again there is no information in the company file to indicate that any vendors' shares were issued.
NAS, BT2/953/5; BT2/1104.

The prospectus of the Hermand Company states that the vendor, James Thornton was to receive £11,000 for the assets. The relevant agreement is not in the file, and the first SCS does not state that any shares were issued free of charge. However, Thornton is shown as holding 900 shares, and it has been assumed that these were part of the payment for the assets transferred.[8]

Robert Bell received 6,500 fully paid £10 shares in the Broxburn company as part-payment for the works mines and leases transferred to the company. This agreement was amended later and Bell transferred 750 of these shares to the company. These shares were held in the names of Steel and Kennedy on behalf of the company; they remained as part of the issued capital and as part of the shares not paid for in cash.[9]

In the case of the Binnend company, the second SCS, dated 29 July 1880 has been used. This company originally had a nominal capital of £130,000, and in 1878 had issued 12,200 shares with £3 called on each. (In 1880 the nominal capital was reduced to £39,000 and 13,000 shares were issued with £3 called on each.)[10]

The companies formed between 1877 and 1885 had 2,172 holdings, net issued capital with a nominal value of £886,455: an average of £408. Tables 8.1(a)–(d), 8.2(a)–(d) and 8.3(a)–(d) give for each company the year of formation, the nominal and issued capital, the amount of shares issued for other than cash, the denomination of shares and, derived from the first SCS submitted after incorporation[11] (with the exception of the Uphall, Holmes Broxburn and Binnend companies), the number of shareholders, the amount of the largest holding and the percentage of the issued capital represented by this. The issued capital per share-

Table 8.3(b) Limited companies: number of shareholders, average holding, largest holding and proportion of net issued capital, 1877–1885

Year	Company	Shareholdings			
		Number	Average £	Largest holding £	Percentage of net issued capital
1877	Broxburn	132	758	13000	13.00
1878	Clippens	7	2857	10000	50.00
1878	Binnend	53	492	13800	52.87
1880	British Oil & Candle	8	1500	5000	41.67
1880	Walkinshaw	192	484	2500	2.69
1881	Burntisland	194	603	10000	8.55
1882	Midlothian	151	463	11000	15.86
1883	Westfield	66	288	2800	14.73
1883	West Lothian	313	239	2700	3.60
1883	Bathgate	48	262	1500	11.90
1883	Pumpherston	173	404	5600	8.00
1883	Lanark	198	505	7000	7.00
1884	Holmes	144	347	9580	19.16
1884	Linlithgow	328	384	14960	11.87
1885	Annick Lodge	49	128	1000	15.93
1885	Hermand	116	168	2000	10.26
		2172		112440	12.68

Table 8.3(c) Limited companies: shareholdings with a nominal value of £1,000 or more, and proportion of net issued capital, 1877–1885

Year	Company	Shareholdings		
		No. £1000 or more	Nominal value £	Percentage of net issued capital
1877	Broxburn	28	68900	68.90
1878	Clippens	7	20000	100.00
1878	Binnend	3	18300	70.11
1880	British Oil & Candle	3	11000	91.67
1880	Walkinshaw	38	44300	47.64
1881	Burntisland	43	74950	64.06
1882	Midlothian	17	38100	54.43
1883	Westfield	3	6300	33.16
1883	West Lothian	16	20550	27.40
1883	Bathgate	4	4500	35.71
1883	Pumpherston	17	33900	48.43
1883	Lanark	28	58300	58.30
1884	Holmes	13	27890	49.58
1884	Linlithgow	34	68010	53.98
1885	Annick Lodge	1	1000	15.94
1885	Hermand	2	3000	15.39
		257	499000	56.29

holder has been calculated. The number of shareholders with shares of a nominal value of £1,000 or more and the total nominal value of these holdings has been calculated. The number of holdings of £100 or less, and the total value of such holdings, is given.

It has been argued that the limited company made available for investment large amounts of money held by a multitude of small savers. William Court, on the other hand, is of the opinion that this new form of investment was open to the upper and middle classes, although in some industries it might affect working-class savings. Payne has questioned the reality of the appeal of Scottish limited companies to the small investor, pointing out that relatively few companies before 1895 had capital in shares of £1 or less: the most favoured denominations were between £10 and £25. Mathias argues that shares were acquired by a relatively small group of well-established investors and not thousands of small investors. He also considers that the process of launching a company was so expensive as to exclude any but well established concerns from seeking limited liability. Cottrell agrees that in the case

Table 8.3(d) Limited companies: smallest shareholding, number of shareholdings with a nominal value of £100 or less, total nominal value and proportion of net issued capital, 1877–1885

Year	Company	Shareholdings			
		Smallest £	No. £100 or less	Nominal value £	Percentage of net issued capital
1877	Broxburn	50	25	2160	2.16
1878	Clippens	1000	–	–	–
1878	Binnend	3	26	1251	4.79
1880	British Oil & Candle	50	4	300	2.50
1880	Walkinshaw	50	34	3060	3.29
1881	Burntisland	30	45	3840	3.28
1882	Midlothian	20	53	4580	4.25
1883	Westfield	50	21	1600	8.42
1883	West Lothian	50	158	12100	16.13
1883	Bathgate	20	22	1850	14.68
1883	Pumpherston	50	63	5700	8.14
1883	Lanark	20	79	6680	6.68
1884	Holmes	10	56	4060	7.22
1884	Linlithgow	10	142	11270	8.94
1885	Annick Lodge	10	33	2050	32.66
1885	Hermand	10	70	5010	17.58
			831	65511	7.39

of some small companies, exorbitant fees were charged by promoters. However, he goes on the state that Chadwick's normal fee was 1 per cent of a company's nominal capital. Hannah attributes a lessening of hostility to limited liability to the growth of a wider market involving solicitors, accountants and bankers in the issue of shares to investors.[12]

The preliminary expenses of the Broxburn company amounted to £1,351, half of which was to be paid by Robert Bell. The Pumpherston share issue was handled by a firm of solicitors.[13] Copies of the prospectuses of thirteen companies formed between 1871 and 1885 indicate in all cases that applications for shares were to be made to solicitors, bankers, stockbrokers or accountants. The stock exchanges were controlled by stockbrokers, and quotations were more likely to be awarded where the issue of shares had involved stockbrokers.[14]

In the shale industry, the first limited company – the Broxburn Shale Oil Company – was formed in 1862 with shares of a nominal value of £200. Between 1862 and 1869, 11 more concerns were established: one with shares of a nominal value of £500, three of £100, and two of £50. Five companies issued shares with a nominal value of £10. The largest company, Young's Paraffin Light & Mineral Oil Company Limited, was formed to take over James Young's interests at Bathgate and Addiewell. With 74 holders of shares with a nominal value of £582,500, Young's was the largest in the industry in terms of share capital, and remained so for the rest of the nineteenth century. The largest shareholder was Young himself with shares worth £100,000, but these were not vendors' shares. He was to be paid some £400,000 in cash. The smallest holding was £1,000, and the average, £7,871.[15] It is clear that this company made its appeal to the wealthier sections of society.

Six other companies issued shares with nominal values of £50 or more. In only one of these do we find a shareholder with shares worth £100 or less. This was the Mid Calder Mineral Oil Company Limited, and in this case the holder of one £100 share was David Simpson, a Bathgate bank agent, who may be presumed to be a relative of the principal shareholder.[16] This company was formed to take over the assets of the private partnership of Hare, Simpson and McKinlay: S.B. Hare was the landowner; James Y. Simpson was the discoverer of the anaesthetic properties of chloroform and had a family connection with Bathgate; and William McKinlay was the manager of the works and mine. These three held 64 out of the 85 shares in the new company. The remaining shares were held by people presumed to be associated with the principal shareholders: John McKinlay, a farmer at Hardhill, Bathgate; David Simpson; David James Simpson, a Doctor of Medicine, Edinburgh; and A.M. Hare, WS, of Edinburgh (see Chapter 10 on the relationship between these shareholders). This company has all the appearance of a partnership adopting the limited company form to secure its benefits.

The same may be said of the other five concerns in this group. None had more than the 15 shareholders of the Broxburn Shale Oil Company. Of these, seven were the subscribers to the Memorandum of Association, holding 69 of the 80 shares issued. Glasgow Oil, formed to take over the plant erected by Broxburn Shale, had nine shareholders, all of whom were subscribers to the Memorandum of Association. Four of them had been shareholders in Broxburn Shale. The Glentore company never issued any shares beyond the two £100 shares taken up by each of the seven subscribers. The Airdrie Mineral Oil Company issued 15 £500 shares to nine individuals, of whom seven were subscribers, holding 13 of the shares. Eight of the nine shareholders lived in Fife. The Oakbank company was formed to purchase and develop the works hitherto operated by Mid Calder Oil and had ten shareholders, of whom seven were subscribers, holding 370 of the 400 £50 shares. It seems clear, therefore, that the companies discussed here were essentially private partnerships with the protection of limited liability. Even in the case of the largest, Young's, the 74 shareholders were recruited without public advertisement. The company's prospectus was headed 'For Private Circulation only'.[17]

A different pattern might have been expected in the five companies that issued shares at £10. However, four of them had 12 or fewer shareholders. The Monklands Oil Refining Company issued 800 shares: holdings of 200, two of 100, one of 85, two of 70 and three of 40 made up 745 of the total. There was only one holding of £100 or less: five shares held by the secretary to the company. The Monklands Oil & Coal Company was formed to purchase works, etc from William Smith, a Glasgow merchant. Five hundred £10 shares were issued to the seven subscribers in numbers ranging from 10 to 250. However, the first SCS, submitted about one year after the company's formation, lists nine shareholders. Two of the subscribers no longer hold shares, and four additional names appear, each holding ten shares to a value of £100. Two merchants, a publisher and a farmer do not appear to be among the ranks of the small saver. The Capeldrae Oil & Coal Company issued its 140 £10 shares to its seven subscribers: 20 to each. The Scottish Oil company issued 100 £10 shares to each of seven subscribers. Although these companies between them had five shareholdings of £100 or less, it does not appear that they were anything other than partnerships seeking the protection of limited liability.[18]

The last concern in this group was rather different. The Dalserf Coal, Coke & Oil Company was formed to take over the works, etc of the Dalserf Coal Company from its three partners. The partners received 1,250 £10 shares. The remaining 1,260 shares were issued to 32 shareholders, the largest holdings being six of 100 shares each. The smallest were two of five shares each. In all, there were seven holdings of £100 or less, totalling £600.[19] The holdings of five shares were held by an accountant and a clerk; and the holdings of ten shares by a clerk, a commission agent, an agent, a cashier, a coal merchant and a coal agent. There is a faint indication here that the £10 share was beginning to attract the smaller investor.

This process continued in the companies formed between 1871 and 1876, listed in tables 8.2(a)–(d). The five concerns had 461 shareholders with an average holding of £648, compared to the 198 holdings with an average of £3,510 in the earlier group. This average remains considerably less than that of the earlier group, even if Young's is taken out: 124 shareholders averaged £906 each. The number of shareholders was considerably larger than in the companies formed up to 1869, ranging from 61 in the Straiton company to 138 in the West Calder concern. The denomination of shares continued to fall. Three of the companies issued shares at £10, one at £5 and one at £1. The number of shareholdings of £100 or less increased substantially to 120, over a quarter of the total. The value of these small shareholdings was £9,415, or 3.15 per cent of the total net issued capital. The average holding was £78.46. There was considerable variation between the companies. In the

Uphall company, 14 such holdings amounted to £1,350, or 1.48 per cent of the net issued capital and an average of £96.43; in the Midlothian Mineral Oil Company, 56 holdings (more than half the 104 shareholders) amounted to £3,475, or 17.47 per cent of the company's net issued capital, an average of £62.05.

The sixteen companies formed between 1877 and 1885 had in their first year of existence[20] £886,455 of net issued capital, which was subscribed by 2,172 shareholders with an average holding of £408 – a significant reduction on the previous periods. One company, the Clippens, which was a straightforward conversion of a family-owned firm, issued shares with a nominal value of £100 to seven individuals, 1,000 of 1,200 shares being issued to James Scott, the previous proprietor. Of the remaining 15 companies, one issued shares at £5, the rest at £10; 831 shareholders (more than a third of the total) held shares to the value of £100 or less, a total value of £65,511, or 7.39 per cent of the total. In the Broxburn company, 25 out of 132 shareholders held shares to the value of £2,160, 2.16 per cent of the total and an average of £86.40 At the other extreme, 33 of the shareholders in the Annick Lodge company (almost two thirds of the total number) held shares with a nominal value of £2,050, 32.66 per cent of the total and an average of £62.12. It is clear that, over the years, smaller shareholdings were an increasing factor in limited companies, although they remained a relatively insignificant part of the total capital.

It must be emphasised that there were some substantial holdings, and also that the limited company form was necessary to raise the large amounts of capital required as the industry developed. The works of E.W. Binney & Co. cost £3,000 in 1851, and it is conceivable that many of the small plants operating in the period up to 1877 cost even less. The Dalmeny works was valued at £3,591 in 1870, and it was by no means the smallest in the Almond valley.[21] The annual value in 1870–1 was £500. In 1871, the shale oil works at Roman Camp, consisting of mines, 51 horizontal retorts and refining apparatus, was valued at £2,800.[22] From 1870 to 1873 the annual value was £100. In the same year, the annual values of works in the Broxburn area included £35 for Bell's Stewartfield works, £200 for Miller's works, £150 for Poynter's, and £409 for the Albyn works of the Glasgow Oil Company. Up to 1877, people of moderate means were able to invest in the oil industry either as individuals or as members of small partnerships. After 1877 this was no longer possible: a works with a comparatively modest usage of 300 tons of shale per day required a capital outlay of the order of £70,000.[23] Capital on such a scale was, as has been pointed out by Professor Mathias, more readily raised by means of the limited liability company.[24]

Tables 8.1(a) to 8.3(d) show that in all three periods the amount of capital raised from holders of shares with a nominal value of £1,000 or more was a substantial part of the whole. Among the 12 companies formed between 1862 and 1869, Young's had 74 shareholders, all of whom had shares with a nominal value of £1,000 or more. Nine of the remaining 11 concerns had 43 such holders with shares of a nominal value of £87,150, 77.54 per cent of the total and an average of £2,027. The five companies formed between 1871 and 1876 had 116 shareholders with holdings of £1,000 or more, totalling £236,590, 79.24 per cent of the total and an average of £2,040. The 16 companies formed between 1877 and 1885 had 257 holdings with a nominal value of £1,000 or more, a total of £499,000, 56.29 per cent of the total and an average of £1,942. The average amount of these larger shareholdings remained fairly constant over the three periods. The proportion of capital subscribed by them fell significantly but remained above half of the total.

The shareholdings of the 16 companies formed between 1877 and 1885 have been analysed in Table 8.4.

This table shows that over half of the shareholders in the 16 companies formed between 1877 and 1885 had holdings with a nominal value of £200 or less. The combined value of their holdings amounted to only 15.81 per cent of the total. This does, however, indicate that limited companies were seen as a suitable investment by individuals other than the members of the middle and upper classes, as argued by Court and Mathias. On the other hand, the small investors identified by Flinn held a relatively insignificant proportion of the total value: 54.08 per cent of the nominal value was held by 257 shareholders, only 11.83 per cent of the total; 73.43

Table 8.4 Shareholdings in limited companies formed between 1877 and 1885 by nominal value

Nominal value £	Number of holders	Proportion %	Nominal value	Proportion %
1–100	831	38.26	65511	7.10
101–200	438	20.16	80334	8.71
201–300	229	10.54	63530	6.88
301–400	91	4.19	35760	3.88
401–500	238	10.96	118750	12.87
501–600	35	1.61	20770	2.25
601–700	26	1.20	17280	1.87
701–800	21	0.97	16420	1.78
801–900	6	0.28	5350	0.58
901–999				
1000–	257	11.83	499000	54.08
	2172	100.00	922705	100.00

Note: The total nominal value shown in the table – £922,705 – differs from that in Table 8.3(a): £886,455. This is because it was not possible to identify the vendors' shares in the Lanark and Holmes companies.

per cent – almost three quarters – of the nominal value was held by 583 share-holders with more than £400 of shares, only 26.85 per cent of the shareholders.

Although the proportion of capital raised from holders of large amounts of shares fell over the period, it remains true that the bulk of the capital raised by limited companies came from people able to invest what were then large sums. Tables 8.1(a) to 8.3(d) also provide data on the largest shareholder in each company. In some concerns, the largest shareholder was the vendor (or vendors). It is considered that these individuals made no actual cash investment at the time of incorporation, and in all cases the largest shareholder has been taken as the person making the largest cash commitment. From 1862 to 1870, the largest shareholders varied from the £200 of the Capeldrae and Glentore companies to the £100,000 of Young's company. If we ignore the radically different figure for Young's, the median figure is £2,000.

The proportion of capital invested by the largest shareholder varied from the 8 per cent of the Dalserf company to the 45 per cent of Monkland Oil & Coal. The median figure is 25 per cent. In the second period, 1871–6, the largest holdings range from the £2,000 of the Dalmeny company to Straiton's £11,100. In this case, the median is £5,000. The proportion invested by the largest shareholder ranged from the 4.63 per cent of the West Calder company to 18.50 per cent in the case of the Straiton company. The median was 10.96. In the third period, 1877–85, the range was from Annick Lodge's £1,000 to Linlithgow's £14,960, and the median is between £5,000 and £5,600. The proportion invested by the largest holder ranged from 2.69 per cent in the Walkinshaw company to 52.87 per cent in the Binnend. The median is between 11.87 per cent and 11.90 per cent.

It is interesting that in very few instances did the holdings of the largest shareholders even approach absolute control of the concerns. This was sometimes left to the holders of the 'vendors' shares', and will be discussed later in consideration of the industry's management.

Social composition of shareholders

The Summary of Capital and Shares provides the names and addresses, sometimes detailed, but often containing only the town of residence, of the shareholders. The form also required an occupation or designation to be stated, but this was not always provided. Information on the designation or occupation of shareholders was extracted from the first SCS for each company (the second in the case of the Uphall, Binnend and Holmes companies). The two Caledonian companies were omitted because of lack of information.[1] It has been pointed out that, as the occupations given in the SCS were provided by the shareholder, they were essentially an exercise in self-classification. They must be treated with caution, because the shareholders might claim higher status than their situations warranted.[2] However, for the present purpose, this is the only source available and it must be used, although the possibility of such bias must be borne in mind.

This information is analysed in Tables D(a)–(c), Appendix 2, arranged in three groups: companies formed from 1862 to 1870; from 1871 to 1876; and from 1877 to 1885. Within each group the shareholders are allocated to broad descriptions corresponding to major divisions in Scottish society. The first is a miscellaneous group, which includes those shareholders for whom no designation or occupation was given in the SCS. It also includes people with no known occupation, such as 'gentlemen', 'noblemen', 'spinsters' and 'widows'. The second covers those engaged in commercial activity and includes merchants of all kinds, stockbrokers, bankers, various agents, brokers and wholesale dealers. The main problem here is the large number described simply as 'merchant'. Stana Nenadic confines this designation to men conducting business from offices, counting houses or warehouses.[3] However, it might have been an occupational title assumed by a small retailer.

Another problem may be illustrated by reference to particular cases. John Orr Ewing is included in this analysis as a merchant because of his being so described in the SCS for Young's company. He is also described as such in the *Dictionary of Scottish Business Biography* (*DSBB*).[4] However, it is clear from the entry there that he was in turn a yarn agent, the principal of a calico printing firm, and latterly involved in producing dyed yarns and cloths. When he died in 1878, his estate was valued at £460,000, and it is at least arguable that his name should have been placed in the industry group. A contrary case is that of George Boyd Thornton, who described himself as an India rubber manufacturer. It is clear from the entry in the *DSBB* that, although such manufacture was indeed part of his business, his main emphasis was as much on the wholesale and retail sale of other firms' India rubber clothing and sporting goods as it was on manufacture.[5] Thornton might well have been included in the merchant group. However, these individuals have been allocated in accordance with the entries in the SCS because it is clear from the examples given that there was, at that time, some overlap between the commerce and industry groups. Coal merchants are also problematical: people described as such might well be simply self-employed sellers of coal to households, but there were also large-scale retail and wholesale traders in this field. The available data cannot distinguish between them.

The professional group is largely self-descriptive. Factors might have been placed here, but there is a case for their inclusion in the group connected with the land. Commodity factors were considered essentially to be brokers, and they were placed in the commercial section. The professional group includes teachers, professors, doctors, lawyers, churchmen, engineers, architects, and so on. Those involved in the public service include Inspectors of Poor, Inspectors of Mines and law court officials. They, as well as members of the armed services, might well have been placed in the professional group, but it was thought best to treat them separately.

People in the industry sector were in most cases clearly defined in the SCS, although, as indicated above, there was some crossover with the commerce group. To this group were allocated people involved in production that cannot strictly be described as manufacture, such as coal masters and builders. This group therefore contains industrialists of all kinds.

In addition to shopkeepers, the retail section includes the various service trades such as plumbers and joiners. All of these were considered to be employers or self-employed. In the case of an individual described simply as, for example, a joiner, it is obviously impossible to decide whether he is in the retail category or one of the 'working class'. In such cases, the decision has been made on the basis that, in the absence of information to the contrary, such individuals are placed in the 'retail/ service' group. The employed group comprises all those who are not employers or self-employed, and who cannot strictly be defined as working class. It is subdivided into 'managerial' and 'other'. Managers are easily identified, but this group also contains shipmasters, master mariners and station masters; 'other' includes salesmen, commercial travellers and law, commercial and bank clerks. The working-class section is also subdivided into upper and lower groups. The first comprises skilled workers and those in supervisory positions, such as foremen and oversmen. Clerks, not more fully described, were included here although it could be argued that they are proper to the employed, other group. It was considered however. that the majority of clerks, other than law, mercantile or bank clerks had much in common with the supervisory grades of the working classes. A small number of individuals were found to be in domestic service. The last category contains those connected with the land, e.g. proprietors, farmers, farm managers etc. A sub-group was set up to comprise those connected with the land in subordinate positions but only two individuals were found to be included.

The totals for the different groups in Tables D (a)–(c), Appendix 2, are given in Tables 9.1(a)–(c).

The first point to note here is the increase in the absolute number of share-holders over time. Twelve companies formed between 1862 and 1870 had 198 share-holders, an average of 16. The highest was 74 and the lowest 7. Five companies formed between 1871 and 1876 had 461 shareholders, an average of 92. The highest was 138 and the lowest 61. Sixteen companies formed between 1877 and 1885 had 2,172 shareholders, an average of 135. The highest was 328 and the lowest 7.

Also of note is the number of different occupations. In the period 1862–70, there were 74 different designations; in 1871–6, there were 99; and in 1877–85, there were 290. This in itself indicates a significant spread of interest in investment in limited companies over the period. Tables 9.1(a)–(c) show that in 1862–70 the miscella-neous, commerce, professional and industrial sectors contained 168 shareholders, 84.85 per cent of the total, holding 97.29 per cent of the nominal value of the shares. From 1871 to 1876, these groups, in which it can be said the wealth of the nation was concentrated, made up 380 shareholders, 82.44 per cent of the total, holding 85.35 per cent of the shares by value. In 1877–85 they constituted 1,650 shareholders, 75.96 per cent of the total, holding 87.32 per cent of the total nominal value of shares.

Table 9.1(a) Shareholders in companies formed between 1862 and 1870: occupational groups

Group	No. of share holders	Proportion %	No. of shares	Proportion %	Nominal value of shares £	Proportion %
Miscellaneous (4)	10	5.05	525	5.09	32300	4.65
Commerce (18)	86	43.43	4955	48.02	325050	46.78
Professions (13)	50	25.25	3307	32.05	286300	41.20
Public Service – 1 (6)	6	3.03	140	1.36	7700	1.11
Armed Forces (1)	2	1.01	40	0.39	400	0.06
Manufacturing (14)	22	11.11	878	8.51	32350	4.66
Employed – 1 (5)	6	3.03	193	1.87	4000	0.58
Employed – 2 (3)	4	2.02	100	0.97	1000	0.14
Working Class – 1 (1)	3	1.52	40	0.38	400	0.05
Land – 1 (9)	9	4.55	141	1.36	5400	0.77
	198	100.00	10319	100.00	694900	100.00

Note: The numbers in brackets are the number of different occupational descriptions in each group.

Table 9.1(b) Shareholders in companies formed between 1871 and 1876: occupational groups

Group	No. of shareholders	Proportion %	No. of shares	Proportion %	Nominal value of shares £	Proportion %
Miscellaneous (7)	193	41.87	40986	49.40	122005	40.86
Commerce (21)	85	18.44	14324	17.26	64575	21.63
Professions (21)	75	16.27	5863	7.06	28120	9.42
Public Service – 1 (4)	6	1.30	1673	2.02	16715	5.60
Armed Services (3)	6	1.30	300	0.36	1850	0.62
Manufacturing (14)	27	5.86	8113	9.78	40130	13.44
Retail (11)	21	4.56	7615	9.18	10650	3.57
Employed – 1 (5)	6	1.30	605	0.73	1500	0.50
Employed – 2 (8)	12	2.60	585	0.71	1350	0.45
Working Class – 1 (1)	12	2.60	1953	2.35	2405	0.81
Domestic Service (2)	2	0.43	15	0.02	150	0.05
Land – 1 (2)	16	3.47	934	1.13	9120	3.05
	461	100.00	82966	100.00	298570	100.00

There were significant variations over the three periods in the make-up of this overall group of wealth holders. In period (a), the miscellaneous group contained ten individuals, making up only 5.05 per cent of shareholders and 4.65 per cent of share value. In period (b), 193 shareholdings constituted 41.87 per cent of the total of 461, holding shares with a nominal value of £122,005, 40.86 per cent of the total. The reason for this substantial increase lies in the very much greater numbers of males and females for whom a designation or occupation was not given in the SCS. A total of 141 such men held shares with a nominal value of £84,480, and 38 females held £7,475. Together with three widows and a governess, 42 females – 3.14 per cent of the total number of shareholders – held shares with a nominal value of £9,375, 9.11 per cent of the total.

There is some evidence to indicate that these males were not all without occupation. In an exercise to assess the level of multiple ownership of shares among holders of shares with a nominal value of £1,000 or more, it was found that 14 individuals were given no designation in one company but were provided with a specific occupation in another. It is impossible to be precise, but it is clear that not all of those without an entry in the 'occupation' column of the SCS were in fact unoccupied. It is also of note that in period (b) a significant number of women were shareholders.

In period (b) the number of shareholders in the commerce sector was 85 – 18.44 per cent of the total – and they held 21.63 per cent of the value of shares, less than

Table 9.1(c) Shareholders in companies formed between 1877 and 1885: occupational groups

Group	No. of shares	Proportion %	No. of shareholders	Proportion %	Nominal value of shares £	Proportion %
Miscellaneous (13)	715	32.92	31820	32.74	310390	33.64
Commerce (62)	416	19.15	19737	20.31	195585	21.19
Professions (27)	287	13.21	9555	9.83	103150	11.18
Public Service – 1 (9)	10	0.46	245	0.25	2450	0.26
Public Service – 2 (6)	9	0.41	83	0.09	640	0.07
Armed Forces (4)	8	0.37	380	0.39	4700	0.51
Manufacturing (56)	232	10.68	24248	24.95	196600	21.31
Retail (28)	144	6.63	3235	3.33	31760	3.44
Employed – 1 (28)	85	3.91	2216	2.28	21955	2.38
Employed – 2 (13)	65	2.99	1427	1.47	13930	1.51
Working Class – 1 (29)	140	6.45	2036	2.09	19895	2.16
Working Class – 2 (4)	6	0.28	50	0.05	500	0.05
Domestic Service (3)	4	0.19	20	0.02	140	0.02
Land – 1 (6)	49	2.26	2121	2.18	20860	2.26
Land – 2 (2)	2	0.09	15	0.02	150	0.02
	2172	100.00	97188	99.99	922705	100.00

Note: The nominal value of shares in Table 9.1(c) – £922,705 – differs from that in Table 8.3(a): £886,455. This is because it is not possible to identify the shares sold by the vendors in the Lanark and Holmes companies.

half the proportions in period (a). For the professions, 75 shareholders – 16.27 per cent – held 9.42 per cent of the value, again very substantially less than the proportions held in period (a). These changes must have been due in part at least to the increase in the numbers of individuals with no listed occupation. However, it is also true that the industrial sector in period (b) contained 27 shareholders – 5.86 per cent of the total – a substantial drop from period (a); but these shareholders held 13.44 per cent of the total share value, more than double the figure for period (a). Some smaller sectors also contributed to the change. The public sector and armed services had 12 shareholders – 2.60 per cent of the total – with 6.22 per cent of value, but this may well have been a distortion due to the presence of three members of parliament holding shares worth £16,000. The retail trade had 21 shareholders – 4.56 of the total – owning 3.57 per cent of the value. Land contributed 16 shareholders with 3.05 per cent of share value. These sectors together held 98.19 per cent of the nominal value of shares. Thirty-two people – 6.94 per cent of the total –

employed in various capacities, ranging from managers of various kinds to domestic servants, held the remainder of the shares: 1.81 per cent.

In period (c) the miscellaneous, commerce, professional and industrial sectors had 1,650 shareholders – 75.97 per cent of the total – and held 87.32 per cent of the nominal capital. The retail sector now had 144 shareholders – 6.63 per cent of the total – holding shares worth 3.44 per cent of the nominal value. Land contributed 49 holders – 2.26 per cent of the total – and 2.26 per cent of the value. Along with the public service and armed forces sectors, these groups made up 1,870 shareholders, holding 93.86 per cent of the nominal value of shares. In the groups made up of employed people, a total of 302 shareholders held shares worth 6.14 per cent of the nominal value. Although this remains a small proportion of the total investment, it is a substantial improvement on the previous periods and indicates that shareholding in this industry was beginning to appeal to a wider cross-section of the population. The increase was spread across all elements of the employed population. Of particular note is that 85 managerial employees now made up 3.91 per cent of shareholders and held 2.38 per cent of share value, while those identified as working class numbered 146, with 6.73 per cent of shareholders holding 2.21 per cent. Also of note in this period is that 126 unspecified female shareholders, together with 10 widows, 13 spinsters and 8 women with occupations, a total of 157, held 3.87 per cent of the nominal value. This was a smaller proportion of the shareholders than in period (b) – 7.23 per cent compared with 9.11 – but a slightly higher proportion of the value: 3.87 per cent compared with 3.14.

Cottrell discusses the social composition of shareholders in a sample of 78 English companies in 1885 and concludes that the bulk of subscribed capital came from the unoccupied, trade and the professions. His table shows that these categories, with the addition of a land group, account for 82.62 per cent of the subscribed capital. Employed people of all kinds accounted for 2.94 per cent; the remainder was made up of institutional and corporate holdings, together with bearer shares and unknown holders. If these last categories are set aside, 96.46 per cent of capital was held by the moneyed classes and 3.43 per cent by employed people of all grades.[6]

In the shale industry, it is shown above that the equivalent proportions for companies formed between 1877 and 1885 were 94.19 per cent and 5.81 respectively. The Scottish shale companies appear to have drawn their capital from social groups similar to those subscribing to a wide range of English concerns. There are two points worthy of note. In the shale companies the 'miscellaneous' group, which corresponds to Cottrell's 'unoccupied', is almost twice as large as in the English sample. As discussed above, not all of the individuals failing to disclose an occupation were, in fact, unoccupied. Commerce makes a smaller contribution in the shale industry, as does the professional sector, and it may be that the size of the unoccupied sector in the shale companies has contributed to this imbalance. It must also be borne in mind that Cottrell's analysis was based on paid-up capital, while this work on the shale companies has been based on the nominal value of shares taken up. At the time of the first SCS, it was often the case that only a small proportion of the capital had been called up, leaving the remainder to be called in the succeeding year. The nominal value of shares therefore expressed the shareholders' financial commitment in the purchase of the shares, rather than the actual payment made at the time of submission of the SCS.

It is clear that the shale companies secured their initial share capital largely from the wealth-holding members of Scottish society. Over the period from 1862 to 1885, the range of occupations was extended; it is also the case that sectors such as the retail trade and various grades of employed people assumed a greater role as time went on. One point worthy of note in the working-class sector is that, in the first two time periods, the upper section only contained clerks. In the last period, 1877 to 1885, the preponderance of clerks – 75 – continued, but there were 28 other designations covering 65 individuals.

It seems reasonable to conclude that the limited companies in the shale industry during 1862–85 began to appeal to a wider range of investors, although it is clear, even at the end of the period, that the bulk of the share capital remained in the hands of the wealthier groups in Scottish society.

Female shareholders

Before leaving this discussion, the number of female shareholders may be worthy of some further consideration, although the Summaries of Capital and Shares provide little information about women shareholders. Only two women held shares in the companies formed between 1862 and 1870, possessing 110 Young's shares worth a nominal £11,000. In 1871–6, 38 women with no designation and three widows held 4,610 shares with a nominal value of £9,275. In addition, a woman designated as a 'governess' held 10 shares in the Uphall company. From 1877 to 1885, 126 women with no designation – 13 spinsters and 10 widows – held 3,483 shares with a value of £34,705. In eight cases, the women were described as having occupations: governess, matron at Perth General Prison, bleacher, dressmaker, hotel keeper, farmer, teacher, and one holding belonging to two women with the same surname and address and described respectively as grocer and teacher. It is clearly impossible to draw any firm conclusions from such a small sample. All that can be said is that these eight women included a governess and a dressmaker (seamstress), two examples of the few occupations open to middle-class women in the mid-nineteenth century.[7] The occupations of the remaining six may indicate that wider opportunities were becoming available by the 1870s and 1880s.

For most of the nineteenth century, married women were unable to own property: on marriage, any property was assumed to belong to the husband. This situation was not remedied until the early 1880s, although an act passed in 1870 provided a small but real improvement.[8] The shale industry developed in a period which straddled this point in time and it is possible that the Summaries of Capital and Shares of the various concerns will shed some light on the experience of married women in share ownership.

The SCS in many cases added 'Mrs' or 'Miss' before the names of women shareholders, and this has been used to discuss the proportions of married and single women at various periods in the history of the industry.[9] From 1862 to 1870, there were only two women shareholders out of a total of 198. Both held Young's shares. Mary Ann Young of West Calder was fairly obviously a relative of James Young, and Mrs Jane Arthur of Paisley was clearly the wife of James Arthur, one of the directors of the company. Their holdings may well have been influenced or even financed by their male relatives. However, Mrs Jane Arthur was a prominent advocate of women's rights at this time and may have been expected to have an opinion on the investment. She was active in the suffrage movement and 'she had the full support of her husband and other male members of the family'.[10]

From 1871 to 1876, 42 women held shares in five companies. In 17 cases the marital status is not given. Of the remaining 25, eight were recorded as Mrs and 16 as Miss. One holding was in the names of two women described as Misses. One Miss was shown as employed as a governess, and three of the Mrs were described as widows. Of the 25 holdings, 20 were held by single women. Seventeen Misses and three widows made up 80 per cent of the total number of women shareholders, and they held 92.14 per cent of the shares.

From 1877 to 1881, 40 female shareholders were identified. Again, in 17 cases marital status was not indicated. Of these, one was identified as a governess and one as matron of Perth General Prison. One holding was in the names of a man and woman at the same address, both identified as grocers. Five were identified as spinsters and one as a widow. Two of those prefixed Mrs were further described as widow. There were therefore three widows, five spinsters and seven shareholders with the prefix Miss, making a total of 15 single women; 14 shareholders were given the prefix Mrs. There was a slight preponderance in favour of single women in terms of numbers. They also held just over 50 per cent of the nominal value of shares.

In the companies formed between 1882 and 1885, shares were held by 118 women. Of these, 41 had no prefix that would indicate marital status. Eight of these were described as spinsters, leaving 33 for whom no marital status is known. Fifty-six were prefixed as Mrs, but seven were further described as widows. Twenty-one were prefixed Miss and, together with eight spinsters and seven widows, made up a total of 36 single women out of the 85 for whom marital status is known, i.e.,

Advertisement from list of products of Broxburn Oil Company, Petroline, 1884

Advertisement from list of products of Broxburn Oil Company, various candles, 1884

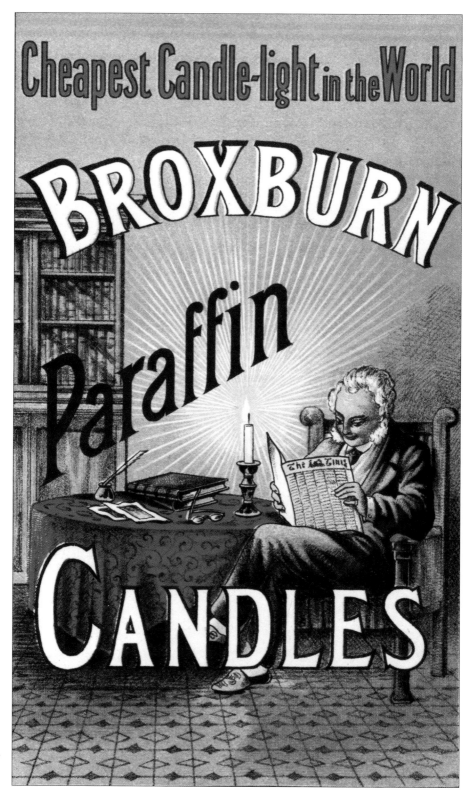

Advertisement from list of products of Broxburn Oil Company Limited, paraffin candles, 1884

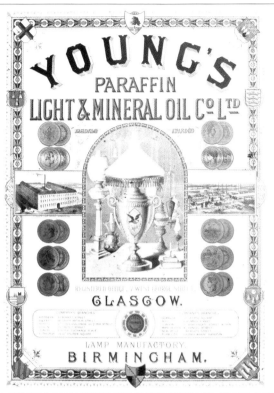

Left. Young's Paraffin Light & Mineral Oil Company Limited advertisement, c. 1880s

Below. Young's Paraffin Light & Mineral Oil Company Limited stand at Glasgow International Exhibition, 1901

The Brown Retort showing at left the large mesh shale being fed into the retort (Mr Brown the inventor standing), c. 1890. (A) Automatic feed, (B) pipe conveying exhaust heat to boilers, (C) oil burner for heating furnace, (D) furnace surrounding retort, (E) revolving retort

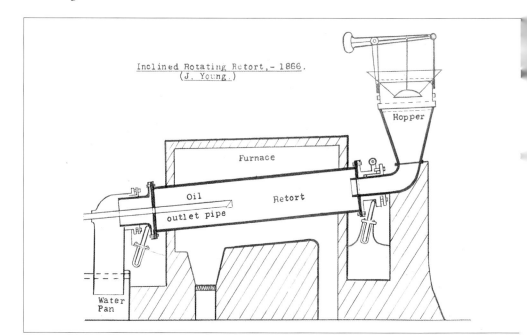

Diagram of workings of Inclined Rotating Retort (James Young), 1866

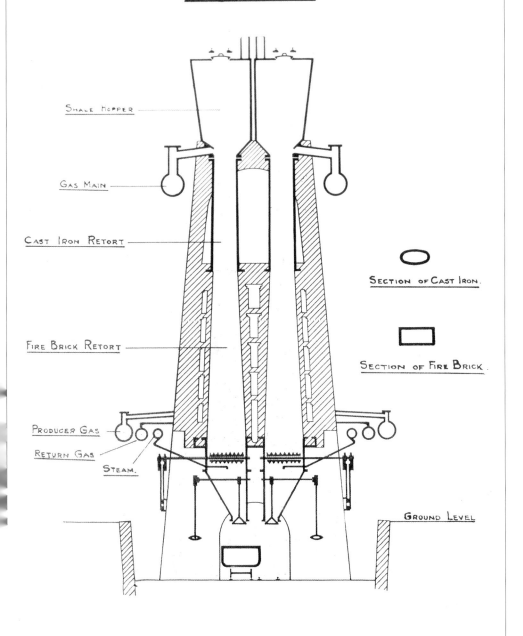

Diagram of workings of Broxburn Retort (Henderson), 1901

Fraser Pit, Diesel locomotive with train of loaded shale tubs, 1920

Shoring up the pit roof

Horse-drawn paraffin cart, 1920

Paraffin delivery vehicle, 1920

Portrait of James Young, 1860s

Sketch of Sir John Pender, owner of
Blackburn House and founder of the
shale oil works in Seafield, c. 1889
(West Lothian Libraries)

Above. Diesel Locomotive, Burngrange Pit

Left. Electric Boring Tool, Burngrange Pit

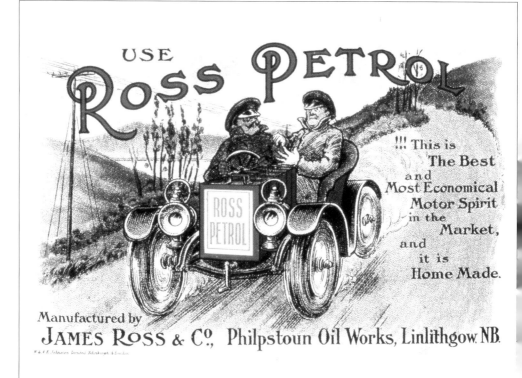

James Ross & Company Advert, 1906

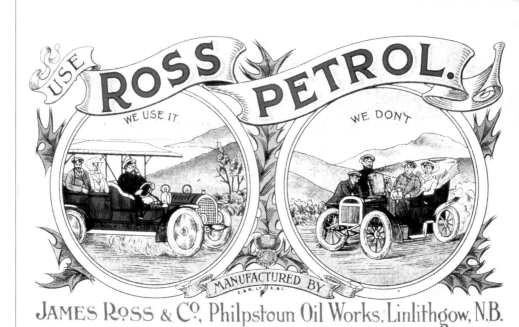

James Ross & Company Advert, 1906

ift to and from the surface

Broxburn Hayes Craig Mine: two shale miners underground with naked flame lamps.
(West Lothian Libraries)

Philpstoun Oil Works on the bank of the Union Canal, 1920

Dean's Crude Oil Works, Livingston Station, 1920

Westwood Pit, West Calder, a view of the surface arrangements, 1920

Westwood Works, general view, possibly early twentieth century

Broxburn Oil Works, looking west over Greendykes Road, 1900s
(West Lothian Libraries)

West Lothian Oil Company (1883–1892) workmen standing beside a steam locomotive belonging to the company, c. 1890 (West Lothian Libraries)

group of pit-ponies exhibited at the West Lothian Agricultural Society's Show, 1929

East Calder, West End, 1920

Main Street, Broxburn, 1920

42.35 per cent. They held 41.49 per cent of the shares belonging to the 85 women. The 49 women prefixed as Mrs made up 57.65 per cent of the total and held 58.51 per cent of the shares. Married women at this time were obviously beginning to be more active in financial dealings. The occupations listed were farmer, hotel keeper, dressmaker, teacher, and, as mentioned above, two women of the same surname at the same address and described as grocer and teacher.

Before leaving this aspect of shareholding it was thought desirable to look at the Tarbrax Oil Company, formed in 1904, nearly twenty years after the last of the other concerns. This company has not previously been considered. It was essentially a creation of the directorate of the Pumpherston company, and initially shares were offered only to Pumpherston shareholders. It was also the only company to offer both ordinary and preference shares at flotation. For these reasons it was not included in the general analysis of shareholders, but it is thought that a study of the female shareholders might be rewarding. Seventy-seven share-holdings held by women comprised 9,905 preference and 3,098 ordinary shares, 28.3 per cent of the 35,000 preference shares offered and 5.25 per cent of the ordinary shares. Six holdings were held by women whose marital status could not be identified. The remaining 71 held 7,605 preference and 2,368 ordinary shares. Thirty-eight married women made up 53.52 per cent of these, and held 4,180 preference and 1,568 ordinary shares: 54.96 per cent and 66.21 per cent respectively. Twenty-seven women prefixed Miss, five widows and a spinster made up 33 single women, 46.48 per cent; they held 3,425 preference and 800 ordinary shares, 45.04 per cent and 33.79 per cent respectively. In an analysis of 12 English companies incorporated between 1873 and 1908, Maltby and Rutterford found a similar bias towards lower-risk securities among women shareholders.[11]

It is perhaps worthy of note that in the period from 1862 to 1885, three sharehold-ings were held jointly by a man and woman who had the same surname and address. Seven similar holdings were found in the Tarbrax company. Five holdings were found in the names of women with the same surname and address, and eight in the case of Tarbrax. This indicates possible joint action by families, a supposition reinforced by the presence in some companies of female and male shareholders sharing an address and a surname. The two female shareholders in Young's company fall into this category. Thirty-four such examples were found in compa-nies formed in the period up to 1885, and there were 18 cases where more than one female shareholder is listed at the same address.

The shale companies show that, in the later nineteenth century, women were involved in financial affairs. This became more marked as the century went on and was not confined to women of any particular marital status. If anything, the involvement of married women became slightly more obvious with time.

Location

It remains now to consider whether the investor's location influenced the decision to invest in particular companies. Cottrell concludes that for his samples of English companies in 1860, 75.91 per cent of capital came from within ten miles of the companies' registered offices. In 1885 this had fallen to 62.47 per cent, if foreign subscribed capital is ignored.[1] There will be no similar analysis for the shale companies here, but instead a consideration of the relationship between the shareholders' counties/cities of residence and the location of the companies' registered offices, which are detailed below.

Period	Location of Registered Office		
1862–1870	**Glasgow**	**Edinburgh**	**At Works**
	Broxburn Shale	Scottish	Mid Calder Mineral
	YPLMO		Capeldrae Oil & Coal
	Glasgow		Glentore Mineral
	Dalserf Coal Coke & Oil		Airdrie Mineral
	Monklands Oil & Coal		
	Monklands Oil Refining		
	Oakbank		
1871–1876	Uphall Mineral	Straiton Estate (later Oil)	Dalmeny
	Midlothian Mineral		
	West Calder		
1877–1885	Annick Lodge	Bathgate	British Oil & Candle
	Broxburn	Binnend	
	Clippens	Burntisland	
	Holmes	Hermand	
	Pumpherston	Lanark	
	Walkinshaw	Linlithgow	
		Midlothian	
		Westfield	
		West Lothian	

The addresses given for shareholders in the Summaries of Capital and Shares have been analysed by city, county and country of residence to form Tables E(a)–(c), Appendix 2.

In the case of the 12 companies formed between 1862 and 1870, four had their registered offices at the company's works, one had an office in Edinburgh and seven in Glasgow. Those with registered offices at the works, in Edinburgh, and all but two of those located in Glasgow, had small numbers of shareholders (see Table 8.1(b)). Four had only seven – the minimum number of subscribers prescribed by the legislation – and the Broxburn Shale Oil Company had 15. All of these seem to conform to Kennedy's conclusion that, in the last quarter of the nineteenth century, between 60 and 70 per cent of capital formation was performed by small groups of men well known to each other through personal or business contacts.[2]

The seven subscribers and shareholders of the Mid Calder Mineral Oil Company comprised Sir James Young Simpson, who discovered the anaesthetic properties of chloroform, David James Simpson, a Doctor of Medicine who shared an address as Sir James, and David Simpson, agent for the Royal Bank in Bathgate, the town where Sir James Simpson was born. A family relationship may therefore be assumed. Stewart Bayley Hare of Calderhall was the owner of the land on which the Oakbank works were situated, and Alexander MacConnachie Hare was an Edinburgh solicitor. The last two, William and John McKinlay, may also be presumed to have a family relationship.[3] Before the incorporation of the Mid Calder company, the minerals and works were operated by a partnership, Hare, Simpson & McKinlay.[4] It may safely be assumed that the four related persons were required to make up the seven subscribers required by the legislation.

The subscribers for the Glentore Mineral Oil company were, with one exception – a Glasgow solicitor – all people of some status with addresses in and around Airdrie. Those of the Scottish Oil Company were a tobacco manufacturer, a goldsmith, a chartered accountant, a tea merchant and a builder, all with addresses in central Edinburgh. The remaining two were a gentleman residing in Hamilton and the manager of the company. Shareholders of the Airdrie Mineral Oil Company comprised the seven subscribers and two additional individuals. With the exception of a Glasgow accountant, all of the shareholders had addresses in Fife and comprised four farmers, two manufacturers, an oil merchant and an accountant.[5] A similar pattern exists in the rest of the ten companies with small numbers of shareholders.

The two exceptions are Young's Paraffin Light & Mineral Oil Company and the Dalserf Coal Coke & Oil Company, which had 74 and 32 shareholders respectively. Young's, in fact, although set up to raise £600,000 in nominal capital, was essentially a private company. The prospectus is endorsed 'For Private Circulation only', and it is stated that Mr Young and his son had agreed to take 1,350 shares and that 'the whole of the remaining Shares have been subscribed for privately'.[6] The shareholders were widely distributed in geographical terms: 36.94 per cent of the nominal capital was subscribed by residents of Glasgow and its environs, while West Calder (James Young and his family) contributed 27.68 per cent, Edinburgh 9.17 per cent, and England (Manchester and London) 26.04 per cent. The first chairman of the company, John Orr Ewing, has been described as 'one of the small group of businessmen responsible for forming Young's Paraffin Light and Mineral Oil Co Ltd'.[7] This may well merit the conclusion that this company was formed in the manner that Kennedy describes. Another relationship among shareholders is that of James Young with Lyon Playfair, an eminent professor of chemistry; and this, together with Young's scientific reputation – he became a Fellow of the Royal Society of Edinburgh in 1861[8] – may account for five professors subscribing £48,000 of the nominal capital.

The Dalserf company had 32 shareholders, spread fairly widely over Scotland, from Hawick, Penicuik, Edinburgh, Perth, Glasgow, Lanarkshire and Campbeltown. The largest concentration was in Glasgow, where 21 shareholders subscribed £7,150 (56.75 per cent) of the nominal capital. There are no obvious indicators of close-knit groups among the shareholders. Ignoring the vendors, the seven largest holders each held shares with a nominal value of £1,000. They were a papermaker in Penicuik, a civil engineer in Edinburgh, two sharebrokers in Glasgow, a ship-owner in Glasgow, and a solicitor in Perth. Apart from three resident in Glasgow, there is no obvious connection between any of these men in geographical or business terms. Dalserf may be an early, small-scale example of a 'public company'.

Between 1871 and 1876, five companies were formed. The Dalmeny company's registered office was at the works, while Straiton's was in Edinburgh and the remaining three in Glasgow. The number of shareholders was considerably larger than in the previous period, ranging from Straiton's 61 to West Calder's 138. At first sight, the shareholders seem to have been drawn from a wide geographical area, ranging from Aberdeenshire to Wigtownshire, with 14.99 per cent of the nominal capital having been subscribed by people resident outside Scotland (see Appendix 2, Table E (b)).

Despite the presence of three of the five registered offices, only 23.65 per cent of the nominal capital was subscribed by people with Glasgow addresses. Adding addresses in what were possibly commuter areas around the city – Ayrshire, Dunbartonshire and Renfrewshire – increases the total to only 26.75 per cent. Edinburgh provided 28.83 per cent of the nominal capital. The Straiton company, registered in Edinburgh, secured £48,600 (85.56 per cent) of its nominal capital from within the city. Dalmeny, with a registered office at Dalmeny – only a few miles from Edinburgh – had £9,690 (43.09 per cent) of its nominal capital from

Edinburgh addresses. Of the three companies with registered offices in Glasgow, the Uphall secured £16,700 (18.29 per cent) of nominal capital from Edinburgh addresses; Midlothian Mineral £500 (2.53 per cent); and West Calder £10,600 (9.81 per cent).

It is clear, however, that the two cities provided only 52.48 per cent of the nominal capital of the five companies – a little more than half. The area made up of the county of Midlothian (west of the Pentland Hills) and West Lothian provided £52,455 (17.57 per cent of the total), which is explained largely by the shareholdings of four of the subscribers and largest shareholders in the Uphall company who were resident in the county. Together they held £35,830 of the nominal capital of the company. John Peter Raeburn, a Midlothian Mineral director, and his family resided at Mid Calder and held shares with a nominal value of £3,125.

It is possible that there was a relationship between the residence and description of the subscribers and the location of the remaining shareholders, rather than between the latter and the situation of the registered office. The seven Dalmeny subscribers were two sons of Lord Rosebery's factor, residing at Dalmeny, along with William Drummond of 42 Frederick Street, Edinburgh, the secretary to the company; George Roberts, an Edinburgh builder; James Roberts, also an Edinburgh builder; James Mill of 26 Heriot Row, Edinburgh; and William Reid of 7 Palmerston Place, Edinburgh. It is not surprising, therefore, that £19,190 (85.33 per cent) of the company's nominal capital was subscribed by individuals with addresses in Edinburgh, the Lothians, and Dunfermline and Inverkeithing in Fife.

The nine Uphall subscribers included Peter McLagen, MP of Pumpherston; Edward Meldrum of Dechmont, James Young's former partner; and George Simpson, coal master, of Benhar, West Lothian. These three men were the members of the private partnership taken over by the company. In addition, there were Henry Cadell of Grange, Bo'ness, an ironmaster; George P. Gunnis, a Stirling merchant, who later gave an address in Glasgow;[9] W. Mackinnon of Renfield Street Glasgow, a merchant; George Harrison of 31 South Bridge, Edinburgh, a merchant; George S. Keith, MD, of 57 Northumberland Street, Edinburgh; and Stewart S. Robertson of Lawhead, Hamilton, elsewhere described as chamberlain to the duke of Hamilton.[10] It is not surprising, therefore, that £59,130 (64.77 per cent) of the nominal capital was subscribed from Edinburgh and the Lothians. A further £8,050 came from addresses in Lanarkshire, a total of 73.59 per cent. It is of interest here that £10,960 (12.00 per cent) of nominal capital was subscribed in London: £3,000 of this was due to James Wyllie and Farquhar Mathieson, merchants, of 13 Leadenhall Street, both of whom unquestionably possessed Scottish names. May it be presumed that this firm had a Scottish connection?

The seven subscribers for the West Calder company were Charles B. Findlay of Glasgow and London, a merchant; Thomas Reid, a dyer of Ibroxhill, Glasgow;

Geo. W. Clark of Dumbreck, a Glasgow merchant; Thomas D. Findlay, of Easterhill, Lanark, merchant; Lewis T. Merrow, Kennebec House, Lanark, merchant; James Findlay, Hermand, Edinburgh, merchant; James Paul, Glasgow, merchant. Charles Bannantyne Findlay is later in Article 17 described as belonging to Messrs Richardson, Findlay and Co., merchants, London and Glasgow; Thomas Reid is described as provost of Govan; and Thomas Dunlop Findlay, Easterhill, is described as a member of Messrs T.D. Findlay & Co., merchants. Charles Findlay, Thomas Findlay, Reid, Clark and Merrow were among the first directors and were joined by Stewart Robertson and by Richard S. Cunliffe of Randolph, Elder & Co., engineers and shipbuilders, Glasgow. This company was set afloat by members of the merchant community of Glasgow. It is not surprising, therefore, that £89,400 (82.7 per cent) of the nominal capital was secured from addresses in Glasgow, Edinburgh and the central belt of Scotland, with the bulk of this capital – £62,400 (57.72 per cent) – coming from Glasgow. It is also true that 11 London-based shareholders subscribed £11,700 (10.82 per cent) of the capital, which might well be explained by connections between merchants in Glasgow and London. We have already seen that Charles Findlay was a member of a partnership with offices in the two cities. In London, John Fleming of 18 Leadenhall Street held £5,000 of shares, and William Nicol of the same address held £2,000, while Francis Richardson of 7 Mincing Lane held £1,000. Richardson may be assumed to be the Richardson in partnership with Charles Findlay, while Fleming and Nicol, both with Scottish names, may also be assumed to have similar connections.[11]

The seven subscribers to the Straiton Estate (later Oil) Company were James Dick, a retired merchant of 35 Hope Terrace, Edinburgh; William Speedie, an engineer of Summerhill House, Midlothian; Walter Brodie, a plumber of 60 South Clerk Street, Edinburgh; Jno Cockburn, a wine merchant of Kilgraston Road, Edinburgh; John Henry Cooper, a brewer of Mayfield House, Newington, Edinburgh; Ebenezer Erskine Harper, an advocate; and James Sinclair, an Edinburgh builder. It is not surprising that £48,600 (85.56 per cent) of the capital was subscribed in Edinburgh, with a further £2,500 (4.40 per cent) in Midlothian.

It is not possible to state with certainty that the larger numbers of shareholders in these five companies indicates a wider demand among the general public for such investments. Certainly, shareholdings were distributed over a wide geographical area, but there remains some evidence that personal and business contacts between individuals may have remained important. However, companies did advertise their shares. The West Calder company prospectus appeared in the *Scotsman* of 22 April 1872, followed on 24 April by an abridged version, which was repeated on 26 April together with a notice that the subscription list for shares would close on 1 May 1872. This notice was repeated on 27 and 29 April, and on 1 May 1872. The prospectus stated that 'from the applications already made, the

Directors have now at their disposal only from 3000 to 4000 shares'. Only 10,860 of the available 13,000 A shares were ever issued, and it would seem that the advertisement failed in its purpose to the extent of 1,000 to 2,000 shares.

The prospectus for the Dalmeny Oil Company was published in the *Scotsman* on nine occasions between 29 September and 12 October 1871. Unfortunately, it has not been possible to trace similar advertisements for the other three concerns, but these two examples indicate that there was some desire on the part of the companies to appeal to a wider public.

Of the 16 companies registered between 1877 and 1885, one had its registered office at its works, six in Glasgow and nine in Edinburgh. The capital subscribed in the case of these companies was very much more confined to Scottish sources. Shareholders were found in 30 of the 33 Scottish counties; 96.63 per cent of the nominal capital was subscribed by people with Scottish addresses, compared with 85.01 per cent in the previous period; and 90.05 per cent was recruited from addresses in the central belt, with 30.96 per cent from Edinburgh and 27.58 per cent from Glasgow. The higher proportion of holdings in Edinburgh appears to confirm the view that shares were taken up by people resident in the neighbourhood of the companies' registered offices, 9 of the 16 companies having their registered offices in Edinburgh.

Two of the companies, Clippens and British Oil & Candle, were essentially private concerns with small numbers of shareholders. If these are left out of consideration, 9 of the remaining 14 companies had registered offices in Edinburgh and 5 in Glasgow. The total nominal capital of the 5 companies with offices in Glasgow was £325,505. Of this, £137,390 – 42.21 per cent – was raised in Glasgow. Of the rest, £59,690 – 18.34 per cent – was raised in Edinburgh. The nominal capital of the 9 companies based in Edinburgh was £565,200: £221,140 – 39.13 per cent – was raised in Edinburgh; £99,075 – 17.53 per cent – originated in Glasgow. The nominal capital of the 14 companies was raised as follows: 58.08 per cent (£517,295) in Glasgow and Edinburgh; 32.61 per cent (£290,460) in the central belt counties, the Lothians, Fife, Clackmannan, Stirling, Lanark, Ayrshire, Renfrew and Dunbarton; 5.94 per cent (£52,910) from the other Scottish counties; and 3.37 per cent (£30,040) from outwith Scotland. This indicates a widespread knowledge of the availability of the investment opportunities. How was this knowledge disseminated to possibly interested parties? The larger investors may well have been able to rely on personal contact with other people of substance. An examination of investors taking up shares to a nominal value of £1,000 or more might be fruitful.

In the case of the five companies with registered offices in Glasgow, 97 individuals held shares with a nominal value of £1,000 or more. The total was £175,990. Forty-eight shareholders with addresses in Glasgow held shares with a nominal value of £75,050 – 42.64 per cent of the total. Fifteen Edinburgh-based shareholders held shares with a nominal value of £45,400 – 25.80 per cent of the total. One hundred and fifty shareholders in the nine companies with registered offices in Edinburgh held shares with a nominal value of £292,010. Sixty-four shareholders with addresses in Edinburgh held shares with a nominal value of £144,200 – 49.38 per cent of the total; 36 with addresses in Glasgow held with a nominal value of £50,350 – 17.24 per cent of the total. Of the total £468,000 of shares held in blocks of £1,000 or more, shareholders with Edinburgh addresses held shares to a nominal value of £189,600 – 40.51 per cent of the total; while those with Glasgow addresses held £125,400 – 26.79 per cent of the total. Just over two thirds of these shares – £315,000 (67.30 per cent) – was held in the two major cities of Scotland. It is possible – indeed probable – that people with such amounts of money available for investment were known to one another: if not personally, then at least by repute. In Glasgow, they may well have been members of the 'high-profile elite of extremely wealthy merchants and industrialists who mixed together in predominantly professional or commercially oriented societies located around George Square'.[12]

A meaningful analysis of these individuals by occupation and association will require considerable further research. Only very tentative conclusions are possible. A common occupation was 'merchant', of whom there were ten in Edinburgh and six in Glasgow. It is not inconceivable that the members of these groups might have been known to each other. Similarly, six coal masters based in Glasgow may have been in contact. There is some evidence also that some shareholders might have had other interests in the shale industry. John Hurll held 250 shares in the Broxburn company. He was a manufacturer of firebrick, which was extensively used in the construction of retort and still flues. Similarly, James and William Wood, who held 200 and 400 shares respectively in the Pumpherston company, were coal masters. In the 1870s and 1880s, the shale industry became a major customer for the coal industry. Robert B. Tennent, who held 560 Pumpherston shares, was an ironfounder; the shale industry was a major user of iron and steel in the construction of retorts and stills.

These are all ways in which the major shareholders – those with the ability to commit to a liability of £1,000 or more – might have been drawn to invest in the shale companies. However, it remains true that a substantial proportion of the industry's capital came from people with smaller resources. The companies in this period (1877–1885) certainly set out to attract both large and small shareholders. Twelve of the fourteen companies under consideration advertised their shares in the *Glasgow Herald* and the *Scotsman*. These prospectuses were not always completely successful. In 1883, the Bathgate, Pumpherston and Hermand companies were promoted. The short-lived journal *The Scottish Financier* stated that the Hermand was certain to be floated, described the directors in fulsome terms and advised investors 'to apply for as many shares as they can take up'. The other two companies were regarded as doubtful prospects.[13] The Hermand company was not floated at that time, and the Bathgate and Pumpherston companies were incorporated. Bathgate secured the take-up of only 2,260 of the 3,500 shares offered, and failed after only a short period, while Pumpherston went on to become the largest and most successful company in the industry.

In 1884, the Linlithgow company was able to issue only 14,000 of 20,000 shares offered; this suggests that potential investors were cautious in their approach to oil company shares. In 1885, when the Hermand company was again promoted, only 2,850 of 14,000 shares were taken up, and even this was achieved only after the vendor, James Thornton, offered a personal guarantee that shares would be redeemed at cost after one year if the holder so desired.[14]

The reorganised Oakbank company also had some difficulty in this respect. The new company had a nominal capital of £90,000 in £10 shares: 4,500 of these were issued to the shareholders in the old company as the purchase price, and 4,500 were offered to the public on 19 January 1886. The prospectus was advertised in the *Glasgow Herald*, *Scotsman* and *Dundee Advertiser*. Brokers were offered a commission of 1 shilling and 6 pence per share for shares that were applied for through them. By 8 March 1886, 3,500 shares were applied for, but the 4,500 new shares were not completely taken up until April 1887.[15]

Over the period from 1862 to 1885, the nominal value of shares declined, commonly to £10 per share. This may well have been a factor in the increasingly widespread shareholdings of the later period, although even then the bulk of the industry's capital was held by the wealthier sections of the population. Shareholdings were increasingly widespread around Scotland, and for a time in other parts of the United Kingdom. There is evidence that some companies had difficulty in persuading investors to place their money with them.

Part 4 Management and success or failure

Introduction

The sources for this section include minutes of board meetings and of annual and extraordinary general meetings of the shareholders. The directors' minutes are informative about day-to-day decisions but discussion is not always recorded. The minutes of the shareholders' meetings are also somewhat sanitised, but details of discussions omitted from the minutes can sometimes be found in newspaper reports. Taken together, these provide a view of the relationship between the directors, management and owners of the business. These records exist only for the four surviving companies. For the remaining unsuccessful limited companies, we must depend on published reports. The local newspapers – the *West Lothian Courier*, the *Linlithgowshire Gazette* and the *Midlothian Advertiser* – as well as the *Scotsman* and the *Glasgow Herald* have been useful here, but data are necessarily limited.

As discussed earlier, the history of the shale industry was dominated by a struggle against competition from industries based on natural petroleum sources in the USA and later in Russia and the Far East. The survival of the industry was to some extent due to factors outwith its control. It was helped by the much larger proportion of wax in shale crude oil, and especially by the presence of ammonia in the shale. However, the number of failures indicates that these were not, of themselves, a guarantee of success and suggest the importance of other factors, internal to the companies themselves. The quality of management was obviously one of these. Part 4 of this book will therefore attempt to examine the management of some of the companies in relation to their success or failure, and also to identify and discuss some of the individuals involved.

James Young and E.W. Binney & Company

The first concern in the industry was, of course, E.W. Binney & Company, a partnership consisting of James Young, Edward Meldrum and E.W. Binney. The management of this company and its transition to limited liability is an obvious starting point and requires detailed consideration. Binney was Young's lawyer;[1] Meldrum was a chemist and colleague. The firm set up at Boghead near Bathgate a plant for distillation cannel coal and refining the resulting crude oil. From the first, Meldrum acted as works manager. Young originally resided at Murrayfield in Edinburgh, but moved to Easterhouse near Glasgow, and then to Sardinia Terrace, Glasgow. In 1861–2 he was resident at Limefield House, to the east of West Calder.[2]

The 1861 Census Enumerators' Books make possible some conclusions about the workforce and the management structure. One boy and 158 men were identified as employees; all but five of these were identified by the addition of 'at chemical works' to the occupation given in the census. The five not so designated were John Gellatly, who is known from other sources to be Young's chemist;[3] Meldrum, described as 'Manufacturing Chemist'; an assistant chemist lodging in a house at the chemical works; a boilermaker; and an oversman over labourers living in houses described as 'at chemical works'. Of these 159 individuals, 141 were described as labourers, three as chemists, and there were two engineers, two foremen or overseers, six clerks, one boilermaker, one cooper, two retortmen, and one boy. A number of craftsmen – engineers, boilermakers, blacksmiths, coopers, etc. – were enumerated in the census. Bremner stated that considerable numbers of such tradesmen were employed at oil works.[4] It is possible – indeed probable – that some of these men were employed at the chemical works but did not indicate this in the census schedule.

In the early 1860s, the company produced over 1 million gallons per year, with a peak of 2 million in 1862.[5] At that time, the management structure was headed by Young and Meldrum as owners and managers, responsible for the overall direction of the company. They had successfully identified uses for potentially embarrassing by-products and had ensured that one of them, burning oil, had become the main source of profit.

The subsidiary management is less clearly defined. Alexander Kirk is described in the 1861 census as an engineer at the chemical works; he has elsewhere been described as the manager of the works at that time. He was responsible for the design of a refrigerating apparatus for separating wax from the oil; this was later also used in breweries. Kirk attended Edinburgh University and was apprenticed to Robert Napier, the shipbuilder, and worked in London before coming to Bathgate. He later returned to Glasgow and became a well-known figure in shipbuilding and engineering. He was the senior partner in R. Napier & Sons, was responsible for the design of the triple expansion marine steam engine, and has been described as 'one of the most able marine engineers of his generation'. He was consulted by the directors of the Oakbank company on the extensions to the works taken over from the Mid Calder company. He became a director and eventually chairman of Oakbank.[6] Recruited by the Bathgate concern in 1860, in 1865 he was manager of the Addiewell works. He planned this works and 'conducted the whole erection of them'.[7] Later, he was manager to Messrs John Elder & Company, Engineers, Glasgow.

In 1861 Norman Henderson, a native of Bathgate, joined the company. He appears in the 1851 census as an 11-year-old handloom weaver,[8] and in the 1861 as an iron pattern maker. His obituary stated that he had previously worked for the Shotts Iron Company, after serving an apprenticeship as a millwright.[9] He was engaged as Kirk's assistant and draughtsman, later becoming manager of Oakbank works and then general works manager and a director of the Broxburn company. He was responsible for a number of important improvements in the processes of the industry.

It is clear, therefore, that, at the time of the conversion to limited company status, the firm had at its head two men, Young and Meldrum, with considerable experience as practising chemists. Meldrum, in charge of the Bathgate works, had the assistance of two very competent engineers. The management was therefore in the hands of persons fully capable of understanding and developing the process as well as the necessary plant and equipment. With a workforce of probably less than 200, it is unlikely that management as a distinct discipline would have been thought necessary. Drucker believes that this becomes necessary when a concern has between 300 and 1,000 employees, but concedes that the complexity of operations is also important.[10] The Bathgate operation was a not a simple one. It involved the distillation of the initial raw material to produce crude oil, which then had to be treated with chemicals and further distilled to produce the main product, burning oil. A distinct but related activity was involved in the separation of the paraffin wax, and in refining this to make it suitable for candle production.

John Gellatly, a chemist, was recruited by Young on 1 February 1859, when he was said to have 'started work ... on oil'.[11] It is possible to speculate that he was employed in monitoring the quality of the product and the way it was produced. An assistant chemist was also employed. Two men in supervisory positions were enumerated in 1861: William Meek, aged 45, is described as 'foreman, chemical works', implying that he was concerned with the oversight of the processes; and

Thomas Murray, aged 39, was described as 'oversman over labourers'. He may well have been responsible for controlling the work of the less skilled elements of the process, such as the firing of boilers, retorts, etc.

Six clerks were enumerated in 1861 as employed at the chemical works. One of these, Alexander Birnie, occupied a house of four rooms at Durhamtown. In January 1866 Young went to Bathgate and talked to Birnie about an unfinished report from a Mr Maclure: this may also indicate that Birnie was in charge of the Bathgate office. As Mr Birney, he is named in the minute of agreement by which Young bought out his partners as 'their present clerk'. He next appears in the minutes of the limited company's board as having breached his engagement with the company, which in itself indicates that he occupied more than a minor position within the organisation. He then appears as manager of the Uphall Mineral Oil Company, confirming that he was of some importance in Young's at Bathgate.[12]

There appears to have been some concern over the qualities required of a manager at the time of the transfer. In March 1866, Young recorded that he wished to take Napier from Bathgate to manage Addiewell in succession to Kirk. This was opposed by John Moffat, a director, because Napier was a chemist and they needed someone to build a works. Later, Napier was appointed manager at Bathgate.[13] At the same time, it is clear that the concern, both before and after the transfer, had among its staff qualified chemists able to contribute their expertise to the development of the firm's products. Before the transfer Young had a laboratory at Limefield House, where he had the assistance of two chemists. Both of these men, John Calderwood and William MacIvor, transferred to the limited company.[14]

The management in 1861 consisted of Meldrum, two engineers, a chemist and assistant chemist, two foremen and six clerks, one of whom held a superior position. Between 1861 and the end of 1864 when the partnership was dissolved, the annual value of the Bathgate works rose from £891 to £1,020 in 1863–4 and to £2,012 in 1864–5.[15] This indicates substantial development, which may well have increased the management requirement. Certainly, by 1866, after the transfer to the limited company, the workforce at Bathgate had increased to 427.[16]

The employment of six clerks in itself indicates some organising and recording of activities at the works, and possibly of sales. There was also a substantial presence in Glasgow. In 1852–3, the Glasgow Post Office Street Directory lists on page 344 a John Young as 'Sole agent in Glasgow for James Young's patent mineral oil'. On page 235, the firm E. Meldrum & Co. at 6 Graeme Street is listed as 'oil merchants'. In subsequent editions, the directory lists the firm at Great Dovehill Street, and in 1862–3 at Craignestock Place, where it is clearly described as 'paraffin and mineral oil manufacturers, Craignestock Pl, Glasgow and chemical works, Bathgate.'

F.. Meldrum & Co. was, in fact, another partnership of Binney, Meldrum and Young and was dissolved at the same time as E.W. Binney & Company.[17] Young, himself, initially resident in Edinburgh, was by early 1854 living in Glasgow and clearly involved in the selling and distribution of the company's products. He noted in his diary for 24 February 1855 that he had carted empty barrels to McFarlane Street before breakfast. On Saturday 3 March, he noted that over 8,000 gallons had been sent out that week.[18]

In the agreement between Young and the limited company, there is mention of the ten stations of the Paraffin Light Company throughout the country, and also to Young's property in South Frederick Street, Glasgow. There is some evidence that Young had been building up this sales network independently of the partnership. In July 1859 Binney wrote to Young that 'you ought not to allow Mr Rowatt as your servant to open the shale question which our firm has been doing its best to keep quiet so many years'.[19] Rowatt was at this time manager of the Paraffin Light Company at Lochrin, Edinburgh, and the tone of Binney's letter seems to indicate that this was an independent enterprise of Young's.[20] Correspondence from July 1862 to April 1863 about what Young describes as the Manchester concern is extant and concludes with a reference to the Paraffin Light Company.[21]

The board of directors and the shareholders

The transfer of ownership of Young's business to the limited company meant that the ultimate control of its activities passed from Young to a board of directors. The company was at the time of incorporation, and for the rest of the nineteenth century, the largest in the industry. It is also the concern for which data are most readily available. Discussion of the industry's management will therefore, to some extent, be concentrated on this company.

However, before dealing with this, it will be helpful to discuss the board of directors in the context of the shale industry generally, and in so doing consider the possible influence of the 'vendors'. Almost 40 per cent (39.99 per cent) of the paid-up capital of concerns established between 1877 and 1914 was issued to vendors as payment or part-payment for assets transferred to the companies (see Appendix 1, Table B). This is substantially less than the proportion for companies generally. It has been estimated that almost 60 per cent of the paid-up capital of companies created between 1885 and 1914 was issued to vendors, and that this enabled them to keep control.[1] The position of the individual companies in the shale industry is given in Table 12.1.

The proportion of vendors' shares ranged from the 2.5 per cent of the Burntisland company to British Oil & Candle's 97.5 per cent. In only three cases did the proportion exceed 50 per cent. British Oil & Candle was essentially a private company, with only eight shareholders; its assets were sold to the Lanark company in 1883. The Clippens company was formed in 1878 to take over the Clippens works near Paisley, set up by James Scott, formerly the proprietor of the largest cotton-spinning works in Scotland.[2] This was originally a private company with only seven shareholders. However, by 1883 the issued capital had been increased to £210,000, of which James Scott, although still the largest shareholder, held only £48,000, 22.86 per cent.[3]

The Uphall company was formed in 1871 to take over the assets of a partnership. The 54.4 per cent of issued capital given to the three partners was made up of £90,000 of B and C shares deferred to the A shares in terms of dividend, etc. Only £18,710 was in the form of fully paid A shares. The three partners were directors. The company was re-organised in 1876 with the cancellation of the £30,000 of C shares, and was eventually absorbed by the larger Young's company in 1884.

Three companies issued between 40 and 50 per cent of their capital to vendors. All three were small concerns that did not thrive and were wound up soon after

Table 12.1 Shares issued free of charge to vendors, 1862–1885

Company	No. of vendors	Value £	Percentage of issued capital	No. of vendors on board	Value of shares held £	Percentage of issued capital
Young's (a)	1	100000	17.17	1	100000	17.17
Dalserf	3	12500	49.8	1	4700	18.73
Uphall Mineral	3	108710	54.4	3	108710	54.4
Dalmeny	2	4510	16.7			
Midlothian Mineral	1	7000	26.03	1	7000	26.03
West Calder	2	30000	21.72	2	6500	4.71
Broxburn	1	57500	34.85	1	57500	34.85
Clippens	1	103000	85.83	1	103000	85.83
Binnend	1	12900	33.08	1	12900	33.08
British Oil & Candle	3	11700	97.5	3	11700	97.5
Walkinshaw	7	17640	11.34	2	7140	6.45
Burntisland (b)	1	3000	2.5	1	3000	2.5
Westfield	1	6000	24.0			
Bathgate	1	10000	44.25			
Pumpherston	1	20000	22.22	1	20000	22.22
Lanark	1	30000	30.0			
Holmes	1	6250	11.11			
Linlithgow	5	14000	10.0	3	8000	6.00
Hermand	1	9000	31.58	1	9000	31.58
Annick Lodge	4	5500	46.71	1	1565	13.29

Notes:
(a) James Young originally undertook to purchase £100,000 of shares, but later agreed to accept cancellation of the uncalled liability on these shares as part of the purchase price.
(b) These shares were for John Waddell's services in the transfer of the Binnend assets to the Burntisland company.

formation. The Binnend, Westfield and Lanark companies were creations of George Simpson and went quickly into liquidation. The Broxburn company is of interest in the sense that, although comprising only 34.85 per cent of the issued capital, the £57,500 share issue to Robert Bell was one of the largest in the industry. Bell became a director, but he started to dispose of these shares in 1879 and by 1881 had transferred £47,410 of his original holding.

The remaining companies gave vendors amounts ranging from 10 per cent to 31.58 per cent of issued capital. For the Pumpherston, Linlithgow and Holmes companies, the transaction was in respect of mineral leases only. The companies then proceeded to construct mines and works on greenfield sites

It seems clear that, with the exception of Uphall, vendors' shares, although in many cases a major holding, did not amount to complete control. However, it is clear from Table 12.2 that in most cases these substantial holdings made up an often greater proportion of the shares held by directors.

Table A of the First Schedule to the Companies Act of 1862 provided a model set of Articles of Association. Article 52 provided that the number of directors and the names of the first directors of a company were to be determined by the subscribers to the Memorandum of Association. Article 53 stated that until directors were appointed, the subscribers were deemed to be the directors. Articles 58 to 61 provided for the subsequent election of directors at general meetings of shareholders.

It has been observed that 'the notion that the Board is a committee chosen by the shareholders to supervise the conduct of the business is found to be a delusion'.[4] Drucker considered that, by the late twentieth century, the idea of 'the board' had become a fiction. It was either simply a committee of the management, or it was ineffectual. However, he goes on to observe that in the nineteenth century, share ownership was confined to small numbers of people holding substantial amounts of the total capital. The board did represent their interests, since each member had a substantial stake in the company.[5] The position in the shale industry is shown in Table 12.2, which gives the value of shares held by directors of the various companies.

In terms of statistics, the shale oil companies can be seen to accord with Drucker's view. The 12 companies formed between 1862 and 1869 had relatively small numbers of shareholders. Four had the minimum of seven required by the legislation. Only four had numbers in double figures: the 12 of the Monklands Oil Refining Company; the 15 of the Broxburn Shale Oil Company; the 32 of the Dalserf Coal Coke & Oil Company; and the 74 of Young's Company. In only three concerns did the directors hold less than half the issued shares. The lowest proportion was the 32.67 per cent of shares held by the directors of the Dalserf company. In this case, the five directors included three of the largest shareholders. The Scottish Oil Company's three directors held 42.85 per cent of the share capital, but the seven shareholders each held £1,000 of issued capital, and the three directors with £1,000 each may be held to represent them. The eight directors of Young's company held £280,000 of the £582,500 of issued capital: 48.01 per cent. The directors included the largest shareholder – Young himself, with £100,000 of shares – and four other shareholders with £20,000 or more.

In only one of the five companies formed between 1871 and 1876 – the Uphall Mineral Oil Company – did the directors hold more than half the shares. Three of the directors were the vendors and had accepted deferred shares as payment. It is, therefore, possible to speculate that it was in their interests to ensure that the company was viable. The highest proportion among the other four companies was

Table 12.2 Scottish shale oil companies: shareholdings of directors

Company	Formed	Qualification shares	No. of directors	No. of shareholders	Shares held by directors £	Proportion of issued capital %	Proportion of directors' shares held by vendors %
Broxburn Shale	1862	£400	3	15	11400	71.25	
Mid Calder Mineral	1864		4	7	7400	87.05	
Young's PL & MO	1866	£2000	8	74	280000	48.01	35.76
Capeldrae Oil & Coal	1866		7				
Scottish	1866		3	7	3000	42.85	
Glasgow	1866	£2500	3	9	15000	60.00	
Dalserf	1866	£500	5	32	8200	32.67	57.32
Monklands Oil Refining	1866		3	12	4000	50.00	
Monklands Oil & Coal	1866	£500	3	9	3850	77.00	
Glentore	1866	£200	7	7	1400	100.00	
Airdrie Mineral	1866	£500	7	9	6500	86.67	
Oakbank	1869	£2000	3	10	15000	75.00	
Uphall Mineral	1871	£1000	7	99	151790	75.90	93.41
Dalmeny	1871	£500	4	64	3000	13.34	
Midlothian Mineral	1871	£250	4	104	12250	38.93	57.14
West Calder	1872	£1000	7	138	18700	17.3	34.78
Straiton Estate	1876	£1000	4	59	11950	19.92	
Broxburn	1877		6	134	40840	24.75	32.81
Clippens	1878	£500	3	7	114000	95.00	90.35
Binnend	1878	£150	4	54	21780	55.84	59.24

Company	Formed	Qualification shares	No. of directors	No. of shareholders	Shares held by directors £	Proportion of issued capital %	Proportion of directors' shares held by vendors %
British Oil & Candle	1880	£500	4	8	1170	97.50	100.00
Walkinshaw	1880	£1000	6	192	12540	11.33	56.94
Burntisland	1881	£1000	7	194	30200	25.16	9.94
Midlothian	1882	£250	6	128	8600	12.29	
Westfield	1883	£500	4	66	9500	55.88	
West Lothian	1883	£500	5	313	3750	6.25	
Bathgate	1883	£200	5	48	3900	17.25	
Pumpherston	1883	£1000	5	172	31050	34.50	64.41
Lanark	1883	£500	4	198	10450	14.93	
Holmes	1884	£1000	4	144	4000	8.00	
Linlithgow	1884	£1000	3	328	30810	22.01	45.44
Annick Lodge	1885	£125	6	49	2190	20.00	71.46
Hermand	1885	£500	3	117	11300	39.65	79.65

Source: Company files; NAS, BT2 series; Registrar of Companies, company files.

the 38.93 per cent of shares held by the four directors of the Midlothian Mineral Oil Company. The four directors of the Dalmeny Company held only 13.34 per cent of the shares. In this period also, all of the companies except the Straiton issued fully paid shares to vendors in payment or part-payment for assets taken over.

In the 16 companies formed between 1877 and 1885, the proportion of shares held by directors ranged from 6.25 per cent (the West Lothian Company) to 97.5 per cent (British Oil & Candle). This last company, and Clippens at 95 per cent, with eight and seven shareholders respectively, were effectively private partnerships seeking the protection of limited liability. Of the remaining 14 concerns, the two in which the directors held more than half the shares were the Binnend and Westfield companies. These were promotions by George Simpson, and the large holdings by directors owed something to his methods, which are discussed later. The remaining 12 concerns had directors holding from 6.25 per cent in the Linlithgow company to 39.65 per cent in Hermand.

Young's, Oakbank and Broxburn survived until 1919, when they were absorbed into Scottish Oils. For all three, the minutes of the annual general meetings of shareholders have survived and afford the means of examining the relationship between directors and shareholders. For the Pumpherston company and some of the failed concerns, it is possible to extract similar information from newspaper reports.

Young's was founded in 1866. The seven subscribers were all subsequently share-holders, but one, Peter White, did not become a director. Six subscribers and two other shareholders made up a board of eight. They served for periods ranging from 3 to 46 years. Between 1866 and 1919, when the board resigned to make way for nominees of the Anglo-Persian Oil Company, 30 different individuals held office. The six directors in 1919 had been in office for 2, 5, 12, 13, 24 and 33 years respectively.[6]

The Oakbank company, formed in 1869, followed a similar pattern. There were actually two companies, the original being wound up and reorganised as a new concern in 1886. Over the 17 years of its existence, eight people were directors of the original company. Three of these were elected in the discussions that took place regarding the reorganisation. The company in the beginning had three directors, one of whom resigned after 10 years; the other two survived until the reorganisation, along with one elected in 1875 and another in 1881. The new company began in 1886 with seven directors, three of whom had been directors of the old company. Until 1919, 10 people served as directors: four survived to 1919, two of whom had held office for 33 years, since the formation of the company, one for 22 years, and one for 18.[7]

The Broxburn company, from its formation in 1877 until the amalgamation in 1919, lasted for 42 years. The six original directors held office for 5, 13, 18, 19, 19 and

22 years respectively. Of the five directors in 1919, two had served for eight years, one for nine, one for 14 and one for 23 years.[8]

The Pumpherston company, formed in 1883, had 11 individuals as directors in the 36 years of its independent existence. The first board consisted of five members who held office for 12, 17, 26, 28 and 32 years. The five directors in 1919 had served for 2, 3, 16, 19 and 31 years.[9]

It is clear that the boards of these four companies enjoyed a substantial element of continuity in their membership. Information for the remaining, less successful concerns is not so readily available, but it is possible to surmise that there may well have been a similar situation in at least some of them. The Uphall company was formed in 1871 and reorganised as a new concern in 1876. Four of the six original directors in 1871 survived to be part of the board of the new company. One of them was among the three directors co-opted to the Young's board after the amalgamation in 1884. In 1914, one of the directors of the Dalmeny company had previously been a member of the board of the original company before the 1896 reorganisation. Another was the son of James Jones, and had succeeded his father as managing director and secretary. When Clippens was finally wound up in 1908, A.C. Scott, one of the original shareholders and a director since 1885, remained a member of the board. The six directors of the Linlithgow company listed in 1901 included two members of the first board appointed in 1884.[10]

Discussion of the relationship between shareholders and directors presents some difficulty. The minutes of shareholders' meetings available for three of the companies often consist of not much more than the report by the directors, a statement by the chairman, and a record of decisions regarding dividends and the report. The Broxburn company was unusual in that, from its inception to his death, William Kennedy, its first managing director, provided a financial statement, about which he made explanations and answered questions. Unfortunately, there are no detailed records of these statements. Young's company, from 1872 until 1883, provided, along with the directors' report, a revenue statement for each financial year since the formation of the company. This provided the make in gallons of burning oil; average price of burning oil; total sales of all products; proportion of management expenses to sales; dividends paid; and amounts spent on maintenance and written off for depreciation. This practice ceased in 1884 after the amalgamation with Uphall . Sometimes there are mentions of questions by shareholders on particular points. The minutes are supplemented by newspaper reports of meetings which, on occasion, give more detail of any discussion that took place. In most cases the newspaper reports are, in fact, the only source.

Most of the comment, question and disagreement expressed by shareholders was in respect of the size or lack of dividends, the health of the company, and the stock exchange price, etc., all matters affecting the financial health of the individual shareholder. At the annual meeting in 1885, a Broxburn shareholder observed that 'the accounts appear to be a little cooked'. He considered that the directors could safely declare 5 per cent more of dividend, and went on to say that 'posterity had done nothing for them and they did not want to accumulate money for those who might succeed them'.[11] At the meeting in 1900, a shareholder complained of the dividend not being 20 per cent instead of 15, and suggested that too much had been added to the reserve fund. Another asked when the Pumpherston shares had ever before been higher than Broxburn.[12] Also in 1900, a number of Oakbank shareholders made strong representations that the dividend should have been more than the 7.5 per cent proposed by the directors. In all of these and similar instances, the views of the directors were eventually accepted.

There were also objections by shareholders to the method of re-electing directors. In 1869 Peter White, a Young's shareholder, suggested that one or more of the directors should retire each year. Discussed at the 1870 annual meeting, this was opposed by the directors and not adopted by the company. In the discussion, James Arthur, a retiring director, said that 'the shareholders would not take away the idea that the directors clung to their office; from the great claim it made on his time he would gladly retire'. He was re-elected.[13] In 1888, at Oakbank's annual meeting, it was suggested that a director should step down each year, to ensure 'fresh blood'. Charles Fraser, a director, said: 'For some companies anyone may be able to act as a director, but for an oil company so much practical and technical knowledge is required that a director ignorant of the working of the affairs of an oil company would be a great disadvantage.'[14]

Among the five surviving concerns there is only one example of shareholders' dissatisfaction being pursued to a vote. At the annual meeting in 1871, the appointment of John P. Kidston to a vacancy on the board of Young's was carried by 12 votes to 7. This may have been less an expression of dissatisfaction among shareholders generally than an attempt by James Young to embarrass the board. Kidston was proposed by the board; Dr Fleming was proposed by Young.[15] The reasons for Young's attitude to the board will be discussed later.

The less successful concerns might well have been expected to experience unrest among their shareholders, and indeed there are some examples among those companies for which information is available. The second general meeting of the Lanark company in December 1884 was well-attended. The company had lost £8,000 the previous year, and many questions were asked about this, directors' share dealings, the price paid for the assets taken over, and the condition of the retorting plant. A committee of shareholders was appointed to confer with the directors, but the report was adopted, an amendment for non-approval not having found a seconder. In 1892 there was a large attendance of shareholders at the annual meeting of the Linlithgow company. The *Scotsman*'s report of the meeting largely concerns complaints about works management, financial management, and the overall management. At the end of the meeting, the retiring directors were re-elected.[16]

The second annual general meeting of the West Lothian company experienced a large attendance of shareholders and was reported at length in the *Scotsman* of 5 June 1886, and the *West Lothian Courier* of 5 and 12 June, with the heading 'STORMY PROCEEDINGS'. The directors had reported a debit balance of £10,373 for the year,[17] and the meeting also had before it the report of a committee of shareholders and another by William Fraser on the company's mines and crude oil works. The committee's report set out in detail a number of deficiencies in the management and the financial record keeping and control, giving examples of what it considered to be 'the loose and defective character of the management ... management of such an character ... was calculated to produce those results which we now all deplore'.[18] The discussion was described as 'most animated' and 'lasted from one o'clock till close on five'. Several shareholders called for the resignation of the board – one saying that 'a more incapable board of directors never had their legs under a board table', which was greeted with applause. Much similar sentiment was expressed, including reference to the influence of George Simpson as not having been beneficial.

The meeting ended with the resignation of the directors, with the exception of one who was not present. A new board was elected, which, however, contained one of the resigning directors.[19] This is the only example in the industry of a shareholders' revolt that resulted in a change of directors. In the shale industry, it seems that the board of directors was 'a self-elected oligarchy'.[20]

The management structure of the refining companies

Formation of companies

The first, and possibly the most important, action of directors on behalf of a company was, of course, the purchase of the business from previous owners or the setting up of a new enterprise. The way they handled this transaction provides an indication of the directors' fitness. In the case of Young's company, the vidimus of the capital account when the company was formed shows that Young was to be paid £473,243: £50,000 was to be paid in cash on 2 January 1866, the remainder in payments of £50,000 each half year after 31 December 1865 up to 4 July 1870, the bills bearing interest at 5 per cent.[1] The sum was made up of :

Bathgate works	£100,000
Addiewell works	£67,091
Addiewell coal & shale pits workmen's houses etc.	£31,176
Casks	£4,540
Stock in hand of coal & shale	£8,924
Oils, paraffin, lamps etc. in stock	£111,512
Goodwill of business, coal & shale leases	£150,000
Total	£473,243

At a board meeting on 8 February 1866 cheques for £50,000 and £253, and nine bills payable at six-month intervals, were signed in favour of Young in payment of the purchase price. These cheques and bills totalled £523,726 and, obviously, included interest. This sum was later challenged as excessive, and in 1869 Young agreed to forego all interest on the money owed him by the company, including interest already paid, a total of £53,487. He also agreed to accept as part-payment the sum of unpaid calls on his shares (these not being due at the time), amounting to £39,000. Young had made a substantial concession, but it remained true that the company had paid some £470,000 for the assets taken over.[2]

Did the directors act prudently? The Bathgate works cost £100,000. In December 1864 Young bought the Bathgate works from E.W. Binney & Company for £32,000, and it is possible to argue that the £100,000 paid by the limited company was grossly excessive. However, the agreement between the partners stipulated that the value on which the sale was based was the breaking-up value.[3] This would, of course, be considerably less than its value as a going concern. The works had, in fact, been reported as being on the market with no prospect of a sale,[4] and this may explain the relatively low price paid by Young.

The remaining assets taken over were subject to verification by Alexander Moore and William Brown, Glasgow accountants. Moore had a previous association with Young.[5] They were to assess the value of the partially completed Addiewell works by reference to Young's books. The stocks of finished products and material in course of production were valued according to an inventory at prices agreed in the third clause of the agreement between Young and the company.[6]

The main incentive to those setting up the limited company and taking over Young's business was, of course, the very high level of profit achieved by Young and his partners. The 24th article of the agreement provided for evidence to be furnished that the profits of the partnership in the three years ending 31 December 1864 amounted to an average of £57,000 per annum, and that the profit earned by the Paraffin Light Company's stations in the year ending 29 April 1865 was £12,000. These figures were to be verified by William Brown. On 5 January 1866 the directors received a report on the profits of Young's business. No details were given in the minute, but the report was considered 'thoroughly satisfactory'.[7] The continuation of such a level of profitability meant that a substantial part of the payments to Young could have been made out of profits.

It is not clear to what extent the directors could have been aware of the threat posed by the growing American oil industry. In fact, imports of American oil, particularly of illuminating oil, fell in 1865.[8] Importations of American oils were reported in the *Times*,[9] and it is possible that this information was available to potential investors in the Scottish industry. The price of Young's oil in London in the first eight months of 1865 was 2 shillings and 3 pence per gallon. In September it rose to 3 shillings, in October to 3 shillings and 4 pence, and in December to 3 shillings and 6 pence.[10] These two factors may well have been enough for the directors to justify to themselves the promotion of the limited company.

The company immediately faced difficulties. In 1866 imports of American illuminating oil trebled to 230,853 barrels, and the price of Young's oil in London fell from 3 shillings and 6 pence per gallon in January to 1 shilling and 8 pence in December The average price for the year was 23.21 pence per gallon. The company nevertheless made a profit of £35,504, out of which interest on the purchase price had to be paid. The shareholders were informed that the depressed state of the market had 'prevented the disposal of the products of the Company's works to the extent and at the prices anticipated and requisite for meeting the expenses incurred in completing the new works at Addiewell'. These difficulties continued, and in the period up to 30 April 1868 a loss of £13,026 was incurred.[11]

Similar detail is not available for other concerns, but some comparisons are possible. Of the £473,243 paid by Young's company, £198,267 was for the Bathgate and Addiewell works. The rest was for goodwill, the distribution network, stock in hand, and mineral leases. For this figure, the company acquired crude oil and refinery works that dealt with 57,826 tons of shale in the six months ending 31 October 1867, an average of over 2,000 tons per week.[12] The data for Young's and seven other refining companies are summarised in Table 13.1.

Two of the three earliest concerns, Young's and the West Calder, incurred capital costs of about £100 per ton/week of capacity. The exception here was the Oakbank, which had in fact the lowest initial cost of all eight companies. A possible explanation is that the other two companies took over going concerns. Oakbank acquired a moribund works at a cost of £5,600. The previous owners, the Mid Calder Mineral Oil Company Limited, had a paid-up capital of £22,129, and it must be presumed that the new company had something of a bargain.[13] In October 1867, the Young's directors had decided not to offer for the Oakbank works. A report by Young stated that the works consisted of 64 new vertical retorts, 64 old verticals

Table 13.1 Relative capital costs

Company	Cost £	Shale per week Tons	Capital cost per ton/week £
Young's (1866) (a)	198267	2000	99.13
Oakbank (1869) (b)	31000	1000	31.00
West Calder (1872) (c)	80000	800	100.00
Broxburn (1877) (d)	147000	2500	58.80
Burntisland (1881) (e)	130400	2250	57.95
West Lothian (1883) (f)	95317	1800	52.95
Pumpherston (1883) (g)	87397	2000	43.69
Linlithgow (1884) (h)	151422	3000	50.47

Sources:

(a) BP Archive, YP, SHMB 1, Fo. 62.
(b) BP Archive, OOC, GMB Fos 4/5 and 20; OOC Ledger No. 9, Fo. 34.
(c) NAS, BT2/416/3; *Scotsman*, 22 April 1872.
(d) *Scotsman* 10 May 1879; BP Archive, BOC, GMB 1 Fo. 29 et seq., Fo. 35 et seq.
(e) *Scotsman* 26 May 1885; NAS, BT2/1049A/2.
(f) BT2/1285/8; WLC, 5 June 1886.
(g) WLC, 30 May 1885; AR0649 (Prospectus).
(h) BP Archive, AR 0648 (Directors' Report, 4 June 1886); WLC, 12 June 1886; NAS, BT2 1351/5 and 6.

and 21 horizontal retorts, together with the necessary refining plant.[14] Such a plant would have been fully capable of using 1,000 tons of shale per week, and the purchase price of £5,600 would have left an ample margin for improvement out of the ultimate expenditure of £31,000.

It must be emphasised here that some of these figures involve conjecture. In some cases it is not clear whether the costs include the purchase of shale leases. The Oakbank company apart, the trend in the later concerns was for the capital costs to be about half, or less, of those of the earlier firms. This gave rise to comment within the industry itself. For example, the Lanark Oil prospectus stated that the company, along with other recent formations, had a distinct advantage over the older companies in this respect.[15] However, it cannot be said that there was a relationship between the level of capital expenditure at formation and the length of life of the companies. Young's company, which had one of the highest, was the longest-lived concern in the industry. The Broxburn company, which had the highest figure among the later companies, also lasted until the amalgamation in 1919. Conversely, the Oakbank and Pumpherston companies, which had the lowest and second lowest ratios, were also among the survivors to 1919. Of the other companies, the West Calder lasted six years, the West Lothian seven years, the Burntisland nine, and the Linlithgow seventeen. The reasons for this may be the actual worth of the assets acquired or constructed under the supervision of the directors. This is discussed in some detail in Chapter 15.

The initial financial arrangements were not the only source of problems for the early directors. The type and quality of the plant to be used was important. In the case of the three early concerns, this was already in place as the companies were established to take over established works. Of the five later concerns, Pumpherston and Linlithgow set out to build completely new works. The West Lothian company had purchased a small refinery and shale leases at a different site. Burntisland had purchased a crude oil works and refinery commenced by Simpson in 1878, which in 1881 remained incomplete.[16] The Broxburn company had acquired virtually all of the crude oil works in and around Broxburn, a small refinery and the shale leases.

An important element in the choice of plant was the retort. As indicated earlier, the type of retort used changed at relatively frequent intervals during the life of the industry. The Broxburn directors settled on the retort designed by their manager, Norman Henderson, in 1873.[17] This was an immediate success, and the company paid a succession of dividends of 25 per cent. The Burntisland company, in taking over the partially completed works of the failed Binnend company, found itself committed to the Henderson retort, and again it was the basis of some successful years.[18] By the time the Linlithgow company was established in 1884, the Young and Beilby retort had come into use. This was superior to the Henderson in that it gave a much higher yield of ammonia.[19] However the Linlithgow directors, possibly because of the proximity of their shale field to that of the Broxburn, decided to invest in the Henderson retort.[20] This decision left the company with perfectly sound retorts that quickly became unsuited to the most profitable shales. The Pumpherston and West Lothian companies opted for the new retort, and in Pumpherston's case it was the basis for a solid start to what eventually became the most successful concern in the later years of the industry. The first two benches built for the West Lothian company were, however, badly constructed, and this was one of the causes of the company's lack of success.[21]

Directors and day-to-day management: Young's Paraffin Light & Mineral Oil Company Limited

It has been stated that, in the last quarter of the nineteenth century, boards of directors of non-family firms behaved very like family concerns in their attitude towards salaried managers. They reserved to themselves the overall conduct of business, and employed salaried managers only at a functional or departmental level.[22] I hope to show that the shale industry did not long adhere to this model.

The reports of annual meetings are, of course, very useful in terms of the light shed on the directors' activities in general terms as they affected shareholders. However, they are not so informative on the directors' contribution to day-to-day affairs. The minute books of directors' meetings would, of course, be a valuable source, but for most of the concerns they have not survived. For the four surviving refining companies, the first and last of the series of minute books have been preserved. For the Oakbank 1869 company, the minute book from 2 February 1875 to 18 January 1882 has survived. These suffer from the defects inherent in the minutes of any organisation: almost invariably there is no record of discussion, and the minute simply records the decisions made. The basis of these decisions was often a report by one or more of the directors or by the managers, but the actual reports are rarely given in the minutes. However, the board's minutes can provide a view of the activities of the directors and their relationship with the day-to-day managers of the concern. Some of the commercial records of the four limited companies which survived to 1919 to form Scottish Oils Limited have been preserved. These consist mainly of the general or private ledgers and journals. The subsidiary records have only rarely survived, but their existence can be deduced from the ledgers and journals. A considerable amount of papers and correspondence survives, but mainly for Young's company. Some of the detail of these records has been used in discussing, in Part 1, the industry's development. Here we are concerned with their structure and what they may have contributed to the management of the concerns. In considering the management of the industry, it may be best to concentrate on these four concerns for which some company records have survived. The first of these is of course Young's Paraffin Light & Mineral Oil Company.

On 1 January 1866, the limited company took possession of the works at Bathgate, the partially completed works at Addiewell and the ten paraffin light stations throughout the country. These were listed in the company's first journal as London, Manchester, Birmingham, Bristol, Hull, Newcastle-on-Tyne, Edinburgh, Glasgow, Aberdeen and Dublin.[23] In the case of Young's, we are fortunate in that a complete run of the minutes of the shareholders' meetings has been preserved. Minute books of the directors' meetings from December 1865 to June 1868, from July 1917 to October 1919, and a private minute book of meetings from September 1881 to July 1919, are also available.

Initially, there were eight directors:

1. James Young of Limefield
2. John Pender, MP, Manchester
3. John Orr Ewing of Levenfield
4. Professor Lyon Playfair, Edinburgh
5. John Moffat, Ardrossan
6. James Arthur of Barshaw
7. James King, Younger of Campsie
8. Hugh Bartholemew, Glasgow

Young's connection with the oil industry needs no elaboration. He was undoubtedly the board member most experienced in the production and distribution of the company's products, having been at the head of the concern since its foundation in 1851. John Pender (later Sir John), a native of Dunbartonshire, son of a textile merchant, moved to Manchester and accumulated considerable wealth in the cotton trade. He later became a major figure in international telegraph communications and in the electrical industry. He was MP for Totnes and later for Wick Burghs. He remained a director until his death in 1896, when it was said of him that, although unable to attend board meetings very frequently, his experience and influence were valuable to the company.[24] John Orr Ewing was the first chairman of the company and remained so until 1874, relinquishing his seat on the board at the AGM on 16 June 1875. He died in 1878. He was a major figure in the Vale of Leven dyeing industry, with considerable experience and expertise in both the production and commercial sides of his business.[25] Professor Lyon Playfair was the distinguished chemist and politician who introduced Young to the oil industry.[26] John Moffat was listed as a chartered engineer in the first SCS. His death was notified in the 1882 Directors' Report. James Arthur of Barshaw was a director until his death in 1886. He was an extremely successful manufacturer, wholesaler and retailer of men's clothing, with branches in London, Edinburgh and Newcastle and factories in Glasgow, Londonderry and Leeds.[27] James King was the son of John King of the Hurlet and Campsie company, manufacturers of dyestuffs for the textile industry, but his main interest was in building up a varied investment portfolio, which had a value of £676,338 at his death in 1911.[28] He remained a director until his death, and was chairman from 1895 until 1907. Hugh Bartholemew was a director until he declined re-election in 1871. A friend of Young, he was an engineer and manager of the City and Suburban Gas Company of Glasgow, and it was he who sent the sample of cannel coal that brought Young to Bathgate.[29] These men were fairly obviously members of the 'large and experienced business class' identified as one of the key factors in Scotland's Victorian success.[30]

The eight original directors of the company held 2,800, almost half, of the 5,825 shares issued. They had made a substantial financial commitment. The prospectus indicated that £25 per share was to be called up during 1866. Between them, the directors were liable to pay £70,000 in respect of their shares. George Readman was appointed auditor with a seat on the board. William McEwan was appointed a director in December 1866; in the first Summary of Capital and Shares, he is described simply as a merchant resident in Glasgow. James Young junior became a director in February 1867.[31]

The legislation conferred significant powers upon directors. Table A of the First Schedule to the Act of 1862 states at Article 55 that the business of the company was to be managed by the directors. Any restriction on their exercise of the powers of the company had to be contained in the Act itself, or in the Articles of Association of the company. Articles 1 to 51 were concerned with the shares and with the procedures for general meetings. Articles 52 to 54 and 57 to 71 related to the selection, qualification, disqualification, rotation and proceedings of directors, and provided at Article 65 for the removal of a director by a resolution of the company in general meeting. As has been shown above, this ultimate sanction was only rarely exercised by the shale companies. Certain obligations regarding dividends, accounts and audit were imposed on the directors by Articles 78 to 94. The articles of Young's company did not apply these model articles, but Articles 9 and 10 adopt much of the sense of those replaced.

Important differences were:

- The requirement to circulate a printed copy of the balance sheet was replaced by the necessity of placing it before a general meeting;
- The requirement that the company's books should be available to any shareholder was replaced by a statement that such access was possible only with a written order from the board; and

- The arrangements for audit, set out in considerable detail in Articles 83 to 94 of Table A, were condensed to a simple statement at Article 10 that the accounts, books and balance sheet were to be examined once at least in every year by an auditor or auditors to be appointed by the directors for the first year, and by the general meeting thereafter.

The Young's articles also provided at Article 11 for one of the directors to be appointed managing director, with suitable remuneration.[32]

The Young's directors met on 56 occasions in 1866, 55 in 1867, and 24 in the period up to 24 June in 1868.[33] Most of these meetings were held at the company's offices in Glasgow, but occasionally the location was the Bathgate or Addiewell works, when the meeting ended with an inspection of the works. The first chairman of directors was John Orr Ewing, who remained in post until 1874. He is credited with supervising the 'transition from the personal management of James Young to that of the directors and their managers'.[34]

On 28 December 1865, the directors resolved to set up two committees: a works committee consisting of Young, Moffat, Playfair and Bartholemew; and a finance committee made up of Pender, Orr Ewing, Moffat and Arthur – the chairman of directors to be a member of both. The board minutes provide no indication that these committees actually functioned until February 1867, when the two committees were again established and their responsibilities set out in some detail. The lack of action on this matter is confirmed by the appointment of an ad hoc committee to arrange for a manager at Addiewell, a matter that might have been considered appropriate for a works committee.[35]

From the start, the directors made important decisions without reference to the shareholders. Before the company was formally established, it was decided to build 270 additional cottages and to sink pits. In April 1866 a report by Lyon Playfair suggested the removal of candle-making from Bathgate to Addiewell, and 24 machines were authorised at Addiewell. Later that month it was agreed to build 150–200 new retorts at Addiewell. In May 1866, 156 more new retorts were authorised, to achieve the production originally agreed upon – 4 million gallons per year.[36]

In addition to making such major decisions, the individual directors were actively involved in running the company. The board members were men with considerable experience in trade and industry. James Young himself was the largest shareholder and is said to have acted as general manager, along with his son, James junior. It is not clear, from the board minutes, that such an appointment was ever made, although James Young junior received a payment of £500 on 31 December 1866 for one year's salary. However, the minutes demonstrate that demands were made on most of the directors in the day-to-day management of the company. At one of its earliest meetings, it was minuted that Mr King was to enquire about the possibility of a market for solid paraffin in France. Such remits became more frequent towards the end of 1866. In October 1866 the orders for Bathgate and Addiewell were remitted to Mr Bartholemew, and he was also, along with Mr King, entrusted with a tender for supplies. James King and the auditor, George Readman, were asked to see 'Mr Robinson and other parties with a view to sales being made on the Continent'. During the period up to 17 June 1868, when the minute book closes, James King was asked to perform such tasks on eight occasions; Lyon Playfair on three; Hugh Bartholemew on ten; John Moffat on four; William McEwen on seven; John Orr Ewing on four; and James Arthur on four. James Young was mentioned twenty times and his son eight. The Youngs were called upon for matters mostly related to the works at Bathgate and Addiewell. For example, Young senior was asked to deal with a difficulty in retaining men at the works at their present rates of pay, the problem of limiting oil production, and the making of white and scentless oil. Young junior was entrusted with the engagement of foremen and the arrangements for making sulphate of ammonia at Bathgate.[37]

At the meeting on 14 February 1867, the committees proposed at the beginning were formally set up.

It was agreed that there should be a Committee composed of Messrs Young, Young Jnr, Playfair, Bartholemew, King and Moffat, called the 'Manufacturing Committee' Mr James Young Jnr Convenor – three to be a quorum – to take superintendence of the manufacturing of all the articles produced by the Company so as to secure as far as possible thorough economy in the production combined with a first class quality of each article. Minutes to be kept of the business transacted at each meeting which are to be laid before the Board at their first meeting thereafter.

That in the Finance Committee there should be Five Directors – Mr Bartholemew to be the additional member – two a quorum – to meet as required for the following business, viz.

In the first week of each month statements of the financial position of the Company to be laid before the meeting; 1st shewing the assets and liabilities for the month; 2nd a vidimus shewing an estimate of the assets and liabilities for the three following months; 3rd a list of all outstanding debts.

In the last week of each month, All accounts for payment to be initialled by the Storekeeper at the Works, the Manager of the Works & thereafter submitted to and initialled by the General Manager and afterwards by one of the Committee for payment. Minutes of meetings to be kept and laid before the Board at their first meeting thereafter, along with all statements which have been under consideration. The Chairman of the Board to be ex officio a member of each committee.

From this point onwards, the board minutes become more formal in that they generally start with a statement of minutes presented and approved. At most meetings these were confined to those of the board and the finance committee, which met on the same day as the directors. The finance committee minutes were presented for approval on 54 occasions between March 1867 and June 1868; those of the manufacturing committee on only seven. In October 1867 and again in April 1868, it was minuted that the manufacturing committee should meet on a fixed date each month.[38] However, this appears to have had little effect and minutes of the committee appeared only when there had been a specific remit from the board.

The creation of a committee structure did not mean the cessation of remits to individual directors or small ad hoc committees. These continued, but in 1867 and 1868 these remits were often to a director or directors, along with the general manager or a works manager. At the same time there is a greater clarity in the nature of information submitted to the board. During 1866, the board received for consideration documents described simply as Works Returns and Branches Returns. From July 1867, they were described as abstract of make, stock and sales; abstract of sales at each branch; bank balances; Addiewell stock; Bathgate stock; and calls paid and unpaid. The first presentation of these must have caused some embarrassment to officials: 'The stock sheets being examined, several serious errors were pointed out & Mr Hill was instructed to make out a correct statement of all stocks & see that they are accurate in future.'[39] Later, estimates of receipts and payments and assets and liabilities were called for.[40]

In its early activities, the board may well have had considerable assistance from James Young, but there is evidence that the relationship was not entirely harmonious. In his diaries Young complains about John Moffat in particular.[41] In October 1868, Young recorded that he disagreed with Moffat regarding a forecast of production, going on to say that Moffat and Ewing left together and that he (Young) thought a plot was in hand.[42] The price paid to Young was challenged more or less unsuccessfully. Young did agree to forego payment of interest, but the principal sum remained payable and was a substantial burden on the company. After the negotiations leading to this settlement, Young left the board in 1869, but for some time he remained a critic of aspects of its policy, particularly in relation to the flashpoint of burning oils.[43] Correspondence between Young and the board dating from July to October 1871 ends with a letter dated 13 October 1871 from the board to Young, which concludes:

But what has been the part played by Mr Young. Simply that, from the very outset of the concern down to the present moment he has so conducted himself towards the directors, as if they were his personal enemies, and towards the company generally as if its interests were antagonistic to his own, whereas upon every principle of honour he was bound to be its warmest friend.

Mr Young, as was natural, was one of the original Board and a director he might have continued for it was the wish of his colleagues to act harmoniously with him but influenced by prejudices for which the Directors are unable to entertain any respect, he chose to retire from the Board and the disposition to thwart and to annoy which he manifested while a Director, he seems bent upon manifesting now that he is only an ordinary shareholder.[44]

Introduction of top management

Initially, Young acted as general manager.[45] However, in June 1866 Alexander Moore was appointed to fill the dual roles of secretary and general manager. Moore was a Glasgow chartered accountant who had acted for Young before the limited company was formed. He was of some repute in the profession; in 1878 he acted in the formation of the Distillers Company Limited.[46]

Henry Hill was appointed general manager in November 1866. Moore remained secretary until February 1867, when he was replaced by Mr O.T.B. Gardner, previously the company's cashier. Moore then became the company's auditor. Hill was described as having been 'long connected with the management of Price's Patent Candle Company Limited', which had been registered as a public joint stock company in 1847 under the Joint Stock Companies Act of 1844. In 1848 it was incorporated by a private Act of Parliament. Hill therefore had experience in a company managed by a board of directors.[47]

From 1867 onwards, the company's top management consisted of the general manager, in overall charge of the business and a secretary, who was also the cashier, in charge of the head office. Their duties were clearly set out in the following scheme:

General Manager

I. To take the general supervision & direction of the business of the Company, with a view to the harmonious working of the whole in the most economical and efficient manner.

II. To take charge of the finances of the Compy [sic] with a view to the regular collection of outstanding accounts & provision for the Compy/s liabilities.

III. To make all purchases and sales for the Company in Glasgow and elsewhere either personally or by instructions to the Works, Branch Managers
and agents; to apportion the duties of the various employees engaged
commercially in the Company's service, and arrange their remuneration,
all subject to the approval of the Board; and to direct all commercial
transactions of the Branches or Agents, subject to agreements made with
the latter by the Board.

IV. To visit the Works and Branches when necessary.

V. To take the instructions of the Directors or Committees of their number
on all matters connected with the business of the Company.

Secretary and Cashier

I. As Secretary: – To call all meetings of Directors and Committees & such
others as may be required by the Company's act 1862.

To present all business for Consideration to the Committees &
meetings of the board.

To attend all meetings of the Directors & of the various Committees
also all meetings of shareholders, and keep minutes of the proceedings at
the same.

To conduct all correspondence arising out of the meetings of the
Board, or Committees, & issue remits from the former.

To conduct the general correspondence of the Registered Office
subject to the Approval of the General Manager.

II. As Cashier: – To take charge of the whole receipts and payments of the
Company.

To direct the whole Book-keeping arrangements of the company,
subject to the approval of the General Manager.

To carry out the arrangements of the General Manager, in the event of
his absence at any time, in accordance with his instructions.

To prepare and present all statements and returns required by the
Board or Committees.[48]

It is not clear how long Henry Hill remained with the company. In 1872 the directors' report to the annual general meeting states that Mr D.J. Kennelly had been
appointed to the board in 1871 in place of Mr Bartholemew, who had declined his
re-election at the AGM in 1871. In 1874 the directors reported that Mr Kennelly had
resigned his position as managing director. It seems likely that Kennelly was
appointed in 1871 as managing director, but it is not clear whether he was replacing
Hill. What is clear, however, is that Kennelly left in 1873 and that the directors

decided to replace him with a general manager.[49] John Fyfe, previously superintendent of stores at the St Rollox depot of the Caledonian Railway Company, was appointed general manager of 'their whole business' for five years. It is not clear what qualities he brought to the company, but as stores manager of one of the two largest railway companies in Scotland he obviously had significant organisational abilities and also a knowledge of the country's transport system. He became managing director in 1882 and remained with the company until shortly before his death in 1915.[50] At the time of Fyfe's appointment, the top level of head office staff comprised Fyfe himself; Gardner, secretary; Smith, bookkeeper; Love, general salesman; and Coleman, lubricating oil salesman.[51]

The Uphall takeover in 1884 obviously added to the organisation's size and complexity. Shale usage increased from 300,000 tons in 1883 to 507,395 tons in 1892, and to 818,912 tons in 1914. Turnover increased from £420,593 in 1883 to over £650,000 in 1914, although this was an extended period of falling prices for the industry's main products.[52]

After the takeover of the Uphall company, Fyfe set out, in a letter of 28 October 1884, Young's management structure. Control was vested in one central figure, himself, and the company's activities were organised in departments controlled by senior officials responsible to him. In the registered office he delegated to the secretary the bulk of correspondence with the public and branches, leaving only 'the most important as well as obviously those to the Works and Pits' to be dealt with by himself. The bookkeeper had acquired an assistant from the Uphall office and was now more of an accountant responsible for the supervision of accounts and their preparation for submission to the board. The head office was clearly in the course of developing a separate accounting department.

Fyfe reached the age of 65 in 1900, and the hierarchy was adapted to cater for this and for the firm's development. In 1907 R.W. Meikle was appointed assistant secretary, and in 1912 Thomas Wylie Steven was appointed assistant general manager, although he was expected to continue with the more important duties of secretary. At the time of the latter appointment Fyfe was 77 years old, and it is probable that it was made in preparation for his retirement. He was to have retired on 31 December 1915, having extended his service because of the Great War, but he died shortly before that date.[53] Steven was appointed general manager on 3 November 1915, but was killed in a traffic accident on 1 November 1916.[54] His position was not filled, but his duties were shared out between three new posts. Angus Kerr, previously the accountant, was appointed commercial manager; William Cowan, previously manager of the Glasgow branch, became sales manager; and J.W. Anderson, manager at Addiewell, became general works manager, based at Addiewell. Kerr was appointed general manager in 1919.[55]

Oakbank, Broxburn and Pumpherston oil companies

For the other three refining companies that survived to make up Scottish Oils Limited, the BP Archive is less informative than for Young's company. The minute books and records described above are available, but very little correspondence has survived.

The Oakbank Company initially had three directors: Robert Fraser, a merchant resident in Glasgow; and John Ferguson Cathcart and Archibald Ritchie Gillespie, merchants in Leith. However, the Glasgow Post Office directories show the firm of Gillespie, Cathcart and Fraser, commission merchants and sugar brokers, at 54 Miller Street, which became the registered office of the new company.[56] The directors were obviously already closely associated. In setting up the company, the directors had acquired and improved the works at Oakbank for a relatively modest sum.

The Broxburn company was established in 1877. The first directors were Robert Bell, John Hurll, William Kennedy, James Steel, John Waddell and William Weir.[57] Bell was the lessee of the shale seams in and around Broxburn, and in addition to mining shale for sale he had acquired most of the oil works there that had ceased operation by 1877. Bell was a major figure in the Lanarkshire mining industry and came to Broxburn in 1858 with the intention of mining ironstone. His discovery of shale seams led to the start of oil production there. He has been described as the 'leading figure in the second generation' of the industry.[58] John Hurll was a member of the family of fireclay manufacturers. James Steel was a native of Wishaw, where he was a successful builder; he moved to Edinburgh in 1866, established a major house-building firm in the last quarter of the nineteenth century, and was lord provost from 1900 to 1903.[59] John Waddell was a railway contractor on a large scale in Scotland and the north-east of England.[60]

The Pumpherston company, formed in 1883, had five directors. James Wood, born in Paisley, the son of a handloom weaver, set up as a coal merchant in 1860. From his offices in Glasgow in the 1870s and 1880s, he ran an increasingly successful business as a colliery owner, centred on Armadale and Bathville in West Lothian.[61] James Craig was described as 'late of Messrs J. & F. Craig, Engineers, Paisley'.[62] This firm was heavily involved in the construction of retorts and other plant for the shale industry. Robert Browne Tennent was an iron founder at Whifflet, near Coatbridge.[63] John Paterson was described as a merchant of 62 Princes Street, Edinburgh: the firm of Romanes and Paterson still trades at that address. The managing director was William Fraser.

The first directors' minute book of the Oakbank company has not survived, and it is not possible to compare the frequency of its early directors' meetings with those of Young's company. However, the directors met on 18 occasions in each year

1875–7; 21 times in 1878 and in 1879; 19 in 1880; and 24 in 1881.[64] The Broxburn board met 16 times in 1878; 16 in 1879; 17 in 1880; 15 in 1881; and 14 in 1882.[65] The Pumpherston directors had 24 meetings in 1884; 27 in 1885; and 43 in 1886. Apart from 1886, when Pumpherston had considerable problems with finance and works management, the directors of the three newer companies met much less frequently than those of Young's in its early years. The minute books also show that there were very few remits to individual directors compared with Young's early years. The newer concerns had begun to rely on management structures similar to the ones it had taken Young's company some years to develop.

Initially, Oakbank had William Kennedy as general manager. He left in 1877 to set up Broxburn Oil and was succeeded by G.B. Hogarth, who died in 1884. J.M. Storrar, a chemical merchant, was appointed in his place. After the 1886 reorganisation, Storrar left the company on 31 March 1886 and Charles Fraser, one of the directors, was appointed managing director. John Wishart, secretary to the old company, was appointed secretary to the new company in 1886. He was elected a director in 1897, having previously been general manager. He remained in post until the amalgamation in 1919. The first secretary was Charles Bryce. There were six secretaries in the years after the foundation of the company, the last being Robert C. Miller, who held office from 1893 to 1919.[66]

William Kennedy was managing director of the Broxburn company from the beginning, assisted in the registered office by the secretary and a sales manager.

The managing director of the Pumpherston company was William Fraser, who had been mining manager and latterly overall manager of the Uphall works. His brother Archibald was appointed secretary and commercial manager.[67]

The most detailed exposition of what directors expected of their senior officials is the one issued by the Young's board. The Broxburn board simply required that William Kennedy, as managing director, should

> devote his whole time and attention to the management of the business of the company, subject to the direction and control of the Board of Directors for the time being and shall not be at liberty while acting as managing director to be personally engaged either directly or indirectly in any other company or business but without prejudice to his holding shares in any joint stock or limited company.[68]

The Pumpherston directors were even more sparing of words. The managing director was 'to have the superintendence and management of the affairs of the company and to have power generally to do everything requisite for the successful prosecution of the business of the company'.[69] It must be assumed that this lack of specification was related to the fact that Kennedy and Fraser took a prominent part in promoting their companies. It must have been expected that they would be closely involved in running the new concerns. Certainly, Fraser is listed in the Pumpherston prospectus as managing director.[70] These two men remained at the head of their respective companies until their deaths, Kennedy in 1899 and Fraser in 1916.

Both men had considerable experience in the shale industry, but in different fields. William Kennedy, after an apprenticeship with a Biggar merchant, came to Glasgow in 1853 at the age of 16. By 1856 he was selling paraffin oil and lamps in many towns in Scotland and Ireland. In 1861 he joined the West Calder Oil Company, remaining there until 1869 when he joined Robert Fraser in forming the Oakbank company.[71] Unlike Fyfe, he had been involved in the oil trade almost from its inception. Fraser had been a colliery manager in Glasgow and at Carnbroe. He moved to the Uphall company, where he remained for seven years: first as manager of the company's mines, and latterly for two and a half years of the oil works.[72] The two men had experience of different aspects of the oil industry and might have been expected to be deficient in some respects. However, Kennedy had the benefit of having as works manager Norman Henderson, a former Oakbank colleague. Fraser was assisted in his company's commercial affairs by his brother Archibald, first as secretary and commercial manager, and later as secretary and general manager; Archibald Fraser had previously been a bookkeeper with Robert Addie and Sons, ironmasters.[73]

These men occupied positions of power within their companies. Wishart was described in 1918 as part of a two-man band with his chairman, Robert Moore.[74] The importance of Kennedy and Fraser in their companies is clearly demonstrated by their prominent role in shareholders' meetings. An informative statement on management policy was submitted to the Pumpherston directors by Archibald Fraser, the company secretary, when he accepted the additional responsibilities of general manager. Fraser requested and received an assurance that he would have 'the entire control of every department of the company's business'. He also asked that there would be 'no interference on the part of the Directors either directly or indirectly' with any part of the business under his control. In effect, he asked that the activities of the directors be confined to the boardroom, where the business of the company would be reported to the board's weekly meetings. He also asked that his brother William be appointed as consulting director to advise him on a daily basis.[75] The brothers remained in control of the company until William's death in 1916.

Supporting staff

The registered offices provided support for management. Young's company, in the first year after the Uphall takeover, spent £1,609 on salaries in its registered office.

In the year ending 30 April 1915, £5,996 was expended. In 1884, the Uphall company had, in its Glasgow office, four clerks with salaries ranging from £13 to £78, and two in obviously superior positions, earning salaries of £150 and £200. These two, and two of the others, were retained in Young's service after the amalgamation. In 1883 the Broxburn company had eight clerks with salaries totalling £581 per annum. In 1914 such salaries amounted to £2,289. In 1884, the original head office staff of the Pumpherston company comprised a cashier, a bookkeeper and a salesman. By 1903, the clerical staff at the works and in the head office numbered 50. In 1914 charges incurred at head office amounted to £18,911 and included £8,557 in salaries. The reorganised Oakbank company in 1886 had a head office staff consisting of a cashier, a bookkeeper with two assistants, an invoice clerk with one assistant, a corresponding clerk, a German clerk and two junior clerks.[76]

Young's inherited a substantial head office structure, which it expanded as the company developed. The other three companies obviously began with relatively small organisations, but these grew as the companies expanded to their fullest extent.

Sales and distribution

Young's company acquired from Young ten Paraffin Light stations in various places in the United Kingdom. James Hurst, Young's agent in Manchester, was also recruited, and a presence in Paris was added soon after the takeover.[1] Papers in the BP Archive indicate that agencies were established in Norway, Denmark, Germany, Belgium, Holland, Switzerland and Italy.[2] The pattern of sales in the various branches and locations is shown in Table 14.1.

The pattern varied over the years, but it is clear that a substantial proportion of sales was made in Scotland, and that this increased over the years to 1913–14, from 17 per cent to nearly half. The proportion of sales made in England and Wales fell over the same period from 75 per cent to 36 per cent. Ireland's contribution varied, but ended at about the same level; sales made in foreign countries also varied. One interesting point is that there was, over the years, an increasing concentration in the two largest branches: Glasgow and London. Their joint share of the market rose from 41 per cent in 1867–8 to 58 per cent in 1913–14. Glasgow's share of Scottish sales was less than half in 1867–8 but rose in 1871–2 to 72 per cent, and to 76 per cent in 1913–14. London's share of English sales fell from 43 per cent in 1867–8 to 23 per cent in 1887–8, but rose to 55 per cent in 1913–14.

This may have resulted from the increasing concentration of population in London and south-east England, and in the Glasgow area. The changing product profile was possibly important. In 1871–2, burning oil at 52 per cent and candles at 16 per cent made up two thirds of the company's sales. These were goods ready for retail sale and may well have been more readily distributed through branches near to the final customer. By 1913, the proportion of sales attributed to these items had fallen to 31 per cent. At the same time, sulphate of ammonia accounted for 32 per cent of sales (see Chapter 4, Table 4.2). This fertiliser was more likely to be sold by contracts negotiated at the main offices of the company. It is also possible that the increasing use of the telephone and telegraph made it easier for large customers to communicate directly with the company rather than through branches or agents. The number of telegraph messages transmitted in the United Kingdom rose to 'over 50 million in 1886–7, 66 million in 1890–91, and over 90 million at the end of the century.'[3]

Each of the branches had a manager. Between 1871 and 1881, the number of commercial travellers in the United Kingdom rose from 20,000 to over 40,000.[4] There is evidence in the miscellaneous correspondence in the BP Archive that

Table 14.1 Branch sales, Young's Paraffin Light & Mineral Oil Company Limited

Branch	1867–8 £	1867–8 %	1871–2 £	1871–2 %	1887–8 £	1887–8 %	1894–5 £	1894–5 %	1913–14 £	1913–14 %
Aberdeen	12895	5.28	14366	3.42	29097	6.54	29338	6.16	49339	7.41
Birmingham	10935	4.48	15691	3.73					18087	2.72
Belfast					14683	3.30	11879	2.50		
Bristol	14222	5.83	26667	6.35	38876	8.73	29166	6.13	27862	4.18
Dublin	17090	7.00	28895	6.87	38926	8.75	31624	6.64	23388	3.51
Edinburgh	8561	3.51	9978	2.37	21050	4.73	22779	4.79	28907	4.34
Foreign			36490	8.68	28850	6.48	56653	11.91	41488	6.23
Glasgow	20140	8.25	64019	15.23	112408	25.25	144438	30.35	253499	38.06
Hull	19078	7.81	13760	3.27	26372	5.92	24012	5.05	12237	1.84
Hurst	33600	13.76	18669	4.44	6085	1.37	5077	1.07		
London	80019	32.77	98818	23.51	44771	10.06	45834	9.63	133659	20.07
Manchester	17269	7.07	39815	9.47	49270	11.07	40092	8.43	46961	7.05
Newcastle	9364	3.84	34500	8.21	24073	5.41	24382	5.12	20167	3.03
Paris	977	0.40	18688	4.45	10658	2.39	10565	2.22	10495	1.56
	244152	100.00	420356	100.00	445119	100.00	475839	100.00	666089	100.00
Scotland		17.04		21.02		36.52		41.30		49.81
England & Wales		75.56		58.98		42.56		35.43		36.17
Ireland		7.00		6.87		12.05		9.14		6.23
Foreign & Paris		0.40		13.13		8.87		14.13		7.79
Glasgow & London		41.02		38.74		35.31		39.98		58.13
Glasgow % of Scotland		48.42		72.45		69.14		73.49		76.41
London % of England		43.37		39.86		23.64		27.18		55.49

Note: The 1867–8 and 1871–2 figures are for 'credits' to the branches, and the totals are a little more than the sales figure for these years: £205,841 and £399,205 (source: BP Archive, YP, SHMB 1, Directors' Report, April 1872). The proportions are the important element here.

Source: BP Archive, YP Ledgers Nos 1, 2, 8 and 12.

commercial travellers were employed to sell the company's products.[5] In 1918, the staff of the branches, in addition to managers, was made up of 37 men and 17 women.[6]

The other three companies followed Young's in setting up distribution networks. In 1878, William Kennedy was authorised to make arrangements for selling products, including the 'engaging of travellers etc.' In 1882, Kennedy was able to state that the company had branches or representatives in London, Newcastle, Manchester, Hull, Dublin, Belfast and Dundee.[7]

The records of the Broxburn company do not provide the same detail about sales as those of Young's, but it is clear that a significant proportion was attributable to the London branch. In 1883–4, total sales were £313,538, of which £82,502 or 26.31 per cent was achieved in London; in 1893–4, the figures were £99,709 out of £303,957 – 32.8 per cent, and in 1912–13, £174,401 out of £553,320 – 31.51 per cent.[8]

Similar information on the Oakbank network is not available, but the company's first ledger, dating from 1869, has over 300 accounts, with addresses ranging from Scottish villages such as Larkhall, Biggar, Inverary and Maybole to cities like Glasgow, Manchester, Leeds, Liverpool and Dublin, and to Mannheim, Hamburg, Naples, Copenhagen, Leghorn and Munich on the continent. Over half of the accounts had Scottish addresses. In 1886 the reorganised company appointed agents in Newcastle and district, Liverpool and district, and in Manchester. In 1896, the accounts indicate the maintenance of stocks of paraffin wax in Genoa, Naples, Leghorn and Venice. At Marseilles, stocks were held of wax, engine and cylinder oils, and there were stocks of engine oil at Havre.[9]

The Pumpherston directors appointed agents in Belfast, Dundee, London and Newcastle. After a visit to the continent by the secretary, agencies were established in Rouen, Paris, Lille, Berlin, Magdeburg, Leipsig, Vienna, Frankfurt and Cologne. The Pumpherston company did not establish a network like that of Young's, but by 1912 it had depots in Glasgow, Dundee and Manchester.[10]

Table 14.2 Deliveries of liquid products by the four refining companies in 1913

	Gallons	Scotland %	England %	Ireland %	Foreign %
Naphtha	5292075	73.71	23.89	1.09	1.31
Burning Oil	18069681	66.81	12.88	4.56	15.75
Gas & Fuel Oils	15285218	64.13	31.28	1.05	3.54
Lubricating Oils	6520901	41.03	44.72	1.01	13.24
Total	45167875	62.99	24.99	2.45	9.57

Source: Comparative statement of production and deliveries.

It is clear that all four of the companies that survived to become part of Scottish Oils in 1919 distributed their products widely throughout the United Kingdom and Europe.

At that time, liquid products made up less than half of the value of the industry's sales. In the year ending March/April 1913, solid products – paraffin wax, candles and sulphate of ammonia – made up 58 per cent of the sales of the four companies.[11] Sulphate of ammonia was used as a fertiliser in German sugar beet farming, in the West Indies sugar cane industry, and in the manufacture of compound fertilisers. It is not possible to distinguish the destinations of these products for the industry as a whole, but Broxburn's Ledger No. 18 shows that, in the year ending 31 March 1913, 22 per cent by value of the company's production of sulphate of ammonia was dealt with by their London branch; 67 per cent of sales of paraffin scale and wax, and 49 per cent of candles, were also handled in London.

Advertising

The shale oil industry developed at a time when the removal of duties on newspaper advertising in 1855, and the effects of the Great Exhibition of 1851, are believed to have caused a great increase in the level of advertising of industry's products.[12] In its first year of operation ending on 31 December 1866, Young's spent £1,756 on advertising,[13] a very small amount compared with the expenditure of £80,000 per annum by Pears' soap, or Lever's £2 million over 20 years. However, it compares favourably with that of Wills, the tobacco manufacturer, whose advertising expenditure rose from £800 in 1871 to £2,400 in 1880.[14] This level was not maintained, gradually falling until 1915, when it was only £33.[15] A similar, although less marked, pattern is apparent in the Broxburn company. In the year ending 31 March 1880, £99 was spent; in 1881, £65; and in 1882, £288. In 1889, the figure reached £368. Expenditure then ranged from £39 in 1890 to £58 in 1891, before rising to £137 in 1895. Next came an increase from £50 in 1899 to £87 in 1898, and from £86 in 1912 to £108 in 1914.[16]

The reason for a relatively generous initial expenditure may be that in the 1860s, burning oil and paraffin wax candles were among 'the many new inventions which appeared' and 'were made known to potential customers and had their benefits extolled by means of advertisements'.[17] An advertisement by Young's company in 1866 is worth reproducing in full:

Young's Hard Paraffin Candles

———-

These beautiful, transparent and highly illuminating Candles realise the prophecy of Baron Liebig, 'That it would certainly be esteemed one of the greatest discoveries of the age if anyone could succeed in condensing coal gas into a white, dry, solid, odourless substance, portable and capable of being placed in a candlestick.' 'This very problem,' says Professor Hoffman in his report of the Great Exhibition of 1863 [sic] 'Mr Young has accomplished.'

Wholesale from

Young's Paraffin Light and Mineral Oil Company Limited
Lochrin Works, Edinburgh
Retail from
Innes & Grieve, St Andrew Square
D Foulis, 61 George Street
Jas. Miller, 70 Princes Street[18]

This is clearly an attempt by Young's to penetrate a market previously dominated by Price's Patent Candle Company and 'composite' candles made from stearine and coconut oil.[19]

In the late 1870s and early 1880s, the Broxburn company faced a different challenge. Young's company and the American oil industry had established a market for the new illuminant. Broxburn had to break into this, and also into the market for paraffin wax candles. This explains the early, relatively heavy, expenditure on advertising.

These two products, burning oil and candles, were examples of branded products whose advertising became important in the second half of the nineteenth century.[20] Burning oil was distributed in casks and could not be described as packaged for retail sale. The casks were, however, branded with the producer's trademark.[21]

The means adopted by the shale companies were ones common to the period. The Young's directors decided to continue the use of Young's trademarks. A candles show card was approved.[22] The Broxburn directors also approved a show card for customers,[23] and newspapers were used as indicated above. An advertisement appeared in 1880 for Broxburn's petroline: it was described in the *West Lothian Courier* as a pure crystal burning oil – 'Brilliant, Safe, Inodorous, Economical and sold by all respectable dealers'. The same newspaper printed advertisements for burning oil sold by the Pumpherston and Linlithgow companies.[24]

The shale oil concerns also utilised various exhibitions. Young's spent £72 on a case for exhibits at the Paris Exhibition; and in 1878, an exhibit of Oakbank samples received an honourable mention there. In 1885, Young's was present at the International Inventors' Exhibition in London; while Broxburn earned gold medals at an exhibition in Antwerp. Two years later, the Broxburn and Linlithgow companies displayed their products at an exhibition in Manchester; and Young's, Broxburn and Pumpherston attended the 1901 International Exhibition in Glasgow.[25]

The companies also made use of the trade press. In 1879, the Broxburn directors decided to advertise in the *Oil Trade Review*.[26] The Oakbank Company seems to have confined its advertising in later years to cylinder oils, in which it specialised. In 1886, it paid £19 for advertising in the *Oil & Colourman's Journal*, and £5 for the *Liverpool Journal of Commerce*. W.H. Smith & Son is mentioned in connection with these payments, and may well have acted as agent in the transactions.[27] Clippens, Broxburn and Linlithgow also used the trade press.[28]

The shale companies appear, therefore, to have made use of the advertising available in the period. The gradual decrease over time in expenditure may be explained by an increasing reliance on the companies' branch networks and their staff of commercial travellers. It is also true that, in the 1890s and later, the companies relied more on sulphate of ammonia and wax, which were generally sold by contract at prices agreed in advance of production.

Management of the mines and works

The directors and top management performed one very important function with regard to the mines and works. The shale oil industry was more complex than that based on natural crude oil. The shale had to be mined, taken to the retorts and distilled. The crude oil, naphtha and ammonia had then to be refined to provide saleable products. At the refinery, there had to be a sufficient supply of crude oil; this in turn required sufficient supplies of shale at the retorts, which meant ensuring that there was adequate mining capacity. The directors had to ensure that suitable initial decisions were made about mines and works.

This balance between mines, retorts and refinery had to be maintained as companies developed. Young's directors in 1883 leased shale fields at Newliston to ensure supplies of shale more suited to market conditions than their West Calder fields. This was followed by the acquisition of the Uphall company and the expansion of its works to deal with the new supplies of shale.[1] When the Broxburn directors decided to create a new crude oil works at Roman Camp to deal with hitherto unused seams of shale at Drumshoreland, they took steps to make sure that the Broxburn refinery was able to deal with the greater quantity of crude oil.[2] In 1897, the directors were able to report that: 'Every department is now admirably arranged to accomplish the maximum amount of work at greatly reduced costs.'[3] They also stated that there had been in that year the greatest output of finished products in the company's history.[4] Similar action by directors of the Oakbank and Pumpherston companies was at times taken in relation to expansion and diversification.

Young's discovery that it was possible to extract oil from cannel coal was the first and possibly the only example of entrepreneurial innovation. Any subsequent developments were in the nature of improvements in Young's process, the identification of uses for by-products or wastes, and the necessary arrangements for their exploitation. These arrangements were the responsibility of the directors and top management, and might well be described as entrepreneurial action by the firm as a corporate body. The data here are insufficient to warrant in-depth discussion of current and recent work on corporate entrepreneurship; however, it has been suggested that middle managers have an important role in this regard.[5] This is true of the shale industry: Alexander Kirk, Norman Henderson, George Beilby and James Bryson were management figures responsible for important innovations leading to new developments and directions in the industry.

Works management

The quality of management over the works and mines was obviously of considerable importance. Inefficient management and outright fraud have been identified as serious problems in the development of large firms in the first half of the nineteenth century.[6] Oil works in the Lothians and Renfrewshire were at some distance from head offices in Glasgow or Edinburgh, and they might have been similarly exposed. Some companies, in fact, did experience difficulties, which are discussed in the following pages. However, in general, the surviving refining companies were able to recruit men who were worthy members of what has been described as 'the newly rising profession of industrial managers'.[7]

The Young's directors had some difficulty in establishing a works management structure. By breaking up the partnership, the continuing concern – and, later, the limited company – was deprived of the services of Edward Meldrum, a central figure in the management of the Bathgate works and the distribution network. Shortly after the transition to limited liability status, Alexander C. Kirk, the manager at Bathgate and Addiewell left for Glasgow to pursue a career of some distinction in shipbuilding and engineering. Norman Henderson, his assistant, left to manage the Mid Calder Company's Oakbank works, and he eventually became the inventive genius behind the success of the Broxburn company. Alexander Birnie, the partnership's clerk at Bathgate, left to become manager of the Uphall Oil Company. These defections must have had serious effects on the new limited company, and until these men were replaced there was a considerable dependence on Young and his son.

Kirk did remain as manager at Addiewell for some three months after the formation of the limited company. His position was advertised in 'Scotch and English' newspapers in July 1866, appearing in the *Scotsman* of 9, 10 and 11 July 1866.[8]

Manager wanted for Oil Works at West Calder

The Directors of Young's Paraffin Light and Mineral Oil Company Limited are prepared to receive applications for the situation of manager of their extensive works at Addiewell. A Party having had experience in the management of Public Works required.

Applications, which will be treated as confidential, to be addressed to the Directors and lodged with the Secretary at the office of the company, 7 South Frederick Street, Glasgow, on or before the 14th instant.

Robert Scott, manager of the Coltness Iron Works, was selected and offered a salary of £500 per annum with a free house for a period of three years. He took up the post on 22 August. In the 1871 census he is described as Manager of Oil Works, and farmer of 68 acres: in 1867 Scott had taken a lease for five years of Auchenhard estate, and he may not have given his whole attention to the oil works. In 1872, his health appears to have become an issue; he may not have been entirely satisfactory, and was replaced by John Calderwood in October of that year.[9]

Young's then had a succession of three managers at Addiewell. John Calderwood had been a chemist with James Young before the formation of the limited company, and was employed by the company as such at Addiewell and Bathgate. He was works manager from 1872 to 1880, when he left to become general manager of Price's Patent Candle Company in London. He was succeeded by William McCutcheon, who had been works engineer and then Calderwood's assistant. In 1898 he was succeeded by J.W. Anderson, formerly with Barclay's Engineering Works at Kilmarnock. Anderson became general works manager in 1916 and remained with the company until 1919.[10]

After the takeover from Young, the Bathgate works was managed by a chemist, Napier, about whom nothing more is known. In 1871 the manager was Robert Lavender, a 41-year-old Englishman.[11] John Bagshaw is listed as assistant to Lavender in 1873 and as manager in 1884; he was also English. He was 37 in 1873, was recruited by Lavender as engineer and draughtsman at Bathgate, and had previously been engaged in planning and constructing the Belvedere Oil Works on the south bank of the River Thames below Woolwich. In 1888, after retorting and refining had ceased at Bathgate, he became manager at Uphall works, where he remained until his death in January 1917.[12]

The Oakbank company's first works manager was Norman Henderson, who had managed the Oakbank works for the Mid Calder Oil Company, having been recruited from Young's in April 1866.[13] He acted as assistant to Alexander Kirk at Bathgate from 1860, and so had considerable experience in the industry. While at Oakbank, he designed the retort that bore his name and was later the basis of Broxburn's success. When he left in 1877 to become manager at Broxburn, he was succeeded by George Beilby, a chemist with the company since 1869. After the reorganisation in 1886, the company had some difficulty with its management and Beilby left the company, with suggestions of mismanagement.[14] A replacement proved difficult to find and Robert Calderwood was appointed interim works manager in addition to his position as mining manager, a post he had held since 1869.[15] The failure to declare a dividend in 1892 was attributed to a falsification of returns by the retort manager, which led to an underestimate of the amount and cost of shale used.[16] However, in the first decade of the twentieth century the company had the services of Alexander Thomson, who had previously managed the Pumpherston, Lanark and Caledonian companies. Thomson later became the chief constructional engineer of Scottish Oils Limited.[17]

The first manager of the Broxburn works was Norman Henderson, previously manager at Oakbank. He remained with the company, latterly in a consultative capacity until his death in 1917. In addition to experience in oil works management, he was also a talented engineer. While with the Broxburn company, he designed important improvements to the industry's processes. He made significant changes to his original retort to cope with the demand for sulphate of ammonia, and was responsible for a system of continuous distillation that considerably reduced the cost of refining, and a sweating process for the purification of wax scale. He was awarded a gold medal at the Exhibition of Industry, Science and Art held in Edinburgh in 1886.[18]

The Pumpherston experience illustrates the difficulties faced by the companies in the early 1880s, when a number of concerns were floated. The company's first manager was Alexander C. Thomson, who had been assistant works manager with the Walkinshaw company in Renfrewshire. Walkinshaw had been formed in 1880 to take over two oil works in Renfrewshire, and it was intended to spend £50,000 in increasing their capacity to 3,000,000 gallons of crude oil per year. Thomson's involvement in this would have made him well qualified for the post at Pumpherston, but he resigned in October 1884 after differences with the managing director and the board. It must be said that he left an almost completed works, which in the first four months of 1885 made a gross profit of £5,348. He later had a very successful career in the industry.[19]

The company experienced some difficulty in filling the position. On 19 December the board considered applications, but found none suitable. G.D.H. Mitchell was appointed on 30 March 1885: he had been chemist at Oakbank for some years, and in 1881 had acted as works manager in the absence of George Beilby, for which he was awarded £10 by the directors.[20] Mitchell proved extremely unsatisfactory, however. In 1886 the poor quality of semi-refined wax became a problem. To make things easier for the manager, the board appointed an assistant,[21] but during the summer and autumn of 1886 relations between Mitchell and the board worsened to the extent that the board decided to revise Mitchell's contract to make him carry out his duties properly. This decision was strongly opposed by William Fraser, who resigned from the board and as managing director, ending his letter of resignation by putting on record that he had 'urged the Board for the last twelve months to get rid of this man who has done so much already to crush the company and who will do more if he has the opportunity of so doing.'[22]

The board persevered with Mitchell, but he agreed to resign on 5 April 1887 if required to do so by the directors. Communications continued to be strained, and Mitchell also behaved strangely towards the works staff, ultimately refusing for several days to allow the cashier access to the works. Eventually, he was dismissed and James Bryson was appointed in his place. A native of Coatbridge, he had served an engineering apprenticeship with the Summerlee Iron Company, later working with Scott's Shipbuilding and Engineering Company at Greenock, the Carron Iron Company, and the Gartsherrie Iron Company, from which he moved to Pumpherston. He was elected to the board in 1903 and in 1916, on the death of William Fraser, he became joint managing director with Fraser's son, also William. He remained with the company until 1919, becoming general works manager of Scottish Oils Limited after the amalgamation. Bryson designed the retort that bears his name and was the industry's mainstay in the years up to the Great War.[23]

The four companies had five refineries, each with a manager; the Uphall and Addiewell works of Young's company also had assistant managers. The associated crude oil works were under the control of the relative refinery manager, but where these were at a distance from the refinery a manager was appointed. Young's had the Hopetoun crude works near Winchburgh, built by the Uphall company. Pumpherston had crude oil works at Deans and Seafield in West Lothian, and later at Tarbrax in Lanarkshire. The Broxburn company had the Roman Camp crude oil works. In the early twentieth century, Oakbank established the Niddry Castle crude oil works at Winchburgh. All of these had managers.

Chemists

James Young was a chemist whose training had enabled him to make the discovery that led to the establishment at Bathgate of what has been called 'the first real oil works in the whole world'.[24] Chemistry was to remain an important element in the industry's management during the various phases of its development. Mackie discusses the chemists' role by noting that, in the nineteenth century, chemical firms were founded by men like Young, who had developed the necessary processes. Later, development work was often carried out by consultants, leaving industry's own chemists to undertake analysis and quality control.[25] He cites in particular the examples of the alkali, steel and brewing industries; and at first sight his observations may also be true of the shale industry. In 1900 Daniel Steuart, Broxburn's chief chemist, commented: 'Oil-works chemists are too busy with pressing practical problems to have time for purely scientific investigations.'[26] However, the paper in which he states this makes it very clear that Steuart himself had a wide knowledge of the state of research in the composition of different crude oils. It is also true that the 'pressing practical problems' were somewhat more complex than routine analysis.

Oil shale appeared in 21 distinct seams with different qualities. The same shale could also vary in different areas of the seam and also with the depth. The changing nature of the demand for the various products of the industry meant that the value of seams changed over time. Steuart provides a detailed description of work carried out on the composition of various shales by himself and other chemists in the industry.[27] Between 1863 and 1865, numerous experiments on shales were carried out at Young's Limefield laboratory.[28]

Shale crude oil was much more difficult to refine than natural petroleum, which required only one distillation and one treatment with vitriol and soda to produce burning oil. Shale crude oil, because of the violent process it undergoes in the retorts, required three or four distillations.[29] Chemists were involved in quality control at many stages of manufacture, and this often involved more than simple analysis. The industry was new in the second half of the nineteenth century: standards had to be set and maintained; and burning oil, one of the more important products, required constant attention, particularly with regard to its flashpoint. In addition to routine analysis, oil works chemists developed methods and apparatus for the necessary tests.[30] Solid paraffin wax became a highly important product, and required very careful examination to ensure quality, consistency and freedom from impurities. Again, oil works chemists were involved – not simply in the day-to-day testing, but also in devising methods and equipment.[31]

The number of chemists employed by the industry in the period up to the Great War cannot be established with any precision, but some qualified conclusions can be drawn. From a variety of sources, 42 individuals have been identified. Obviously, not all were employed for the entire period. In 1890 the Scottish Mineral Oil Association suggested that the chief chemists of each member company should meet to discuss the problems encountered in the analysis of paraffin scale. In the resulting paper, ten individuals were identified as 'chief chemists', suggesting that there may have been as many as 20 chemists in the ten refining works involved.[32] Young's company, at its works at Addiewell and Bathgate in 1871, had the services of William McIvor and John Calderwood, who had previously worked with Young at his Limefield laboratory. J.J. Coleman was also at Addiewell at the time George Alston was enumerated as a 'chemist's assistant at oil works' in 1871. In 1891, the company had the services at Addiewell of William Blair Syme and two assistants. At Uphall, John Stuart Thomson, appointed in 1884 as chief chemist in 1891, had two assistants.[33]

In 1869 the Oakbank company employed John Galletly and George Thomas Beilby; in 1883, J.O. Morrison and G.D.H. Mitchell were in post. The Pumpherston company had Edwin M. Bailey as a junior chemist from 1886 to 1891, along with, at various times during that period, J.O. Morrison, James Snodgrass and Mr Milburn. The Broxburn company in 1891 had Daniel Rankine Steuart as chief chemist, with one assistant, John Woodrow.[34]

It seems clear, therefore, that the four refining companies that survived to the amalgamation in 1919 made use of chemical expertise in managing their operations. There is also some evidence that the companies which failed in the 1890s and early

1900s employed chemists. The Lists of Members in the *Journal of the Society of Chemical Industry* show that Clippens had Nigel McPhie in 1884 and John Gray in 1887, while the Burntisland company had D.A. Sutherland in 1887 and Mr Milburn in 1891.[35] The available sources also show that there were laboratory facilities at the various works. Journal Number 2 of the Broxburn Oil Company has a laboratory account for the year ending 31 March 1880, and the Pumpherston company's Private Ledger Number 1 has a similar account. I.J. Redwood expressed his thanks in 1886 to his employers (Young's) for the use of the Addiewell laboratory.[36]

There was some movement between the various refining companies, and also to concerns outside of the shale industry. For example, John Galletly is first encountered in Young's service at Bathgate in 1859, next appearing at Oakbank in 1869 and last seen at Addiewell from 1881 to 1886. R. Denholm left the Broxburn company in 1905 for a position with the Assam Oil Company.[37] Some chemists moved into management within the industry. George Beilby became manager at Oakbank, John Calderwood was appointed as manager at Addiewell in 1872, and G.D.H. Mitchell left Oakbank to be a rather unsuccessful manager at Pumpherston. James Snodgrass left Pumpherston in 1889 to become manager of the Caledonian Oil Company, and Nigel McPhie managed Clippens' Straiton works in 1885.[38]

Robin Mackie indicates the difficulties in establishing the qualifications of people enumerated as chemists in 1911.[39] This is also a problem in the shale industry, but a number of the chemists were men of some distinction. R.H. Findlater of the Broxburn company and John Gray of Clippens were both Fellows of the Institute of Chemistry (FIC); Burntisland's D.A. Sutherland was a Fellow of the Chemical Society (FCS). Four men in particular deserve a little more recognition, and sufficient information is available to provide this.

Edwin M. Bailey qualified as an analytical chemist in Glasgow and was appointed as a junior chemist at the Pumpherston works in 1886. From 1894 he served the company as chief chemist, until his appointment as chief chemist at the new Scottish Oils laboratory at Middleton Hall. He was frequently consulted on the quality of crude petroleum from fields in Borneo, Burma, New Zealand, Trinidad and Peru.[40]

John Calderwood studied chemistry under Professor George Wilson at Edinburgh University, in Germany, and later with Dr Angus Smith at Manchester, before joining Young as a research chemist at Limefield in 1863. He was elected a Fellow of the Royal Society of Edinburgh in 1879, proposed by James Young, Lyon Playfair, Professor Alexander Crum Brown and Sir James Dewar. After a successful transfer in 1872 to management of the Addiewell works, he was persuaded in 1880 to become manager (later managing director) of Price's Patent Candle Company Limited, at that time the largest manufacturer of wax and candles in the United Kingdom. The company was in some difficulty, and Calderwood is credited with transforming its fortunes. Calderwood was an original member of the Society of Chemical Industry, a Member of Council of the Society in 1886 and 1889, and a Vice-President in 1894.[41]

Daniel Rankine Steuart studied under professors Crum Brown and P.G. Tait, as well as with Crum Brown's assistant, William Dittmar, at Edinburgh University. He then went to Munich to study with Erlenmeyer. He came back to Scotland, working under Dittmar at the Andersonian in Glasgow for two years. He was appointed assistant chemist at the Oakbank works in 1876, and became chief chemist to the Broxburn company on 1 January 1878. He retired in 1920. He was well known in the shale and petroleum industries, publishing numerous papers on shale and shale oil, and particularly associated with the concerns expressed in the last quarter of the nineteenth century on the safety of lamp oils. He was a member of the Philosophical Society of Glasgow, elected a Fellow of the Institute of Chemistry in 1878, and a Fellow of the Chemical Society in 1881. He was a member of the Chemistry Advisory Committee of Heriot-Watt College, and elected a Fellow of the Royal Society of Edinburgh in 1916.[42]

George Thomas Beilby came to Oakbank in 1869 as assistant to John Galletly, having been educated at Edinburgh University. In the 1870s and early 1880s, his research on the presence of nitrogen in various minerals led to his designing with William Young (the Clippens works manager) a retort that greatly increased the recovery of sulphate of ammonia from shale. This Young & Beilby retort, and its many derivatives, was a major factor in the survival of the industry in the face of competition from natural petroleum, which did not produce this valuable fertiliser. Beilby went on to design a column still to improve methods of recovering ammonia from the crude liquid produced by the retorts. This improvement in extracting ammonia was a major contribution by an oil works chemist to the industry's success. Beilby went on to achieve distinction in different branches of the science: he studied fuel economy and smoke prevention in coal consumption, and was director of Fuel Research from 1917–23. He was a Fellow of the Institute of Chemistry and of the Chemical Society; and President of the Society of Chemical Industry in 1899, and of the Institute of Chemistry from 1909 to 1912. He was awarded honorary doctorates by the universities of Glasgow, Birmingham and Durham, and was chairman of the Royal Technical College of Glasgow 1907–23. He was a Fellow of the Royal Society, and was knighted in 1916.[43]

Two men who achieved some distinction in other disciplines within the industry were educated in chemistry. Alexander Cunningham Thomson managed the Pumpherston, Caledonian and Oakbank companies before becoming chief constructional engineer with Scottish Oils. He studied chemistry at the Andersonian College in Glasgow, and was subsequently briefly employed as a chemist at Uphall and Walkinshaw.[44] William Fraser, son of the Pumpherston founder, studied in the

Department of Technical Chemistry at Glasgow's Royal Technical College. He later joined his father in the Pumpherston company's management, and ended his career as chairman of the Anglo-Iranian Oil Company, later the British Petroleum Company Limited (now BP plc).[45]

Contemporary opinion held that deficiencies in technical and scientific education contributed to what was seen as a decline in industrial performance after the 'Mid Victorian Boom'.[46] This view was generally accepted by later historians. For example, Chandler attributes the continuing influence of 'gentlemen' in British industrial management to the failure of British scientific and technical education.[47] Sanderson, however, considers this view unnecessarily gloomy.[48] He accepts that, initially, British industry and education may have lagged behind other countries, particularly the United States and Germany, but that by 1890 Britain had started to catch up. The period up to 1914 then saw the establishment of provincial colleges, which were to become civic universities, and of municipal technical colleges. He concludes that we must doubt the assumption that defects in educating the workforce were responsible for the British economy's decline before 1914.

Shale oil was an example of a successful industry in this period. Among the chemists and managers, a significant number were educated at colleges and universities. The University of Edinburgh in the 1850s, 1860s and 1870s figured in the careers of Alexander Kirk, John Calderwood, George Beilby and Daniel Steuart, all of whom made significant contributions to the industry's development. The Andersonian Institute, or Anderson's University, in Glasgow educated James Young, Lyon Playfair and A.C. Thomson. From the 1790s, it provided classes in science and technology, later becoming the Royal Technical College, now Strathclyde University.[49] In 1870, Young endowed the Young Chair of Chemical Technology at Anderson's University, the oldest chair of applied chemistry in the United Kingdom.[50] Glasgow's Royal Technical College produced William Fraser, later Lord Strathalmond, chairman of the British Petroleum Company Limited. It seems, therefore, that the shale industry in the years before the Great War had links with the established Scottish universities and colleges, to their mutual benefit.

Subordinate management at the works

In 1887 before Bryson's appointment, the Pumpherston directors sought the opinion of William Young, the manager of the Clippens company and one of the designers of the Young & Beilby retort. He advised that, in oil works then in operation, it was difficult to recruit a manager 'possessing all the necessary qualifications for the proper management of the various departments': it was necessary to divide the works into departments and have one qualified man running the crude department, and another overseeing the refining.[51] This had, in fact, been the practice in

Young's company for some years: in 1871, the Addiewell works had a retort foreman and a foreman oil refiner. When the refining of scale into paraffin wax assumed importance, this was treated as a separate department, and Young's employed a foreman paraffin refiner in 1871.[52] By 1891, all four of the refining companies that survived up to the 1919 amalgamation had developed management structures organised in this manner. In locations where sulphate of ammonia became the most important product, a separate foreman was in charge of its manufacture, as at Pumpherston.[53]

The large staff of coopers required for despatching liquid products in casks and barrels was also supervised by foremen. Many other tradesmen of different kinds were required for the maintenance of the plant, buildings and workmen's houses. In the larger establishments, each trade had its own foreman. In 1891, Young's had the services of a foreman joiner, foreman engine fitter, foreman cooper, foreman mason, and a traffic manager.[54]

Clerical staff at the works

Clerical staff were also required at the various works, in most cases headed by a cashier. In 1891, the census returns for the parishes concerned show cashiers in post at Addiewell, Uphall, Hopetoun and Broxburn; one was also in post at Pumpherston in 1887.[55] It is not possible to be completely certain about the size of the clerical staffs at the various works. A photograph of the Addiewell oil works' clerical staff published in 1949 is supposed to have been taken about 64 years before, i.e., about 1885. It gives the names of 20 male clerks and the cashier, W.R. Scott.[56] It is clear that the company had a substantial clerical work force at its Addiewell works and associated mines.

By 1918, the clerical workforce at Young's three works comprised: at Addiewell, 18 males and 8 females; at Uphall, 15 males and 14 females; and at Hopetoun, 3 males and 2 females. At the associated mines, 5 men and 1 woman were in post.[57] In 1903, Pumpherston had a substantial clerical workforce at its mines and in its head office. In June of that year, an excursion to Garelochhead involved 50 members of the works' and head office clerical staff.[58]

Mines

The manufacturing side of the industry, of course, included the shale mines. These were under the general supervision of the relevant works manager, but mining required very different skills from those involved in oil production. Caldwell describes the methods used in working oil shale, and in so doing provides an insight into the management responsibilities involved. The productive miners worked in teams of two or three. One of the men contracted to work a 'place' at an agreed price per ton. He was responsible for working it safely and properly, paying the wages of his 'drawer' and additional 'faceman', if one was required.[59] This would seem to leave little responsibility for management, apart from negotiating the price. However, in the 'stoop and room' method of working described in Chapter 2, a number of factors required care. The levels and upsets forming the 'rooms' had to be driven in the correct direction, and the rooms had to be of suitable dimensions for the nature of the seam. The size of the 'stoops' was important for the stability of the mine. In steeply inclined workings, the stoops had to be considerably larger than in level seams because the inclination effectively reduced the area supporting the roof. This could cause a 'creep' or 'crush', which could very quickly destroy a working.[60] Although the miners may have been self-employed, mine management had considerable responsibility for ensuring that the work was properly carried out.

The companies and therefore the managers were responsible for the 'oncost' work: the maintenance of roadways; ventilation; and keeping the mines free of water. An important function was providing and maintaining the underground haulage system. Some mines relied on the 'drawers' to take the filled hutches to the pit or mine bottom. In others, horses were used. In many mines and pits, mechanical haulage was the norm and involved various forms of self-acting inclines and endless rope systems.[61] It is clear, therefore, that considerable management effort was required to ensure the right level of shale output to keep the retorts working.

Young's demonstrated some anxiety about appointing their first mine manager, a decision that was subject to the approval of Mr McCreath, a mining engineer.[62] Oakbank's first mining manager was Robert Calderwood, who had a long association with the mining industry as an engine keeper, coal miner, overseer and manager. Before arriving at Oakbank he had operated, on lease from Robert Fraser, a small oil works at Drumcross, near Bathgate. When he retired in 1890, he was replaced by James B. Sneddon, who had been assistant manager since 1886 and had apparently survived criticism from Charles Fraser in 1888. Aged 28 in 1891, Sneddon remained with the company until the amalgamation in 1919, and was later agent for the Western Group of Mines for Scottish Oils Limited. He was awarded the OBE in 1935.[63]

The Broxburn company's initial mining manager was Alexander Kennedy, a native of Govan who spent much of his early working life in the Monklands area of Lanarkshire, where he managed the Airdrie ironstone pit of Robert Addie & Sons. He came to Broxburn in 1866 to manage the shale mines worked by Robert Bell, becoming mining manager to the Broxburn Oil Company in 1877, holding this post until his retirement in 1905.

Pumpherston appointed William Wilson as its first mining manager. He had been manager of the mines at Uphall under William Fraser. He was replaced in 1884 by James Caldwell, who was recruited from Robert Addie & Sons, Airdrie and remained with the company until his retirement in 1920.[64]

For the early years, little is known of the organisation of individual pits or of the management structure at the mines belonging to the larger concerns. However, the tragedy at Uphall's Starlaw pit in April 1870 throws some light on management practice at that time. Seven men out of the 56 employed underground died because of a fire in the only shaft. A roadsman, John Pate, 'exercised a general supervision of the underground workings' under Robert Watt, the manager, and a fireman, Robert Moffat, was also employed.[65] Pate and the engineman seem to have organised the early efforts which brought all but 7 of the 56 men to the surface before the winding rope burned through. Birnie, the Uphall works manager, and Simpson, one of the partners, arrived later to take charge. It seems to have been the case that Pate was in day-to-day control of workings involving 56 men, but it is not clear whether Watt was the manager of the mine or in overall charge of the oil works and mine. A roadsman, 'reddsman' or 'brusher' was employed to keep roadways clear and to 'brush' dangerous or obstructing material from the roof and sides of roads. It is interesting to note that Pate and Moffat were designated simply as 'miners' in 1871.[66] These two men seem not to have differentiated their roles in the pit from those of other workers.

Shale mines were brought under the same system of control as coal mines by the Coal Mines Regulation Act of 1872. This required that any colliery employing more than 30 men must have a certificated manager. Boards were set up to examine candidates for certificates in seven topics covering the whole range of mining practice. The Inspector for Scotland East District reported that two examinations had taken place in 1873, with 60 candidates passing and 14 failing. The examinations were therefore more than a perfunctory exercise. However, it was stated that 'certificates of service have also been granted to those who were managers prior to the passing of the Act'. The 1887 Coal Mines Regulation Act provided for first and second class certificates, the latter being appropriate for under-managers and subordinate officials.[67]

These regulations were concerned with the safety of the miners. Here, it is of more interest to use the inspectors' annual reports as a valuable source in uncovering how the management structure developed within the shale industry's mining section. The Inspector for the Scotland East area, Ralph Moore, provided in each annual report a list of mines in his area. From 1875 onwards, this included the names of the proprietor and the manager, and the numbers of men employed above and below ground at each mine or pit.

In 1875 there were 19 mines or pits belonging to seven concerns. Each concern had one manager. Three of these were in charge of one mine or pit; one was in charge of two; one in charge of three; one in charge of four; and one oversaw seven mines or pits. The total number of underground miners was 911, an average of 48; and there was an average of one manager to 130 men. The smallest pit or mine had 15 underground workers and the largest 106. Only four had fewer than 30 underground workers and of these, three were managed by men responsible for a number of units.[68]

By 1885 the number of mines and pits had risen to 44. Three managers had only one mine or pit to supervise; four had two; five had three; and one had six. Two men shared the responsibility for Young's 12 Addiewell pits and mines. The mines and pits were larger there: 3,538 underground miners worked in the 44 openings, an average of 80. The smallest employed 11 men, while 13 openings had 100 men or more. Eight had 30 or fewer men, all of whom were associated with other workings. There was an average of one manager to 236 men.[69]

The 1885 Census of Wages provides information on the subordinate management in the mines. Although 17 schedules were issued for completion by employers in the shale industry, only six were returned, but these covered 1,670 (43 per cent) of the men employed. Thirteen out of 1,555 underground workers were described as oversmen,[70] and there might well have been 30 such men in the industry as a whole. Their existence went some way towards compensating for the increase in number of miners per manager.

In 1913, only six concerns remained. There were 41 mines or pits staffed by 14 managers and 40 under-managers. With 4,634 underground workers, there was an average of 86 workers per management official. The managers generally were responsible for more than one opening, but they had the assistance of an under-manager for each. The list of mines fails to give details of the men employed in each opening; although a total for the mines under a given manager is sometimes listed. Nevertheless, it is clear that mines and pits had become larger. Two had 293 and 297 underground workers respectively, and the average was 113.[71]

There is little doubt that the shale mines' management structure was strongly influenced by legislation and the Mines Inspectorate, but it is also evident that, judging by the numbers of officials involved, management became more rigorous as the industry developed. This may have been one reason for the survival of the fitter companies and the failure of the rest.

Remuneration

The individuals involved in management were obviously of considerable importance to the success of the companies, and the nature and level of their rewards is of interest. At the top of any salary scale were the general managers or managing directors. John Fyfe was recruited as general manager of Young's in 1873 with a salary of £1,200, increasing over three years to £1,500. By 1905, when he had been managing director for over 20 years, his salary was £2,500 per annum with a bonus equivalent to the dividend on shares worth £10,000.[1] Between 1901 and 1914 the company failed to pay a dividend in only two years. Fyfe's bonus over the 14 years amounted to £5,850, an average of £417 per year. He may have been exceptionally well rewarded: his successor, T.W. Steven, had a salary of £1,400 per annum, with a bonus equivalent to the dividend on £5,000 worth of shares.[2]

As managing director of the Broxburn company, William Kennedy's initial salary was £750 per annum, plus the dividend on a notional paid-up capital of £2,500. In the years from 1880 to 1886 the company paid dividends of 25 per cent, and Kennedy's bonus would have added £625 to his salary; in 1889 his salary increased to £1,200. Although not so successful as in earlier years, the company failed to declare a dividend in only four years up to 1914. Dividends ranged from 5 per cent to 20 per cent, and would have added appreciably to his salary. William Love, Kennedy's successor, was paid £1,400 in 1914.[3]

When William Fraser died in 1916, his son, also William, was appointed joint managing director of the Pumpherston company with a salary of £1,050 plus a commission of 1 per cent of net profit. It is not clear how the profit was to be established, but the amount distributed as dividend on ordinary shares in 1917 was £114,200.[4] One per cent of that figure amounts to £1,142, slightly more than Fraser's basic salary.

John Wishart, general manager and director of the Oakbank company, was paid £1,000 as a bonus for the year ending 31 March 1901. For the years ending 31 March 1913 and 31 March 1914, he received £750.[5]

It seems clear that, in the years up to the Great War, the most senior figures in the industry's management enjoyed salaries and bonuses of in excess of £1,000 per annum. Fraser identifies this, in 1914, as the entry point to the 'comfortably off middle class'.[6]

Apart from the general managers, the senior officials in head offices were the company secretaries. In 1867, O.T.B. Gardner of Young's was paid £400 per annum.

In 1878, Oakbank's Peter W. Turner was paid £150, rising to £175 with a bonus of 2.5–4 per cent of commercial profits. As the companies grew in size, administration became more complex and secretaries were more highly rewarded. In 1886, John Wishart had a salary of £225 per annum. In 1914, William Montgomerie was paid £750 as secretary of the Broxburn company. In 1919, R.C. McCulley of the Pumpherston company had his salary increased from £700 to £850.[7]

In 1887, the cashier and bookkeeper at Oakbank's head office were each paid £90 per annum. Senior clerks had between £50 and £80; juniors from £15 to £35. At Young's registered office, there were at various times accountants paid from £300 to £380, bookkeepers from £200 to £250, and a chief clerk paid £200. The clerical staff were paid from £40–£50 for juniors, £65–£100 for more senior clerks, and £115–£155 for the clerks working for the managing director and secretary. In industry and commerce generally in 1909, 23 per cent of clerks earned more than £160 per annum; those earning less than this figure averaged £80. Only one of the 18 clerks in Young's registered office had more than £160 – i.e., 5 per cent. The remaining 17 averaged £82. Young's clerks therefore seem to have been paid about or perhaps slightly above the national average. The Oakbank clerks were paid considerably less, but there may well have been a general increase between 1887 and 1913.[8]

Works managers were paid at various rates according to the size and complexity of the operation. Henderson had £300 per annum at Oakbank in 1875, with a bonus equivalent to the dividend on £1,000 of shares. In 1885, when the works was being extended, Beilby had £150 for one quarter's salary – i.e., equal to £600 per annum. In 1880, John Calderwood, manager of Addiewell works, had a salary of £500 plus a bonus of £160. His successor, William McCutchon, received £500, with a bonus of £30, in 1884. At the same time, the manager of the Bathgate works, which was being run down, received £350. J.W. Anderson, McCutchon's successor at Addiewell, was appointed in a period of difficulty for the company, and indeed for the industry. He was paid £300, rising to £350, plus a bonus equivalent to the dividend on £1,000 of stock. When he was appointed general works manager, based at Addiewell, he enjoyed a salary of £700 per annum.[9]

When Norman Henderson was appointed manager of the Broxburn works, his salary was £400 plus the dividend on 200 paid-up shares. This rose to £525 in 1880. In 1887 he is recorded as receiving £750 and commission of £300, and in 1889 his salary was £850. His successor, Cuthbertson, was paid £700 in 1914, while Henderson himself received £200.[10]

A.C. Thomson, the first manager of the Pumpherston company's works, had a salary of £400, rising to £500. His successor, G.D.H. Mitchell, received from £500 to £600. I have no information on James Bryson's salary, but in 1916, before his appointment as joint managing director, he was in receipt of a 1 per cent commission on the company's net profits, which was probably worth over £1,000.[11] Bryson, and to a greater extent Henderson, must also have benefited from royalties on inventions that were widely adopted in the industry. In fact, this caused some resentment. In 1889, the Hermand chairman was reported as saying that 'it was disgusting to find they could hardly move in any direction without having to pay excessive royalties to men who, as managers of works, had procured patents for everything connected with the trade'.[12]

Assistant managers were paid considerably less than their principals. In 1873 McCutchon, as assistant to Calderwood at Addiewell, was paid £250 per annum; and Bagshaw at Bathgate received £180. Chemists played an important part in process development and control. They were rewarded with salaries roughly in line with those of assistant works managers. For example, in 1889, W.B. Syme, chemist at Addiewell, was paid £250 per annum; at Uphall, J.S. Thomson had the same. Daniel Steuart of the Broxburn company, who achieved considerable distinction in the field, had a salary of £485 per annum by 1914, and an assistant earning £275.[13]

Information about the salaries of works clerical staff is regrettably scarce. Matthew Cowan, the first head clerk at Broxburn, was paid £100 per annum, and his assistant £1 10s. per week. In 1884, the chief clerk at the Uphall works was paid £160 per annum.[14]

The salaries of mining managers varied greatly. Thomas Prentice, in charge of a number of Young's mines around West Calder, was paid £450 per annum. J. Hardie at Uphall was paid £260. Alexander Kennedy, Broxburn mining manager, was offered a salary of £150, with the alternative of £1 10s. (£1.50) per 1,000 tons of shale; this would have provided a salary of slightly over £200. In 1916, his successor at Broxburn was paid £360 per annum, and the Roman Camp manager £350.[15]

On the distribution side, the salaries of branch managers varied with the importance of the branch. At the start, Young's salaries ranged from the Glasgow and Bristol managers' £150 per annum to the £250 enjoyed by the London manager. In 1901, the assistant manager of Young's London branch was paid £300 per annum, with a commission of ¼ per cent on sales in excess of £50,000. In 1901, London branch sales were £103,077, which would have added £132 to his salary. In 1907 the assistant manager of the Glasgow branch received £250 per annum, with a commission of ⅛ per cent on sales over £75,000. In 1905 sales at the branch were £132,756, which would have added £72 to his salary. In 1889 the manager of the Hull branch had a salary of £250 per annum, with a commission of 1 per cent on sales over £15,000: in 1901, sales at that branch totalled £21,937 and would have added £69 to his salary. A commercial traveller at Young's London branch was paid £160 per annum, rising to £180 after three years; a traveller in Manchester district received £150.[16]

Income tax in the late nineteenth century was levied on incomes greater than £160 per annum. By the late nineteenth century, income tax payers included such as those in occupations such as 'skilled mechanics, bank clerks, solicitors' clerks, board school teachers, county council clerks, sanitary inspectors, police inspectors, curates, and commercial travellers among others. The average earnings of income tax payers were £855 in 1880 and £838 in 1913.'[17] The salaries of sales staff and the management of works and mines ranged from around £150 per annum to over £700. The lower paid were in the bottom end of the middle classes, and the higher paid in the middle ranks.

The works managers were assisted by foremen overseeing various productive departments and the squads of tradesmen required to maintain the works and property. They were paid at rates considerably higher than the men they super-vised. In 1886, 6 of the 12 active concerns in the industry submitted returns to a Board of Trade Census of Wages. Five foremen were paid an average of 41s. and 5d. per week; 16 received between 30s. and 35s., an average of 32s. and 2d. The stillmen, refiners, retortmen, sulphate of ammonia makers, and pressmen were paid between 22s. and 24s. 9d. per week. Tradesmen received between 26s. and 31s. 2d. The highest paid were the coopers, whose work was essential to the distribution of the products. They were also protected by a very strong trade union organisation.[18]

A wages record for the Uphall company from 1 November 1881 to 4 October 1882 has survived. It deals only with men employed on maintenance work and reveals that they worked for ten hours each day from Monday to Friday, and seven hours on Saturday, a total of 54 hours per week. They were paid fortnightly at daily rates.

It can be seen that, where a comparison is possible, the weekly rates given in the Census of Wages do not differ radically from those at Uphall in 1882. The census also provides the means for comparing wage levels in the shale industry with those in industry more generally. The average wage of 3,021 men in the shale industry was 25s., compared with 24s. 7d. in the 38 trades dealt with in the report. The industry ranked 14th out of the 38. Possibly of more significance is that 54.4 per cent of shale oil workers earned between 25s. and 30s. per week, compared with a general average of 20.5 per cent of workers in other trades.[19] At each works, the associated mines were in the charge of a manager, assisted by under managers and oversmen. The mining managers were responsible to the management of the associated works and were paid at rates somewhat lower than these managers. The oversmen received from 33s. to 40s. and 1d. per week, when the miners they supervised were paid from 27s. to 32s. per week, a substantial difference.[20]

The works officials and foremen were rewarded in ways other than higher pay. Managers, chemists and cashiers were accommodated, often rent-free, in relatively substantial houses. In 1891, the Addiewell manager, William McCutcheon, lived in Breich Villa a house of nine rooms; the assistant manager, James Maxwell, had Beechwood cottage with eight rooms; the chemist, William B. Syme, resided in the seven-room Elm Cottage; and the cashier, William R. Scott, was allocated

Table 16.1 Wages at Uphall Oil Company Limited's Uphall Works, 1882, compared with Census of Wages, 1886

Description	Various daily wage rates					Weekly rates	Rates per census wages
Fitter	5s.	4s. 8d.	4s. 6d.	4s. 4d.	4s. 2d.	25s. to 30s.	26s.
Boilermaker	5s.	4s. 8d.	4s.			24s. to 30s.	27s. 10d.
Plumber	5s.	4s. 2d.	3s. 8d.			22s. to 30s.	
Tinsmith	3s. 4d.					20s.	
Bricklayer	5s. 4d.	4s. 6d.	3s. 4d.			20s. to 32s.	
Slater	4s. 8d.					28s.	
Blacksmith	4s. 8d.	4s. 4d.				26s. to 28s.	26s. 11d.
Joiner	4s. 8d.	3s. 4d.				20s. to 28s.	
Cooper	5s.					30s.	31s. 2d.
Mason	5s. 5d.					32/6	
Surfaceman	3s. 8d.	3s. 4d.				20s. to 22s.	
Platelayer	3s. 4d.					20s.	
Hammerman	3s.	2s. 4d.				14s. to 18s.	18s. 2d.
Scavenger	2s. 8d.					16s.	
Labourer	4s.	3s. 4d.	3s. 2d.	3s.	2s. 10d.		
				2s. 8d.	2s. 6d.	15s. to 24s.	17s. 4d.
Fitters' Labourers	2s. 8d.	3s	3s. 4d.			16s. to 20s.	18s. 1d.
Foremen							
Bricklayer	6s. 4d.					38s.	
Joiner	5s. 6d.					33s.	30s.
Labourer	5s.					30s.	to 41s. 5d.
Boilermaker	5s. 6d.					33s.	

Source: Uphall Oil Company Limited, Time Abstract Book No. 2, Fortnight ending 23 Aug. 1882.

Hawthorn Cottage, also boasting seven rooms. Similar arrangements were made by other companies. At Broxburn, Norman Henderson, the works manager, occupied Broxburn Lodge, a house of 14 rooms, while works chemist Daniel Steuart lived at Osborne Cottage, with 12 rooms. At Pumpherston James Bryson, the manager, and James Caldwell, the mining manager, occupied cottages of five rooms each.[21]

The foremen also benefited from better quality housing. The houses provided for the workmen were generally of one room or two. At Addiewell, there were 290 two-apartment and 70 single-apartment houses. There were 14 houses of 3 rooms in Farady Place for foremen. The Pumpherston company provided 27 single-apartment and 173 two-apartment houses. For foremen, 19 houses of 3 rooms were provided.[22]

The importance of capable foremen and officials was recognised in other ways. At Addiewell, in the early years of Young's company, the foremen were engaged on individual contracts, often for a period of years. The Broxburn directors authorised 'gifts' to their foremen in 1880, which were not to exceed £100 in total. The following year the same bonuses were again authorised, and the directors were of the opinion that 'it would be advisable to have agreements with the principal men'. In 1882 bonuses totalling £153 were paid to foremen, and £20 to the chemist. The company's officials were similarly rewarded. In 1880, Mr King, the secretary, was allowed an 'honorarium' of £50. At the annual meeting in 1883 a shareholder suggested that the firm's officials deserved some recognition for their efforts. This was taken up by the directors, who reported that bonuses had been paid to these men, who had been 'instrumental in bringing the company to its present prosperous position'. In 1910, the Oakbank company paid a bonus of £500 to John Wishart, the managing director, and £446 to officials and foremen; in 1911 the amounts were £250 and £224. The dividend in 1910 was 10 per cent, and in 1911 5 per cent.[23] It seems, therefore, that these bonuses varied according to the company's performance.

Company accounts as an aid to management

Sidney Pollard has stated that the 'practice of using accounts as direct aids to management was not one of the achievements of the British industrial revolution'.[1] It has also been assumed by some historians that the high profit margins in the Industrial Revolution industries made it unnecessary for manufacturers to pay attention to costs. These views have been challenged, particularly in the cases of textiles and iron, where there was in fact keen competition.[2] James Young and his partners in the 1850s and early 1860s certainly enjoyed high levels of profit, but American exports soon produced a highly competitive market. In fact from the 1870s onwards, the shale industry's product prices were established by reference to those set by the large imports of American petroleum products into Europe.

The industry naturally had to look to controlling its costs. This is discussed in some detail in Chapter 2; here it is sufficient to point out that, to some extent, costs as well as prices were subject to external influences. Wages were a major consideration. The Pumpherston company paid the men at its three works £87,442 in the year ending 30 April 1899, 34.82 per cent of sales totalling £251,085 for the same period.[3] Shale miners' wages were obviously influenced by the much larger coal industry. It is also important that the shale industry was not able to take advantage of cost accounting to dispense with unprofitable products, as the Carron Company did with nails, anchors and anvils.[4] In the shale industry, none of the products could be obtained without the others; all that could be achieved was a change in the proportions, by using different shales or the development of new plant.

It has been suggested that 'historians, untrained in accounting, have difficulty dealing with the increasing sophistication and complexity of accounting',[5] an assertion that is certainly true in this case. In earlier chapters, I used surviving records to show how the industry developed and how its product profile changed to cope with competition from America. What remains to be done is to examine these records in an attempt to establish how they helped management and directorial decision making. Without a full understanding of the principles and methods of accounting, it is possible only to make some very tentative observations.

The surviving accounts relate almost entirely to the four refining companies that survived to become part of Scottish Oils Limited in 1919. They comprise directors' minute books for the first few and last few years of these companies' independent existence; for the Young's, Oakbank and Broxburn companies, the minute books of shareholders' meetings; and for all four companies, journals and private or general ledgers.

The early ledgers contained accounts for the firms' customers, but also accounts for the various aspects of the companies' business. Later volumes are concerned solely with the firms' internal activities. For example, Young's Ledger No. 2 has 35 accounts relating to Addiewell, 15 to Bathgate, 7 to Craignestock, 3 to Lochrin, 13 to branches, 1 to James Hurst, an agent in Manchester, 19 to sales and branch expenses, and 13 to individual products. The other companies had a similar breadth of accounts. The ledgers are supported by the journals, which survive with some gaps in the runs for Oakbank, Broxburn and Pumpherston. The journals are effectively summaries of the activities for set periods. Those of the Broxburn and Oakbank (1869) companies are made up fortnightly; the others monthly. The journals and ledgers were supported by subsidiary ledgers and day books that have not survived but whose existence can be deduced from the ledgers and journals. For example, Young's Journal No. 13 contains monthly summaries of product sales derived from an Oil Day Book and a Lamp Day Book. Journal No. 8 (1900–1) of the Oakbank 1886 company contains references to Journal Jotter No. 2, the purchase day book, sales day book, empty barrel book, cost returns, refinery abstract, cash book, works pay sheets, works cash statements, and works journal. It is clear, therefore, that a mechanism existed for management to exercise control of financial affairs.

The ledgers contain separate accounts for the various products, the operations that produced them, and for various subsidiary activities such as cooperages and the various trades involved in maintenance: for example, joiners, smiths, plumbers, and so on. Ledger No. 7 of the Pumpherston company can be used as an example. In the year ending 30 April 1901, the shale account shows that shale costing £58,597 was delivered to the crude oil account (the retorts). The crude oil accounts show that retorting involved manufacturing costs of £20,613 and repairs of £1,861. Crude oil costing £80,932 was transferred to the general refining account. The Seafield crude oil account shows that shale costing £30,770 was retorted with manufacturing costs of £10,286 and repairs of £2,326. The Deans accounts show that shale costing £29,341 was used with manufacturing costs of £10,094 and repairs of £1,110. The Seafield and Deans crude oil was transferred to a crude oil purchased account, where it was aggregated with purchases from Hermand and Philpstoun. From this account, crude oil costing £87,137 was transferred to the general refining account, along with £80,932 from the Pumpherston crude oil account, making a total cost to the refining account of £168,069. The general refining account shows manufacturing costs of £29,130 and repairs of £4,140. The credit side of the general refining account contains the large item of £209,453 by sundry accounts. This is the total of debits to the general refining account in the ledger accounts for burning oil, £58,884; lubricating oil, £100,646; naphtha, £15,540 and paraffin scale, £34,383.

These accounts list other costs, including carriage and freight, agents' commission, rolling stock repairs, tank hire, casks purchased, and sundry accounts.[6]

It seems clear, therefore, that these shale oil concerns maintained records detailing production and distribution costs. Overhead costs remain to be accounted for. Fleischman and Parker emphasise the importance of allocating these costs in product pricing.[7] This was not critical in the case of the shale industry, because prices were set for all the major products by market forces outwith the control of management. However, an understanding of such costs was essential in order to assess profit or loss. Young's records indicate that overhead costs at their works were dealt with in the manufacturing accounts of their Addiewell, Bathgate, Craignestock and Uphall works. Other charges, such as advertising, branch expenses, office salaries, rent, interest, etc., were dealt with as specific items in the annual profit and loss account.[8]

The Oakbank company included in its profit and loss account the balance of a works charges account which included items such as salaries, laboratory expenses, etc. The office charges account included the registered office and sales costs. Interest and bad debts had separate entries.[9] The Broxburn company included in its profit and loss account items for registered office charges, interest and branch expenses. Works charges were apportioned to shale, crude oil, refinery, sulphate of ammonia, and candle house accounts according to a set formula. The balance of the locomotives and railway accounts were dealt with similarly.[10] The Pumpherston company showed its products accounts in debit to 'sundry accounts', which included overheads such as salaries, insurance, agencies' expenses, general charges, travelling expenses, etc. The products accounts were debited in proportion to their sales.[11]

For each of the four companies, the end result was an annual profit and loss account and balance sheet that enabled management and directors to meet shareholders with statements regarding the company's affairs. More importantly, it enabled management and directors to maintain control over the day-to-day running of the company. For example, the Broxburn directors received profit and loss statements at regular intervals.[12]

Audit

Auditing of company accounts, apart from railway and banking companies, was not compulsory until 1900, and only in 1947 did the law demand that it had to be carried out by registered accountants.[13] However, it can be shown that the four refining companies that survived to 1919 had appointed auditors from the beginning.[14] Similar appointments were made by most of the companies set up after 1877 and which did not survive. All of the appointments were of men or firms described as 'CA'. In the second half of the nineteenth century, accountancy became increasingly professionalised and subject to regulation with regard to the training and qualification of practitioners. This movement started in Scotland with the formation of the Royal Society of Accountants in Edinburgh and the Royal Institute of Accountants and Actuaries in Glasgow in 1853.[15] The designation 'CA' must have been seen by shareholders as an indication that the audit was carried out professionally and competently, although the experience of the West Lothian company, described in Chapter 19, might well suggest otherwise.

The shale oil industry: managerial capitalism?

In *Scale and Scope* (1990), Chandler discusses the transition from owners' personal management of their enterprises to the control of salaried managers divorced from the ownership. The development of the railway as a new means of transport encouraged the growth of mass marketing and mass production, and led to the adoption by other industries of the management techniques developed in response to the complexities of the railway networks. To achieve success in this new environment, firms were required to invest in production facilities, marketing, distribution, and management.

This change was particularly evident in the United States and in Germany, which rapidly overtook Britain, the world's first industrial nation, in terms of industrial output. Chandler attributes Britain's failure to participate fully in these developments to a commitment to personal capitalism, and to personal management by the founders of firms and their families. He was able to concede, however, some exceptions to his thesis of failure within British industry. These included new consumer goods industries, and industries such as rubber, glass, explosives, chemicals and rayon.[1] The shale oil industry was also new, and two of its main products – burning oil and candles – were very much consumer-oriented.

Economies of scale and scope: marketing

Chandler states that the benefits of these developments included economies of scale and scope. The progress of Rockefeller's Standard Oil is cited as an example of economies of scale. In 1870, increases in the size of plants and stills had reduced the cost of refining crude oil from 5 to 3 cents per gallon. In 1885, by concentrating production in a reduced number of refineries, this had been reduced to 0.452 cents – less than 10 per cent of the original cost.[2] The venture into crude oil production and the acquisition of marketing facilities meant that Standard had become vertically integrated by the end of the century.[3]

Economies of scope – those deriving from the manufacture of additional products – were, in the case of Standard Oil, achieved by refining the complete range of petroleum products. The early industry concentrated on illuminating oil. The heavier fractions, containing the raw materials for lubricating oils and wax, were sold off to specialist refiners. However, by the 1890s Standard Oil had diversified to claim a substantial share of the markets for lubricating oils and paraffin wax.[4]

Chandler has been criticised for a failure to take into account the contribution of smaller concerns to the developments in the economy.[5] The shale oil industry was from the first a very minor competitor for the American industry, and particularly for Standard Oil. In 1862, after some 11 years of operation, the Bathgate works produced and refined 2,000,000 gallons of crude oil per annum. The American industry at the same time operated on 3,000,000 barrels of crude oil, equivalent to over 100 million gallons.[6] In 1899, Standard's refineries processed 46 million barrels of crude oil.[7] In the years before the Great War, the shale industry at its peak refined some 70 million gallons, equivalent to 2 million barrels. It seems impertinent in the extreme to compare such a minnow with the leviathan that was Standard Oil. However, as has been shown, Standard in the 1890s viewed the shale industry as a significant competitor with respect to one important product: paraffin wax.

It is also the case that, despite its relatively small scale, the Scottish shale industry's development was similar in some ways to the American. Although it began on a much smaller scale than the American industry, significant economies were achieved from the start. The first innovation was the adoption of the vertical, continuously operating retort. After that, successive improvements in the retorting process reduced the cost of this section of the process from 6od. (£0.25) per ton in 1869 to 12d. (£0.05) in 1897. These later retorts also had a significantly higher yield of sulphate of ammonia, an increasingly valuable product. The cost of refining the crude oil fell from 2.2d. (£0.009) per gallon in 1869 to 0.77d. (£0.003) in 1889.[8] These improvements in methods were accompanied by a sixfold increase in throughput from 541,273 tons per annum in 1876 to 3,279,903 tons in 1913. Such economies meant that the shale industry was able to cope with significant reductions in product prices. In 1864, the products of a ton of cannel coal fetched £13.50; in 1869 those of a ton of shale realised £1.25; and in 1911 the figure was only £0.49.

These economies, and the associated expansion, secured the industry's survival, but not of all of its constituent concerns. Of the 12 refining companies active in the 1880s, only four survived to the amalgamation in 1919. Prospectuses found for some of the failed companies indicate an intention to undertake significant expansion. For example, the Burntisland company was to extend the works taken over from the defunct Binnend company, enabling them to deal with 300 tons of shale per day.[9] The Lanark company took over the refinery at Lanark and the mines and crude oil works at Tarbrax, with the intention of expanding the latter to deal with 100,000 tons of shale per year.[10]

The failed companies may be credited with having attempted to take advantage of economies of scale. However, in all cases the results fell considerably short of the achievement of the four survivors. In the absence of records for any of the lapsed companies, the only available measure of the relative achievement of the companies is the number of underground miners employed. Those in the Eastern District of Scotland are shown in Table 18.1.

It can be seen that only the Clippens company attained the size of the smallest of the four survivors. However, this company failed because of difficulties with water. The remaining concerns remained on a small scale compared with the survivors, and only two lasted until the twentieth century.

There were also economies of scope. The early ventures at Alfreton and Bathgate were intended to produce lubricants. The lighter fractions were something of a liability until the invention of a suitable lamp. After that, burning or illuminating oil became the most important product until the invention of a candle-making machine made paraffin wax profitable. In the 1880s, significant economies of scope could be achieved by an increase in the production of sulphate of ammonia, which had become important as a fertiliser. In the more successful concerns, this was achieved by the use of the new Young & Beilby retort available from the early 1880s, and the Bryson retort from the mid-1890s. The less successful concerns, such as the Linlithgow company, were inhibited by a lack of finance.

Several different versions of the new retort were developed to cope with leakages at the joint between the iron and brick sections. Some of these were failures, and the Hermand, West Lothian and Lanark companies experienced problems.[11] Some, at least, of these problems can be attributed to deficiencies in management.

Table 18.1 Underground workforce of refining companies

Company	Active	Maximum no. of underground miners	
		Year	Number
Pumpherston	1883–1919	1914	1229
Young's	1866–1919	1885	948
		(1914	919)
Broxburn	1877–1919	1914	933
Oakbank	1869–1919	1914	614
Clippens	1878–1897	1885	601
Linlithgow	1884–1902	1888	353
Burntisland	1881–1893	1891	331
Caledonian	1889–1901	1895	270
West Lothian	1883–1891	1890	260
Lanark	1883–1886	1885	123
Midlothian	1882–1885	1884	102

Source: Inspectors of Mines Reports (PP); Lists of Mines (Home Office).

The choice of plant must be considered one of the first concerns of a board of directors.

Chandler also identifies investment in marketing and distribution as essential for success.[12] The four surviving concerns in the shale industry were not deficient in this respect (see Chapter 14).

Divorce of ownership and management

The third, and possibly most important, requirement identified by Chandler is management, and the divorce between ownership and control. When the firm of Rockefeller Andrews & Flagler was incorporated as the Standard Oil Company in 1870, John D. Rockefeller and three others were the active management and held two thirds of the stock.[13] Over the period to 1879, Standard's stock was increased to 35,000 shares of $100 each, held by 37 individuals, to accomplish the takeover of 40 or so concerns in the industry.[14] Eight men associated with these 40 concerns had significant share holdings in Standard Oil. Along with the four original partners, they were important figures in Standard's management. Together, these 12 men held 25,080 of the 35,000 shares.[15] When the Standard Oil Trust was created in 1882, the nine trustees were the 'chief active managers of the combination'; the ownership 'lay mainly in the hands of the executives'.[16] This close association of ownership with control was to change by the end of the century. Rockefeller retired in 1896–7, and his early associates had either died, lost contact with Standard, or begun to interest themselves in projects outside of Standard Oil. Rockefeller's son, John Davison junior, who might have been expected to assume a position in Standard Oil, devoted himself to managing the family fortune, and particularly to philanthropic activities.[17]

By the end of the century, therefore, the management of Standard Oil was effectively divorced from its ownership. Chandler notes that, in the American oil industry by the 1920s, all firms were 'administered by experienced, full time, career managers, the great majority of whom held only a tiny percentage of stock in the companies they operated'. In the former Standard companies, members of the Rockefeller family were not even 'outside directors'.[18]

The four refining companies that survived to make up Scottish Oils in 1919 were limited companies, the survivors of 43 such concerns established in the industry. The companies legislation required that the first directors were to be appointed by the subscribers to the Memorandum and Articles of Association. Thereafter, they were to be elected by the shareholders in general meeting. In fact, in only one instance was this privilege exercised by shareholders; in every other case, the annual general meeting ended with the election or re-election of directors as proposed by the existing board. In the case of Young's, established in 1866 with

74 shareholders, the directors held 48.01 per cent of the shares, and so could be considered to have a substantial stake in the ownership of the company as well as exercising control. The three directors of the Oakbank company, formed in 1869, had 75 per cent of the original shares.

Young's company divided its £100 shares into 10 of £10 each in 1872. The shares were listed on the Glasgow Stock Exchange as early as 1871; and by 1872 the exchange was inclined to refuse listings for companies that had not placed two thirds of their capital with the public. These are, therefore, clear indications that the company's ownership was becoming more widespread. The first chairman, John Orr Ewing, held 250 £100 shares – £25,000 – when the company was formed. At his death in 1878, this had been reduced to 1,250 £10 shares, or £12,500. The Oakbank company divided its £50 shares into 50 of £1 each in 1873; by 1885 there were 255 shareholders of 90,000 £1 shares. The largest holding was 5,430, and the four directors – two of whom had served from the start – held 14,538 shares. The ownership of these two companies had become more widespread, while the control remained ultimately in the hands of the directors.[19]

The ownership of Broxburn and Pumpherston shares was more widespread from the start. In Broxburn's case, the vendor, Robert Bell was given 6,500 £10 shares free of charge as payment for the assets transferred. The remaining 10,000 shares were held by 132 shareholders, the 5 remaining directors holding 2,825. Bell transferred 1,550 shares on 30 April 1879; 2,191 on 5 November 1879; and 1,000 on 10 November 1880. The company's capital was increased to 20,000 £10 shares in 1881, and at that time there were 301 shareholders. The vendors of the shale leases to the Pumpherston company, the Fraser brothers, were given 2,000 shares, with £7 10s. paid on each. The remaining 7,000 shares were held by 173 shareholders. The directors held 3,105 shares, of which 2,000 were those given to the Fraser brothers. The board held a minority of the shares, but the managing director, Fraser, had a substantial interest, along with his brother.[20]

The shares of these four companies became more widely held as time went on. The Oakbank company was reorganised in 1886, and in January 1897, 237 shareholders were paid £3,371 25s. in dividends. The largest payment was £189 to the National Bank of Scotland. The six directors received £578, 17 per cent of the total. They had a significant interest in the firm, but their holding was far from a majority. In 1919, when the companies were absorbed into Scottish Oils Limited, 1,129 holdings of 111,982 shares in Young's were transferred to Scottish Oils Limited, as were 2,030 holdings of 282,479 shares in the Pumpherston company, and 1,372 holdings of 224,980 Broxburn shares.[21]

The freedom accorded to directors in the conduct of company business is discussed in Chapter 12. Here, it is intended only to reinforce this conclusion by looking at the attendance record of shareholders at general meetings. Information is available only for the Broxburn company and the reorganised Oakbank company. In 1878, only 20 of the 133 shareholders attended Broxburn's first general meeting. In the 12 years to 1890, an average of 29 members attended 12 general meetings; from 1891 to 1900, there was an average attendance of 29 at 10 meetings; from 1901 to 1910, an average of 25 at 9 meetings; and from 1911 to 1919, an average of 20 members at 9 meetings. In 1918, the 19 members attending held 11,330 shares, and in 1919, 21 members held 13,280.[22] In 1919, only 21 out of 1,372 shareholders attended, representing 13,280 of 235,000 ordinary shares.[23]

Between 1887 and 1900, 13 general meetings of the Oakbank company attracted an average attendance of 13 members; between 1901 and 1910, 10 meetings had an average attendance of 21; and between 1911 and 1919, the average was 25. The only available information regarding number of members reveals that, in 1897, there were 237.

It seems clear, therefore, that the majority of shareholders were content to leave the conduct of the companies in the hands of the directors. We must now look more closely at the relationship between the directors and the salaried managers of the companies. The management structure of the companies is fully discussed in Chapters 12 to 19; and although, because of its relatively small size, the shale oil industry did not require such an elaborate management system as that of Standard Oil, it is clear that there were similarities. The production facilities and distribution centres were all under professional management. The four surviving refining companies had registered offices in Glasgow. These were obviously much more modest than 26 Broadway, but they served as the centres of the companies' operations. Here we are concerned with the relationship between the directors and senior management.

This is perhaps best illustrated by the letter written to Young's directors by John Fyfe in 1884. He establishes that the company's four works had 'fairly competent resident management', and that the secretary and the accountant were able to conduct the head office's day-to-day business, leaving Fyfe to look after 'the larger interests of the company involved in prices, costs, processes, economies, visits to the works and pits'. He ends by stating that 'many larger concerns than Young's Company are content to have one Chief Official with strong Departments'. Fyfe, recruited from the Caledonian Railway Company, had been general manager of the company since 1873, and managing director since 1882. In the context of Chandler's emphasis on the importance of the railways in this discussion, it is possibly not without significance that John Orr Ewing was for many years a director of the Edinburgh and Glasgow Railway, and took a prominent part in its management. He was also a promoter and director of the Caledonian and Dunbartonshire Railway. James Scott of the Clippens company also played a prominent role in railway development in Scotland.[24]

In 1887, Archibald Fraser, Pumpherston's secretary and commercial manager, was asked to be general manager. The directors accepted that he would have the entire control of every department of the company's business, and that they would not interfere. Their duties would be confined to the boardroom, where 'as far as necessary and practicable all the business (including the appointments of responsible officials, such as mining manager, works manager, sales manager etc.) will be passed before the Board at the regular weekly meetings'.[25]

Chandler distinguishes between 'inside' and 'outside' directors in company hierarchies. Inside directors were full-time managers, while outside directors were men with other interests and only a part-time role in representing the interests of shareholders.[26] This pattern developed early in the shale industry. William Kennedy, of the Broxburn company, and William Fraser of Pumpherston were managing directors from the beginning. Young himself and his son were for some years involved in the management, and were on the board of the limited company. This gave way to a salaried management at the top and, with Fyfe's appointment in 1873, the structure began to be settled. In 1882, Fyfe was elected to the board and became managing director. The directors' report commented: 'The additional influence thereby conferred on Mr Fyfe will be beneficial to the company, besides being a mark of confidence to which he is fully entitled.'[27] The distinction between board members developed differently in the various companies. Fyfe remained the only salaried manager on the Young's board. The Oakbank company appointed its general manager, John Wishart, to the board in 1897, while Broxburn elected its works manager, Norman Henderson, to the board in 1895.[28]

When Fyfe retired in 1915, he was replaced by Thomas Steven as general manager, who did not, however, have a seat on the board. William Kennedy died in 1899 and was replaced by William Love as managing director. Love had been manager of the company's London branch since its foundation.

The case of the Pumpherston company was rather different. From 1887, when Archibald Fraser became general manager, effective control of the company was exercised by the two brothers. Archibald Fraser joined the board in 1900, and with the addition of James Bryson in 1903 and William Fraser junior in 1913, four of the board members were actively involved in the management, and three of them were members of the founding family.[29] When William Fraser died in 1915, William Fraser junior and James Bryson became joint managing directors. In 1919 there were five directors. William Fraser, Archibald Fraser and James Bryson remained in office. From 1913 to 1919, the 'inside directors' had a majority on the board.

A firm indication of these men's positions in their companies' structure is provided by the fact that, during the discussions with Standard Oil on imports of paraffin wax, the lead was invariably taken by the salaried managers, not by the outside directors. Fyfe attended a private meeting with Standard Oil's E.T. Bedford on behalf of Young's company, as did Kennedy for the Broxburn. Relations with the government during the Great War were conducted on behalf of the Pumpherston company, and of the industry generally, by William Fraser junior.

The less successful concerns

It is appropriate now to examine some of the concerns that did not survive to become part of Scottish Oils, in an attempt to identify factors which might account for their different fates. The information available about the companies formed before 1870 is, in the main, confined to the company files in the National Archives, and it does no more than indicate that a company did stop trading. For the later companies, failure to secure economies of scale and scope has already been discussed (see Chapter 18). The directors of these companies held shares ranging from 6.25 per cent of capital in the Linlithgow company to 25.16 per cent in the Burntisland (see Chapter 12, Table 12.2). The owners of these companies were therefore no more in control than those of the successful concerns.

A very important undertaking when a company was formed was the acquisition or construction of the assets which would form the basis of operations. In some cases, the directors may have acted imprudently in taking over assets, particularly where there was a large payment in cash. The Walkinshaw company paid £15,006 in cash and £14,996 in shares out of a subscribed capital of £102,000 for mines and works that required considerable improvement. The Linlithgow company paid £15,500 to vendors for shale leases from a subscribed capital of £112,000. West Calder paid £50,000 in cash and £30,000 in shares out of a paid-up capital of £138,000 for works requiring some improvement. The Midlothian Oil Company Limited acquired mines and works from the Straiton Oil Company for £66,000, leaving only a small margin out of the nominal capital of £100,000 for the expansion plans set out in the prospectus.[1]

George Simpson

In a number of cases, imprudence on the part of directors was compounded by vendor cupidity. The career of George Simpson is illuminating in this respect. The Binnend company in 1878 paid Simpson £22,000 in cash and £12,900 in shares for works and mines capable of dealing with only 80 tons of shale per day.[2] In 1883, the Lanark company paid Simpson £40,000 out of a paid-up capital of £90,000 for works at Whitelees and Tarbrax, which were later described as not worth the value placed on them and as requiring complete rearrangement and reconstruction.[3]

In 1868, Simpson and Young's former partner, Edward Meldrum, constructed a mine and oil works at Boghall to the east of Bathgate.[4] The partnership became part of the Uphall Mineral Oil Company, which was incorporated as a limited company in 1871. This operated with some small success until taken over by Young's company in 1884. It is the only concern with which Simpson was associated that achieved anything like long-term prosperity.

In considering Simpson's career it must be borne in mind that, after the general introduction of limited liability in 1856, 'the British corporate code was the most permissive in Europe'.[5] Simpson's activities would today have been restricted by legislation, but nothing he did in the nineteenth century was outside the law.

In 1861, he was a coal master at Benhar on the boundary between West Lothian and Lanarkshirel, and in 1866–7, he owned an oil works there. In 1867–8 this was worked by the Caledonian Oil Company, a partnership of Simpson, Christian Salvesen and others, producing crude oil from cannel coal for shipment to a refinery owned by Salvesen at Mandal in Norway. The company ceased to operate in 1870, and most of the other partners sold out cheaply to Simpson.[6] In 1871, Simpson sold the works to the Uphall Oil Company Limited, and in 1877 the directors reported that the Uphall works were being expanded by the removal of plant from Benhar which had not been in use for some years.[7]

In June 1878, the Broxburn company contracted with Simpson to supply shale to crude oil works that he would erect at Broxburn. In November 1878, this contract was assigned by Simpson to the Benhar Coal Company Limited, and in 1880 it was decided to free the company from the contract by purchasing the crude oil works at Broxburn and the refinery at Benhar. The cost was £40,000 plus £6,000 for stocks. The Broxburn company worked the two plants until 1882, when the Benhar refinery was discontinued in favour of expansion at Broxburn. In October 1883, the Benhar works was sold to James Thornton for £6,500; the East crude works at the same time was valued at £3,493.[8] The Broxburn company does not appear to have profited from its association with Simpson.

Simpson again acquired the Benhar works and transferred it, along with shale leases at Deans, near Bathgate, to the newly formed West Lothian Oil Company Limited. The negotiated price was £28,500, and Simpson originally agreed to accept up to 1,500 shares with £7 paid on each as part of this. Applications were made for five times the 7,500 shares offered, and Simpson agreed, at the directors' request, to waive this part of the agreement in order to allow the allocation of these shares to applicants. Simpson therefore received £28,500 in cash for the leases at Deans and the plant at Benhar. This was in respect of works described by the Broxburn chairman as requiring considerable expenditure to make it anything like perfect. By 20 February 1885, £7 had been paid on each of the 7,500 shares issued, a total of £52,500.[9] Simpson had received 54 per cent of this, leaving only £24,000 for the development of mines and works and for working capital.

Simpson's reputation was the subject of comment in the financial press of the time. The *Scottish Financier* noted that:

> Our old friend George Simpson, of Benhar notoriety, is once more to the front. I had always thought him buried for good. He was the vendor of the Lanark Oil Company, and apparently so satisfactorily to himself that this week he makes his bow in connection with the 'West Lothian.' I suppose he thinks that in these times of cheap money anything with the word 'oil' in it will go down.[10]

Advice available to investors

Simpson's activities and the failure of other concerns argue a certain level of investor naivety. In considering the number of failures among the limited companies, the late 1870s and early 1880s was apparently a period in which investment opportunities were sought by those who held a considerable accumulation of capital.[11] Some of this found a home in the shale industry. Between 1880 and 1885, 13 limited companies were formed in the industry, only one of which survived to be included in the amalgamation of 1919. The advice available to investors at this time has been described as of doubtful merit.[12] This certainly seems to have been the case in respect of the shale industry. In 1883, six oil companies were offered to the public, four of them in the months of October and November.[13] An indication of the quality of financial advice available may be derived from the November 1883 issue of the *Scottish Financier*, which contains the following:

> Within the last week, the prospectuses of no fewer than three new oil companies have been issued to the public, viz. these: – The Bathgate, the Pumpherston, and the Hermand. Of these three there is no doubt that the last named will meet with the most favour. This company is certain to be floated, and I strongly recommend investors to apply for as many shares as they can take up. The Directors are all well known, honourable men, who must thoroughly believe in the success of the Company or their names would not be found in the prospectus. It is doubtful whether the other two companies will meet with the success that is desired for them, as the public are beginning to think that 'enough is as good as a feast,' and in this case the public are correct.

The Pumpherston company had offered 7,000 shares to the public and received applications for 26,418.[14] It was a consistently well-run concern, and in the early twentieth century it became the largest in the industry. The Bathgate company fulfilled the *Scottish Financier's* bleak forecast. Only 2,260 of 3,500 shares offered were taken up, and the company was wound up in October 1885.[15] The Hermand company, so highly spoken of, was not incorporated until September 1885, when a further, more successful, attempt at flotation was made.[16] It seems that the *Scottish Financier* was correct only in its suggestion that investors had become more careful. Another source of advice was from stockbrokers. The Edinburgh firm Walker & Watson issued a monthly circular dealing with companies in the shale industry. In January 1889 it recommended the Pumpherston, Holmes and Linlithgow companies to investors.[17] Of these, only the Pumpherston went on to achieve consistent success.

Management deficiencies

It seems clear that, in its short life, the Lanark company had to contend with the problems of an inflated purchase price paid for works in poor condition, and that substantial amounts of capital had been required to improve matters. Its management was ineffective at board level, and also at the works. There were complaints that the Tarbrax and Whitelees works did not operate harmoniously together, and suggestions that directors were interested in profiting by dealing in the company's shares.[18] It is clear that the shares were the subject of considerable dealings on the stock exchanges. In the 12 months ending on 6 January 1886, 16,047 shares were transferred.[19] Only 10,000 shares were issued, so some shares must have been transferred more than once.

There were similar management deficiencies in the West Lothian company. Reports of the general meeting of 4 June 1886 illustrate the main factors in the company's failure. The whole capital of the company had been called up – £10 per share.[20] The directors reported a deficit on 15 months' working of £10,373, with no allowance made for depreciation. A shareholders' committee reported that 'the past management has been extremely loose and defective. There has been an entire absence of method, order and arrangement in the conduct of the Company's affairs and in the records of the Company's operations.' The works records were found to be in order, but the commercial accounts were extremely deficient. These were held partly in the secretary's office in Hope Street and partly in the commercial office in Frederick Street. Neither had been properly kept, with the result that no fortnightly, monthly or quarterly profit and loss account had been available that would allow the directors to monitor progress. The committee commented on the secretary's rare attendance at board meetings: this obligation, together with the maintenance of accounts at his office, he delegated to a clerk. The secretary was an Edinburgh lawyer, and presumably he carried out his duties alongside other claims on his time.[21] There was also a submission by William Fraser of the Pumpherston company, setting out the deficiencies in the working of the company's shale. The poor quality of the shale was later described as the principal cause of the company's failure.[22] This again reflects badly on the directors who had purchased the shale leases from Simpson.

Some concern was expressed regarding the state of the company's shares on the stock exchange, and there were accusations of attempts made to manipulate the shares for personal gain.[23] There is some evidence of 'stagging' in the company's shares and in those of other companies. It is of interest to note that in the last Summary of Capital and Shares for this company, 6,217 shares were held by banks: Royal Bank, 1,700; Bank of Scotland, 1,977; British Linen, 520; Commercial, 1,860; and Clydesdale, 160.[24] The financing of share speculation by banks in the late nineteenth century has been identified. Is it possible that these shares had been offered as security for loans? This was a not uncommon practice at this time.[25]

The West Lothian management deficiencies were addressed by a new board elected on 4 June 1886. The registered office was reorganised and moved to Glasgow, but the press continued to express doubts.[26] No dividends were paid, and the company was placed in liquidation in 1892 with debts of £45,842.[27]

Defective management at the top level and at the works can be identified in some of the unsuccessful concerns that did not suffer from Simpson's influence. When the Midlothian company was taken over by Clippens, the directors attributed the lack of success in part to defective management at the works.[28] There is also some evidence of mismanagement in the day-to-day running of the Linlithgow company. Until 1890, the head office was in Edinburgh, but it was then moved to Glasgow, because this 'would bring them into closer contact with the principal buyers in their trade'.[29] At the same time the secretary, John Young, was appointed general manager.[30] In 1892, the secretary explained to the shareholders that the retorts had been badly used and required considerable expenditure on repairs. A change of management was called for: the late manager had not got on very well with the men, and it had been difficult for the board to interfere with his authority as manager. At the same meeting, a shareholder complained that the company's financial affairs were not looked after as they ought to be: payment of the company's accounts had been neglected, and the company had 'got into disgrace'.[31] The mine manager, James Beveridge, was appointed works manager and remained in post until the demise of the company. The published reports of company meetings after 1892 give no further indications of management problems.

Other causes of failure

Some other causes of failure are discussed briefly in Chapter 4. The Clippens Oil Company is an example. The company was formed in 1878 to take over a pre-existing private concern that had works and mines in Renfrewshire. In 1881, a substantial crude oil works was set up at Pentland, in the parish of Lasswade, Midlothian. By 1885, 4,000 tons of shale per week were dealt with and, apart from purchases, supplied the requirements of the Clippens refinery. This move to the east may well have been the result of difficulties in refining crude oil from the Renfrewshire shales to meet newer standards of purity.[32]

The company initially enjoyed some success, and until 1886 paid dividends of between 5 and 12 per cent (see Tables 2.3 and 2.4). The Midlothian Company's mines and works were close to the Pentland works, and when the Midlothian concern experienced difficulties in 1885, it was taken over. By 1887, Clippens had become one of the larger concerns in the shale industry. In the year ending 31 March 1887, the throughput was 185,000 gallons of crude oil per week; in the year ending 31 March 1891, sales of £285,000 were achieved.[33] In the same year, the Oakbank company sold £108,000 of products; Pumpherston £168,000; Broxburn £333,000; and Young's £543,000.[34] Clippens appears to have been well managed. Newspaper reports of company meetings indicate that crude oil refining produced between 70 and 73 per cent of finished products; this compared not unfavourably with Broxburn's performance in 1885 of 70 per cent.[35] For much of its life, the company had as its works manager William Young, one of the designers of the Young & Beilby or Pentland retort, which was the mainstay of the industry in the second half of the 1880s and the first half of the 1890s.[36] The company's products were highly regarded in the trade. In 1887, the Pumpherston directors considered that, although their company could not guarantee a quality of semi-refined wax equal to Clippens, it should aim for that standard.[37]

However, from 1886 onwards the company experienced severe water problems in the mines, along with the difficulties associated with steeply inclined seams. The company was placed in liquidation in 1892, but an arrangement with creditors and debenture holders led to the formation of a new company.[38] This new company survived the problems of the middle 1890s. In the year ending 30 September 1896, the company reported a net profit of £1,443, and in the first six months of the following year it also achieved a positive balance. The company appeared to have recovered. However, in 1897 it became involved in a dispute with the Edinburgh and District Water Trust, which led to the closure of its mines and works.[39] They were never reopened. The company survived by working limestone mines, but was eventually wound up in 1908.

Conclusion

The four refining companies that survived to the start of the Great War were completely vertically integrated in that they mined and retorted the shale, refined the crude oil and distributed the finished products. It is clear that these four companies had management structures leading upwards from the workmen on the production side through foremen and works and mine managers to a general manager or managing director. All four had a distribution network in the United Kingdom and in Europe, also under the control of the general manager or managing director. At the head office, this functionary, through the company secretary, controlled the accounting procedures and financial affairs of the company. The apex of the structure was, of course, the board of directors.

From 1900 to 1914 the four companies paid over £2 million in dividends to shareholders and bond holders. In the financial year that ended in the spring of 1914, £175,744 was distributed, slightly above the average for the period.[1]

These four companies were able to rely on the crude oil production of the Dalmeny Company and the private partnership of James Ross & Company when their own resources were inadequate. These six concerns were the only survivors of the multitude of individual enterprises, partnerships and limited companies set up in the 1860s, 1870s and 1880s. The concentration had involved a sixfold increase in production, and survival as an industry had been achieved despite often brutal competition from American and other oil producers. The industry well merits Professor Campbell's citation of it as an example of the successful application of technical advance in late nineteenth-century industry.[2]

Postscript: 1914–1982

The first year of the Great War had adverse effects on the industry. Exports of wax and sulphate of ammonia were seriously disrupted, and there was a serious labour shortage. The industry came very much under government influence. The navy was increasingly dependent on oil as fuel; when Winston Churchill became First Lord of the Admiralty in 1911, he noted that 56 oil-fuelled destroyers had been built or were under construction.[1] The importance to the war effort of the shale oil industry was frequently acknowledged. Early in 1918, there was even a suggestion from the Admiralty that the government should take over the industry.[2]

Sulphate of ammonia was also important, and distribution eventually came under the control of the Ministry of Food. Ammonia was also required for the manufacture of explosives; the government partly funded a plant at the Deans works to make concentrated ammonia liquor.[3]

Despite all the problems involved, the Great War was, in financial terms, nevertheless very successful for the industry. The company minute books and published financial reports show that, in the four financial years ending in the spring of 1919, £869,534 was distributed to shareholders and bond holders. At the same time, provision was made for the excess profits duty of 50 per cent (raised to 80 per cent in 1917) that was imposed late in 1915.[4] In addition, £291,601 was set aside for depreciation and £207,689 for improved plant accounts. The Pumpherston and Broxburn companies also added £110,000 and 24,819 respectively to their general reserve funds. The four companies had investments and other reserves totalling £1,115,039.

During the Great War, William Fraser junior played an important part in liaising with government departments and other bodies, particularly in matters relating to the production of fuel oil, ammonia for munitions, and sulphate of ammonia for food production. He was made a CBE in June 1918. At the amalgamation in 1919, he became managing director of Scottish Oils Limited, and in 1923 a director of the parent company Anglo-Persian, becoming its deputy chairman in 1928 and chairman in 1941. In addition, as one of four managing directors he was responsible for production and United Kingdom distribution. He was knighted in 1939 and became Baron Strathalmond of Pumpherston in 1955.

However, the industry faced severe problems. In 1914, world production of petroleum was 404 million barrels. The shale industry produced about 2 million barrels: 0.5 per cent of the total. By 1918, shale production had remained virtually static, while world petroleum production rose to 514 million barrels; in 1926 the figure was 1,096 million.[5] The shale oil industry was, therefore, an increasingly insignificant part of a rapidly expanding world oil industry. In the years before the Great War, the industry could survive, and at times prosper, partly because of profitable by-products, mainly sulphate of ammonia. In the post-war period, its price was affected by competition from a Swedish process for converting atmospheric nitrogen into fertilisers and raw materials for explosives. In discussions on the future of the industry, John Wishart of the Oakbank company claimed that Oakbank was losing 3 shillings and 6 pence on every ton of shale used. It was also claimed that the industry as a whole had made a loss of £16,716 in April 1919.[6]

The industry had never been slow to seek ways of reducing costs. In the years before the Great War, this had largely been achieved through improvements in the retort, the basic equipment of the industry. Economies were now to be achieved by alterations in the industry's structure. In the last years of the Great War, and under pressure from the government, a joint selling organisation – the Scottish Oil Agency Limited – was formed, with a consequent reduction in the costs of distribution.[7] In July 1919 a similar arrangement was proposed for the manufacturing side. In 1914 the government had acquired a controlling interest in the Anglo-Persian Oil Company Limited;[8] it was now proposed that Anglo-Persian should, by the creation of a new subsidiary, Scottish Oils Limited, take over the shale oil companies. This, it was thought, would result in economies similar to those achieved on the selling side by the Scottish Oil Agency. Anglo-Persian would also be able to supply imported crude oil to keep the refineries fully employed.[9] By January 1920, over 99 per cent of the ordinary shares in the four companies had been transferred to Scottish Oils Limited.[10]

The five shale companies continued to exist. Their ordinary share capital had simply been acquired, apart from a small number of shares by Scottish Oils Limited in exchange for its 7 per cent preference shares. The preference shares of the shale companies remained in public hands. The ordinary share capital of Scottish Oils Limited (1,000,000 £1 shares) was held entirely by Anglo-Persian. In effect, Anglo-Persian controlled Scottish Oils, and this in turn controlled the five shale oil companies. It should be remembered that the value of the pound was considerably greater in 1919 than it is today. The combined value of the shale companies – £2,797,836 – corresponds to almost £65,000,000 at 1998 prices: Anglo-Persian had gained control of a substantial business. In addition to the mines and works, it also acquired control of the substantial reserves built up by the shale companies in the years up to and including the Great War. These amounted to some £1,200,000.[11]

Despite the difficulties facing the industry, the immediate post-war period was not entirely unsuccessful. This was due, in part at least, to the amalgamation; which, a report to the Board of Scottish Oils Limited claimed, resulted in efficiency savings of nearly 20 per cent. In 1921, the five shale companies paid ordinary dividends totalling £120,000; in 1922, £63,000; and in 1923, £138,000. However, in 1924 no ordinary dividends were declared, and only refunds of the wartime excess profits duty enabled the shale companies to report small credit balances, after paying dividends to their preference shareholders. It was clear that the shale industry was approaching a crisis. This is best illustrated by the fact that, in 1914, the average value of the products of a ton of shale amounted to 12 shillings and 6 pence (£0.625), while the costs of production were 9 shillings and 11 pence (£0.49), leaving a substantial element of profit. In 1924 and 1925, the average value was 12 shillings and 5 pence (£0.624): it differed very little from the 1914 figure, but the costs of production had risen to 14 shillings and 2 pence (£0.70). The industry as a whole was operating at a considerable loss.[12]

Meanwhile, Scottish Oils Limited commenced refining the crude oil supplied by the Anglo-Persian company. In 1919, the shale refineries at Addiewell and Uphall were closed because of an excess of refining capacity. Scottish Oils adapted the Uphall plant for the treatment of Persian crude oil supplied from Grangemouth – initially by rail, but in 1924 a pipeline was brought into use. At the same time, a refinery was built at Grangemouth. This came on stream in 1924, and refined over 25,000 tons of Persian crude oil per month, roughly equivalent to the total capacity of all the shale oil refineries. The Uphall refinery was closed in 1936, and the refining of imported crude oil was concentrated at Grangemouth.[13]

The situation was exacerbated by the ending in March 1925 of the contract with the Admiralty for the supply of fuel oil for the navy. In September 1925, management suggested closing the most unremunerative works and mines. William Fraser, managing director of Scottish Oils, proposed that a 10 per cent cut in wages would allow the remaining mines and works to keep operating until March 1926, 'in the hope that conditions might improve'. If this proposal was not accepted, the only alternative was to shut down the whole industry. The miners and oil workers rejected this by 5,063 votes to 929, and went on strike on 10 November. A committee of enquiry was appointed, with representatives from both sides and a neutral chairman. In the end, a 5 per cent reduction in wages was proposed, and the employers insisted that some mines and works would not restart. This was accepted by the men by 3,875 votes to 915, a majority of over 400 per cent.[14]

Because of the time required to put the plant, particularly the retorts, into working order, it was not possible to resume work until January and February 1926. Mines and crude oil works at Pumpherston, Dalmeny, Broxburn and Tarbrax, and the refinery at Broxburn, did not restart.[15] The closures meant a reduction of some 30 per cent in capacity. From 1919 to 1924, around 2.75 million tons of shale were mined and processed annually, only marginally less than the 3 million tons of the best pre-war year.[16] By 1927, all hope of restarting the closed mines and works was abandoned, and the industry had declined to the extent that only 2 million tons were used.[17]

The closure of the uneconomic sections of the industry did not secure profitability. Despite the men's acceptance in October 1927 of a further cut of 5 per cent in wages, the Board of Scottish Oils was informed in January 1928 that: 'Notwithstanding that the costs of mining and retorting shale had been brought to the lowest and yields to the highest that they have touched in recent years, the losses in operations for the month of November . . . amounted to £10,000 without charging depreciation.'[18]

In April 1928, the government's need for additional revenue led to the imposition of a duty of 4 pence per gallon on light oils. Home-produced oils were exempt, giving the shale industry a price advantage over imported oils. This preference, which eventually rose to 1 shilling and 3 pence, was initially confined to motor spirit but was later extended to diesel oil used in road vehicles (DERV).[19]

This was a considerable advantage, and inspired some confidence for the future, but did nothing to alter the basic situation of the shale industry. With a production of about 200,000 tons of crude oil per year, the shale companies existed within a world oil industry dealing with nearly 200 million tons per year. Throughout the 1930s, the shale industry had to meet the prices set by the large oil concerns, and also suffered the effects of oil 'dumping' from 'certain European oilfields' at very low prices.[20] Despite this, the industry was able to respond positively to the opportunity presented by the new duty on imported oils. In September 1928, it was decided to erect at Pumpherston, at a cost of £100,000, four cracking plants, which 'had been designed with a view to dealing with products from shale in order that the fullest advantage may be taken of the duty on imported motor spirit'.[21] This was, however, combined with further contraction in overall operations. In July 1931, the works and mines at Philpstoun were closed. During the 1930s, further closures took place at Seafield and Oakbank. In 1938, there remained five crude oil works at Niddry Castle, Hopetoun (Winchburgh), Roman Camp, Deans and Addiewell. The total throughput of shale was about 1,500,000 tons per year, little more than half that of 1924.[22]

This contraction had, of course, a significant effect on employment. The total number in 1925 was 7,500, a significant decrease from the 9,000 at the end of the Great War. After the closures of 1925, the workforce in 1926 was 5,347, falling gradually to 4,537 in 1931. In 1932 there was a sharp decrease to 3,384, but numbers rose to 4,226 in 1933 and remained at about this figure until 1938.[23] This increase was the result of the introduction in 1932 of a 'spread-over' scheme, which involved large sections of the workforce working for three weeks out of four. In the fourth 'idle week', they were able to draw unemployment benefit. The result was the sharing to some extent of the hardship occasioned by the economic depression of the 1930s.[24]

Some of the displaced men secured employment in the Grangemouth refinery and at Middleton Hall, which had become the head office and central workshops for Scottish Oils.[25] Some men also transferred to the Anglo-Persian refinery at Llandarcy in South Wales. Some miners, of course, found employment in the coal fields.[26] There was, nevertheless, a considerable amount of unemployment. The National Union of Shale Miners and Oil Workers claimed that there were 922 unemployed shale miners and oil workers in the area at the end of 1936.[27]

During the 1930s, the company began to use the spent shale in making bricks. The shale mines themselves were large users for stoppings and other work underground. Vast sections of the offices, laboratories, and so forth at Grangemouth are constructed of this very distinctive pink brick. The Pumpherston works, where the shale crude oil refining was concentrated, had many examples of the use of the new brick, one of the most prominent being the workmen's baths, built in 1937. During the 1939–45 war, a works canteen was built.[28]

As mentioned earlier, the introduction of duty on imported light oils made it necessary to increase production of such oils, particularly motor spirit. When the duty was extended to gas oil used in diesel engines, Pumpherston introduced a diesel distillation unit to maximise production and make full use of the benefit conferred by the duty relief.

Westwood and expansion at Pumpherston

The industry, after a few bad years at the start of the 1930s, returned to profit in the period 1936–8.[29] In 1938, it was decided to increase capacity by constructing a completely new crude oil works at Westwood, near West Calder, along with an increase in refining capacity at Pumpherston. Overall the cost was to be some £800,000, of which £135,000 was to be spent at Pumpherston.[30] A new crude oil distillation plant consisted of a tube still, from which the oil vapours were led through a vertical tower, where the various fractions were taken off at different levels. Two of these were eventually erected at Pumpherston; the works now had the capacity to deal with about 200,000 tons of crude oil per annum.

English crude and the final decline of shale oil

The 1939–45 conflict meant that, although the industry was important to the war effort, planned further expansion at Westwood was postponed and, in fact, was never carried out. The story of the shale industry from 1945 onwards is one of gradual decline. By 1951, the Deans and Hopetoun crude works had been closed, leaving only Westwood, Niddry Castle, Roman Camp and Addiewell. In 1944, there is the first mention of English crude oil at Pumpherston refinery. This was the result of exploration and drilling by the Anglo-Iranian Oil Company. A small amount of oil was produced by wells at Formby in Lancashire and at Cousland near Dalkeith, but the main production was from wells in Nottinghamshire, at Eakring and Egmanton. By 1948, over 4,000 tons per month were refined at Pumpherston. In 1956, it was dealing with 70,000 tons of Eakring and Egmanton crude oils, and 72,500 tons of shale crude oil per annum. In January 1957, Pumpherston refined 1,676,078 gallons of English crude oils and only 1,466,446 gallons of shale crude.[31] English crude oils were now, and would remain, the larger element of the Pumpherston refinery throughput.

Liquid detergent production

The other significant development at Pumpherston in the immediate post-war period was the construction of the Detergent Plant. This produced a liquid detergent from a feedstock derived from the wax extraction process. The liquid was sold in bulk to other manufacturers, but it was also bottled at the plant under the name 'Iranopol', later changed to 'By-Prox'. Although women had been employed in the works offices for some considerable time, and some worked at the brick presses, the Detergent Plant was the first location in the refinery to give employment to more than a few women.[32]

In 1928, the shale oil industry was assisted by a duty preference over imported light oils at the rate of 4 pence (£0.017) per gallon. By 1951, this had risen to 9 pence (£0.0375) per gallon and extended to include gas oil used in diesel-engined road vehicles. In 1951 the benefit to the industry was £760,000, at a time when the annual wage bill was £1,500,000.[33] The preference was later raised to 1 shilling and 3 pence (£0.0625) per gallon, and was obviously a significant element in the industry's finances. Britain's entry into the European Free Trade Association in 1962 made it necessary for this favourable treatment of indigenous industry to cease, and the preference was withdrawn. This meant the immediate cessation of shale mining, retorting and the refining operations at Pumpherston.

The Detergent Plant and the wax extraction process were carried on using a feedstock from Llandarcy, and Pumpherston products became important in dealing with oil pollution at sea. However, this ceased in 1982, and nothing now remains of what was once the major industry in the Almond Valley.

Shale oil companies: capitalisation

Table A Capital employed in the shale oil industry by limited companies, 1863 to 1914

Year	Company name	Paid up in year £	Capital total £	Invested cumulative total £	Company	Capital lost in year £	Total £	Cumulative total £	Net active capital £
1863	Broxburn Shale	10000	10000						
1864	Mid Calder	8500	8500	18500	Broxburn Shale	10000	10000	10000	8500
1866	Mid Calder	4800							
	Scottish	1200							
	Glasgow	7000							
	Capeldrae	1400							
	Young's	106175							
	Glentore	1400	121975	140475				10000	130475
1867	Mid Calder	8829							
	Scottish	1600							
	Glasgow	12000							
	Capeldrae	2910							
	Young's	39450							

Year	Company name	Paid up in year £	Capital total £	Invested cumulative total £	Company	Capital lost in year £	Total £	Cumulative total £	Net active capital £
	Dalserf Coal Coke & Oil	24125							
	Airdrie Mineral	3750							
	Monklands Oil Refining	2400							
	Monklands Oil & Coal	5000	100064	240539				10000	230539
1868	Glasgow	4750			Glentore	1400			
	Young's	101875			Mid Calder	22129			
	Monklands Oil Refining	800	107425	347964	Scottish	2800	26329	36329	311635
1869	Young's	70375							
	Oakbank	12000			Monklands Oil Refining	3200			
	Airdrie Mineral	3750	86125	434089	Dalserf Coal Coke & Oil	24125	27325	63654	370435
1870	Young's	111500							
	Oakbank	20000	131500	565589				63654	501935
1871	Young's	57250							
	Oakbank	8000							
	Dalmeny	17774							
	Uphall Mineral	122820	205844	771433				63654	707779

Year	Location				Location				
1872	Midlothian Mineral	18412							
	Uphall Mineral	52562							
	West Calder	79930	150904	922337				63654	858683
1873	Uphall Mineral	6360							
	West Calder	26630							
	Dalmeny	1126							
	Midlothian Mineral	8478	42594	964931	Glasgow	23750	23750	87404	877527
1874	Capeldrae	690	690	965621	Airdrie Mineral	7500	7500	94904	870717
1875	Uphall Mineral	17908							
	West Calder	31980	49888	1015509				94404	920605
1876	Oakbank	5000	5000	1020509	Midlothian Mineral	26890	26890	121794	898715
1877	Uphall	350	350	1020859				121794	899065
1878	Broxburn	84180							
	Clippens	120000			Capeldrae	5000			
	Binnend	33120			West Calder	138540			
	Straiton	34275	271575	1292434	Uphall Mineral	30000	173540	295334	997100
1879	Broxburn	65820	65820	1358254				295334	1062920
1880	Binnend	2400							
	Straiton	11188	13588	1371842				295334	1076508

Year	Company name	Paid up in year £	Capital total £	Invested cumulative total £	Company	Capital lost in year £	Total £	Cumulative total £	Net active capital £
1881	British Oil & Candle	12000							
	Burntisland	61460							
	Broxburn	29750							
	Straiton	1087							
	Walkinshaw	94027	198324	1570166	Binnend	35520	35520	330854	1239312
1882	Oakbank	15000							
	Clippens	33750							
	Midlothian	33000							
	Walkinshaw	3723							
	Straiton	6192	91665	1661831	Monklands Oil & Coal	5000	5000	335854	1325977
1883	Oakbank	15000							
	Clippens	37500							
	Burntisland	40990							
	Westfield	14880							
	Midlothian	23000							
	Straiton	4058	135428	1797259	British Oil & Candle	12000	12000	347854	1449405
1884	Midlothian	24000							

Year	Works	Output							
	Young's	119000							
	Clippens	7500							
	Westfield	6370							
	West Lothian	35740							
	Bathgate	22600							
	Pumpherston	25500							
	Linlithgow	35700			Uphall	170000			
	Walkinshaw	16580	292990	2090249	Straiton	56800	226800	574654	1515595
1885	Broxburn	20000							
	Burntisland	17000							
	Westfield	3750							
	Lanark	90000							
	West Lothian	16760							
	Pumpherston	10500							
	Walkinshaw	33320							
	Linlithgow	75723							
	Holmes	30000			Bathgate	22600			
	Annick Lodge	8125	305178	2395427	Midlothian	80000	102600	677254	1718173
1886	Clippens	48900							
	Burntisland	25500							
	WestLothian	47500							
	Pumpherston	40500							
	Holmes	5000							

Year	Company name	Paid up in year £	Capital total £	Invested cumulative total £	Company	Capital lost in year £	Total £	Cumulative total £	Net active capital £
	Linlithgow	48577							
	Hermand	8510			Lanark	40000			
	Oakbank	50250			Westfield	25000			
	Lanark	10000							
	Annick Lodge	1235	285972	2681399	Oakbank	75000	140000	817254	1864145
1887	Pumpherston	30770							
	Hermand	15715							
	Oakbank	13450			Lanark	60000			
	Walkinshaw	200	60135	2741534	West Lothian	25000	85000	902254	1839280
1888	Broxburn	100000							
	Holmes	5000							
	Young's	37496							
	Oakbank	3800	146296	2887830	Young's	427500	427500	1329754	1558076
1889	Pumpherston	3230							
	Young's	2100							
	Hermand	4275	9605	2897435	Annick Lodge	9360	9360	1339114	1558321
1890	Clippens	9409							
	Hermand	6000							
	Young's	13282	28691	2926126	Linlithgow	50000	50000	1389114	1537012
1891	Pumpherston	51007							

Year	Company				Company				
	Clippens	1091							
	Linlithgow	18037			Walkinshaw	147850			
	Hermand	265000			West Lothian	75000			
1892	Young's	35586	370721	3296847	Hermand	34500	257350	1646464	1650383
	Burntisland	25050							
	Pumpherston	19353							
	Linlithgow	19984							
	Clippens	750							
	Hermand	32225							
1893	Young's	73017	170379	3467226	Clippens	181230	181230	1827694	1639532
	Linlithgow	28530							
	Hermand	6362			Clippens	77670			
	Young's	111854	146746	3613972	Burntisland	170000	247670	2075364	1538608
1894	Hermand	174							
	Young's	1212	1386	3615358	Linlithgow	49484	49484	2124848	1490510
1895	Hermand	750							
	Young's	136	886	3616244				2124848	1491396
1896	Pumpherston	21330							
	Dalmeny	37800	59130	3675374				2124848	1550526
1897	Pumpherston	8310							
	Hermand	245							
	Holmes	9475	18030	3693404				2124848	1568556
1898	Holmes	6775	6775	3700179				2124848	1575331

Year	Company name	Paid up in year £	Capital total £	Invested cumulative total £	Company	Capital lost in year £	Total £	Cumulative total £	Net active capital £
1899	Hermand	246							
	New Hermand	46984	47230	3747409	Hermand	305002	305002	2429850	1317559
1900	New Hermand	6922	6922	3754331	New Hermand			2429850	1324481
1902	Oakbank	28500			Holmes	56250			
	New Hermand	18156	46656	3800987	Linlithgow	127067	183317	2613167	1187820
1903	Oakbank	20000	20000	3820987	New Hermand	72062	72062	2685229	1135758
1904	Oakbank	60750							
	Tarbrax	27206	87956	3908943					1223714
1905	Tarbrax	43994	43994	3952937				2685229	1267708
1906	Tarbrax	33800	33800	3986737				2685229	1301508
1907				3986737	Oakbank	6750	6750	2691979	1294758
1909	Tarbrax	15000	15000	4001737				2691979	1309758
1910	Tarbrax	15000							
	Oakbank	100000	115000	4116737				2691979	1424758
1913	Pumpherston	225000	225000	4341737	Tarbrax	135000	135000	2826979	1514758

Note: In the 'Company name' column, 'Oil Company Limited' should be read as added to each name given. The full title of Young's Company is Young's Paraffin Light & Mineral Oil Company Limited.

Source: Annual Summaries of Capital and Shares (SCS) in Limited Company files. Files of lapsed or dissolved companies are held in the National Archives of Scotland, West Register House in Repertory BT2; files of extant concerns are held by the Registrar of Companies at Argyle House, 37 Castle Terrace, Edinburgh.

Table B Capital in the shale oil companies

Period	Nominal £	Capital issued £	Paid up £	Not paid in cash £	Proportion of total paid-up %	Net paid £	Cash payments £	Proportion of net paid-up %
1862–70	826400	697400	589750	12500	2.12	577250	400000	69.29
1871–6	612000	448790	367502	150220	40.88	217282	60490	27.84
1877–1914	2266000	1747100	1494977	597889	39.99	897088	262066	29.21
1862–1914	3704400	2893290	2452229	760609	31.02	1691620	722556	42.71

Note: The figure for issued capital in the first Summary of Capital and Shares is reduced to take account of shares forfeited in the early years of a company's existence.

Young's 100 × £100 shares = £10,000.

Midlothian Mineral 915 × £5 shares = £4,155

Straiton Estate 4,000 × £1 shares held by James Dick on behalf of the company transferred to Reserve Fund; 800 × £1 subsequently issued to shareholders. Issued capital reduced by £3,200.

Table C Initial paid-up capital in limited companies and additions after formation

Company	Initial paid-up capital	New ordinary shares	Calls on existing shares	Preference shares	Total paid-up capital
Broxburn Shale	10000				10000
Mid Calder	8500	13629			22129
Young's	486625	244856	148827		880308
Capeldrae	1400	2880	720		5000
Scottish	2800				2800
Glasgow	23750				23750
Dalserf	24125				24125
Monklands Oil Refining	2400		800		3200
Monklands Oil & Coal	5000				5000
Glentore	1400				1400
Airdrie	3750		3750		7500
Oakbank	20000	40000	15000		75000
Uphall Mineral	181742		18258		200000
Dalmeny	18900	18900		18900	56700
Midlothian Mineral	26890				26890
West Calder	105670	500	32370		138540
Straiton	34300		22500		56800
Broxburn	150000	49750		100000	299750
Clippens	120000	127650	11250		258900
Binnend	35520				35520
British Oil & Candle	12000				12000
Walkinshaw	94027	7973	17850	28000	147850
Burntisland	102450	42500	25050		170000
Midlothian	56000	24000			80000
Westfield	17500		7500		25000
West Lothian	52500	17500	30000		100000
Bathgate	22600				22600
Pumpherston	76500	189500	19500	150000	435500
Lanark	90000		10000		100000
Holmes	40000		16250		56250
Linlithgow	112000	48000	39345	27206	226551
Annick Lodge	9360				9360

Company	Initial paid-up capital	New ordinary shares	Calls on existing shares	Preference shares	Total paid-up capital
Hermand	24225	10275			34500
Oakbank (new)	67500	109250		100000	276750
Hermand (1892)	265000		40002		305002
New Hermand	42795	2127	8990	18150	72062
Tarbrax	105000	5000	15000	10000	135000
	2452229	954290	482962	452256	4341737

Note: 'Oil Company Limited' should be added to each company name.
Source: BT2 files in National Archives of Scotland for lapsed companies; Registrar of Companies files for live concerns.

Shale oil industry shareholders: occupations and residence

Table D(a) Occupations of shareholders in shale oil industry limited companies formed 1862–1870

Occupation or designation	Shareholders	No. of shares	Nominal value £
MISCELLANEOUS			
Gentleman	4	185	10000
In trust	1	30	300
Unspecified (male)	3	200	11000
Unspecified (female)	2	110	11000
	10	525	32300
COMMERCE			
Merchant	47	3399	263050
Merchant (commission)	1	3	600
Merchant (iron)	5	422	11850
Merchant (oil)	5	123	9200
Merchant (tea)	1	100	1000
Merchant (timber)	1	20	4000
Merchant (coal)	1	10	100
Banker	10	277	21500
Bank agent/manager	1	1	100
Broker, cotton	1	15	1500
Factor	1	10	1000
Publisher	2	60	5100
Shipowner	2	150	1500
Commission Agent	1	10	100
Shipping agent	1	20	200
Insurance broker	2	100	1000
Stock/sharebroker	3	210	3000
Agent	1	25	250
	86	4955	325050

Occupation or designation	Shareholders	No. of shares	Nominal value £
PROFESSIONS			
Accountant	7	143	10450
Actuary	1	20	2000
CA	2	150	6000
Chemist	2	1500	150000
Clergyman/minister	1	50	500
Doctor/MD/Physician/Surgeon	5	78	6000
Engineer	8	365	37000
Engineer, railway	2	60	3000
Professor	5	480	48000
Secretary	1	10	1000
Solicitor/WS/SSC/law agent/ writer	14	321	21050
Mining engineer	1	30	300
Civil engineer	1	100	1000
	50	3307	286300
PUBLIC SERVICE (1)			
Director, Geological Survey	1	25	2500
Deputy Inspector General of hospitals	1	25	2500
Government inspector of alkali works	1	10	1000
Inspector of poor	1	20	200
Royal Mint official	1	10	1000
Town clerk	1	50	500
	6	140	7700
ARMED SERVICES			
Major/Captain/ Lieutenant	2	40	400
	2	40	400
MANUFACTURING			
Manufacturer	5	48	9800
Manufacturer, oil	1	10	500
Manufacturer, paper	1	2	200
Manufacturer, pianoforte	1	20	200

Table 9D(a) *Continued*

Occupation or designation	Shareholders	No. of shares	Nominal value £
Manufacturer, starch	1	20	2000
Manufacturer, tobacco	1	100	1000
Builder	1	100	1000
Coalmaster	4	295	10750
Distiller	2	30	1200
Goldsmith	1	100	1000
Shipbuilder	1	40	400
Wagon builder	1	50	2500
Bleacher	1	50	500
Dyer	1	13	1300
	22	878	32350
EMPLOYED (1)			
Manager, colliery	1	20	200
Manager, iron works	1	20	200
Manager, oil works	2	123	3300
Railway officer	1	20	200
Colliery agent	1	10	100
	6	193	4000
EMPLOYED (2)			
Bookkeeper	2	75	750
Oil salesman	1	15	150
Cashier	1	10	100
		100	1000
WORKING CLASS (1)			
Clerk	3	40	400
	3	40	400
LAND (1)			
Chamberlain, duke of Hamilton	1	10	1000
Farmer	8	131	4400
	9	141	5400
	198	10319	694900

Table D(b) Occupations of shareholders in shale oil industry limited companies formed
1871–1876

Occupation or designation	Shareholders	No. of shares	Nominal value £
MISCELLANEOUS			
Gentleman	9	25250	25250
Nobleman	1	200	2000
Unspecified (male)	141	9926	84480
Unspecified (female)	38	2900	7475
Widow	3	1710	1800
In Trust	1	1000	1000
	193	40986	122005
COMMERCE			
Merchant	42	5723	39390
Merchant (coal)	1	10	100
Merchant (East India)	1	50	500
Merchant (manure)	1	20	200
Merchant (oil)	3	1136	2360
Merchant (wine)	1	3450	3450
Merchant (retired)	1	100	100
Agent, commission	2	2010	2100
Agent, house	1	50	500
Agent, ship and insurance	2	40	200
Banker	12	450	3625
Bank agent/manager	2	100	750
Broker	1	100	1000
Broker, insurance	1	100	1000
Broker, produce	1	50	500
Broker, Russia	2	100	1000
Broker, ship	1	400	4000
Factor	3	40	400
Share dealer	1	10	50
Stockbroker/sharebroker	4	350	3000
Warehouseman	2	35	350
	85	14324	64575

Table 9A(b) *Continued*

Occupation or designation	Shareholders	No. of shares	Nominal value £
PROFESSIONS			
Accountant	7	397	2610
Architect	4	195	1950
Barrister/advocate	1	20	100
CA	2	70	700
Chemist	1	20	200
Chemist, analytical	1	100	100
Clergyman/minister	12	501	3360
Doctor/MD	5	275	2750
Surgeon	1	5	25
Engineer	6	720	1800
Engineer, civil	1	500	500
Engineer, mining	1	15	150
Professor	1	50	500
LLD	1	100	1000
PhD	1	25	250
Secretary	3	325	1450
Writer	3	170	1700
Solicitor/WS/SSC/law agent	18	2170	6925
Surveyor	2	125	1250
Teacher/schoolmaster	3	60	600
Rector, grammar school	1	20	200
	75	5863	28120
PUBLIC SERVICE (1)			
Deputy Inspector General of hospitals	1	20	200
Member of Parliament	3	1600	16000
Sheriff-Clerk Depute	1	3	15
Sheriff Substitute	1	50	500
	6	1673	16715
ARMED SERVICES			
Captain RN	1	50	250
Major/Captain/ Lieutenant	4	200	1100

Occupation or designation	Shareholders	No. of shares	Nominal value £
Surgeon Major	1	50	500
	6	300	1850
MANUFACTURING			
Manufacturer	2	35	350
Manufacturing, chemist	2	1053	10530
Manufacturer paper	1	25	250
Builder	2	70	700
Coalmaster	6	1430	14300
Confectioner	1	100	1000
Contractor	2	550	1000
Distiller	4	4125	5250
Ironfounder/ironmaster	2	400	4000
Miller	1	100	500
Printer and publisher	1	50	500
Seedsman	1	50	500
Shipbuilder	1	100	1000
Spinner, flax	1	25	250
	27	8113	40130
RETAIL			
Baker	1	50	500
Bookseller	1	10	50
Clothier	4	2315	2450
Decorator	1	100	1000
Draper	1	20	100
Grocer	3	1045	1350
Gunmaker	1	15	150
Ironmonger	1	100	1000
Plumber	5	3100	3100
Shoemaker	1	750	750
Watchmaker	2	110	200
	21	7615	10650
EMPLOYED (1)			
Manager	1	500	500
Manager, brewery	1	10	50

Table D(b) *Continued*

Occupation or designation	Shareholders	No. of shares	Nominal value £
Manager, railway	1	25	250
Agent, colliery	2	60	600
Agent, station	1	10	100
	6	605	1500
EMPLOYED (2)			
Agent	1	100	100
Agent, insurance	1	100	100
Cashier	3	30	300
Clerk/solicitor's/law/ commercial/ mercantile/ bankteller	3	35	350
Commercial traveller	1	10	100
Traveller	2	300	300
Mineral check grieve	1	10	100
	12	585	1350
WORKING CLASS (1)			
Clerk	12	1953	2405
	12	1953	2405
DOMESTIC SERVICE			
Gardener	1	5	50
Governess	1	10	100
	2	15	150
LAND (1)			
Chamberlain, duke of Hamilton	1	300	3000
Farmer	15	634	6120
	16	934	9120
TOTAL			
	461	82966	298570

Table D(c) Occupations of shareholders in shale oil industry limited companies formed 1877–1885

Occupation or designation	Shareholders	No. of shares	Nominal value £
MISCELLANEOUS			
Executor	1	5	50
Gentleman	8	650	6500
Householder	1	50	500
In trust	3	26	260
Minor	1	10	100
Banks	4	595	5950
Nobleman	7	660	6600
Portioner	2	60	600
Spinster	13	227	2270
Unspecified (male)	536	26226	254575
Unspecified (female)	126	3049	30365
Unspecified (male/female joint holders)	3	55	550
Widow	10	207	2070
	715	31820	310390
COMMERCE			
Merchant	153	8056	80265
Merchant (cement)	2	20	200
Merchant (china)	1	50	500
Merchant (coal)	15	1007	9720
Merchant (commission)	2	70	700
Merchant (corn/grain)	6	200	2000
Merchant (flour)	1	50	500
Merchant (foreign)	1	15	150
Merchant (hardware)	1	20	200
Merchant (iron)	18	596	5885
Merchant (iron) & ironmonger	1	40	400
Merchant (iron & oil)	1	10	100
Merchant (iron & wood)	1	50	500
Merchant (jute)	1	15	150
Merchant (leather)	5	230	2300
Merchant (lime)	1	10	100

Table D(c) *Continued*

Occupation or designation	Shareholders	No. of shares	Nominal value £
Merchant (metal)	2	70	700
Merchant (oil)	14	1020	10050
Merchant (ostrich feather)	1	10	100
Merchant (potato)	3	70	700
Merchant (provision)	2	15	150
Merchant (seed)	2	60	600
Merchant (spirit)	1	30	300
Merchant (tea)	7	310	3100
Merchant (timber)	13	680	6660
Merchant (wine)	9	620	6200
Merchant (wool)	1	50	500
Merchant (yarn)	1	10	100
Merchant (cork)	1	45	450
Merchant (retired)	1	100	1000
Agent	2	40	400
Agent, commercial	1	25	250
Agent, commission	9	297	2970
Agent, manufacturer's	1	5	50
Agent, property/estate	4	35	350
Agent, shipping	5	385	3850
Agent, steamship	1	10	100
Auctioneer	5	105	1050
Banker	28	944	9265
Bank accountant	5	65	650
Bank agent/manager	15	430	4300
Broker, insurance	2	200	2000
Broker, metal	5	475	4750
Broker, produce	1	15	150
Broker, ship	3	130	1300
Broker, steamship	3	130	800
Broker, wool	1	50	500
Coal importer and steamship owner	1	50	500
Dealer, tea	1	150	1500

Occupation or designation	Shareholders	No. of shares	Nominal value £
Drysalter	2	135	1350
Factor	5	110	1000
Factor, engineer's	1	20	200
Publisher	3	135	1350
Shipowner	8	447	4470
Silk mercer	2	40	400
Steamship owner	3	95	950
Stockbroker/sharebroker	16	1125	11250
Tallow Chandler	1	80	800
Warehouseman	9	315	3150
Warehouseman, grocery	1	5	50
Wholesale grocer	2	130	1300
Wholesale stationer	2	30	300
	416	19737	195585
PROFESSIONS			
Accountant	28	1070	10700
Actuary	1	1	10
Analyst	1	25	250
Architect	8	247	2120
CA	20	895	9775
Chemist	9	112	1120
Chemist, analytical	1	50	500
Clergyman/minister	22	436	4360
Doctor/MD/physician/surgeon/ dental surgeon	35	1205	11930
Engineer	33	1641	15360
Engineer, civil	3	140	1400
Engineer, electrical	1	25	250
Engineer, gas	4	130	1300
Engineer, mining	11	330	3265
Engraver	1	10	100
Inspector of Schools	1	10	100
Organist	1	10	100
Sculptor	2	32	320
Sculptor, monumental	1	10	100

Table D(c) *Continued*

Occupation or designation	Shareholders	No. of shares	Nominal value £
Secretary	10	605	15050
Solicitor & banker	2	60	600
Solicitor/WS/SSC/law agent/writer/ barrister/advocate	68	2252	21850
Surveyor	3	40	400
Teacher/ schoolmaster	17	174	1740
Teacher (female)	1	5	50
Treasurer	1	10	100
Valuator	2	30	300
	287	9555	103150
PUBLIC SERVICE (1)			
Agent of Government of Canada	1	40	400
Assessor of taxes	2	60	600
Baillie	1	15	150
Chief Constable	1	10	100
Inspector of mines	1	60	600
Inspector of poor	1	10	100
Procurator Fiscal	1	10	100
Registration Examiner	1	20	200
Town Clerk	1	20	200
	10	245	2450
PUBLIC SERVICE (2)			
Excise Dept (Inland Revenue)	4	35	350
Excise Officer (retired)	1	5	50
Harbour master	1	10	100
Matron	1	25	75
Police constable	1	3	15
Postmaster	1	5	50
	9	83	640
ARMED SERVICES			
Major/Captain/ Lieutenant	2	40	400
Major-General	1	200	2000
Military officer (retired)	2	30	1200

Occupation or designation	Shareholders	No. of shares	Nominal value £
Surgeon Major	3	110	1100
	8	380	4700
MANUFACTURING			
Manufacturer	30	1729	16520
Manufacturer (retired)	2	270	2700
Manufacturer, boot	3	15	150
Manufacturer, brick	2	55	550
Manufacturer, carpet	1	100	1000
Manufacturing, chemist	9	4950	15650
Manufacturer, earthenware/potter	1	30	300
Manufacturer, fireclay	2	290	2900
Manufacturer, floorcloth	1	30	300
Manufacturer, glass	6	375	3750
Manufacturer, indiarubber	1	120	1200
Manufacturer, iron	1	5	50
Manufacturer, iron tube	2	120	1200
Manufacturer, leather/currier	1	20	200
Manufacturer, malleable iron	1	50	500
Manufacturer, oil	4	750	7500
Manufacturer, paper	5	335	3350
Manufacturer, power loom	1	60	600
Manufacturer, sacking	1	50	500
Soap maker	1	10	100
Manufacturer, steel	1	15	150
Manufacturer, tile	1	40	400
Manufacturer, tube	5	317	3030
Bleacher	1	50	500
Brassfounder	1	10	100
Brewer	6	1280	12800
Brick and tile maker	4	160	1400
Brick builder	3	30	300
Builder	14	1736	16240
Calico printer	1	100	1000
Candlemaker	1	10	100

Table D(c) *Continued*

Occupation or designation	Shareholders	No. of shares	Nominal value £
Clothier	1	30	300
Coalmaster	41	6793	59710
Contractor	14	475	4470
Contractor, mining	1	8	80
Contractor, railway	2	655	6550
Contractor, sinking	1	20	200
Cooper	4	210	1050
Distiller	7	770	7450
Dyer	3	90	900
Engineer and shipbuilder	1	80	800
Fancy paper box maker	1	10	100
Ironfounder/ironmaster	22	1582	15820
Meter maker	1	5	50
Mineral borer	4	60	600
Printer	3	21	210
Printer and publisher	1	10	100
Proprietor of slate mines	1	50	500
Sailmaker	2	50	500
Seedsman	3	30	300
Shipbuilder	1	100	1000
Shipbuilder (retired)	1	10	100
Spinner	1	50	500
Tanner	1	5	50
Twister	1	10	100
Upholsterer	1	12	120
	232	24248	196600
RETAIL			
Baker	15	386	3860
Baker, pastry	1	4	40
Bookseller	2	20	200
Butcher/flesher	5	230	2250
Chemist and druggist	3	43	430
Clothier	4	130	1300

Occupation or designation	Shareholders	No. of shares	Nominal value £
Confectioner	2	81	810
Co-operative society	1	50	500
Draper	20	352	3520
Fruiterer	1	3	30
Grocer	32	662	6495
Grocer and wine merchant	1	20	200
Grocer and teacher (2 females)	1	10	100
Gunmaker	1	70	700
Hatter	3	35	350
Hotel/innkeeper	6	150	1500
Ironmonger	16	374	3565
Joiner	3	25	250
Painter	1	12	120
Pawnbroker and jeweller	1	20	100
Plumber	2	30	300
Restaurateur	1	4	40
Saddler	1	30	300
Shoemaker	2	22	220
Slater	1	20	60
Stationer	11	223	2230
Watchmaker	6	209	2090
Wine and spirit merchant	1	20	200
	144	3235	31760
EMPLOYED (1)			
General manager, railway	2	150	1500
Manager	17	552	4570
Manager, colliery	14	209	2075
Manager, colliery (assistant)	1	10	100
Manager, engine works	1	40	400
Manager, factory	1	5	50
Manager, furnace	1	20	200
Manager, iron works	2	110	1100
Manager, gas works	3	85	850
Manager, mill	1	20	60

Table D(c)

Occupation or designation	Shareholders	No. of shares	Nominal value £
Manager, mining	6	61	610
Manager, oil works	8	340	4300
Manager, railway	2	110	1100
Manager, store	2	13	130
Manager, sugar house	1	20	200
Manager, works	1	40	400
Managing clerk	1	20	200
Agent, colliery	2	77	770
Agent, railway	1	5	50
Agent, station	1	10	100
Designer	1	20	200
Hydropathic superintendent	1	12	120
Inspector, coal traffic	1	10	100
Inspector, railway	2	15	150
Private secretary	1	20	200
Shipmaster/master mariner	4	127	1270
Shipmaster, retired	1	50	500
Stationmaster	6	65	650
	85	2216	21955
EMPLOYED (2)			
Bookkeeper	4	40	400
Cashier	17	430	4200
Clerk/solicitor's/law/commercial/ mercantile/ bankteller	6	55	550
Commercial traveller	15	274	2740
Traveller	1	20	100
Iron selector	1	12	120
Newspaper reporter	6	85	850
Salesman	2	40	260
Salesman, cattle	1	100	1000
Salesman, colliery	8	256	2560
Salesman, flour	1	10	100
Salesman, iron	2	85	850
Shorthand writer	1	20	200
	65	1427	13930

Occupation or designation	Shareholders	No. of shares	Nominal value £
WORKING CLASS (1)			
Blacksmith	2	12	110
Boilermaker	1	30	90
Cabinet maker	1	12	120
Candlemaker	3	28	280
Carpenter, house	1	5	50
Clerk	74	1429	14240
Colliery oversman	3	40	400
Dressmaker (female)	1	6	60
Engineer	10	84	715
Engine driver	3	15	150
Engine keeper	2	15	150
Foreman	1	5	50
Foreman, cooper	1	10	100
Foreman, retort	1	10	100
Grocer's assistant	1	4	40
Joiner	4	35	350
Messenger	1	5	50
Miner	7	57	570
Miner, coal	3	30	300
Oil refiner	4	36	360
Painter	2	17	170
Pit sinker	1	5	50
Plasterer	2	20	200
Plumber	1	10	100
Power loom tenter	2	15	150
Shopman	1	8	80
Storekeeper	5	71	640
Sulphate maker	1	10	100
Tailor's cutter	1	12	120
	140	2036	19895
WORKING CLASS (2)			
Labourer	3	20	200
Locomotive fireman	1	5	50

Occupation or designation	Shareholders	No. of shares	Nominal value £
Office porter	1	15	150
Packer	1	10	100
	6	50	500
DOMESTIC SERVICE			
Butler	2	12	70
Governess	1	6	60
Groom	1	2	10
	4	20	140
LAND (1)			
Factor	2	40	400
Farmer	36	1331	12960
Farmer and limeburner	1	50	500
Farm manager	2	35	350
Proprietor	6	640	6400
Steward	2	25	250
	49	2121	20860
LAND (2)			
Dairyman	1	5	50
Taxman of salmon fisheries	1	10	100
	2	15	150
Totals	2172	97188	922705

Table E(a) Shareholders by residence, 1862–1870

City	No. of shareholders	No. of shares	Nominal value £	Proportion
Scotland				
Edinburgh	33	1802	80850	11.64
Glasgow	97	3583	198150	28.51
County				
Argyll	1	20	200	0.03
Ayrshire	4	282	28400	4.09
Clackmannanshire	1	20	200	0.03
Dunbartonshire	3	268	27300	3.93
Fife	12	75	7800	1.12
Midlothian (east)	1	100	1000	0.14
Midlothian (west) and West Lothian	10	1874	171650	24.70
Lanarkshire	12	372	9700	1.40
Perthshire	2	110	1100	0.16
Renfrewshire	5	110	11000	1.58
Roxburghshire	1	50	500	0.07
Scotland	182	8666	537850	77.40
London	12	723	70350	10.12
Manchester	3	860	86000	12.38
England	15	1583	156350	22.50
Overseas	1	70	700	0.10
Total	198	10319	694900	100.00

Table E(b) Shareholders by residence, 1871–1876

City	No. of shareholders	No. of shares	Nominal value £	Proportion %
Scotland				
Aberdeen	16	1365	4650	1.56
Dundee	3	60	600	0.20
Edinburgh	133	52399	86090	28.83
Glasgow	83	8070	70600	23.65
County				
Aberdeenshire	2	26	230	0.08
Argyll	1	40	400	0.13
Ayrshire	4	145	950	0.32
Bute	1	100	1000	0.33
Clackmannan	3	270	2700	0.90
Dunbartonshire	2	150	1500	0.50
Dumfriesshire	1	25	250	0.08
Fife	8	375	2850	0.95
Kincardine	1	20	100	0.03
Kirkcudbright	1	20	100	0.03
Lewis	5	18	90	0.03
East Lothian	6	100	800	0.27
Midlothian (east)	7	2755	4550	1.53
Midlothian (west) and West Lothian	33	5583	52455	17.57
Lanarkshire	15	1015	10150	3.40
Moray	3	60	600	0.20
Peeblesshire	1	10	100	0.03
Perthshire	5	80	750	0.25
Renfrewshire	5	1130	6800	2.28
Rossshire	1	20	200	0.07
Roxburghshire	18	472	2560	0.86
Selkirkshire	1	50	500	0.17
Stirlingshire	4	75	650	0.22
Wigtownshire	6	220	1600	0.54
Scotland	369	74653	253825	85.01

City	No. of shareholders	No. of shares	Nominal value £	Proportion %
England				
City				
Liverpool	5	305	3025	1.01
London	54	6684	32950	11.04
Manchester	1	5	50	0.02
County				
Bedfordshire	2	60	300	0.10
Berkshire	1	50	250	0.08
Cumberland	2	70	450	0.15
Devon	3	130	650	0.22
Durham	1	20	200	0.07
Hampshire	3	308	3040	1.02
Hereford	1	20	200	0.07
Northumberland	4	110	550	0.18
Suffolk	3	100	650	0.22
Sussex	1	20	100	0.03
Warwickshire	1	60	300	0.10
Yorkshire	3	16	155	0.05
England	85	7958	42870	14.36
Ireland				
Dublin	3	30	250	0.08
Provinces	4	325	1625	0.55
Ireland	7	355	1875	0.63
Total	461	82966	298570	100.00

Table E(c) Shareholders by residence, 1877–1885

City	No. of shareholders	No. of shares	Nominal value £	Proportion
Scotland				
Aberdeen	15	207	2070	0.22
Dundee	114	2707	27070	2.93
Edinburgh	499	32483	285630	30.96
Glasgow	524	24891	254465	27.58
County				
Aberdeenshire	5	350	3500	0.38
Angus	14	540	5400	0.59
Argyll	3	120	1200	0.13
Ayrshire	47	1417	13145	1.42
Banffshire	3	50	500	0.05
Berwickshire	2	20	200	0.02
Bute	5	54	540	0.06
Clackmannan	12	448	4480	0.49
Dunbartonshire	24	1418	14180	1.54
Dumfriessshire	9	175	1750	0.19
Fife	169	7165	71300	7.73
Invernessshire	4	85	850	0.09
Lewis	2	20	200	0.02
East Lothian	10	276	2760	0.30
Midlothian (east)	24	796	7260	0.79
Midlothian (west) and West Lothian	257	7661	74650	8.09
Kirkcudbright	2	40	400	0.04
Lanarkshire	174	8206	71690	7.77
Mull	3	130	1300	0.14
Orkney	1	25	250	0.03
Peeblesshire	9	135	1350	0.15
Perthshire	31	689	6715	0.73
Renfrewshire	50	1846	18635	2.02
Rossshire	4	60	565	0.06
Roxburghshire	16	264	2640	0.29
Selkirkshire	10	410	4100	0.44
Shetland	1	10	100	0.01
Stirlingshire	36	1325	12550	1.36

City	No. of shareholders	No. of shares	Nominal value £	Proportion
Wigtownshire	3	22	220	0.02
Scotland	2082	94045	891665	96.63
England				
City				
Liverpool	8	156	1560	0.17
London	17	647	6470	0.70
Manchester	2	80	800	0.09
County				
Bedfordshire	1	50	500	0.05
Berkshire	2	155	1550	0.17
Cumberland	2	30	300	0.03
Durham	6	95	950	0.10
Gloucestershire	3	115	1150	0.12
Hampshire	5	230	2300	0.25
Hertfordshire	1	5	50	0.01
Isle of Man	6	443	4430	0.48
Kent	1	10	100	0.01
Lincolnshire	1	50	500	0.05
Middlesex	1	30	90	0.01
Nottinghamshire	1	10	100	0.01
Surrey	2	40	300	0.03
Warwickshire	2	90	900	0.10
Yorkshire	11	325	3170	0.35
England	72	2561	25220	2.73
Wales				
Cardiff	1	10	100	0.01
Ireland				
Dublin	0	0	0	
Provinces	6	382	3820	
Ireland	6	382	3820	0.42
Overseas	3	80	800	0.09
Illegible, or otherwise unable to be assigned to counties	8	110	1100	0.12
Total	2172	97188	922705	100.00

Notes

Introduction

1 P. Kinchin and J. Kinchin, 1988, *Glasgow's Great Exhibitions, 1881, 1901, 1911, 1938*, Bicester, White Cockade, 30.
2 John Butt, 1965, 'The Scottish oil mania of 1864–6', *Scottish Journal of Political Economy*, 12, 195–209; 209.
3 R.H. Campbell, 1971, *Scotland since 1707: The Rise of an Industrial Society*, Oxford, Basil Blackwell, 247.
4 Harold F. Williamson and Arnold R. Daum, 1959, *The American Petroleum Industry: The Age of Illumination 1859–1899*, Northwestern University Press, Evanston, 333.
5 *Scotsman*, 30 Dec. 1893, 28 Dec. 1898, 28 Dec. 1900.
6 A.D. Chandler, *Scale and Scope: The Dynamics of Industrial Capitalism*, Cambridge, Mass., Harvard University Press, 1990, 298–304.
7 J.H. Bamberg, *The History of the British Petroleum Company*: Volume 2, 1928–54, Cambridge, Cambridge University Press, 509–11.

Chapter 1 1862–1877

1 H.M. Cadell and J.S. Grant-Wilson, 1906, 'The geology of the oil shale fields', in *The Oil Shales of the Lothians*, Glasgow, HMSO, 11–12.
2 D.R. Steuart, 1889, 'The manufacture of paraffin oil', *Journal of the Society of Chemical Industry*, 8, 100–110; 100; J.B. Sneddon, W. Caldwell, and J. Stein, 1938, 'Seventy-five years of oil shale mining', *Oil shale and Cannel Coal, Proceedings of a conference held in Scotland, June 1938*, London, The Institute of Petroleum, 57.
3 Steuart, 'Manufacture of paraffin oil', 100–1.
4 George Beilby, 'Thirty years of progress', 'Thirty years of progress in the shale oil industry,' *Journal of the Society of Chemical Industry*, 16, 876–86; 877.
5 Steuart, 'Manufacture of paraffin oil', 101.
6 Beilby, 'Thirty years of progress', 876.
7 H.R.J. Conacher, 1927, 'History of the Scottish oil-shale industry', in *The Oil-Shales of the Lothians*, Edinburgh, HMSO, 251.
8 John Butt, 1964, 'James Young, Scottish philanthropist and industrialist', Unpublished PhD Thesis, Glasgow University, 99.
9 Conacher, 'History of the Scottish oil-shale industry', 251
10 N.M. Henderson, 'The history of shale retorts at Broxburn', *Journal of the Society of Chemical Industry*, 16, 984–8; 984; H.M. Cadell, 1913, *The Story of the Forth*, Glasgow, James Maclehose and Sons, 208–9.
11 Rivers Pollution Commission, Fourth Report, 1871, Parliamentary Papers (PP) 1872, Part IV, 321.
12 Butt, 'James Young', 160–1.
13 Ibid., 147.
14 Ibid., 50, 147.
15 BP Archive, AR 1007, Copy Minute of agreement between James Young and Young's Paraffin Light & Mineral Oil Company, 1865, 25–6.
16 Butt, 'Scottish oil mania', passim.
17 Butt, 'Scottish oil mania', 197.

18 H.R.J. Conacher, 1938, 'The mineral oil industry in Scotland, its raw materials and methods', in *Oil Shale and Cannel Coal*, London, The Institute of Petroleum, 304.

19 Butt, 'Scottish oil mania', 208.

20 D.R. Steuart, 1912, 'The chemistry of the oil shales', in *Oil Shales of the Lothians*, Edinburgh, HMSO, 137–8.

21 R.A. Church, 1975, *The Great Victorian Boom, 1850–1873*, London, Macmillan/Economic History Society.

22 S.B. Saul, 1969, *The Myth of the Great Depression, 1873–1896*, London, Macmillan, 14.

23 BP Archive, YP, SHMB 1, 4 Feb. 1867.

24 Williamson and Daum, *American Petroleum Industry*, 75–6, 309, 117, 107, 181–4.

25 Ibid., 291.

26 Steuart, 'Chemistry of the oil shales', 137.

27 Williamson and Daum, *American Petroleum Industry*, 322, 327.

28 S.E. Morison, H.S. Commager and W.E. Leuchtenburg, 1983, *A Concise History of the American Republic*, 2nd edition, New York, Oxford University Press, T10–T13.

29 Massimo Livi-Bacci (tr. Carl Ipsen), 1992, *A Concise History of World Population*, Blackwell, Oxford, 139.

30 Williamson and Daum, *American Petroleum Industry*, 489.

31 Ibid., 489, 521.

32 D. Thomson, 1966, *Europe since Napoleon*, Harmondsworth, Penguin, 112.

33 P. Mathias, 1983, *The First Industrial Nation: An Economic History of Britain, 1700–1914*, London, Methuen, 415.

34 Aldcroft, Derek H., 1994, 'The European dimension to the modern world', in Derek H. Aldcroft and Simon P. Ville (eds), *The European Economy 1750–1914*, 10.

35 D. Kynaston, 1976, *King Labour: The British Working Class, 1850–1914*, London, Allen & Unwin, 67.

36 J.F.C. Harrison, 1990, *Late Victorian Britain, 1875–1901*, London, Fontana, 59.

37 Mathias, *First Industrial Nation*, 423.

38 J.C. Stamp, 1916, *British Incomes and Property*, London, London, P.S. King, 448; quoted in W.H. Fraser, 1981, *The Coming of the Mass Market, 1850–1914*, London, Macmillan, 23.

39 A.L. Bowley, 1920, *The Change in the Distribution of National Income, 1880–1913*, Oxford, Clarendon Press, 21; quoted in Fraser, *Coming of the Mass Market*, 24.

40 Mathias, *First Industrial Nation*, 345.

41 Fraser, *Coming of the Mass Market*, 16–23.

42 Ibid., 17.

43 John F. Wilson and Andrew Thomson, 2006, *The Making of Modern Management*, Oxford, Oxford University Press, 220.

44 Williamson and Daum, *American Petroleum Industry*, 29.

45 P. Horn, 1995, *Labouring Life in the Victorian Countryside*, Stroud, Alan Sutton, 24–5.

46 Checkland, 1969, *The Rise of Industrial Society in England, 1815–1885*, London, Longmans Green, 248–9, 269–70; William Donaldson, 1986, *Popular Literature in Victorian Scotland*, Aberdeen University Press, 1–3.

47 Williamson and Daum, *American Petroleum Industry*, 1959, 323

48 Butt, 'James Young': 340

49 BP Archive, YP, SHMB 1, Directors' Report, 1873.

50 Williamson and Daum, *American Petroleum Industry*, 492.

51 Graham P. Anderson, 1892, *The Rural Exodus*, London, Macmillan, 90.

52 B. Borrows, 1998, *Lengthening the Day: A History of Lighting Technology*, Oxford, Oxford University Press, 49.

53 I.R.C. Byatt, 1979, *The British Electrical Industry, 1875–1914*, Oxford, Clarendon Press, 3.

54 Derek Matthews, 1986, 'Laissez-faire and the London gas industry in the nineteenth century: Another look', *Economic History Review*, 39, 244–63; 246.

55 Francis Goodall, 2002, 'Gas in London: A divided city', *The London Journal*, 27, 2, 34–50; 42.
56 Maud Pember Reeves, 1979, *Round about a Pound a Week*, London, Virago.
57 Judith Flanders, 2003, *The Victorian House*, London, Harper Collins, 172.
58 Anon., 1888, *Memoirs and Portraits of One Hundred Glasgow Men*, vol. 2, Glasgow, James Maclehose and Sons, 342, 'James Young'.
59 BP Archive, OOC, GMB, 20 June 1871.
60 BP Archive, OOC, GMB, 16 June 1874.
61 BP Archive, YP, SHMB 1, 16 June 1875.
62 Statistical Abstract for the United Kingdom, 1861–75, *PP*, 1876, 28–9.
63 Statistical Abstract for the United Kingdom, 1876–90, *PP*, 1890–1, 58–9.
64 BP Archive, YP, SHMB 1, 18 June 1872.
65 Williamson and Daum, *American Petroleum Industry*, 328, 335.
66 Ibid., 325.
67 Ibid., 178.
68 Ibid., 333.
69 J.S. Jeans, 1872, *Western Worthies*, Glasgow, Star Office, 68.
70 Butt, 'Scottish oil mania', 204.
71 I. Redwood, 1897, *A Practical Treatise on Mineral Oils and their By-products*, London, E. & F.N. Spon, 26–7.
72 Steuart, 'Chemistry of the oil shales', 137.
73 Ibid.
74 Conacher, 'History of the Scottish oil-shale industry', 257.
75 Jeans, *Western Worthies*, 68.
76 BP Archive, YP, SHMB 1, Directors' Report, y.e. 30 April 1872, Appendix.
77 Williamson and Daum, *American Petroleum Industry*, 335.
78 Butt, 'James Young', 340; Conacher, 'History of the Scottish oil-shale industry', 249.
79 BP Archive, YP, SHMB 1, Directors' Report, y.e. 30 April 1873.
80 BP Archive, OOC, GMB, 15 June 1875, 20 June 1876.
81 BP Archive, OOC, GMB, 15 June 1875.
82 *Scotsman*, 20 Jan. 1874.
83 Rivers Pollution Commissioners, Fourth Report, 1871, 23.
84 Steuart, 'Chemistry of the oil shales', 139, 138.
85 BP Archive, YP, SHMB 1, Directors' Report, y.e. 30 April 1878.
86 BP Archive, BOC, Registrar's File 792/3, Schedule to Agreement between Bell and new company.
87 Inspectors of Mines Reports (IOM Report), PP, 1877, 137.
88 IOM Report, 1876, xiii, 62–3.
89 Valuation Rolls, County of Renfrew, 1875–6, Part 1, Parish of Kilbarchan, 2, Item 5; 5, Item 17; Part 2, Abbey Parish, 14, Item 21.
90 IOM Report, PP, 1876, 184.

Chapter 2 1877–1887

1 NAS, Hare of Calderhall papers; BP Archive, OOC, Statement of value of shale; IOM Report, PP, 1877, 137; BP Archive, YP, SHMB 1, Directors' Report, y.e. 30 April 1878; IOM Report, PP, 1876, 184; 1877, 180; BP Archive, YP, SHMB 1, Directors' Reports, y.e. 30 April 1876 and 1877; Dalmeny Estate Papers, Cash Ledger No. 3, Fo. 474; BP Archive, OOC, GMB, Minutes of AGM, 20 June 1876, 15 May 1877; *Scotsman*, 24 May 1877.
2 Church, *Great Victorian Boom*, 9.
3 Saul, *Myth of the Great Depression*, 32.

4   Bowley's and Feinstein's figures are both quoted in G.R. Boyer, 2004, 'Living Standards, 1860–1939', in R. Floud and P. Johnson (eds), *The Cambridge Economic History of Modern Britain*, Cambridge University Press, 284.

5   Saul, *Myth of the Great Depression*, 14.

6   Williamson and Daum, *American Petroleum Industry*, 495–6 and 815, note 5.

7   See *West Lothian Courier* (*WLC*), 2 Feb. 1884.

8   *WLC*, 25 Aug. 1888.

9   Williamson and Daum, *American Petroleum Industry*, 495.

10   NAS, Hare of Calderhall papers, Oakbank Oil Company monthly statements of sales of burning oil, GD266/81/66; 81/61; 81/58; 81/54; 81/55; 81/5–53; 82/20–54, especially 82/40.

11   *WLC*, 24 June 1876.

12   NAS, Hare of Calderhall papers, OOC, Statements of value of shale, GD266/80/1.

13   Young's figures calculated from data in BP Archive, SHMB 1, Directors' Report, 30 April 1873; see also YP, SHMB 1, Directors' Report, 30 April 1872, Appendix; OOC, GMB, 15 June 1875, Directors' Report to 6th AGM.

14   Beilby, 'Thirty years of progress', 882.

15   Williamson and Daum, *American Petroleum Industry*, 496.

16   Ibid., 489.

17   OOC, GMB, 15 June 1875; BP Archive, YP, SHMB 1, y.e. 30 April 1872.

18   In 1874, American exports of lubricating oil to Europe totalled 27,800 barrels. An American barrel contained 42 American gallons or 35 imperial gallons; 27,800 × 35 = 973,000 imperial gallons.

19   BP Archive, YP, Journal No. 10, Fos 457–8; OOC 1869, Ledger No. 9, Fo. 126.

20   IOM Report, PP, 1879, 101 and 211; and 1884, 39 and 85.

21   BP Archive, OOC 1869, DMB, 6 November 1876.

22   Beilby, 'Thirty years of progress', 882.

23   Ibid.; BP Archive, OOC 1869, GMB, 15 June 1875.

24   BP Archive, YP, SHMB 1, Directors' Report, y.e. 30 April 1874.

25   *WLC*, 24 June 1876.

26   BP Archive, YP, SHMB 1, Directors' Reports, y.e. 30 April 1877 and 1878.

27   *WLC*, 21 June 1879

28   BP Archive, OOC 1869, GMB, 15 May 1877; OOC 1869, GMB, 18 May 1880.

29   Sources of figures: BP Archive, YP, SHMB 1, y.e. 30 April 1878; NAS, BT2/303/18; derived from a report on The Manufacture of Paraffin Lamps, *WLC*, 2 Nov. 1878; NAS, Hare of Calderhall Papers, OOC, Statements of output of Calderhall and Calderhouse shale, GD266, 81/67 & 68; OOC, Statement of value of shale, GD266/80/1; calculated from data in *WLC*, 2 Nov. 1878 and BP Archive, YP, SHMB 1, y.e. 30 April 1878.

30   BP Archive, YP, Ledger No. 5; OOC 1869, Ledger No 9.

31   BP Archive, OOC, Ledger No. 9, Fos 137–42.

32   BP Archive, YP, Journal No. 5, Fo. 265; Journal No. 10, Fos 457–8.

33   BP Archive, YP, Journal No. 5, Fos 267–8; Journal No. 10, Fos 462–3.

34   BP Archive, YP, SHMB 1, y.e. 30 April 1874.

35   *WLC*, 25 June 1881.

36   BP Archive, YP, Journal No. 5, Fo. 265; Journal No. 10, Fos 457–8.

37   Conacher, 'History of the Scottish oil-shale industry', 249, 258.

38   Steuart, 'Manufacture of paraffin oil', 109–110.

39   Beilby, 'Thirty years of progress', 882, 883; Williamson and Daum, *American Petroleum Industry*, 483.

40   *PP*: Mines and Quarries, General Report and Statistics, 1905, Part III, Output, 256; Mining and Mineral Statistics, 1882, 103; Mining and Mineral Statistics, 1894, 89; Mines and Quarries, General Report, 1910, 276.

41   BP Archive, OOC 1869, GMB, 15 June 1875.

42 BP Archive, YP, Journal No. 5, Fo. 262.
43 BP Archive, YP, Journal No. 13, Fo 177.
44 *WLC*, 3 Dec. 1887, Broxburn miners' dispute.
45 NAS, Hare of Calderhall Papers, Box 84, Bundle 90.
46 BP Archive, YP, SHMB 1, 4 Feb. 1867; YP, SHMB 1, 18 Feb. 1870.
47 BP Archive, YP, Journal No. 5, Fo. 262.
48 BP Archive, OOC 1869, GMB, 15 May 1875.
49 BP Archive, POC, DMB 29 May 1884.
50 *Scotsman*, 8 Feb. 1869
51 BP Archive, YP, SHMB, 20 June 1871; OS 1-inch sheet 31, 1904.
52 BP Archive, OOC 1869, GMB, 20 May 1885; OOC 1886, DMB 1, 16 Aug. 1886.
53 W. Caldwell, 1906, 'Methods of working the oil shales', in *Oil Shales of the Lothians*, 110 et seq.
54 Mining and Mineral Statistics (PP), 1886, 95; 193–4.
55 IOM Report, PP, 1876, 184; 1877, 180; and 1878, 226.
56 Conacher, 'History of the Scottish oil-shale industry', 250.
57 Redwood, *Practical Treatise*, 263–5.
58 Beilby, 'Thirty years of progress', 876–7.
59 *WLC*, 17 Dec. 1881, Report of Court of Session judgement, Henderson v Clippens Oil Company Ltd.
60 Beilby, 'Thirty years of progress', 877
61 *WLC*, 31 May, 7, 14, 28 June and 5 July 1879, 17 Dec. 1881.
62 Beilby, 'Thirty years of progress', 877.
63 Ibid., 877–8.
64 Redwood, *Practical Treatise*, 71–6.
65 Henderson, 'History of shale retorts', 984.
66 Beilby, 'Thirty years of progress', 877.
67 BP Archive, OOC 1869, GMB, 15 June 1875.
68 BP Archive, OOC, GMB, 21 May 1878.
69 Beilby, 'Thirty years of progress', 878.
70 *Scotsman*, 12 May 1880; BP Archive, YP, SHMB 1, Directors' Report, y.e. 30 April 1883.
71 *Scotsman*, 24 May 1877.
72 BP Archive, OOC 1886, BMB 1, 13 Sept. 1886.
73 IOM Report, PP, 1879, 256.
74 Registrar of Companies, File No. 792.
75 BP Archive, BOC, GMB 1, 7 May 1878.
76 Ibid., 16 Mar. 1878.
77 Sources of figures: BP Archive, BOC, Journal No. 2, Fo. 292; Journal No. 3, Fos 651, 684, 725, 732; *Scotsman*, 11 May 1887.
78 *WLC*, 2 Nov. 1878. Young's company gave its production of paraffin (crude and refined) in pounds. For the present purpose this has been converted to gallons at a specific gravity of .810 or 8.1 pounds to the gallon (BP Archive, YP, Journal No. 10, Fos 160–1).
79 BP Archive, BOC, Journal No. 3, Fos 247, 8, 250.
80 BP Archive, BOC, Journal No. 3, Fo. 247.
81 BP Archive, YP, Journal No. 10, Fos 182 to 444 passim.
82 BP Archive, BOC, Journal No. 2, Fos 294–95; reports of company affairs in the *Scotsman* newspaper; BOC, GMB 1; BOC, GMB 1, Directors' Report, 10 May 1881; GMB 1, Directors' Report, 9 May1887.
83 IOM Report, PP, 1882, 234; and 1876, 184.
84 NAS, BT2/953/7.
85 IOM Report, PP, 1882, 234–5.
86 NAS, BT2/993.

87 VR, County of Renfrew, 1877–8, Parish of Kilbarchan, item 108; and County of Renfrew, 1883–4, Parish of Kilbarchan, item 116.

88 NAS, BT2/1049A/2, Schedule to agreement between J Waddell and company; *Scotsman*, 22 May 1883, 27 May 1884; *WLC*, 16 May 1885, 22 May 1886.

89 Beilby, 'Thirty years of progress', 878.

90 *WLC*, 23 June 1883.

91 NAS, BT2/135; Beilby, 'Thirty years of progress', 878; *WLC*, 22 May 1886.

92 Conacher, 'History of the Scottish oil-shale industry', 253.

93 *WLC*, 6 Jan. 188.

94 *Scotsman*, 18 May 1882; BP Archive, OOC, GMB, 10 May 1883; YP, SHMB 2, 17 June 1885.

95 BP Archive, YP, SHMB 1, Directors' Report, y.e. 30 April 1881.

96 *WLC*, 6 Jan. 1883.

97 *Ibid.*, and 3 Jan. 1885.

98 Mineral Statistics (PP), 1883, 96; 1889, 187.

99 Beilby, 'Thirty years of progress', 878.

100 Steuart, 'Manufacture of paraffin oil', 102.

101 George Beilby, 1884, 'On the production of ammonia from the nitrogen of minerals', *Journal of the Society of Chemical Industry (JSCI)*, 3, 216–24; 216.

102 Beilby, Ibid., 216–24, and 'Thirty years of progress', 879, 881; Report of International Inventors' Exhibition, London, *JSCI*, 4, 1885, 472–4; Conacher, 'History of the Scottish oil-shale industry', 254.

103 For company formations and liquidations, etc, see: NAS, BT2/1229, BT2/1292; Registrar of Companies, File No. 1295; NAS, BT2/1267, BT2/1285, BT2/1267, BT2/1342, BT2/1351, BT2/1485.

104 IOM Report, PP, 1886, 193–4.

105 NAS, BT2/993; BT2/1431.

106 Mining and Mineral Statistics (PP), 1882, 103; 1886, 95.

107 BP Archive, YP, SHMB 2, 16 June 1886.

108 *WLC*, 5 June 1886.

109 BP Archive, OOC 1869, GMB, 21 May 1884.

110 Ibid., 1886, GMB 1, 27 May 1887.

111 IOM Report, PP, 1887, 153.

112 *Scotsman*, 24 April 1886; 11 May 1886.

113 BP Archive, BOC, Journal No 2, Fo. 292; *Scotsman*, 11 May 1887.

114 *Scotsman*, 22 May 1886.

115 *WLC*, 5 June 1886.

116 Ibid.; BP Archive, YP, SHMB 2, 16 June 1886.

117 *Scotsman*, 20 and 25 May 1886.

118 Ibid., 4 June 1887.

119 Ibid., 11 May 1889.

120 BP Archive, BOC, GMB 1, Directors' Report to AGM 18 May 1887; Ledger No. 4, Fos 105, 117; Ledger No. 6, Fos 151 and 119; Ledger No. 4, Fo. 133; Ledger No. 6, Fos 134–6.

121 *Scotsman*, 11 May 1887.

122 *WLC*, 2 Jan. 1886.

123 Ibid., 5 Mar. 1887.

124 Ibid., 25 June 1887.

125 *Scotsman*, 25 Dec. 1884; NAS, BT2/1267/9.

126 *WLC*, 3 Jan. 1885.

127 *Scotsman*, 23 Dec. 1886, 22 Dec. 1887; *WLC*, 24 Dec. 1887.

128 *WLC*, 4 and 18 June 1887.

129 *Scotsman*, 20 May 1887.

130 *WLC*, 21 May 1887.

131   Ibid., 18 June 1887.
132   Ibid., 6 Jan. 1883; Johnston, 2000, 43–5.
133   The details of this scheme are set out fully in a report of this meeting in the *West Lothian Courier* of 2 July 1887.
134   *WLC*, 9 July 1887.
135   Ibid., 13 Aug. 1887.
136   Ibid., 6 and 13 Aug., 17 Sept 1887.
137   Ibid., 1 Oct. and 3 Dec. 1887.
138   Ibid., 20 Aug. 1887.
139   Ibid., 24 Sept. 1887.
140   Williamson and Daum, *American Petroleum Industry*, 660; Mining and Mineral Statistics (PP) 1887, 71; 1888 and 1889, 187; *WLC*, 13 Aug. 1887.
141   *WLC*, 6 Aug. 1887.
142   Ibid., 15 Oct. 1887.
143   Ibid., 3 Dec. 1887.
144   *WLC*, 24 and 31 Dec. 1887.

Chapter 3 Paraffin wax and Standard Oil, 1888–1899

1   BP Archive, YP, Ledger No. 5; SHMB 1, 16 July 1879; YP Ledger No. 8.
2   Williamson and Daum, *American Petroleum Industry*, 274–5, 249.
3   See *JSCI*, 46, 1887, 630–1.
4   Beilby, 1884, 'On the production of ammonia', 216.
5   BP Archive, OOC, Ledger No. 9, Fos 137–42.
6   Williamson and Daum, *American Petroleum Industry*, 471, 429, 473, 475.
7   Allan Nevins, 1953, *Study in Power*, Charles Scribner's Sons, New York and London, vol. 2, 10–11, 12.
8   Ron Chernow, 1998, *Titan: The Life of John D. Rockefeller, Sr.*, London, Little, Brown, 286.
9   Williamson and Daum, *American Petroleum Industry*, 557, 473, 563, 564, 568.
10   *WLC*, 31 Dec. 1887, 14 Jan. 1888.
11   BP Archive, YP, SMB, 8 Feb. 1866
12   BP Archive, SHMB 1, Directors' Report, 30 April 1872
13   *JSCI*, 6, 1887, 632.
14   *JSCI*, 6, 1887, 632–3; *PP*: Statistical Abstract, 1880–94, 94–5; Census of Production, Preliminary Tables, Part 3, 24; Statistical Abstract, 1899–1914, 192–3.
15   BP Archive, YP, Journal No. 13, Fos 172 to 382; Ledger No. 4, Fo. 105; *JSCI*, 4, 1885, 471.
16   Mining and Mineral Statistics (PP), 1883, 96; 1888, 72.
17   Conacher, 'History of the Scottish oil-shale industry', 257 states that the agreement made in 1888 restricted Scottish production to 24,000 tons.
18   Annual Statement of the Trade of the United Kingdom with Foreign Countries and British possessions (PP), 1877, 54; 1888, 71.
19   Ibid., 1877–1900.
20   *JSCI*, 11, 1892, 851.
21   BP Archive, AR 0822, Memorandum of Agreement between Thompson & Bedford and the Scottish Companies, 30 Jan. 1892; Nevins, *Study in Power*, vol. 2, 288.
22   *WLC*, 11 May 1888.
23   BP Archive, OOC 1886, DMB 1, 1 and 13 Feb., 12 Mar. 1888.
24   *WLC*, 2 Jun. 1888.
25   Ibid., 5 Jan., 19 Jan., 2 Feb., 14 Dec. 1889; 21 Jun. 1890, Report of Young's AGM; and 6 Jun. 1891, Report of Linlithgow company's AGM.

26 *WLC*, 21 Sept 1889.

27 Ibid., 4 Jan. 1890.

28 Annual Statements of the Trade of the United Kingdom (PP), 1888, 71; 1889, 73; 1890, 73; 1891, 75.

29 Mining and Mineral Statistics (PP), 1888, 72 ; 1889, 187; 1890, 74; 1891, 75.

30 Statistical Abstract (PP), 1880–94, 94–5, 100–1.

31 *WLC*, 18 May, 4 May, 11 May and 2 June 1888.

32 Ibid., 25 May 1889.

33 Ibid., 5 Jan., 2 Feb. 1889.

34 Ibid., 1 June 1889.

35 *WLC*, 18 and 25 May, 15 and 22 June, 1889; *Scotsman*, 10 May 1889; *WLC*, 1889; Steuart, 'Manufacture of paraffin oil': 110.

36 Williamson and Daum, *American Petroleum Industry*, 565, 616–19.

37 Nevins, *Study in Power*, vol. 2, 103.

38 Williamson and Daum, *American Petroleum Industry*, 485, 615.

39 BP Archive, Private Report by Mr Fyfe to directors of Young's company, 14 Feb. 1893.

40 Williamson and Daum, *American Petroleum Industry*, 624, 616; Statistical Abstract for Foreign Countries (PP), 1885 to 1894–5, 134–5.

41 *WLC*, 22 June, 1 June 1889.

42 Mining and Mineral Statistics (PP), 1886, 95; 1888, 72.

43 BP Archive, BOC, GMB 1, 18 May 1887; BOC, Ledger No. 6, Fos 58, 60, 61, 68.

44 Mining and Mineral Statistics (PP), 1889, 187; 1890, 74–5.

45 BP Archive, OOC 1886 Ledger No. 1, Fo. 275; No. 2, Fo. 232: BOC Ledger No. 6, Fos 113–4; 121–4; 342; No. 8 Fos 88, 128, 135; POC Ledger No. 2, Fos 238–9, 245–6; No. 3, Fos 234–5, 238–40; YP Ledger No. 8, Fos 52–5, 57–8, 526–7, 529, 532–7, 539.

46 Annual Statement of Trade (PP), 1888, 71; 1891, 75.

47 BP Archive, AR 0822, Memorandum of Agreement . . ., 30 Jan. 1892.

48 Annual Statement of Trade (PP), 1891, 73.

49 BP Archive, POC Statement to the Press, 27 Sept. 1892.

50 BP Archive, YP Ledger No. 8, Fos 57, 58, 528, 529, 534, 537, 539; BOC Ledger No. 8 Fos 88, 121, 128, 135; OOC 1886 Ledger No. 2, Fo. 235; POC Ledger No. 4, Fos 313, 316, 317.

51 Redwood, *Practical Treatise*, 28–37.

52 BP Archive, Private Report by Mr Fyfe . . ., 14 Feb. 1893.

53 T.A.B. Corley, 1983, *A History of the Burmah Oil Company, 1886–1924*, London, Heinemann, 52.

54 BP Archive, POC Statement to the press, 27 Sept 1892.

55 *Scotsman*, 13 May 1892.

56 BP Archive, POC, Ledger No. 4, Fo.313.

57 *WLC*, 20 May 1893.

58 Annual Statements of Trade (PP), 1891, 75; 1893, 80; 1898, 207.

59 For the liquidations, etc., see: NAS, BT2/1285/19; BT2/2469; BT2/808/35; *Scotsman*, 29 Dec., 27 Dec. 1897, and 27 Dec. 1899.

60 Home Office, List of Mines in the United Kingdom of Great Britain and Ireland and the Isle of Man, 1890, 8–11, 18, 29–32; 1896, 7–8, 19–22.

61 *WLC*, 2 May 1896.

62 *Scotsman* 4 May 1896.

63 Robert D. Corrins, 1994, 'The Scottish business elite in the Nineteenth Century: The case of William Baird & Company', in A.J.G. Cummings and T.M. Devine, *Industry, Business and Society in Scotland since 1700*, 73.

64 F.M.L. Thompson, 2000, 'Agricultural, chemical and fertiliser industries', in E.J.T. Collins (ed.), *The Agrarian History of England and Wales*, 1035.

65 R.W. Beachey, 1957, *The British West Indies Sugar Industry in the Late Nineteenth Century*, Oxford, Basil Blackwell, 89.

66 Thompson, 'Agricultural, chemical and fertiliser industries', 1035.
67 BP Archive, OOC 1869, Ledger No. 9, Fo. 135; OOC 1886, Ledger No. 2, Fos 240, 294; YP Ledger No. 5, Fos 47, 49, 433, 441–2, 447, 451–2, 463–4, 469, 474, 482; Ledger No. 8, Fos 57–8, 505–6, 516–7, 522–3, 527, 533–4, 537, 543–4, 573–4, 81; POC Ledger No. 3, Fos 214, 215, 225, 226, 228, 231, 232, 234, 238.
68 *Scotsman*, 12 May 1891.
69 *WLC*, 23 May 1891, 31 May 1890.
70 *Scotsman*, 18 May 1892.
71 *WLC*, 18 May 1889.
72 *Scotsman*, 17 May 1894, 23 May 1895; BP Archive, OOC 1886, Ledger No. 2, Fos 66, 288.
73 *WLC*, 1 June 1889, 21 June 1890; NAS, BT2/1351/25.

Chapter 4 1900–1914: New retorts and expansion

1   *WLC*, 23 May 1896.
2   *JSCI*, 14, 1895, 796–7.
3   For costs, see Bryson, 'The Pumpherston patent retort'; 992; BP Archive, OOC 1886, Ledger No. 4, Fos 44, 50.
4   James Bryson, 1897, 'The Pumpherston patent retort', *JSCI*, 16, 990–3; 990; *WLC*, 21 May 1898, 20 May 1899; BP Archive, OOC 1886, GMB 1, Fo. 142; YP SHMB 2, Fo. 145; *Scotsman*, 12 May 1902, 8 May 1905, 7 May 1906, 6 May 1907, 9 May 1911.
5   *Scotsman*, 1 and 16 June 1904.
6   *Scotsman*, 3 June 1907.
7   Home Office, List of Mines, 1899, 8, 21, 22; 1913, 54, 81, 85; BOC Ledger No. 11, Fos 72, 370; BP Archive, BOC Ledger No. 11, Fos 72, 370; Ledger No. 18, Fo. 103; BOC Ledger No. 11, Fo. 80; BOC Ledger No. 18, Fo. 104; PP: Mines and Quarries, General Report and Statistics, Part 3, Output, 1899, 243; Mines and Quarries, Inspector of Mines Report, Scotland Division, 1913, 7; Home Office, List of Mines , 1899: 7, 8, 19, 21, 22; 1913: 53, 54, 75, 81, 82, 83.
8   *WLC*, 25 April 1902; BP Archive, OOC 1886, Ledger No. 4, Fos. 44, 50; No 8, Fos 120, 330, 336; OOC 1886, Ledger No. 4, Fo. 56; Ledger No. 8 Fo. 304; OOC 1886, Ledger No. 8, Fo. 137.
9   *WLC*, 20 May 1899, 30 May 1902, 5 Jun. 1908.
10 NAS, BT2/4098/14; BT2/5644/11, 16, 19, 20; *WLC*, 1 June 1906; *Scotsman*, 29 May 1909; Home Office, List of Mines, 1899, 8, 21, 22; 1913, 54, 83.
11 NAS, BT2/4179; *Scotsman*, 14 July 1900.
12 NAS, BT2/4179/16; *WLC*, 24 July 1903, 3 Jun. 1904.
13 *WLC*, 19 May 1900; NAS, BT2/1351/39; BT2/1342/23.
14 *Scotsman*, 25 Dec. 1890, 30 Dec. 1891.
15 The term 'crush' seems to be synonymous with the 'creep' described as the most formidable of the difficulties associated with mining. The stoops proved unable to bear the weight of the over-lying strata and allowed the roof and pavement in the rooms to be forced together. It was particularly associated with steeply inclined workings and with a soft pavement (Caldwell, 'Methods of working', 112). The seams at Straiton have been described as 'dipping at a high angle' so that 'mining in these measures is both difficult and costly' (Cadell Grant Wilson, 'Geology of the oil shale fields', 6).
16 *WLC*, 16 May 1891.
17 Butt, 'James Young': 147
18 Beilby, 'Thirty years of progress': 883.
19 BP Archive, OOC 1886, GMB 2, Fos 54–5; *WLC*, 2 Jun. 1911.
20 Geoffrey Jones, 1981, *The State and the Emergence of the British Oil Industry*, London, Macmillan, 33.
21 Chernow, *Titan*, 247.

22 Mineral Statistics (PP), 1891, 76.
23 *JSCI*, 11 (1892), 852.
24 Statistical Abstract (PP), 1899–1914, 146–7.
25 BP Archive, AR1475, Comparative statement showing (1) total production& deliveries of all Scotch companies, (2) other companies' position, (3) Pumpherston company's position, in gallons, for year ending 30 April 1913.
26 *WLC*, 4 Jan. 1890.
27 BP Archive, AR1475, 30 April 1913.
28 Jones, *State and Emergence*, 10, 24, 228.

Part 2 Introduction

1 Margaret Ackrill, 1987, *Manufacturing Industry since 1870*, Oxford, Philip Allan, 7.
2 Initially, discussion is limited to concerns in the Almond Valley, which formed the boundary between the then counties of Midlothian and West Lothian. Firms elsewhere in Scotland will be considered later in dealing with limited companies.
3 Figures derived from lapsed company files and valuation rolls for Midlothian, West Lothian and Lanarkshire.
4 James Young had sold his interests to Young's Paraffin Light & Mineral Oil Co. Ltd. in 1866; Meldrum, Simpson and McLagen sold out to the Uphall Mineral Oil Company Ltd in 1871. This company was reconstructed as the Uphall Oil Co. Ltd in 1876. The private concern, T. & J. Thornton at Leavenseat, and Hermand resumed production in 1878 and was converted to a limited company in 1885.

Chapter 5 1851–1877

1 Butt, 'Scottish oil mania', 202–3.
2 Wray Vamplew, 1975, *Salvesen of Leith*, Edinburgh, Scottish Academic Press, 66.
3 Butt, 'James Young', 104, 99, 142–3; Minute of meeting of the partners of the Bathgate Chemical Works, 16 Dec. 1864.
4 Dalmeny Estate Minerals Ledger, 34.
5 The total rateable value of the private concerns was £6,268; £3,591 multiplied by 6,268 and divided by 164 equals £137,246.
6 Dalmeny Estate Minerals Ledger, 34.
7 Butt, 'James Young', 90–1.
8 Butt, 'Technical change', 518.
9 NAS, BT2/303/1.
10 Census of Scotland, 1871, Mid Calder Parish, District 5, Schedule 85, provides the basis for tracing the birth registrations of Calderwood's seven children. These give his occupations at the times of their births, from 1856 to 1870.
11 For a summary of the debate, see P.L. Payne, 1974, *British Entrepreneurship in the nineteenth century*, London; and for a wide-ranging discussion of the debate as it relates to Scotland, see R.H. Campbell, *The Rise and fall of Scottish Industry, 1707–1939*, Edinburgh, 1980.
12 NAS, BT2.
13 P. Payne, 1980, *The Early Scottish Limited Companies, 1856–1895*, Edinburgh, Scottish Academic Press, Appendix, Table 2, 117.
14 Payne, *Early Scottish Limited Companies*, 3.
15 Payne, *Early Scottish Limited Companies*, 5–7.
16 *WLC*, 18 July 1919; BP Archive, SOL, board meeting minute, 22 Oct. 1919.

17   See Payne, *Early Scottish Limited Companies*, Table 7, 35.
18   NAS, BT2/447, 1872.
19   Payne, *Early Scottish Limited Companies*, 29, 30.
20   Ibid., 32.
21   Ibid., 99.
22   NAS, BT2/222/21; BT2/416/13; BT2/258/13.
23   Payne, *Early Scottish Limited Companies*, 77.
24   Ibid., 44–8; G. Todd, 1932–3, 'Some aspects of joint-stock companies, 1844–1900', *Economic History Review*, 4, 46–71; 67–8.
25   Payne, *Early Scottish Limited Companies*, Table 12, 47.
26   Ibid., 46, note 3.
27   NAS, BT2/343/11 & 12; BT2/416/7 & 9.
28   BP Archive, OOC 1886, DMB 1, 27 Sept. 1886.
29   The files of lapsed companies are held at West Register House, Edinburgh: see NAS, BT2. Those of the four 'live' companies are held by the Registrar of Companies at Castle Terrace, Edinburgh. The 'live' companies are Young's Paraffin Light & Mineral Oil Co. Ltd, which until 1992 operated the detergent plant at Pumpherston Works; the Broxburn Oil Co. Ltd, now known as BP Exploration Ltd; the Pumpherston Oil Co. Ltd; and the Oakbank Oil Co. Ltd, which is now the BP Exploration Company (Associated Holdings) Ltd. The Pumpherston company was dissolved in the late 1990s, but the file remains with the registrar.
30   NAS, BT2/1267.
31   *Linlithgowshire Gazette*, 14 April 1885.
32   NAS, BT2/102/5.
33   BP Archive, YP, SMB.
34   NAS, BT2/343/5 & 8; BT2/379/4 & 6; BT2/701/4 & 6.
35   BP Archive, BOC, DMB.
36   *Scotsman*, 1 Oct. 1880; NAS, BT2/993/7 and 10; *Scotsman*, 26 Oct. 1883; NAS, BT2/1292/6; *Scotsman*, 13 March 1884; NAS, BT2/1342/6; *Scotsman*, 3 May 1884; WLC, 30 Aug. 1884; NAS, BT2/1351/6; BT2/1351/9.
37   It was stated earlier that 43 companies have been identified in the shale industry. Of these, one, the Scottish Mineral Oil & Coal Company, was abortive; the Uphall Oil Company, registered in 1876, was simply a reorganisation involving no new capital; the Burntisland and Clippens companies, registered in 1893, were attempts to revive failing concerns, and again no fresh capital was involved; the Dalmeny company, registered in 1896, was a reorganisation of the existing capital with no fresh money involved; the Caledonian Oil Company, registered in 1898, was also an attempt to continue a failing concern with no fresh capital involved. In the case of this last concern, the original company was registered in London and we have no details of its capital structure. These six companies have not been involved in the present discussion, which is therefore confined to 37 concerns.
38   BP Archive, YP, SHMB 1, Fos 46–7, 17 June 68.
39   NAS, BT2/253/2, Article 9.
40   NAS, BT2/343/2, Article 97.
41   NAS, BT2/343/5 and 8.
42   NAS, BT2/808/12.
43   NAS, BT2 1982/6.
44   NAS, BT2 4179/7.

Chapter 6   Finance for expansion

1   R.C. Michie, 1987, *The London and New York Stock Exchanges, 1850–1914*, London, Allen & Unwin, 110.

2   IOM Report, PP, 1877, xiii; and 1913, 7.

3   BP Archive, ROC, 792/11 & 17.

4   BP Archive, ROC, 792/14.

5   BP Archive, ROC, 792/48

6   NAS, BT2/1049A/12; BT2/1049A/16; *Glasgow Herald*, 31 Jan. 1885; *Scotsman*, 2 June 1883.

7   R.C. Michie, *Money, Mania and Markets*, Edinburgh, John Donald, 131.

8   NAS, BT2/808/10 and 14; Valuation Rolls, Midlothian, 1881–2, Lasswade Parish, 137, items 216 and 230.

9   NAS, BT2/303/4 & 22; *Scotsman*, 22 May 1884; BP Archive, OOC, GMB, 21 May 1884; ROC, 1501/34, Prospectus, 27 June 1901.

10 BP Archive, Volume of documents relating to liquidation of Uphall Oil Company Limited; YP, SHMB 1, Fo. 198, EGM, 15 Feb. 1884; SHMB 2, Fos 3–5, AGM, 20 June 1884, Balance Sheet; *Scotsman*, 24 April 1886; *WLC*, 13 Dec. 1912.

11 *WLC*, 31 May 1912; 1 Nov. 1912

12 YP, SHMB 2, Director's statement to shareholders, 4 June 1887.

13 *Scotsman*, 16 June 1892.

14 Mathias, *First Industrial Nation*, 353–4; P.L. Cottrell, 1983, *Industrial Finance, 1830–1950: The Finance and Organisation of English Manufacturing Industry*, London, Methuen, 164.

15 BP Archive, ROC, 1295/19; *Scotsman*, 11 May 1908; OOC, GMB 2, Fos 13–21; ROC, 792/51; BOC, GMB 1, Fos 99–102; 14 Oct. 1887; NAS, BT2/993/11; *Scotsman*, 20 Dec. 1883; *Glasgow Herald*, 27 Jan. 1885; *WLC*, 6 June 1891; NAS, BT2/1351/16; BT2/4179/9; *Scotsman*, 21 Dec. 1901.

16 Most of the data discussed in the following section are derived from newspaper accounts of directors' reports and general meetings of shareholders of some of the companies. Not all of the companies achieved coverage in the press. The newspapers concerned are the *Scotsman, the West Lothian Courier, the Linlithgowshire Gazette* and, to a lesser extent, the *Glasgow Herald* and the *Midlothian Advertiser*.

17 *WLC*, 9 June 1888, 8 June 1889, 20 June 1891, 1 Oct. 1887, 24 Sept. 1887; *Scotsman*, 2 May 1884, 24 April 1886; *WLC*, 26 April 1890; *Scotsman*, 28 April 1891; NAS, BT2/2533/5; BT2/808/30; *Scotsman*, 4 June 1887, 13 May 1892; *WLC*, 24 May 1901.

18 *WLC*, 16 May 1891, 23 May 1892.

19 Ibid., 21 May 1909.

20 *Scotsman*, 10 May 1910, 9 May 1911.

21 *WLC*, 30 May 1885, 22 May 1886, 4 June 1887, 18 June 1887; ROC, 1295/12 & 15; POC, DMB, Fo. 58, 25 Sept. 1884; POC, DMB, Fo. 73; POC, DMB, 13 Feb. 1885; POC, DMB, 3 June 1885; POC, DMB, Fo. 165; POC, DMB, Fo. 172; POC, DMB Fo. 235, 20 July 1886; POC, DMB, 14 Dec. 1886; POC, DMB, Fo. 329

22 *WLC*, 21 May 1892; directors' reports in *West Lothian Courier*.

23 *WLC*, 31 May 1907.

24 BP Archive, OOC, GMB 1, Fo. 142.

25 BP Archive, OOC 1886, GMB 1; GMB 2, passim.

26 BP Archive, YP, SHMB 1, Fos 79–80, 15 June 1869; YP, SHMB 1, Fos 49 & 123; YP, SHMB 1, Directors' report, y.e. 30 April 1872; YP, SHMB, Directors' Report, y.e. 30 April 1880; YP SHMB, Directors' Report, y.e. 30 April 1881; *WLC*, 25 June 1881.

27 *Scotsman*, 16 June 1892, 31 May 1893.

28 BP Archive, YP, SHMB 2, Fo. 107, EGM, 14 July 1896.

29 Cottrell, *Industrial Finance*, 164.

30 Ibid, 164.

31 Ibid., 167.

32 P.L. Cottrell, 2004, 'Domestic finance, 1860–1914', in Floud and Johnson (eds), *Cambridge Economic History*, 268.

33 I. Donnachie, 1998, *A History of the Brewing Industry in Scotland*, Edinburgh, John Donald, 166–7.

34 P. Payne, 1979, *Colvilles and the Scottish Steel Industry*, Oxford, Clarendon Press, 61.

35 BP Archive, OOC, GMB, Minute of EGM, 22 Sept. 1874.

36 BP Archive, OOC, Journal No. 6, passim.

37 BP Archive, YPLMO, Journal No. 18, passim.

38 *WLC*, 17 Sept. 1887.

39 Charles W. Munn, 1988, *Clydesdale Bank: The First One Hundred and Fifty Years*, London, Collins, 55.

40 Ibid., 127.

41 *Scotsman*, 6 May 1899; BP Archive, OOC 1886, GMB 1, Fos 11/12.

42 Cottrell, *Industrial Finance*, 194.

43 Mathias, *First Industrial Nation*, 323.

44 M. Collins, 1998, 'English bank development within a European context, 1870–1939', *Economic History Review*, 51, 1–24; 1–21, especially 20–1; Cottrell, 'Domestic finance, 1860–1914', 276.

45 S.G. Checkland, 1975, *Scottish Banking: A History, 1695–1973*, Glasgow, Collins, 416–23.

46 R. Saville, 1996, *Bank of Scotland, A History, 1695–1995*, Edinburgh, Edinburgh University Press, 431–3.

47 Checkland, *Scottish Banking*, 506.

48 Royal Bank of Scotland Minute, 10 November, 1878, quoted in Checkland, *Scottish Banking*, 503.

49 M. Collins, 1991, *Banks and Industrial Finance in Britain 1800–1939*, Basingstoke, Macmillan, 49.

50 Munn, *Clydesdale Bank*, 308; BP Archive, YP, SHMB 1, 2 and 3.

51 Munn, *Clydesdale Bank*, 316–7; BP Archive, YP, SMB, 30 Dec. 1865; OOC 1886, GMB 1, Fo. 2, 24 May 1886; OOC 1886, GMB 1, Fo. 28; *WLC*, 18 May 1888.

52 Cottrell, *Industrial Finance*, 253 et seq.; Collins, 'English bank development', 1.

53 S.A. Carlon and R.D. Morris, 2003, 'The economic determinants of depreciation accounting in late nineteenth century Britain', *Accounting, Business & Financial History*, 13, 275–302; 275; J.R. Edwards, 1989, *A History of Financial Accounting*, London, Routledge, 122–5.

54 Wray Vamplew (ed.), 1978, 'The North British Railway Inquiry of 1866', 51.

55 R.A. Church (ed.), *The Dynamics of Victorian Business*, 39.

56 John R. Hume and Michael S. Moss, 1979, *Beardmore: The History of a Scottish Industrial Giant*, London, Heinemann, 92.

57 Quoted in A.C. Storrar and K.C. Pratt, 2000, 'Accountability vs. Privacy, 1884–1907: The coming of the private company', *Accounting Business and Financial History*, 10, 3, 259–91; 273.

58 *Scotsman*, 21 May 1886, 18 May 1894.

59 *Glasgow Herald*, 31 Jan. 1885; *Scotsman*, 22 May 1886, 20 May 1887, 6 June 1888, 12 June 1889, 12 June 1891; *WLC*, 14 June 1890.

60 *Scotsman*, 30 May 1884; *WLC*, 18 June 1887; *Scotsman*, 23 May 1889, 17 May 1890, 21 May 1891, 26 May 1892, 30 May 1894, 3 June 1896, 7 June 1897, 6 June 1899; *WLC*, 3 June 1893; *Glasgow Herald*, 6 June 1895, 7 June 1898, 5 June 1900; *WLC*, 7 June 1901, 5 June 1903, 3 June 1904; *Scotsman*, 2 June 1902.

61 *WLC*, 5 June 1903.

62 BP Archive, BOC, GMB 1, Fo. 24–5.

63 *Scotsman*, 11 May 1897. The directors' report states that depreciation of £323,500 had been written off since the formation of the company. To this was added the amount given as written off in each subsequent published report until 1903. The total capital expenditure was arrived at by adding the amount shown in each published report to the original cost as calculated from the amount of depreciation set aside in the year ended 30 April 1879.

64 Registrar of Companies, File 792/53.

65 *Scotsman*, 19 May 1886, 11 May 1889, 4 May 1895, 29 April 1896, 3 May 1900, 24 June 1886, 8 June 1889, 29 May 1890, 29 May 1893, 11 June 1894, 29 May 1895; *WLC*, 30 May 1885, 11 June 1887, *WLC*, 9 June 1888, 8 June 1889, 14 June 1890.

66 Carlon and Morris, 'Economic determinants', 276.

67 *Scotsman*, 12 May 1891; *WLC*, 13 Dec. 1912.
68 BO Archive, BOC, GMB 1, y.e. 2 April 1879.
69 *WLC*, 16 May 1891.
70 *Scotsman*, 11 May 1881, 11 May 1885; M.V. Pitts, 1999, 'The rise and rise of the premium share account', *Accounting, Business and Financial History*, 10, 317–46; 318; *Scotsman*, 18 May 1882.
71 *WLC*, 18 May 1889, 19 May 1900, 23 May 1891.
72 Ibid., 23 May 1891.
73 *Scotsman*, 17 May 1894.
74 Ibid., 21 May 1896.
75 *Scotsman*, 30 May 1884
76 Ibid., 18 June 1896
77 *Glasgow Herald*, 5 June 1900; *Scotsman*, 23 May 1901, 2 June 1902, 3 June 1903, 1 June 1904, 31 May 1905, 2 June 1906, 3 June 1907, 3 June 1908, 2 June 1909, 1 June 1913, 1 June 1914.
78 *Scotsman*, 4 May 1896, 10 May 1897, 11 May 1898, 8 May 1899, 7 May 1900, 20 May 1901, 7 May 1902, 11 May 1903, 6 May 1904, 8 May 1905, 7 May 1906, 6 May 1907, 11 May 1908, 10 May 1909, 9 May 1910, 8 May 1911, 13 May 1912, 5 May 1913, 4 May 1914.
79 BP Archive, OOC 1886, GMB 1 Fo. 136.
80 *Scotsman*, 3 May 1894, 23 May 1895, 30 April 1896, 29 April 1897, 28 April 1898, 5 May 1899, 14 May 1900, 11 May 1903, 8 May 1905, 7 May 1906, 27 April 1907, 11 May 1908, 29 April 1909, 11 May 1914; *WLC*, 17 May 1901, 23 May 1913; *Glasgow Herald*, 9 May 1904; *Scotsman*, 18 May 1904.
81 *WLC*, 19 May 1905, 18 May 1906, 17 July 1908.
82 BP Archive, YP, SHMB 2 Fo. 185.
83 BP Archive, YP, SHMB 2, Fos 185, 191, 210; YP, SHMB 3 Fo 1; *Scotsman*, 30 May 1910, 3 June 1912, 1 June 1914.
84 *WLC*, 21 May 1909.
85 *Scotsman*, 29 April 1909.
86 Ibid., 2 June 1909.
87 *Scotsman*, 10 May 1909.
88 Cottrell, *Industrial Finance*, 259, 262.
89 BP Archive, BOC, Ledger No. 8 Fos. 62, 72, Fos 103, 385.
90 BP Archive, POC Ledger No. 4, Fos. 283–5, 290, 343; *WLC*, 13 Dec. 1912; BP Archive, POC, Journal No. 12, Fo. 426.
91 BP Archive, OOC, Ledger No. 2 Fos. 66, 288; Ledger No. 8, Fo. 137.
92 *WLC*, 23 May 1896.

Chapter 7 Capital lost

1   Payne, *Early Scottish Limited Companies*, 84, note 4.
2   Sources: NAS, BT2/1267/6; BT2/1285/9; BT2/808/29.
3   BP Archive, YP, SHMB 2, Fo. 22; NAS, BT2/1351/25.
4   NAS, BT2/670/3.
5   NAS, BT2/303/29 and BP Archive, OOC 1869, GMB, 8 Dec. 1885.
6   BP Archive, OOC 1869, GMB, 8 Dec. 1885.
7   *Scotsman*, 4 March 1882, prospectus of the Midlothian Oil Company Limited.
8   Ibid., 24 April 1886.
9   *Glasgow Herald*, 24 June 1885.
10 BP Archive, YP, Documents relating to the liquidation of the Uphall Oil Company Limited.
11 NAS, BT2/1982/6.
12 NAS, BT2/1982/11, 12, 13.
13 NAS, BT2/4179/4 & 7; BT2/4179/18.

14   *WLC,* 13 Dec. 1912.
15   *Scotsman,* 25 Dec. 1912.
16   Payne, *Early Scottish Limited Companies,* 8, 86.
17   BP Archive, OOC 1869, GMB Fo. 45.
18   NAS, BT2/242/2 and 7.
19   NAS, BT2/102/6; BT2/236/6; BT2/258/13.
20   NAS, BT2/253/2.
21   NAS, BT2/1431/14; BT2/953/7.
22   NAS, BT2/1292/7.
23   *Scotsman,* 27 Feb. 1882.
24   NAS, BT2/808/30 & 34; BT2/808/35.
25   NAS, BT2/2533/5; *Scotsman,* 28 Dec. 1898; NAS, BT2/2533/26.
26   NAS, BT2/2469/5.
27   NAS, BT2/2469/5.
28   BP Archive, YP, SHMB 1 Directors' Report, 3 June 1881.
29   NAS, BT2/4179/18.
30   NAS, BT2/1351/40.
31   NAS, BT2/1229/9.
32   NAS, BT2/1285/20.
33   NAS, BT2/1342/25.
34   NAS, BT2/1267/8.
35   Payne, *Early Scottish Limited Companies,* 106–7.
36   Among the survivors, both the Oakbank Oil Co. Ltd and Young's Paraffin Light and Mineral Oil Co. Ltd had undergone major reconstruction, involving considerable reduction in capital. See Appendix 1, Table A.
37   *WLC,* 18 July 1919.
38   BP Archive, BOC, DMB 8, after Fo. 251, Copy of letter of 11 July 1919, from C. Greenaway, Chairman, APOC.
39   Michie, *Money, Mania and Markets,* 201, 213, 215.
40   NAS, BT2/1049A/6; BT2/1049A/7; BT2/1049A/9; BT2/1049A/14; BT2/1049A/15 and 18.
41   H. Withers, 1938, *Stocks and Shares,* London, John Murray, 262–4.
42   NAS, BT2/1049A/9; BT2/1049A/14; BT2/1049A/15.
43   NAS, BT2/1104/4; BT2/1104/5.
44   *Glasgow Stock Exchange Daily Lists.*
45   NAS, BT2/1285/5.
46   John Scott and Michael Hughes, 1980, *The Anatomy of Scottish Capital,* London, Croom Helm, Table 1A, Section A.
47   Registrar of Companies, Files 1295/3 and 1501/41; *Scotsman,* 8 May 1911; *WLC,* 13 Dec. 1912.
48   Scott and Hughes, *Anatomy of Scottish Capital,* Table 2A, Section A.

Chapter 8 Size of shareholdings

1   BP Archive, YP, SHMB 1, 15 June 1870, Fo. 111.
2   NAS, BT2/343/1, 3, 5, 8.
3   NAS, BT2/343/8.
4   Ibid.
5   NAS, BT2/1267/7.
6   NAS, BT2/1285/3; *WLC,* 9 Feb. 1884.
7   NAS, BT2/1342.
8   *Scotsman,* 25 July 1885; NAS, BT2/1485; BT2/1485/5.

9   BP Archive, BOC, DMB, 19 Feb. 1879; *WLC*, 18 Sept. 1880.
10 NAS, BT2/837/6); BT2/837/9.
11 The company files of the Broxburn and Young's companies remain with the Registrar of Companies and access is now difficult. In the case of Young's, I was fortunate enough to obtain a copy of the first Summary of Capital and Shares when the files were more readily available. In the case of the Broxburn company, the details required were taken from the notes of allotment of shares in the directors' minute book. For some companies, the data in these tables may be found to differ slightly from that in other sections. For example, the Dalserf company in its first year issued shares worth £25,100. In the second year 80 shares were cancelled, leaving an issued capital of £24,300, the figure used in the section on the industry's capital. In the case of the Uphall and Holmes companies, the second SCS was used, because a high proportion of the shares were not issued at the date of the first SCS.
12 M.W. Flinn, 1961, *An Economic and Social History of Britain, 1066–1939*, London, Macmillan, 235–7; Court, 1954, 173; Payne, *Early Scottish Limited Companies*, 49–51; Mathias, *First Industrial Nation*, 353; Cottrell, 'Domestic finance, 1860–1914', 265–6; Leslie Hannah, 1983, *The Rise of the corporate Economy*, London, Methuen, 19.
13 *WLC*, 17 May 1879, 16 May 1885; BP Archive, POC, DMB, 8 Jan. and 19 Feb. 1884.
14 Michie, *Money, Mania and Markets*, 191.
15 Registrar of Companies, File 221, SCS dated 12 July 1866.
16 NAS, BT2/174/5.
17 NAS, BT2/102/1 & 5; BT2/247; BT2/251; BT2/231; BT2/303; BP Archive, YP, SMB.
18 NAS, BT2/242; BT2/258/3; BT2/222/2; BT2/236/2.
19 NAS, BT2/253/5.
20 The tables above were, in general, constructed from the first Annual Summary of Capital and Shares for each company, since this represented most nearly the position at the launch of the company. However, in some cases the second Annual Summary has been used. For example, in the case of the Uphall company, less than half of the available shares had been taken up at the time of the first summary, which was submitted less than six months after incorporation (NAS, BT2/303/5) .
21 Dalmeny Estate Minerals Ledger, 34.
22 *Scotsman*, 24 Nov. 1871.
23 *Scotsman*, 27 May 1885, Report of Directors of Pumpherston Oil Co. Ltd, indicated a capital expenditure of £72,597. This included a refining capacity slightly beyond the crude oil production.
24 Mathias, *First Industrial Nation*, 352.

Chapter 9 Social composition of shareholders

1   The first Caledonian company was registered in London and the company file has not been seen. The second company, although registered in Scotland, had the old company as its sole shareholder.
2   Cottrell, *Industrial Finance*, 95.
3   Stana Nenadic, 1991, 'Businessmen, the urban middle classes, and the "dominance" of manufacturers in nineteenth century Britain', *Economic History Review*, 44, 66–85; 68.
4   *DSBB*, 1986 and 1990, Aberdeen University Press, vol. 2, 356.
5   *DSBB*, vol. 2, 230.
6   Cottrell, *Industrial Finance*, 95–6, and Table, 96.
7   D.R. Green and A. Owens, 2003, 'Gentlewomenly capitalism? Spinsters, widows and wealth holding in England and Wales, c.1800–1860'. *Economic History Review*, 55, 3, 510–36; 511.
8   Ibid., 516; A. Cooke et al., 1998, *Modern Scottish History, 1707 to the Present, Volume 2*, East Linton, Tuckwell Press, 162–3; R.J. Morris, 1994, 'Men, women, and property: The reform of the Married

Women's Property Act 1870', in *F.M.L. Thompson (ed.), Landowners, Capitalists and Entrepreneurs*, 190.
9   It is worth noting, however, that in Scotland the title 'Mrs' did not necessarily denote a married woman, but could be applied to any adult female, until well into the twentieth century.
10 *DSBB*, vol. 2, 339; Leah Leneman, 1995, *'A guid cause': The Women's Suffrage Movement in Scotland*, Edinburgh, Mercat Press, 17.
11 Josephine Maltby and Jeanette Rutterford, 2006, ' "She possessed her own fortune": Women investors from the late nineteenth century to the early twentieth century', *Business History*, 48, 220–53; 233.

Chapter 10 Location

1   Cottrell, *Industrial Finance*, 91–4.
2   William P. Kennedy, 1987, *Industrial Structure, Capital Markets and the Origins of British Economic Decline*, Cambridge University Press, 124.
3   NAS, BT2/174/1.
4   Valuation Rolls, Kirknewton Parish, 1863–4, items 74 and 76.
5   NAS, BT2/251/1; BT2/236/1; BT2/231/1.
6   BP Archive, YP, SMB
7   *DSBB*, vol. 2, 358.
8   *DSBB*, vol. 1, 84.
9   NAS, BT2/343/8.
10 NAS, BT2/343/5.
11 NAS, BT2/416/1 and 2.
12 Tristram Hunt, 2005, *Building Jerusalem: The Rise and Fall of the Victorian City*, London, Phoenix, 166.
13 *Scottish Financier*, November 1883, 9.
14 *WLC*, 30 Aug. 1884, 8 Aug. 1885.
15 BP Archive, OOC 1886, DMB 1, 8 March 1886; 25 April 1887.

Chapter 11 James Young and E.W. Binney & Company

1   Butt, 'James Young', 64.
2   University of Strathclyde Archives, T.You 1/23, 1855 Diary; Conacher, 'History of the Scottish oil-shale industry', 242; T.You 1/19, 23 Aug. 1852, T.You 130/1 Fo. 28, and T. You 2/32 & 2/36, letters 9 June 1858 and 7 Jan. 1859 from Binney to Young at Sardinia Terrace; Valuation Rolls, Edinburghshire, 108/7, West Calder Parish, items 215–34.
3   Beilby, 'Thirty years of progress', 876.
4   David Bremner, 1869, *Industries of Scotland*, Edinburgh, A. & C. Black, 490–9.
5   Butt, 'James Young', 108
6   *WLC*, 21 Dec. 1917, Obituary of Norman Henderson; T.J. Byres, 1967, 'Entrepreneurship in the Scottish heavy industries, 1870–1900', in P. Payne (ed.), *Studies in Scottish Business History*, 278; A. Slaven, 1975, *The Development of the West of Scotland, 1750–1960*, London, Routledge & Kegan Paul, 180; Hume and Moss, *Beardmore*, 49; BP Archive, OOC 1869, GMB, Fo. 7; EGM, 16 Nov. 1869; and GMB, 18 May 1880; *Scotsman*, 19 May 1880.
7   BP Archive, Papers concerning a dispute between Young and YPLMO, 21 Aug. 1873.
8   Census for Bathgate, District 4, Schedule 162.
9   *WLC*, 21 Dec. 1917.
10 Drucker, *Management*, 13.
11 University of Strathclyde Archives, T.You 1/25.

12 Census, 1861, Bathgate Parish, District 8, Sch. 105; University of Strathclyde Archives, T.You 1/34, 22 January 1866; BP Archive, GD454/AR1453, 16 Dec. 1864; YP, SMB, 25 April 1866., Fo. 92; Valuation Rols, Linlithgow, Uphall Parish, 1867–8, Fo. 144.

13 University of Strathclyde Archives, T.You 1/34, 8/9 March 1866; BP Archive, YP, SMB, 4 April 1867.

14 University of Strathclyde Archives, Limefield Laboratory Notebook 1863–5; Census, 1871, West Calder Parish, District 6, Schedule 50; BP Archive, YP, SMB, 11 and 19 April 1867.

15 Valuation Rolls, Linlithgow, Bathgate Parish, 1861–2 and 1864–5; BP Archive, AR 1453, Minute of meeting of the partners, 16 Dec. 1864.

16 BP Archive, YP, SMB, Fo. 217, 2 Nov. 1866.

17 *Edinburgh Gazette*, 3 Jan. 1865.

18 University of Strathclyde Archives, T.You 1/23.

19 Letter, Binney to Young, 20 July 1859.

20 Edinburgh Post Office Directory, 1858–9, 183.

21 University of Strathclyde Archives, T.You 130/1, 31 July 1862, 7 Aug. 1862, 1 April 1863.

Chapter 12 The board of directors and the shareholders

1   Mathias, *First Industrial Nation*, 353; Cottrell, *Industrial Finance*, 164.

2   Anon., *Memoirs and Portraits*, vol. 2, 279–80.

3   NAS, BT2/803/13.

4   Withers, *Stocks and Shares*, 58.

5   Peter F. Drucker, 1979, *Management*, London, Pan Books, 536–7.

6   YP, SHMB 1; 2; 3.

7   OOC, DMB, 23 May 1879; OOC, GMB; OOC 1886, GMB 1; 2.

8   BOC, GMB 1; 2.

9   *WLC* and *Scotsman*, reports of company affairs.

10 NAS, BT2/343/2; 670/2; *WLC*, 28 June 1884; Copy of Register of Directors, 1914, NAS, BT2/3346/29, *Scotsman*, 15 May 1885, NAS, BT2/2533/25, *Scotsman*, 3 May 1884; NAS, BT2/1351/37.

11 *Scotsman*, 21 May 1885.

12 BOC, GMB 1 Fo. 184; *Scotsman*, 24 May 1900.

13 YP, SHMB 1, Fos 108–9.

14 OOC 1886, GMB 1, Fo. 27.

15 YP, SHMB 1, Fos 121–2.

16 *Scotsman*, 1 Jan. 1885, 24 May 1892.

17 Ibid., 22 May 1886.

18 *WLC*, 5 June 1886.

19 *WLC*, 12 June 1886.

20 Withers, *Stocks and Shares*, 58.

Chapter 13 The management structure of the refining companies

1   BP Archive, AR 1007, Agreement between Young and company; SHMB 1, Fos 9–10.

2   BP Archive, YP, SHMB 1, Fos 74–80.

3   BP Archive, AR 1453, Minute of meeting, 16 Dec. 1864.

4   *Airdrie & Coatbridge Advertiser*, 3 Dec. 1864.

5   Letter, Young to Rae, 31 July 1862, University of Strathclyde Archives, T.You 130/1, Letter Book, Fo. 145.

6 BP Archive, AR 1007, Copy Minute of agreement, dated 28 and 29 Dec. 1865.
7 BP Archive, YP, SMB, 5 Jan. 1866.
8 Williamson and Daum, *American Petroleum Industry*, 328, Table 13, 4, gives the figures for 1864 as 109,598 barrels of crude and 88,167 of illuminating oil, and for 1865 as 101,280 of crude and 76,631 of illuminating oil – reductions of 7.59 and 13.08 per cent.
9 *Times*, 5 Jan., 13 April, 21 Aug., 25 Aug., and 14 Sept. 1865.
10 University of Strathclyde Archives, T.You 1/32.
11 Ibid.; BP Archive, YP, SHMB 1, Directors' Report, 30 April 1872; SHMB 1, Fo. 25, 4 Feb. 1867; YP, SHMB 1, Fo. 44.
12 BP Archive, YP, SHMB 1, Fo. 62.
13 NAS, BT2/174.
14 BP Archive, YP, SMB, 18 Oct. 1867.
15 *Scotsman*, 26 July 1883.
16 NAS, BT2/837.
17 BP Archive, BOC, GMB 1, Fo. 21, 7 May 1878.
18 NAS, BT2/1049A/2.
19 Beilby, 'Thirty years of progress', 879.
20 *WLC*, 30 Aug. 1884.
21 Ibid., 5 June 1886.
22 Wilson and Thomson, *Making of Modern Management*, 42.
23 BP Archive, YP, Journal No. 1.
24 Anita McConnell, 'Pender, Sir John (1816–1896)', *ODNB*; BP Archive, YP, SHMB 2, 16 June 1897.
25 *DSBB*, vol. 2, 356–8.
26 Graeme J. N. Gooday, 'Playfair, Lyon, first Baron Playfair (1818–1898)', *ODNB* (2004 print edn, and 2008 online edn), 556–60.
27 *DSBB*, vol. 2, 338.
28 Ibid., vol. 1, 111–13.
29 Butt, 'James Young', 74.
30 T.M. Devine, 2005, 'Industrialisation', in T.M. Devine, et al., *The Transformation of Scotland: The Economy since 1700*, 58.
31 BP Archive, YP, SMB, 30 Dec. 1865, 11 Dec. 1866; Registrar of Companies, File 221; BP Archive, YP, SMB, 14 Feb. 1867.
32 BP Archive, YP, SMB.
33 Ibid.
34 *DSBB*, vol. 2, 358.
35 BP Archive, YP, SMB, 14 Feb. 1867, 20 April 1866.
36 Ibid., 30 Dec. 1865, 6 April 1886, 20 April and 24 May 1866.
37 Conacher, 'History of the Scottish oil-shale industry', 247; BP Archive, YP, Journal No. 1, Fo. 300; YP, SMB, 4 Oct. and 9 Oct. 1866, 20 April and 23 Oct. 1866, 16 Aug. 1867, 27 Dec. 1866, 13 Feb. 1868.
38 BP Archive, SMB 4 Oct. 1867, 17 April 1868.
39 BP Archive, YP, SMB, 16 July 1867.
40 Ibid., 13 Sept. 1867.
41 Quoted by E.M. Bailey in his James Young Memorial Lecture on 8 January 1948; BP Archive, AR 1453.
42 University of Strathclyde Archives, T.You 1/36, Young's Diary, 15 Oct. 1868.
43 BP Archive, YP Letter Book, Letter Young to Directors, 3 July 1871.
44 BP Archive, YP, Letter Book, Correspondence between Young and Directors, July to October, 1871.
45 Conacher, 'History of the Scottish oil-shale industry', 247.
46 Ronald Weir, 1995, *The History of the Distillers Company, 1877–1939*, Oxford, Clarendon Press, 37, 45.

47 BP Archive, YP, SMB, 15 Nov. 1866, 4 Feb. 1867; Papers relating to dispute between Young and the Company, 21 Aug. 1873, 30; YP, SHMB 1, 4 Feb. 1867; Price's Patent Candle Company Limited, 1972, *Still the Candle Burns*, 21.

48 BP Archive, YP, DMB, 21 Feb. 1867, Fos. 299–301.

49 BP Archive, SHMB 1, Directors' Report, y.e. 30 April 1874.

50 Glasgow Post Office Directory, 1869–70, 48; BP Archive, AR 0825, YP, Agreement between John Fyfe and Company, 1 July 1873; SHMB 1, Directors' Report, y.e. 30 April 1882; *WLC*, 31 Dec. 1915.

51 BP Archive, AR 0824, YP, Comparison of management structure in 1884 with that in 1873 , 5 Nov. 1884.

52 *WLC*, 23 June 1883; BP Archive, YP, Journal No. 17, Fos 128, 131, 168, 171, 206, 211, 249, 252; Journal No. 25, Fos 126, 128, 173, 175, 213, 215, 254, 257; SHMB 1, Directors' Report; YP, Ledger No. 12, Branch Sales Accounts.

53 BP Archive, YP, DPMB, Minutes 188 and 214, Minute 232; *WLC*, 31 Dec. 1915.

54 BP Archive, YP, DPMB, Minute 236; *WLC*, 3 Nov. 1916.

55 BP Archive, YP, DPMB, 13 Nov. 1916, Minute 248; 26 Feb. 1919, Minute 280.

56 Post Office Directory, 1868–9, 145; NAS, BT2/303/3.

57 Registrar of Companies, File 792/2.

58 William Marwick, 1964, *Scotland in Modern Times*, London, Frank Cass & Co., 75–6.

59 *DSBB*, vol. 2, 168–9.

60 Ibid., 171–2.

61 *DSBB*, vol. 1, 79–81.

62 Registrar of Companies, File 1295/2.

63 Registrar of Companies, ROC file, 1295/4.

64 BP Archive, OOC, DMB.

65 BP Archive, BOC, DMB.

66 *DSBB*, vol. 1, 48; *WLC*, 16 May and 7 Feb. 1885; BP Archive, OOC 1886, DMB 1, 24 March 1886 and 10 Feb. 1886; OOC, GMB, 21 May 1884; *WLC*, 22 May 1897; BP Archive, OOC 1886, GMB 1, Fo. 63; Glasgow Post Office Directory, 1919–20, 494.

67 *WLC*, 15 Sept. 1883; POC, DMB 1, 22 Nov. 1883.

68 BP Archive, BOC, DMB, 14 Nov. 1877.

69 BP Archive, POC, DMB, 8 Jan. 1884.

70 BP Archive, POC, Prospectus, October 1883.

71 See *Oils, Colours and Drysalteries*, 15 July 1895, 493; *DSBB*, vol. 1, 48.

72 *WLC*, 15 Sept. 1883.

73 BP Archive, POC, DMB, Fo. 366, 5 March 1887; ROC, 1295/6.

74 BP Archive, OOC 1886, GMB, Fo. 138–40, 21 May 1918.

75 BP Archive, POC, DMB, Fos 366–70, 1 March 1887.

76 BP Archive, YP, Ledger No. 1, Fo. 214, 31 Dec. 1886; Uphall Oil Company Limited, List of Clerks in Glasgow Office, 14 Feb. 1884; BOC, Journal No. 3, Fo. 576; BOC, Journal No. 10, Fo. 246; POC, DMB 1, 8 July 1884; POC, Journal No. 12, Fo. 543; OOC 1886, DMB 1, 21 April 1886.

Chapter 14 Sales and distribution

1 BP Archive, YP, SMB, Fo. 78, 22 March 1866; and Fo. 69, 1 March 1866.

2 See papers under the reference number GD454.

3 Asa Briggs, 1990, *Victorian Things*, London, Penguin, 380.

4 Wilson and Thomson, *Making of Modern Management*, 221.

5 BP Archive, AR 0730.

6 BP Archive, YP, Letter Book of A. Kerr, Letters to managers dated 27 Feb. 1918.

7 BP Archive, BOC, DMB, Fo. 70, 4 Sept. 1878; *WLC*, 16 Sept. 1882.

8 BP Archive, BOC, Ledger Nos 4, 9 and 18.

9   BP Archive, OOC 1886, DMB 1, 9 Aug. and 11 Oct. 1886; Journal No. 6, Fos 115, 195, 296.
10 BP Archive, POC, DMB, 29 Jan., 17 June and 26 Nov. 1885; Journal No. 12, Fo. 320.
11 BP Archive, BOC, Ledger No. 18; POC, Ledger No. 10; YPLMO, Ledger No. 12; OOC 1886, Ledger No. 8.
12 R.A. Church, 2000, 'Advertising consumer goods in nineteenth century Britain: Reinterpretations', *Economic History Review*, 53, 4, 621–45; 626–7, 629.
13 BP Archive, YP Ledger No. 1, Fo. 41.
14 T.R. Nevett, 1982, *Advertising in Britain: A History*, London, Heinemann, 72–3.
15 BP Archive, YP, Ledger No. 12, Fo. 521.
16 BP Archive, BOC, Journal No. 2, Fos 294–5; Journal No. 3, Fos 252 and 428; Journal No. 4, Fo. 712; BOC, Ledger No. 8, Fos 197–8; Ledger No. 9, Fos 221–2; Journal No. 6, Fos 750–51; Ledger No. 11, Fo. 228; Ledger No. 12, Fo. 221: Ledger No. 18, Fos 242–3; Ledger No. 19, Fo. 203.
17 Nevett, *Advertising in Britain*, 67.
18 *Scotsman*, 16 and 17 Aug. 1866.
19 Price's, *Still the Candle Burns*, 19.
20 Church, 'Advertising consumer goods', 635.
21 Glasgow Post Office Street Directory, 1862–3, 159: advertisement for Young's Patent Paraffin Oil.
22 BP Archive, YP, SMB, 28 Dec. 1865, 9 Oct. 1866.
23 BP Archive, BOC, DMB, 18 June 1879.
24 *WLC*, 1 May 1880, 28 Nov. 1896, 21 Nov. 1896.
25 BP Archive, YP, SMB, 18 Dec. 1866; OOC 1869, DMB, 9 Sept. 1878; *JSCI*, 4, 1885, 470–1; *WLC*, 3 Oct. 1885; *JSCI*, 6, 1887, 630; *JSCI*, 20, 1901, 687.
26 BP Archive, BOC, DMB, 18 June 1879.
27 BP Archive, OOC 1886, Ledger No. 1, Fos 183–4.
28 *Oil & Colourman's Journal*, 1 Jan. 1895, 1, 53, 156.

Chapter 15 Management of the mines and works

1   BP Archive, YP, SHMB 1, Directors' Report, y.e. 30 March 1883; SHMB 1, 14 Dec. 1883; SHMB 2, 16 June 1886.
2   *Scotsman*, 12 May 1891.
3   BP Archive, BOC, GMB 1, 10 May 1897.
4   *Scotsman*, 11 May 1897.
5   S.A. Zahra (ed.), 2005, *Corporate Entrepreneurship and Growth*, is a collection of work on this subject from the 1960s onwards; see also J.S. Hornsby et al., 'Middle managers' perception of the internal environment for corporate entrepreneurship: Assessing a measurement scale', *Journal of Business Venturing*, 17, 253–73.
6   Pollard, 1965, *The Genesis of Modern Management: A Study of the Industrial Revolution in Great Britain*, London, Edward Arnold, passim, especially 1–24.
7   Ibid., 22.
8   BP Archive, AR 1007, 21 Aug. 1873, Papers relating to dispute between Young and the company Article 19, page 31; YP, SMB, 5 July 1866.
9   BP Archive, YP, SMB, 23 Aug. 1866; Livingston Parish, District 1 Schedule 011; YP, SMB, 6 June 1867; letters R Scott to D.J. Kennelly, managing director, 24 July and 8 Aug. 1872; AR 0730, Minute of agreement between YPLMO and John Calderwood, 16 Oct. 1872.
10 BP Archive, AR 0824, YP, Comparison of management structure in 1884 with that in 1873; *WLC*, 5 Feb. 1898; YP, DPMB, 19 Jan. 1898, 13 Nov. 1916, 19 March 1919.
11 Census, Bathgate Parish, District 10, Schedule 51.
12 BP Archive, AR 0824, YP, Comparison of management structure in 1884 with that in 1873; *WLC*, 19 Jan. 1917; Price's, *Still the Candle Burns*, 30.
13 BP Archive, YP, SMB, Fo. 92, 25 April 1866.

14 BP Archive, OOC 1886, DMB 1, 10 Feb. 1886.
15 Ibid., 24 March 1886.
16 BP Archive, OOC 1886, GMB 1, 18 May 1892.
17 *WLC*, 24 Jan. 1930, Obituary of James Bryson.
18 Henderson, 'History of shale retorts', 984–87; *WLC*, 21 Dec. 1917.
19 BP Archive, POC, DMB, 6 Nov. 1883; *Scotsman*, 27 Sept. 1880, 'Prospectus'; BP Archive, POC, DMB, 31 Oct. 1884, and 27 Nov. 1884; *WLC*, 30 May 1885.
20 BP Archive, OOC, DMB, 2 May 1881
21 BP Archive, POC, DMB, 1 April 1886.
22 Ibid., 9 and 23 Nov. 1886.
23 Ibid., 30 Nov. 1886, 11 and 25 Jan., 8 and 15 Feb., 8 March 1887; *WLC*, 5 June 1903, 24 Jan. 1930; BP Archive, AR 1410, Bridgend Church, Mid Calder, Special Memorial Messenger, In Memoriam, Mr James Bryson, March 1930.
24 David Murray, 1959, *'Paraffin Young', The World's First Regular Oil Man*, London, Pall Mall Press, 23.
25 Robin Mackie, 2007, 'Counting chemists', *Journal of Scottish Historical Studies*, 27, 1, 48–74; 67–8.
26 D.R. Steuart, 1900, 'Paraffin oil and petroleum', *JSCI*, 19, 989–92; 989.
27 Steuart, 'Chemistry of the oil shales', 141–57.
28 University of Strathclyde Archives, Limefield Laboratory Notebook.
29 Steuart, 'Chemistry of the oil shales', 179.
30 J. Gray, 1891, 'An apparatus for determining the flash-point of heavy mineral oils', *JSCI*, 10, 348; D.R. Steuart, 1892, 'The flash-point and heat of burning of mineral oils', *JSCI*, 11, 885–93; 1896, 'The standards of minimum flash-point for mineral oil', *JSCI*, 15, 173–9; and 1899, 'The oxidation of mineral oils: notes from Broxburn Oil Works laboratory', *JSCI*, 18, 239–45.
31 D.A. Sutherland, 1887, 'On paraffin scale testing', *JSCI*, 6, 1887, 123–6; J. Stuart Thomson, 1891, 'The determination of impurities in paraffin scale etc.', *JSCI*, 10, 342–7.
32 Thomson, 'The determination of impurities', 342.
33 University of Strathclyde Archives, Limefield Laboratory Notebook, 1863–5; BP Archive, AR 0730, Minute of agreement between YPLMO and John Calderwood, 16 Oct. 1872; Census, 1871, West Calder, District 6, Schedule 50; *JSCI*, 5, 1896, 359; Census, 1871, West Calder, District 1 Schedule 129; Census, West Calder, 1891, District 8, Schedule 4; District 10, Schedule 59; District 4, Schedule 145; BP Archive, AR 0730, Minute of Agreement between YPLMO and Robert Young manager of Uphall works 1 May 1884; Census, 1891, Uphall, District 7, Schedule 104.
34 Beilby, 'Thirty years of progress', 876; *JSCI*, 3, 1884, 223; BP Archive, POC, DMB, 21 Dec. 1886; 28 Dec. 1886; *WLC*, 30 Oct. 1936, 17 Aug. 1889, 7 Nov. 1891; Census, 1891, Uphall, District 1, Schedule 24; District 6, Schedule 177.
35 *JSCI*, 6, 1887, 123–6; *WLC*, 7 Nov. 1891.
36 *JSCI*, 5, 1886, 364.
37 University of Strathclyde Archives, Young's Notebook, 1 Feb. 1859; Beilby, 'Thirty years of progress', 876; Census, 1881, West Calder Parish, District 8, Schedule 63; Valuation Rolls, Midlothian, West Calder parish, 1886–7, 179, item 873; *WLC*, 20 Jan. 1905.
38 Valuation Rolls, Midlothian, 1883–4, Kirknewton Parish, item 61; BP Archive, AR 0730, Minute of agreement between YPLMO and John Calderwood, 16 Oct. 1872; BP Archive, POC, DMB, 30 March 1885; *WLC*, 17 Aug. 1889; Valuation Rolls, Midlothian, Liberton Parish, item 369.
39 'Counting chemists', 52.
40 *WLC*, 30 Oct. 1936, 5 June 1953.
41 *JSCI*, 22, 1903, 986–7; pers. comm., Charles D. Waterston, letter 2 Dec. 2003; Price's, *Still the Candle Burns*, 27; *Times*, 10 Oct. 1881, 11; *JSCI*, 22, 1903, 986–7.
42 Steuart, 1936, *Bygone Days*, Edinburgh, Grant & Murray, 69–73, 95–9.

43 Beilby, 'Thirty years of progress', 876; Beilby, 'On the production of ammonia', 216–24; Conacher, 'History of the Scottish oil-shale industry', 253; Steuart, 'Chemistry of the oil shales', 173, 177–8; *Who was Who, 1916–1928.*

44 *WLC,* 25 Jan. 1929.

45 James Bamberg, 'Fraser, William Milligan, first Baron Strathalmond (1888–1970)', *ODNB.*

46 M. Sanderson, 1999, *Education and Economic Decline in Britain, 1870 to the 1990s,* Cambridge University Press, 14–25.

47 Chandler, *Scale and Scope,* 292–4.

48 Sanderson, *Education and Economic Decline.*

49 Paul Robertson, 1984, 'Scottish universities and industry, 1860–1914, *Scottish Economic and Social History,* 4, 39–54; 41.

50 F.M. Cook, 1971, 'What the oil industry owes to Dr James Young', *Chemistry and Industry,* 585–9; 585.

51 BP Archive, POC, DMB, Fo. 354, 25 Feb. 1887.

52 Census, 1871, West Calder Parish, District 8, Schedules 38, 39, 48.

53 Census, 1891, Mid Calder Parish, District 5, Schedule 5.

54 Census, 1891, West Calder Parish, District 9, Schedules 147, 148, 152, 156, 158.

55 BP Archive, POC, DMB, 1 Feb. 1887.

56 *Midlothian Advertiser,* 30 Dec. 1949.

57 BP Archive, YP, Letter Book of A. Kerr, letters dated 27 Feb. 1918 to J.W. Anderson, W.M.W. Wilson, W. Alison and Peter Wilson.

58 *WLC,* 26 June 1903.

59 Caldwell, 'Methods of working', 107.

60 Ibid., 105, 111–12.

61 Ibid., 128–32.

62 BP Archive, YP, SMB, 22 Feb. 1866; Glasgow Post Office Directory, 1866–7, 212.

63 Census 1871, Mid Calder parish, District 5, Schedule 85, and birth registrations of Calderwood's children; Valuation Rolls, Bathgate Parish, 1868–9, 12, item 517; 1869–70, 7, item 236; Home Office, List of Mines, 1890; BP Archive, OOC 1886, DMB, 5 May and 26 March 1888; Census, Mid Calder Parish, District 6, Schedule 141; BP Archive, AR 1382 Scottish Oils Limited, Management Structure, Chart No. 2 – Mining; *Linlithgowshire Gazette,* 7 June 1935.

64 IOM Report, PP, 1882, 234 ; 1883, 190; BP Archive, POC, DMB, 21 Aug. 1884; *WLC,* 3 Dec. 1920.

65 *Scotsman,* 11 April 1870.

66 Census, Bathgate parish, District 9, schedules 4, 15.

67 R.A. Church, 1986, *The History of the British Coal Industry, Volume 3, 1830–1913: Victorian Pre-eminence,* Oxford University Press, 420; IOM Report, PP, 1873, 142 and 138; Church, *History of the British Coal Industry,* 431.

68 Derived from the information in IOM Report, PP, 1875, 227.

69 Derived from information in IOM Report, PP, 1885, 177–8.

70 Census of Wages Return (PP), vi–vii, 52.

71 Derived from the data in Home Office, List of Mines, 1913, 43 et seq.

Chapter 16 Remuneration

1 BP Archive, AR 0825, YP, Agreements with John Fyfe dated 1 July 1873 and 1 May 1905.

2 BP Archive, YPLMO, Private Minute Book, 3 Nov. 1915.

3 BP Archive, BOC, Directors' Minute Book, 14 Nov. 1887; Journal No. 4, Fortnight ending 30 March 1887; Journal No. 4, 3 April 1889; Journal No. 10, 31 March 1914.

4 BP Archive, POC, DPMB, 25 Jan. 1916; *WLC,* 26 May 1917.

5 BP Archive, OOC 1886, Ledger No. 4, 31 March 1902; Ledger No. 8, Fo. 448.

6 Fraser, *Coming of the Mass Market*, 25 .
7 BP Archive, YP, SMB, 4 Feb. 1867; OOC, 1869, DMB, 23 Sept. 1878; OOC 1886, DMB 1, 21 April 1886; BOC, Journal No. 10, 31 March 1914; POC, DPMB, 25 June 1919.
8 BP Archive, OOC 1886, DMB, 25 April 1887; AR 0824, YP, Comparison of management structure in 1884 with that in 1873, and List of Registered Office Clerks, 2 July 1913; Gregory Anderson, 1976, *Victorian Clerks*, Manchester University Press, 109.
9 BP Archive, OOC 1869, DMB, 2 Feb. 1875; OOC 1886, Ledger No. 1, 26 Dec. 1885; AR 0824, YP, Comparison of management structure in 1884 with that in 1873; YP, DPMB, 19 Jan. 1898, 13 Nov. 1916.
10 BP Archive, BOC, DMB, 14 Nov. 1877; 22 Oct. 1880; Journal No. 4, 30 March 1887, 3 April 1889; Journal No. 10, Fo. 246.
11 BP Archive, POC, DMB, 6 Nov. 1883, 30 March 1885; POC, DPMB, 25 Jan. 1916.
12 *Scotsman*, 17 May 1889.
13 BP Archive, AR 0824, YP, Comparison of management structure in 1884 with that in 1873; YP, Agreements with works officials, 10 July 1889; BOC, Journal No. 10, 31 March 1914.
14 BP Archive, BOC, DMB, 21 Nov. 1877; AR 0824, YP, Letter Robert Young to John Fyfe, 28 Feb. 1884.
15 BP Archive, AR 0822, YP, Agreements with works officials, 10 July 1889; BOC, DMB, 1 Oct. 1879, Fo. 123; BOC, DMB 8, 12 July 1916.
16 BP Archive, YP, SMB, Fo. 103; YP, DPMB, 20 Nov. 1901, 17 April 1907; AR 0728, Agreement dated 1 May 1889; AR 0730, Minute of agreement YP and Charles Frederick Spratt, 1 May 1882, and Minute of agreement YP and Joseph Terry Milnes, 1 May 1881.
17 Fraser, *Coming of the Mass Market*, 23–4.
18 Census of Wages, Report on Mines and Quarries, 52–4.
19 Ibid., Final Report, 470–1.
20 Ibid., Report on Mines and Quarries, 52–4.
21 Census, 1891, West Calder Parish, District 8, schedules 2, 3, 4, and 5; BP Archive, YP, DPMB, 19 Jan. 1898; Census, 1891, Uphall Parish, District 2, Schedule 6, and District 1, Schedule 24; Census, 1891, Mid Calder Parish, District 5, schedules 224 and 225.
22 Royal Commission on Housing in Scotland, Royal Commission on Housing in Scotland, 1921, *Evidence Given before the Royal Commission on the Housing of the Industrial Population of Scotland, Rural and Urban*, Edinburgh, HMSO, 1188–9; Census, 1891, West Calder Parish, District 9, schedules 144–58; Valuation Rolls, Midlothian, 1913–14, Mid Calder Parish, 200–4, items 181, 187, 245, 363–8, 389–98.
23 Butt, 'James Young', 357; BOC, DMB, 5 May 1880, 18 May 1881, 17 May 1882, 5 May 1880; BP Archive, BOC, GMB 1, 16 May 1883 and 21 May 1884; OOC, Ledger No. 8, Fo. 417; *Scotsman*, 9 May 1910, 8 May 1911.

Chapter 17 Company accounts as an aid to management

1 Pollard, *Genesis of Modern Management*, 288.
2 R.K. Fleischman and L.D. Parker, *What is Past is Prologue*, New York and London, Garland Publishing, 1997, 9; Wilson and Thomson, *Making of Modern Management*, 236.
3 BP Archive, POC, Journal No. 6, passim.
4 Fleischman and Parker, *What is Past*, 51.
5 Ibid., 14.
6 BP Archive, POC, Ledger No. 7, Fos 379, 385, 450, 480, 390, 402, 401, 407, 410, 413, 417.
7 Fleischman and Parker, *What is Past*, 34–7.
8 BP Archive, YP, Journal No. 1, Fos 310–13, 31 Dec. 1866; Journal No. 25, Fos 450–2, 30 April 1915.
9 BP Archive, OOC 1886, Journal No. 6, Fo. 309, March 1897.

10   BP Archive, BOC, Journal No. 6, Fos 749–51, 29 March 1899.

11   BP Archive, POC Journal No. 12, Fos 425–6, April 1913, Fo. 543, April 1914.

12   BP Archive, BOC, DMB, 5 Oct. 1881, 1 Feb. 1882, 1 Nov. 1882.

13   Carlon and Morris, 'Economic determinants', 282; Wilson and Thomson, *Making of Modern Management*, 238.

14   BP Archive, YP, SHMB, 1, 2 and 3; OOC 1869, GMB; OOC 1886, GMB 1 and 2; BOC, GMB 1 and 2; POC, newspaper reports of AGMs.

15   R.H. Parker, 1986, *The Development of the Accounting Profession in Britain to the Early Twentieth Century*, San Antonio, Texas, Academy of Accounting Historians, 14–16; Stephen P. Walker, 1996, 'George Auldjo Jamieson, A Victorian "man of affairs" ', in T.A. Lee (ed.), *Shaping the Accountancy Profession: The Story of Three Scottish Pioneers*, 24–5.

Chapter 18   The shale oil industry: managerial capitalism?

1   Chandler, *Scale and Scope*, 1–2, 8, 3, 235, and cited in John F. Wilson, 1995, *British Business History, 1720–1994*, 96–7.

2   Chandler, *Scale and Scope*, 8, 93, 25.

3   Williamson and Daum, *American Petroleum Industry*, 687–96; Chandler, *Scale and Scope*, 95; Chernow, *Titan*, 252 et seq.

4   Williamson and Daum, *American Petroleum Industry*, 624.

5   Barry Supple, 1991, 'Scale and scope: Alfred Chandler and the dynamics of industrial capitalism', *Economic History Review*, 44, 500–14; 508.

6   Williamson and Daum, *American Petroleum Industry*, 290.

7   Ibid., 628.

8   Beilby, 'Thirty years of progress', 882; Bryson, 'The Pumpherston patent retort', 990; Steuart, 'Manufacture of paraffin oil', 110.

9   *Scotsman*, 20 Aug. 1881.

10   Ibid., 26 July 1883.

11   Beilby, 'Thirty years of progress', 880; *WLC*, 8 June 1889; *Scotsman*, 1 Jan. 1885; *WLC*, 2 Jan. 1886.

12   Chandler, *Scale and Scope*, 8.

13   Nevins, *Study in Power*, vol. 1, 83.

14   Matthew Josephson, 1962, *The Robber Barons*, London, Eyre & Spottiswoode, 277.

15   Nevins, *Study in Power*, vol. 1, 386.

16   Ibid., 393, 397.

17   Ibid., vol. 2, 277, 281, 214–15.

18   Chandler, *Scale and Scope*, 104.

19   BP Archive, YP, SHMB 1, Fo. 134; *Glasgow Stock Exchange Daily Lists*, 28 June 1871; Michie, *Money, Mania and Markets*, 207; *DSBB*, 2, 357; BP Archive, OOC, GMB, Fos. 40–3; NAS, BT2/303/29.

20   BP Archive, BOC, DMB, Fos 9–15, 20, 22–3, 27, 35, 38, 52, 56, 63–6; ROC, 792/9, 792/10, 792/14, 1295/4.

21   BP Archive, OOC 1886, Journal No. 6, January 1897; YP, Ordinary Share Transfers Ledger, 10 Nov. 1919; POC, Register of Preference and Ordinary Shareholders, 10 Nov. 1919; BOC, Register of Transfers of Ordinary Shares, No. 4, 10 Nov. 1919.

22   BP Archive, BOC, GMB 1 and 2.

23   BP Archive, GMB 2, Fo. 82.

24   Anon., *Memoirs and Portraits*, vol. 1, 128–9; vol. 2, 278–80.

25   BP Archive, POC, DMB, 5 March 1887.

26   Chandler, *Scale and Scope*, 85.

27   BP Archive, YP, SHMB 1, Directors' Report, April 1882.

28 BP Archive, OOC 1886, GMB 1, 20 May 1897; BOC, GMB 1, 22 May 1895.
29 *WLC*, 2 June 1900, 5 June 1903; *Scotsman*, 31 May 1913.

Chapter 19 The less successful concerns

1 NAS, BT2/1351; BT2/416/3; BT2/701/13; *Scotsman*, 4 March.
2 NAS, BT2/837; *Scotsman*, 7 Dec. 1878
3 NAS, BT2/1267; *WLC*, 2 Jan. 1886.
4 Valuation Rolls, Linlithgow, Bathgate Parish, item 809.
5 Cottrell, 'Domestic finance, 1860–1914', 254.
6 Valuation Rolls, 1860–1 County of Lanark, Shotts Parish; County of Linlithgow, Whitburn Parish, esp. page 59, item 34; Vamplew, *Salvesen of Leith*, 66, 71.
7 NAS, BT2/343/6; *Scotsman*, 24 May 1877.
8 BP Archive, BOC, DMB, 22 May 1878, 5 June 1878, 20 Nov. 1878; *WLC*, 18 Sept. 1880; *Scotsman*, 10 May 1882; BP Archive, BOC, Ledger No. 4, Fos 43, 44.
9 Register of Sasines, 1883, 937, 948 and 955; NAS, BT2/1285/1; BT2/1285/3; *WLC*, 9 Feb. and 24 May 1884; NAS, BT2/1285/6.
10 *Scottish Financier*, October 1883.
11 Michie, *Money, Mania and Markets*, 130–1; Payne, *Early Scottish Limited Companies*, 82.
12 Cottrell, 'Domestic finance, 1860–1914', 269–70.
13 *WLC*, 5 Jan. 1884.
14 BP Archive, POC, DMB, 2 Nov. 1883.
15 NAS, BT2/1292/6.
16 NAS, BT2/1485.
17 *WLC*, 5 Jan. 1889.
18 *Scotsman*, 28 March, 1 Jan. 1885.
19 NAS, BT2/1267/7.
20 NAS, BT2/1285/8.
21 *WLC*, 5 June 1886.
22 *Linlithgowshire Gazette*, 14 Nov. 1891.
23 *WLC*, 12 June 1886.
24 NAS, BT2/1285/17.
25 Checkland, *Scottish Banking*, 510; Saville, *Bank of Scotland*, 457; Michie, *Money, Mania and Markets*, 185–6.
26 *WLC*, 5 Nov. 1887.
27 NAS, BT2/1285/20.
28 *Scotsman*, 30 May 1885.
29 *WLC*, 28 June 1890.
30 Glasgow Post Office Directory, 1891–2, 369.
31 *Scotsman*, 24 May 1892.
32 NAS, BT2/808; Valuation Rolls, Renfrewshire, parishes of Renfrew, Kilbarchan, Abbey, and 1881–2, Edinburghshire, Parish of Lasswade, 137, item 216; *WLC*, 16 May 1885; Conacher, 'History of the Scottish oil-shale industry', 249–50.
33 *Scotsman*, 11 May 1887; *WLC*, 16 May 1891.
34 BP Archive, OOC 1886, Ledger No. 2; BOC, Ledger No. 7; POC, Ledger No. 3; YP, Ledger No. 8.
35 *Scotsman* 11 May 1887; Steuart, 'Manufacture of paraffin oil', 110.
36 *DSBB*, vol. 2, 241–4.
37 BP Archive, POC, DMB, 1 Feb. 1887.
38 NAS, BT2/2533.
39 *Scotsman*, 20 and 29 Dec. 1897.

Chapter 20 Conclusion

1 Company reports in the *Scotsman*, 4, 11 and 21 May 1914, 1 June 1914.
2 Campbell, *Scotland since 1707*, 247.

Postscript: 1914–1982

1 H. Longhurst, 1959, *Adventure in Oil*, London, Sidgwick & Jackson, 51.
2 BP Archive, POC, DMB 2, 16 Jan. 1918.
3 Ibid., 17 Jan. and 2 April 1917.
4 A.J.P. Taylor, 1975, *English History, 1914–1945*, Harmondsworth, Penguin, 71.
5 *WLC*, 20 Jan. 1928.
6 BP Archive, BOC, Directors' Minute Book, No. 8, papers following Fo. 241.
7 BP Archive, OOC 1886, GMB 2, 21 May 1919.
8 R.W. Ferrier, 1982, *The History of the British Petroleum Company*, vol. 1, Cambridge University Press, 210.
9 *WLC*, 18 July 1919.
10 BP Archive, SOL, Minutes of Board Meetings, 11 Dec. 1919, 27 Jan. 1920.
11 *WLC*, 18 July 1919; *Scotsman*, 20 Oct. 2000; BP Archive, SOL, Minutes of Board Meeting, 11 Dec. 1919.
12 BP Archive, SOL, Minutes of Board Meeting, 21 Dec. 1922; Various shale companies, board meetings, 26 May 1924; *WLC*, 25 Dec. 1925.
13 BP Archive, SOL, Minutes of Board Meeting, 28 Jan. 1924; SOL, MD Report, August 1924; *Linlithgowshire Gazette*, 18 Sept. 1936.
14 BP Archive, SOL, Minutes of Board Meeting, 7 April 1925, 29 Sept. 1925, 27 Oct. 1925, 24 November 1925; *WLC*, 4 and 11 Dec. 1925; BP Archive, SOL, Minutes of Board Meeting, 22 Dec. 1925.
15 *WLC*, 25 Dec. 1925.
16 Statistical Abstract for the United Kingdom, PP, 1910–24, 202, Table 79.
17 Ibid., 1924–39, 310, Table 229; *WLC*, 24 June 1927.
18 BP Archive, SOL, Minute of Directors' Meeting, 25 Oct. 1927, 5 Jan. 1928.
19 *WLC*, 15 June 1928.
20 Ibid., 12 June 1931.
21 BP Archive, SOL, Minute of Directors' Meeting,, 25 Sept. 1928.
22 BP Archive, Directors' Minute Book, James Ross & Co., 28 July, 1931; *WLC*, 24 July 1931; BP Archive, SOL, Memorandum to Finance Committee, 22 July 1938.
23 BP Archive, SOL, Record of Accidents, 1927–38.
24 *WLC*, 12 Feb. 1938, 13 Jan. 1939.
25 BP Archive, SOL, Managing Director's Report, September, 1924.
26 My own family provides examples of both of these transfers.
27 *WLC*, 12 Feb. 1937.
28 Ibid., 6 Oct. 1933, 7 Jan. 1938, 4 Aug. 1944.
29 BP Archive, POC, Balance Sheets and Reports.
30 *WLC*, 24 March 1939; BP Archive, SOL, Memorandum to Finance Committee, 22 July 1938.
31 BP Archive, SOL, Memorandum No. 4, 9 Feb. 1951: Scottish Shale Companies; POC, Balance Sheet, 31 December 1944; GD454/AR0936, SOL, Eakring and Formby Crude Oil File: Report dated 24 November 1948, Letter dated 13 July 1956 from G.H. Smith to Commercial Manager, Glasgow, and Statement dated 11 March 1957.
32 *WLC*, 16 April 1948; *Midlothian Advertiser*, 2 July 1948.
33 BP Archive, SOL, Memorandum No. 4, 9 Feb. 1951: Scottish Shale Companies.

Bibliography

Archives

BP Archive

This was formerly held in National Archives of Scotland (NAS), reference GD454, and is now deposited by BPplc with the Almond Valley Heritage Trust in Livingston. It consists of material relating to the shale oil companies that survived to be absorbed by Scottish Oils Limited (SOL) in 1919, and to Scottish Oils Limited itself. The companies, with year of incorporation are:

Young's Paraffin Light and Mineral Oil Company Limited (YP): 1866.

Oakbank Oil Company Limited (OOC): 1869; wound up and reorganised in 1886.

Broxburn Oil Company Limited (BOC): 1877.

Pumpherston Oil Company Limited (POC): 1883.

James Ross & Company (JR): a private partnership until 1919, when it was incorporated as a limited company to facilitate the takeover by Scottish Oils Limited.

The material is catalogued in two series. The AR series consists of documents, papers, photographs and newspaper cuttings. The OS series is made up of bound volumes of minutes, journals and ledgers of the four limited companies and Scottish Oils Limited.

Since the publication of this book, the material has been recatalogued and the catalogue is available online. For access contact BP Archive by email at: bparchive@bp.com

Papers

AR 0105 (2), YP, Letter Book

AR 0531, SOL, Memorandum to Finance Committee, 22 July 1938

AR 0533, SOL, Memorandum No. 4, 9 February 1951, Scottish Shale Companies

AR 00586, 587, POC, Balance Sheets and Reports

AR 0642, Minutes of Board meetings of Scottish Oils Limited (SOL)

AR 0643, Scottish Oils Ltd, Managing Director's Reports to Board

AR 0648, Linlithgow Oil Company Limited, Report by Directors to second AGM, 4 June 1886

AR 0649, POC Prospectus, October 1883

POC Statement to the press with reference to the withdrawal of the company from the Scottish Mineral Oil Association

AR 0728, YP, Letter, Fyfe to Accountant, 5 Sept. 1906

AR 0730, Minute of agreement between YPLMO and John Calderwood, 16 Oct. 1872

Letters R. Scott to D.J. Kennelly, managing airector, YPLMO, 24 July 1872 and 8 Aug. 1872

Correspondence with John Calderwood re Scott, 9 and 10 July 1873

Minute of agreement YP and Joseph Terry Milnes, traveller Manchester, 1 May 1881

Minute of agreement YP and George Thomson, traveller London, 1 March 1882

Minute of agreement YP and Charles Frederick Spratt, traveller London, 1 May 1882 to 30 April 1885

Minute of agreement between YPLMO and Alexander McKay, manager of Paris branch, 30 April 1884 and 1 May 1884

Minute of agreement between YPLMO and Robert Young, manager of Uphall works 1 May 1884 to 30 April 1889

AR 0822, Memorandum of Agreement between Thompson & Bedford and Scottish companies, 30 Jan. 1892

YP, Agreements with works officials, 10 July 1889

AR 0824, Uphall Oil Company Limited, clerks in Glasgow office, 14 Feb. 1884

YP, Letter from Robert Young, manager, Uphall Works to John Fyfe, 28 Feb. 1884

YP, Comparison of management structure in 1884 with that in 1873, 5 Nov. 1884

List of officials taken over by other oil companies; no date, but internal evidence suggests 1880s

YP, List of Registered Office clerks, 2 July 1913

AR 0825, YP, Agreement between John Fyfe and Company, 1 July 1873

YP, Private Report by Mr Fyfe as to his visit to Mr Bedford and Mr Usmar in London, 14 Feb. 1893

YP, List of customers at branches.

YP, Agreement with John Fyfe renewed for 7 years, 1 May 1905

AR 0936, SOL, Eakring and Formby Crude Oil File

AR 1002, 1003, 1004, SOL, Records of Accidents, 1927–1938

AR 1007, Copy minute of agreement between James Young and Young's Paraffin Light & Mineral Oil Company Limited (YP), 28 and 29 December 1865

Papers concerning a dispute between Young and YPLMO, 21 August 1873

AR 1382, Scottish Oils Limited, Management Structure

AR 1410, Bridgend Church, Mid Calder, Special Memorial Messenger, In Memoriam, Mr James Bryson, March 1930.

AR 1453, Minute of meeting of the partners of the Bathgate Chemical Works on the sixteenth day of December 1864

E.M. Bailey, 8 Jan. 1948, James Young Memorial Lecture

AR1475, Comparative statement showing (1) total production and deliveries of all Scotch companies, (2) other companies' position, (3) Pumpherston company's position, in gallons, for year ending 30 April 1913

Bound volumes

OS 0053, YP, Ledger No. 1
OS 0054, YP, Ledger No. 2
OS 0057, YP, Ledger No. 5
OS 0060, YP, Ledger No. 8
OS 0062, YP, Ledger No. 10
OS 0064, YP, Ledger No. 12

OS 0420, YP, Journal No. 1
OS 0424, YP, Journal No. 5
OS 0425, YP, Journal No. 6
OS 0429, YP, Journal No. 10
OS 0432, YP, Journal No. 13
OS 0444, YP, Journal No. 25
OS 0014, OOC, Directors' Minute Book, 1875–82 (DMB)
OS 0015, OOC 1886, Directors' Minute Book No. 1, 1886–8 (DMB 1)
OS 0017, OOC, General Minute Book (GMB)

OS 0018, OOC 1886, General Minute Book No. 1 (GMB 1)
OS 0019, OOC 1886, General Minute Book No. 2 (GMB 2)
OS 0101, OOC, Ledger No.1
OS 0109, OOC, Ledger No. 9
OS 0117, OOC 1886, Ledger No. 1 (new company)
OS 0118, OOC 1886, Ledger No. 2 (new company)
OS 0120, OOC 1886, Ledger No. 4 (new company)
OS 0124, OOC 1886, Ledger No. 8 (new company)
OS 0504, OOC 1886, Journal No. 6 (new company)
OS 0506, OOC 1886, Journal No. 8 (new company)
OS 0008, BOC, Directors' Minute Book (DMB)

OS 0010, BOC, General Minute Book 1 (GMB 1)
OS 0011, BOC, General Minute Book 2 (GMB 2)
OS 0140, BOC, Ledger No. 4
OS 0142, BOC, Ledger No. 6
OS 0143, BOC, Ledger No. 7
OS 0144, BOC, Ledger No. 8
OS 0145, BOC, Ledger No. 9
OS 0147, BOC, Ledger No. 11
OS 0148, BOC, Ledger No. 12
OS 0154, BOC, Ledger No. 18
OS 0155, BOC, Ledger No. 19
OS 0482, BOC, Journal No. 2
OS 0483, BOC, Journal No. 3
OS 0484, BOC, Journal No. 4
OS 0486, BOC, Journal No. 6
OS 0490, BOC, Journal No. 10
BP Archive Ref 192976 BOC, Directors' Minute Book No. 8 (DMB 8)
OS 0005, POC, Directors' Minute Book (DMB)
OS 0007, POC, Directors' Minute Book No. 2 (DMB 2)
OS 0077, POC, Ledger No. 2
OS 0078, POC, Ledger No. 3
OS 0079, POC, Ledger No. 4
OS 0082, POC, Ledger No. 7
OS 0085, POC, Ledger No. 10
OS 0465, POC, Journal No. 12

OS 0030, JR, Directors' Minute Book
Some records were retained at British Petroleum, Grangemouth. These have now been transferred to
    the BP Archive at Warwick University, with the exception of the first item listed:

YP, Secretary's Minute Book of Shareholders' Meetings (SHMB 1), 1866 to 1883 (held at Almond
    Valley Heritage Centre)
YP, Secretary's Minute Book of Shareholders' Meetings No. 2 (SHMB 2) No. 3 (SHMB 3)
YP, Secretary's Minute Book of Board Meetings, 1865–8 (SMB)
YP, Documents relating to the liquidation of the Uphall Oil Company Ltd.

YP, Directors' Private Minute Book, 23 Sept. 1881 to 30 July 1919 (DPMB)
YP, Letter Book of A. Kerr, Commercial (later General) Manager 13 Jan. 1918 to 10 Oct. 1919
YP, Ordinary Shares Transfer Ledger, 3 Sept. 1891 to 25 Sept. 1979
BOC, Register No. 4 of Transfers of Ordinary Shares
POC, Register of Preference and Ordinary Shareholders
POC, Directors' Minute Book Volume 12

Almond Valley Heritage Trust, Livingston Mill, Livingston

Pumpherston Oil Company Limited, Journal No. 6. This was consulted over a period during 1980 at Pumpherston Works by courtesy of Andrew Meek, cashier. I have not been able to locate it since that time.
Uphall Oil Company Limited, Time Abstract Book No. 2, 1 Nov. 1881 to 4 Oct. 1882. This volume has been used as a scrapbook, but enough has survived to be useful.

Registrar of Companies (Companies House), Edinburgh (ROC)

SC000221, Young's Paraffin Light & Mineral Oil Company Limited (YP), 4 Jan. 1866
SC000792, Broxburn Oil Company Limited (BOC) [BP Exploration Company Limited], 6 Nov. 1877
SC001295, Pumpherston Oil Company Limited (POC), 3 Nov. 1883
SC001501, Oakbank Oil Company Limited (OOC) [BP–Japan Oil Development Company Limited], 7 Jan. 1886

National Records of Scotland

National Archives of Scotland

BT2/102, Broxburn Shale Oil Company Limited, 27 March 1862
BT2/174, Mid Calder Mineral Oil Company Limited, 11 June 1864
BT2/222, Capeldrae Oil & Coal Company Limited, 5 Jan. 1866
BT2/231, Airdrie Mineral Oil Company Limited, 13 March 1866
BT2/236, Scottish Oil Company Limited, 12 April 1866
BT2/242, Monklands Oil Refining Company Limited, 28 May 1866
BT2/247, Glasgow Oil Company Limited, 27 June 1866
BT2/251, Glentore Mineral Oil Company Limited, 13 Sept. 1866
BT2/253, Dalserf Coal Coke & Oil Company Limited, 19 Sept. 1866
BT2/258, Monklands Oil & Coal Company Limited, 29 Dec. 1866
BT2/303, Oakbank Oil Company Limited, 2 March 1869
BT2/343, Uphall Mineral Oil Company Limited, 26 Jan. 1871
BT2/370A, Dalmeny Oil Company Limited, 20 Oct. 1871
BT2/379, Midlothian Mineral Oil Company Limited, 22 Nov. 1871
BT2/416, West Calder Oil Company Limited, 22 April 1872
BT2/447, Scottish Mineral Oil & Coal Company Limited, 9 Sept. 1872
BT2/670, Uphall Oil Company Limited, 25 April 1976
BT2/701, Straiton Estate (later Oil) Company Limited, 8 Sept. 1876
BT2/808, Clippens Oil Company Limited, 9 Feb. 1878

BT2/837, Binnend Oil Company Limited, 24 July 1878
BT2/953, British Oil & Candle Company Limited, 13 April 1880
BT2/993, Walkinshaw Oil Company Limited, 14 Oct. 1880
BT2/1049A, Burntisland Oil Company Limited, 5 Sept. 1881
BT2/1104, Midlothian Oil Company Limited, 22 March 1882
BT2/1229, Westfield Oil Company Limited, 13 April 1883
BT2/1267, Lanark Oil Company Limited, 3 Aug. 1883
BT2/1285, West Lothian Oil Company Limited, 5.10.1883
BT2/1292, Bathgate Oil Company Limited, 29 Oct. 1883
BT2/1342, Holmes Oil Company Limited, 4 April 1884
BT2/1351, Linlithgow Oil Company Limited, 26 April 1884
BT2/1431, Annick Lodge Oil Company Limited, 4 Feb. 1885
BT2/1485, Hermand Oil Company Limited, 22 Sept. 1885
BT2/1982, Hermand Oil Company Limited, 11 March 1890
BT2/2469, Burntisland Oil Company Limited, 25 March 1893
BT2/2533, Clippens Oil Company Limited, 23 June 1893
BT2/4098, Caledonian Oil Company Limited, 22 Dec. 1898
BT2/4179, New Hermand Oil Company Limited, 10 March 1899
BT2/5644, Tarbrax Oil Company Limited, 17 June 1904

GD 266/80, Bundle No. 1, Records of Pearson, Robertson & Maconochie WS, Hare of Handaxwood and Calderhall Papers, Oakbank Oil Company Limited, Statement showing value of shale calculated upon the prices obtained for Finished Products, with Rate of Lordship at 1/28th part thereof. From 1876 to 1888 inclusive.
GD266/81/5–7; 9–14; 16–21; 24–29; 32–37; 40–45; 47; 49–55; 57–66; AND
GD266/82/20–22; 25–40; 42–54, Oakbank Oil Company Limited, Monthly Statements of sales of burning oil: August 1876 to October 1884
GD266/81/1; 8; 15; 22; 30; 38; 46; 48; 67–71; AND
GD266/82/41 & 48, Oakbank Oil Company Limited, half yearly statements of output of Calderhall and Calderhouse shale, 12 Nov. 1875 to 9 May 1883
GD266/84, Bundle No. 90, Lease, 1870, between S.B. Hare and Oakbank Oil Company
Register of Sasines
Valuation Rolls for:
    County of Edinburgh, Parishes of Kirknewton, Lasswade, Liberton, Mid Calder, West Calder.
    County of Linlithgow, Parishes of Uphall, Dalmeny/South Queensferry, Kirkliston, Livingston, Bathgate, Whitburn.
    County of Lanark, Parishes of Lanark, Carnwath, Shotts
    County of Renfrew, Abbey Parish and Parish of Kilbarchan

General Register House, Edinburgh (ScotlandsPeople Centre)

Census Enumerators' Books (in digital format) for:
    1851, Bathgate parish
    1861, Bathgate, Livingston, Whitburn parishes
    1871, West Calder Parish
    1891, West Calder, Mid Calder, Uphall parishes

Rosebery Estate Papers, Dalmeny House (Private Collection)

Dalmeny Estate Minerals Register
Dalmeny Estate, Cash Ledger No. 3

University of Strathclyde Archives

James Young Papers

T.You 1/19, Diary 1852
T.You 1/23, Diary 1855
T.You 1/25, Notebook
T.You 1/34
T.You 1/35, Diary 1867
T.You 1/36, Diary 1868
T.You 130/1, Letter Book
T.You 1/31, Notebook kept by W. MacIvor and another chemist of work carried out at Limefield laboratory
T.You 2/32, Letter from Binney to Young, 9 June 1858
T.You 2/36, Letter from Binney to Young, 7 Jan. 1859
T.You 2/73, Letter from Binney to Young, 20 July 1859

Contemporary printed material

Parliamentary Papers (PP)

Annual Statement of the Trade of the United Kingdom with Foreign Countries and British Possessions for the year
  1877, PP 1878, LXXI
  1881, PP 1882, LXVIII
  1886, PP 1887, LXXX
  1888, PP 1889, LXXV
  1889, PP 1890, LXXII
  1890, PP 1891, LXXXII
  1891, PP 1892, LXXVII
  1893, PP 1894, LXXXIV
  1898, PP 1899, XCV

Census of Wages, 1885, Return of Rates of Wages in the Mines and Quarries of the United Kingdom, PP 1890–1, LXXVIII
Census of Wages, Final Report, PP 1893–4, LXXXIII
Census of Production (1907), Preliminary Tables, Part III, PP 1910, CIX
Inspectors of Mines Reports (IOM Reports),
  1873, PP 1874, XIII
  1875, PP 1876, XVII
  1876, PP 1877, XXIII

1877, PP 1878, XX
1878, PP 1878–79, XVIII
1879, PP 1880, XV
1881, PP 1882, XVIII
1882, PP 1883, XIX
1884, PP 1884–1885, XV
1885, PP 1886, LXXI
1886, PP 1887, LXXXIX
1887, PP 1888, XXIX
1913, PP 1914, XLIII

Mines and Minerals, Mining and Mineral Statistics of the United Kingdom of Great Britain and
Ireland with the Isle of Man
1882, PP 1884, LXXXV
1883, PP 1884, XIX
1886, PP 1887, LXXXIX
1887, PP 1888, CVII
1888 and 1889, PP 1890–1, XCII
1890, PP 1890–1, XCII
1891, PP 1892, LXXXVIII
1894, PP 1895, CVII

Mines and Quarries, General Report and Statistics, Part III, Output
1899, PP 1900, CII
1905, PP 1906, CXXXIV, Cd 3196
1910, PP 1911, CII

Rivers Pollution Commission
Fourth Report, 1871, PP 1872, XXXIV

Statistical Abstract for the United Kingdom in each of the last fifteen years,
1861–1875, PP 1876, LXXVII
1876–1890, PP 1890–1, LXXXIX
1880–1894, PP 1895, CIV
1899–1914, PP 1914–16, LXXVI
1910–1924, PP 1926, XXVIII
1924–1937, PP 1938–9, XXV

Statistical Abstract for the Principal and other Foreign Countries in each year from
1885 to 1894–95, PP 1897, XCVI

Royal Commissions

Royal Commission on Housing in Scotland, 1921, *Evidence Given before the Royal Commission on the
Housing of the Industrial Population of Scotland, Rural and Urban*, Edinburgh, HMSO.

University of Strathclyde Library, Special Collections

Glasgow Stock Exchange Daily Lists

Home Office

List of Mines in the United Kingdom of Great Britain and Ireland and the Isle of Man, 1890; 1896; 1899 (issued by the Home Office from 1888 to 1919).

Directories

Glasgow Post Office Directory
Edinburgh Post Office Directory

Maps

Ordnance Survey (OS), 1 inch, Sheet 31, 1904

Newspapers and periodicals

Airdrie and Coatbridge Advertiser
Edinburgh Gazette
Glasgow Herald
Linlithgowshire Gazette
London Gazette
Midlothian Advertiser
Oil & Colourman's Journal
Oils, Colours and Drysalteries
Scotsman (Edinburgh)
Times
West Lothian Courier (*WLC*) (Bathgate)
The Scottish Financier (Glasgow)
Glasgow Stock Exchange Daily Lists

Other primary sources

Anon., 1886, *Memoirs and Portraits of One Hundred Glasgow Men*, Glasgow, James Maclehose and Sons.

Beilby, George, 1884, 'On the production of ammonia from the nitrogen of minerals', *Journal of the Society of Chemical Industry* (*JSCI*), 3, 216–24.

Beilby, George, 1897, 'Thirty years of progress in the shale oil industry', *JSCI*, 16, 876–86.

Bremner, David, 1869, *Industries of Scotland*, Edinburgh, A. & C. Black.

Bryson, James, 1897, 'The Pumpherston patent retort', *JSCI*, 16, 990–3.

Cadell, H.M., 1913, *The Story of the Forth*, Glasgow, James Maclehose and Sons.

Cadell, H.M. and Grant-Wilson, J.S., 1906, 'The geology of the oil shale fields' in *The Oil Shales of the Lothians: Memoir of the Geological Survey of Scotland*, Glasgow, HMSO.

Caldwell, W., 1906, 'Methods of working the oil shales', in *The Oil Shales of the Lothians: Memoir of the Geological Survey of Scotland*, Glasgow, HMSO.

Conacher, H.R.J., 1927, 'History of the Scottish oil-shale industry', in *The Oil-Shales of the Lothians: Memoir of the Geological Survey of Scotland*, Edinburgh, HMSO.

Conacher, H.R.J., 1938, 'The mineral oil industry in Scotland, its raw materials and methods', in *Oil Shale and Cannel Coal: Proceedings of a Conference Held in Scotland, June 1938*, London, The Institute of Petroleum.

Jeans, J.S., 1872, *Western Worthies*, Glasgow, Star Office.

Gray, J., FIC, 1891, 'An apparatus for determining the flash-point of heavy mineral oils', *JSCI*, 10, 348.

Henderson, N.M., 1897, 'The history of shale retorts at Broxburn', *Journal of the Society of Chemical Industry*, 16, 984–8.

Journal of the Society of Chemical Industry.

Redwood, I., 1897, *A Practical Treatise on Mineral Oils and Their By-products*, London, E. & F.N. Spon; new impression, 1914.

Sneddon, J.B., Caldwell, W., and Stein, J., 1938, 'Seventy-five years of oil shale mining', in *Oil shale and Cannel Coal: Proceedings of a Conference Held in Scotland, June 1938*, London, The Institute of Petroleum.

Stamp, J.C., 1916, *British Incomes and Property*, London, P.S. King.

Steuart, D.R., 1889, 'The manufacture of paraffin oil', *Journal of the Society of Chemical Industry (JSCI)*, 8, 100–110.

Steuart, D.R., 1892, 'The flash-point and heat of burning of mineral oils', *JSCI*, 11, 885–93.

Steuart, D.R., 1896, 'The standards of minimum flash-point for mineral oil', *JSCI*, 15, 173–9.

Steuart, D.R., 1899, 'The oxidation of mineral oils: notes from Broxburn Oil Works laboratory', *JSCI*, 18, 239–45.

Steuart, D.R., 1900, 'Paraffin oil and petroleum', *JSCI*, 19, 989–92.

Steuart, D R., 1912, 'The chemistry of the oil shales', in *The Oil Shales of the Lothians: Memoir of the Geological Survey of Scotland*, Edinburgh, HMSO.

Steuart, D.R., 1936, *Bygone Days*, Edinburgh, Grant & Murray Ltd (for private circulation).

Sutherland, D.A., FCS, 1887, 'On paraffin scale testing', *JSCI*, 6, 1887, 123–6.

Thomson, J. Stuart, 1891, 'The determination of impurities in paraffin scale etc.', *JSCI*, 10, 342–7.

Who Was Who, 1916–28, 1992 edn, London, A. & C. Black.

Secondary sources

Ackrill, Margaret, 1987, *Manufacturing Industry since 1870*, Oxford, Philip Allan.

Aldcroft, Derek H., 1994, 'The European dimension to the modern world', in Derek H. Aldcroft and Simon P. Ville (eds), *The European Economy 1750–1914*.

Aldcroft, Derek H. and Ville, Simon P. (eds), 1994, *The European Economy 1750–1914*, Manchester, Manchester University Press.

Anderson, Graham P., 1892, *The Rural Exodus: The Problem of the Village and the Town*, London, Macmillan. Reprinted in Freeman, Mark (ed.), 2005, *The English Rural Poor, 1850–1914*, vol. 3.

Anderson, Gregory, 1976, *Victorian Clerks*, Manchester, Manchester University Press.

Bamberg, J.H., 1994, *The History of the British Petroleum Company: Volume 2, 1928–54*, Cambridge, Cambridge University Press.

Beachey, R.W., 1957, *The British West Indies Sugar Industry in the Late Nineteenth Century*, Oxford, Basil Blackwell.

Borrows, B., 1998, *Lengthening the Day: A History of Lighting Technology*, Oxford, Oxford University Press.

Bowley, A.L., 1920, *The Change in the Distribution of National Income, 1880–1913*, Oxford, Clarendon Press.

Boyer, G.R., 2004, 'Living standards, 1860–1939', in R. Floud and P. Johnson (eds), *The Cambridge Economic History of Modern Britain*.

Briggs, Asa, 1990, *Victorian Things*, London, Penguin.

Butt, John, 1964, 'James Young, Scottish philanthropist and industrialist', Unpublished PhD Thesis, Glasgow University.

Butt, John, 1965, 'The Scottish oil mania of 1864–6', *Scottish Journal of Political Economy*, 12, 195–209.

Butt, John, 1964–5, 'Technical change and the growth of the British shale oil industry (1680–1870)', *Economic History Review*, 17, 511–21.

Byatt, I.R.C., 1979, *The British Electrical Industry, 1875–1914*, Oxford, Clarendon Press.

Byres, T.J., 1967, 'Entrepreneurship in the Scottish heavy industries, 1870–1900', in P. Payne (ed.), *Studies in Scottish Business History*.

Campbell, R.H., 1971, *Scotland since 1707: The Rise of an Industrial Society*, Oxford, Basil Blackwell.

Campbell, R.H., 1980, *The Rise and Fall of Scottish Industry*, Edinburgh, John Donald.

Carlon, S.A. and Morris, R.D., 2003, 'The economic determinants of depreciation accounting in late nineteenth century Britain', *Accounting, Business & Financial History*, 13, 275–302.

Chandler, A.D., 1990, *Scale and Scope: The Dynamics of Industrial Capitalism*, Cambridge, Mass., Harvard University Press.

Checkland, S.G., 1969, *The Rise of Industrial Society in England, 1815–1885*, London, Longmans Green.

Checkland, S.G., 1975, *Scottish Banking: A History, 1695–1973*, Glasgow, Collins.

Chernow, Ron, 1998, *Titan: The Life of John D. Rockefeller, Sr.*, London, Little, Brown and Company.

Church, R.A., 1975, *The Great Victorian Boom, 1850–1873*, London, Macmillan/Economic History Society.

Church, R.A., 1980, 'Problems and perspectives', in R.A. Church (ed.), *The Dynamics of Victorian Business*.

Church, R.A. (ed.), 1980, *The Dynamics of Victorian Business*, London, George Allen and Unwin.

Church, R.A., 1986, *The History of the British Coal Industry, Volume 3, 1830–1913: Victorian Pre-eminence*, Oxford, Oxford University Press.

Church, R.A., 2000, 'Advertising consumer goods in nineteenth century Britain: reinterpretations', *Economic History Review*, 53, 4, 621–45.

Collins, E.J.T. (ed.), 2000, *The Agrarian History of England and Wales, Volume 7: 1850–1914*, Cambridge, Cambridge University Press.

Collins, M., 1998, 'English bank development within a European context, 1870–1939', *Economic History Review*, 51, 1–24.

Cook, F.M., 1971, 'What the oil industry owes to Dr James Young', *Chemistry and Industry*, 585–9.

Cooke, A., Donnachie, I., Macsween, A. and Whatley, C.A., 1998, *Modern Scottish History, 1707 to the Present, Volume 2: The Modernisation of Scotland, 1850 to the Present*, East Linton, Tuckwell Press.

Corley, T.A.B., 1983, *A History of the Burmah Oil Company, 1886–1924*, London, Heinemann.

Corrins, Robert D., 1994, 'The Scottish business elite in the Nineteenth Century: The case of William Baird & Company', in A.J.G. Cummings and T.M. Devine, *Industry, Business and Society in Scotland since 1700*.

Cottrell, P.L., 1983, *Industrial Finance, 1830–1950: The Finance and Organisation of English Manufacturing Industry*, London, Methuen.

Cottrell, P.L., 2004, 'Domestic finance, 1860–1914', in R. Floud and P. Johnson (eds), *The Cambridge Economic History of Modern Britain*.

Court, W.H.B., 1954, *A Concise Economic History of Britain from 1750 to Recent Times*, Cambridge, Cambridge University Press.

Cummings, A.J.G. and Devine T.M., 1994, *Industry, Business and Society in Scotland since 1700*, Edinburgh, John Donald.

Devine, T.M., 2005, 'Industrialisation', in T.M. Devine, et al., *The Transformation of Scotland: The Economy since 1700*.

Devine, T.M., Lee, C.H. and Peden, G.C., 2005, *The Transformation of Scotland: The Economy since 1700*, Edinburgh, University Press.

Dictionary of Scottish Business Biography, 1986 and 1990, eds Anthony Slaven and Sydney Checkland, 2 vols, Aberdeen, Aberdeen University Press.

Donaldson, William, 1986, *Popular Literature in Victorian Scotland: Language, Fiction and the Press*, Aberdeen, Aberdeen University Press.

Donnachie, Ian, 1998, *A History of the Brewing Industry in Scotland*, Edinburgh, John Donald.

Drucker, Peter F, 1979, *Management*, London, Pan Books.

Edwards, J.R., 1989, *A History of Financial Accounting*, London, Routledge.

Ferrier, R.W., 1982, *The History of the British Petroleum Company*, volume 1, Cambridge, Cambridge University Press.

Flanders, Judith, 2003, *The Victorian House*, London, Harper Collins.

Fleischman, R.K. and Parker, L.D., 1997, *What is Past is Prologue: Cost Accounting in the British Industrial Revolution, 1760–1850*, New York and London, Garland Publishing.

Flinn, M.W., 1961, *An Economic and Social History of Britain, 1066–1939*, London, Macmillan.

Floud, R. and Johnson, P. (eds), 2004, *The Cambridge Economic History of Modern Britain, Volume II: Economic Maturity, 1860–1939*, Cambridge, Cambridge University Press.

Fraser, W.H., 1981, *The Coming of the Mass Market, 1850–1914*, London, Macmillan.

Freeman, Mark (ed.), 2005, *The English Rural Poor, 1850–1914*, London, Pickering & Chatto.

Goodall, Francis, 2002, 'Gas in London: A divided city', *The London Journal*, 27, 2, 34–50.

Green, D.R. and Owens, A., 2003, 'Gentlewomenly capitalism? Spinsters, widows and wealth holding in England and Wales, c.1800–1860'. *Economic History Review*, 55, 3, 510–36.

Hannah, Leslie, 1983, *The Rise of the Corporate Economy*, 2nd edn, London, Methuen.

Harrison, J.F.C., 1990, *Late Victorian Britain, 1875–1901*, London, Fontana.

Horn, P., 1995, *Labouring Life in the Victorian Countryside*, Stroud, Alan Sutton.

Hornsby, J.S., Kuratko, D. and Zahra, S.A., 2002, 'Middle managers' perception of the internal environment for corporate entrepreneurship: Assessing a measurement scale', *Journal of Business Venturing*, 17, 253–73.

Hume, John R. and Moss, Michael S., 1979, *Beardmore: The History of a Scottish Industrial Giant*, London, Heinemann.

Hunt, Tristram, 2005, *Building Jerusalem: The Rise and Fall of the Victorian City*, London, Phoenix.

Johnston, Ronald, 2000, *Clydeside Capital, 1870–1920: A Social History of Employers*, East Linton, Tuckwell.

Jones, Geoffrey, 1981, *The State and the Emergence of the British Oil Industry*, London, Macmillan in association with the Business History Trust Unit, University of London.

Josephson, Matthew, 1962, *The Robber Barons: The Great American Capitalists, 1861–1901*, London, Eyre & Spottiswoode.

Kennedy, William P., 1987, *Industrial Structure, Capital Markets and the Origins of British Economic Decline*, Cambridge, Cambridge University Press.

Kinchin, P. and Kinchin, J., 1988, *Glasgow's Great Exhibitions, 1881, 1901, 1911, 1938*, Bicester, White Cockade.

Kynaston, D., 1976, *King Labour: The British Working Class, 1850–1914*, London, Allen & Unwin.

Lee, T.A. (ed.), 1996, *Shaping the Accountancy Profession: The Story of Three Scottish Pioneers*, New York and London, Garland.

Leneman, Leah, 1995, '*A guid cause': The Women's Suffrage Movement in Scotland*, revised edition, Edinburgh, Mercat Press.

Livi-Bacci, Massimo (tr. Carl Ipsen), 1992, *A Concise History of World Population*, Blackwell, Oxford.

Longhurst, H., 1959, *Adventure in Oil*, London, Sidgwick & Jackson.

Mackie, Robin, 2007, 'Counting chemists: The distribution of chemical expertise in Scotland in the first half of the twentieth century', *Journal of Scottish Historical Studies*, 27, 1, 48–74.

Maltby, Josephine and Rutterford, Janette, 2006, ' "She possessed her own fortune": Women investors from the late nineteenth century to the early twentieth century', *Business History*, 48, 220–53.

Marwick, William, 1937, 'The limited company in Scottish economic development', *Economic History*, 4.

Marwick, William, 1964, *Scotland in Modern Times*, London, Frank Cass & Co. Ltd.

Mathias, P., 1983, *The First Industrial Nation: An Economic History of Britain, 1700–1914*, 2nd edition, London, Methuen.

Matthews, Derek, 1986, 'Laissez-faire and the London gas industry in the nineteenth century: Another look', *Economic History Review*, 39, 244–63.

Michie, R.C., 1981, *Money, Mania and Markets*, Edinburgh, John Donald.

Michie, R.C., 1987, *The London and New York Stock Exchanges, 1850–1914*, London, Allen & Unwin.

Morison, S.E., Commager, H.S. and Leuchtenburg, W.E., 1983, *A Concise History of the American Republic*, 2nd edition, New York, Oxford University Press.

Morris, R.J., 1994, 'Men, women, and property: The reform of the Married Women's Property Act 1870', in F.M.L. Thompson (ed.), *Landowners, Capitalists and Entrepreneurs*.

Munn, Charles W., 1988, *Clydesdale Bank: The First One Hundred and Fifty Years*, London, Collins.

Murray, David, 1959, '*Paraffin Young', The World's First Regular Oil Man*, London, Pall Mall Press.

Nenadic, Stana, 1991, 'Businessmen, the urban middle classes, and the "dominance" of manufacturers in nineteenth century Britain', *Economic History Review*, 44, 66–85.

Nevett, T.R., 1982, *Advertising in Britain: A History*, London, Heinemann, on behalf of the History of Advertising Trust.

Nevins, Allan, 1953, *Study in Power: John D. Rockefeller, Industrialist and Philanthropist*, 2 vols, Charles Scribner's Sons, New York and London.

Oxford Dictionary of National Biography (ODNB), 2004 (new edition), eds H.C.G. Matthew and Brian Harrison, Oxford, Oxford University Press.

Parker, R.H., 1986, *The Development of the Accounting Profession in Britain to the Early Twentieth Century*, San Antonio, Texas, Academy of Accounting Historians.

Payne, P. (ed.), 1967, *Studies in Scottish Business History*, London, Cass.

Payne, P., 1974, *British Entrepreneurship in the Nineteenth Century*, London, Economic History Society/Macmillan.

Payne, P., 1979, *Colvilles and the Scottish Steel Industry*, Oxford, Clarendon Press.

Payne, P., 1980, *The Early Scottish Limited Companies, 1856–1895*, Edinburgh, Scottish Academic Press.

Pember Reeves, Maud, 1979, *Round about a Pound a Week*, London, Virago.

Pitts, M.V., 1999, 'The rise and rise of the premium share account', *Accounting, Business and Financial History*, 10, 317–46.

Pollard, Sidney, 1965, *The Genesis of Modern Management: A Study of the Industrial Revolution in Great Britain*, London, Edward Arnold.

Price's Patent Candle Company Limited, 1972, *Still the Candle Burns*, London, Price's Patent Candle Company Limited.

Robertson, Paul, 1984, 'Scottish universities and industry, 1860–1914, *Scottish Economic and Social History*, 4, 39–54.

Sanderson, M., 1999, *Education and Economic Decline in Britain, 1870 to the 1990s*, Cambridge, Cambridge University Press.

Saul, S.B., 1969, *The Myth of the Great Depression, 1873–1896*, London, Macmillan.

Saville, R., 1996, *Bank of Scotland, A History, 1695–1995*, Edinburgh, Edinburgh University Press.

Scott, John and Hughes, Michael, 1980, *The Anatomy of Scottish Capital*, London, Croom Helm.

Slaven, Anthony, 1975, *The Development of the West of Scotland, 1750–1960*, London, Routledge & Kegan Paul.

Storrar, A.C. and Pratt, K.C., 2000, 'Accountability vs. Privacy, 1884–1907: The coming of the private company', *Accounting, Business and Financial History*, 10, 3, 259–91.

Supple, Barry, 1991, 'Scale and scope: Alfred Chandler and the dynamics of industrial capitalism', *Economic History Review*, 44, 500–14.

Taylor, A.J.P., 1975, *English History, 1914–1945*, Harmondsworth, Penguin.

Thomson, D., 1966, *Europe since Napoleon*, Harmondsworth, Penguin.

Thompson, F.M.L. (ed.), 1994, *Landowners, Capitalists and Entrepreneurs: Essays for Sir John Habakkuk*, Oxford, Clarendon Press.

Thompson, F.M.L., 2000, 'Agricultural, chemical and fertiliser industries', in E.J.T. Collins (ed.), *The Agrarian History of England and Wales*.

Todd, G., 1932–3, 'Some aspects of joint-stock companies, 1844–1900', *Economic History Review*, 4, 46–71.

Vamplew, Wray, 1975, *Salvesen of Leith*, Edinburgh, Scottish Academic Press.

Vamplew, Wray (ed.), 1978, 'The North British Railway Inquiry of 1866', in Scottish History Society, *Scottish Industrial History: A Miscellany*, Edinburgh, Printed for the Scottish History Society by T. and A. Constable.

Walker, Stephen P., 1996, 'George Auldjo Jamieson, A Victorian "man of affairs" ', in T.A. Lee (ed.), *Shaping the Accountancy Profession: The Story of Three Scottish Pioneers*.

Weir, Ronald, 1995, *The History of the Distillers Company, 1877–1939*, Oxford, Clarendon Press.

Williamson, Harold F. and Daum, Arnold R., 1959, *The American Petroleum Industry: The Age of Illumination 1859–1899*, Evanston, Ill., Northwestern University Press.

Wilson, John F., 1995, *British Business History, 1720–1994*, Manchester, Manchester University Press.

Wilson, John F. and Thomson, Andrew, 2006, *The Making of Modern Management: British Management in Historical Perspective*, Oxford, Oxford University Press.

Withers, H., 1938, *Stocks and Shares*, 3rd edn, London, John Murray.

Zahra, Z.A. (ed.), 2005, *Corporate Entrepreneurship and Growth*, Cheltenham, Elgar.

Index

Sutherland, D.A. 190
Syme, William Blair 189, 199, 200

Tait, Professor P.G. 191
Tarbrax Oil Company Limited 58, 82, 83, 93, 95, 97, 101, 105, 135
  absorbed by Pumpherston 101
Tarbrax works 5, 18, 31, 58, 188, 208, 215, 218, 225
telephone and telegraph, increasing use of 178
Tennent, Robert B. 85, 142, 174
Thompson & Bedford Limited 46
Thomson, Alexander C. 186, 187, 191, 192, 198
Thomson, Andrew 12
Thomson, John Stuart 189, 199
Thornton, George Boyd 127, 128
Thornton, James 29, 31, 34, 49, 68, 118, 143, 216
Thornton, Thomas 29, 31, 34, 68
Tidewater Oil Company 51
Times, The 162
trade unions 200, 227
Turner, Peter W. 198

Union Bank of Scotland 85, 86, 90
Uphall Mineral Oil Company Limited 17–19, 26, 29, 31, 35, 58, 68, 72, 74–76, 78, 82, 83, 86, 92, 99, 100, 117, 119, 124, 127, 139, 150, 152, 154, 158, 173, 176, 184, 185, 188, 195, 199, 200, 216
  absorbed by Young's 35, 86, 92, 100, 158, 173, 184
  formation of 152
  tragedy at Starlaw 195
  winding up of 72, 83, 99
Uphall Oil Company Limited 72, 99, 216
Uphall works 9, 17, 29, 86, 186, 188, 189, 191, 193, 205, 216, 225
Usmar, Mr (Standard Oil) 52

Vale of Leven dyeing industry 166
vertical retorts 6, 27–29, 32, 33, 66, 94, 208
  introduction of 6, 27, 28, 208

Waddell, John 103, 108, 174
Walker, Andrew 68
Walker & Watson 218

Walkinshaw Oil Company Limited 31, 34, 38, 47, 77, 79, 83, 100, 101, 126, 187, 191, 215
  amalgamation with Hermand 100
Watson Brothers (Armadale) 68
Watt, Robert 195
Weir, William 174
West Calder Oil Company Limited 9, 18, 26, 74, 75, 78, 87, 103–105, 123, 126, 138, 139, 163, 164, 176, 215
  winding up of 75, 103, 104
West Lothian Courier 40–42, 106, 147, 160
West Lothian Oil Company Limited 34, 35, 40, 49, 54, 57, 81, 84, 92, 93, 95, 99, 105, 109, 117, 157, 160, 164, 165, 206, 209, 216, 217–219
  winding up of 54, 105
Westfield Oil Company 34, 105, 153, 157
Westwood shale seams 25
Westwood works 227
White, Peter 157, 159
Whitelees works 215, 218
Whiting refinery, Indiana, USA 50, 52
Williamson, Harold F. 12
Wills' tobacco 181
Wilson, Professor George 190
Wilson, John F. 12
Wilson, William 195
Winchburgh works 82
Wishart, John 60, 175, 176, 197, 198, 202, 213, 224
Wood, James 85, 142, 174
Wood, William 142
Woodrow, John 189
writing down of capital 99
Wyllie, James 139

Young, James 'Paraffin' 1, 5, 7, 13, 66, 68, 77, 78, 86, 122, 134, 138, 148–152, 154, 159, 161, 162, 166–171, 178, 186, 188–190, 192, 203, 213
  disagreements with board 170, 171
  partnership with Binney and Meldrum 148, 151
  patents taken out by 7, 16, 20, 150
Young, James Jr 167–169, 213
Young, John 150, 219